GALILEE AND GOSPEL

Collected Essays

BY

SEAN FREYNE

BRILL ACADEMIC PUBLISHERS, INC.
BOSTON • LEIDEN
2002

Library of Congress Cataloging-in-Publication Data

Freyne, Seán
    Galilee and Gospel : collected essays / Sean Freyne.
        p. cm.
    Originally published: Tübingen : Mohr Siebeck, c2000.
    Includes bibliographical references and index.
    ISBN 0-391-04171-1
        1. Galilee (Israel) in the New Testament. 2. Galilee (Israel)—History. 3.
    Jesus Christ—Person and offices. 4. Bible. N.T. Gospels—Criticism, interpreta-
    tion, etc. 5. Judaism—History—Post-exilic period, 586 B.C.–210 A.D. I. Title.

    BS2545.G34 F74 2002
    225.9'5—dc21
                                                                2002018332

ISBN 0-391-04171-1

© Copyright 2000 by J.C.B. Mohr (Paul Siebeck), P.O. Box 20 40, D-72010 Tübingen.

Preface

This collection of essays is dedicated to Professor Martin Hengel as an expression of gratitude to him for his continuing support and encouragement since he first suggested to me the topic of Galilee in Hellenistic and Roman times in 1972.

My first visit to Tübingen came about through the enthusiastic invitation of Professor Otto Betz who has befriended many visiting students to Tübingen with unfailing kindness and warmth. The *Institutum Judaicum* of the University there has provided me with a friendly and helpful environment for research on several occasions in the intervening years.

The Alexander von Humboldt Stiftung has generously supported my visits to Tübingen and I am happy to be able to acknowledge my appreciation of the courtesy of several General Secretaries of the Foundation and their staff. I trust that the publication of this collection of essays by a prestigious German academic publisher demonstrates the importance of the dialogue in the Humanities between German and visiting scholars that the Foundation continues to make possible.

In the preparation of these essays for publication I have received generous help from the Provost's Academic Development Fund, the Trinity Association and Trust, and the Joint Program for Mediterranean and Near Eastern Studies at Trinity College. My thanks are also due to Peter Kenny and David Edgar, Trinity College, Dublin, for their meticulous care in preparing the manuscript and indices. I am also deeply indebted to my wife, Gail, and to my children, Bridget and Sarah, for whom my preoccupation with Galilee has become a way of life over the years.

I have resisted the temptation to make any large-scale revision to the essays, confining myself to stylistic changes and the addition of new bibliographical information as appropriate. These are indicated by the use of an asterisk in the footnotes.

I also wish gratefully to acknowledge permission to publish the following articles:

Cambridge University Press: 'The Galileans in the Light of Josephus' *Life*,' NTS 26 (1980) 397–413, and 'Galilee-Jerusalem Relations in the Light of Josephus' *Life*,' NTS 33 (1987) 600–609.

The Jewish Theological Seminary: 'Urban-Rural Relations in the Light of the Literary sources,' in *The Galilee in Late Antiquity*, ed. L. Levine (1992).

Scholars Press, Atlanta: 'The Charismatic,' in *Ideal Figures in Ancient Judaism*, ed. J. J. Collins and G. Nickelsburg, Septuagint and Cognate Studies 12 (1982), 223–58; 'Town and Country Once More: the Case of Roman Galilee,' in *Archaeology and the Galilee*, ed. D. Edwards and T. McCollough, USF Studies in the History of Judaism (1997) 49–56.

Eisenbrauns: 'Behind the Names: Galileans, Samaritans, *Ioudaioi*,' in *Galilee through the Centuries: Confluence of Cultures*, ed. E. Meyers (1999) 39–55.

Scandinavian University Press: 'Jesus and the Urban Culture of Galilee,' in *Texts and Contexts. Texts in their Textual and Situational Contexts*, ed. D. Hellholm and T. Fornberg (1996) 597–622.

Wilfiried Laurier University Press: 'Galilean Questions to Crossan's Mediterranean Jesus,' in *Whose Historical Jesus?* ed. W. Arnal and M. Desjardin (1997) 63–91.

E.J. Brill: 'Jesus the Wine-Drinker, Friend of Women,' in *Transformative Encounters. Jesus and Women*, ed. I. R. Kitzberger (1999) 162–80.

Leuven University Press/Presses Universitaires de Louvain/Universitaire Pers Leuven: 'Locality and Doctrine. Mark and John Revisited,' in *The Four Gospels 1992. Festschrift Frans Neirynck*, ed. F. van Segbroeck, C. M. Tuckett, G. Van Belle, J. Verheyden, vol. 3 (1992) 1889–1901.

North Carolina Museum of Art: 'Christianity in Sepphoris and Galilee,' in *Sepphoris in Galilee: Crosscurrents of Culture*, ed. R. Martin Nagy, et al. (1997) 67–74.

Seán Freyne, Trinity College, Dublin   March 2000.

Table of Contents

Abbreviations

Standard abbreviations are used for the biblical books, apocrypha, pseudepigrapha, Dead Sea Scrolls and the tractates of the Mishnah, Tosefta and Talmuds. The Loeb Classical Library translation of Josephus is used.

ANRW	*Aufstieg und Niedergang der römischen Welt*
ASOR	American Schools of Oriental Research
BA	*Biblical Archaeologist*
BAR	British Archaeological Reports
BASOR	*Bulletin of the American Schools of Oriental Research*
BZ	*Biblische Zeitschrift*
CBQ	*Catholic Biblical Quarterly*
CRINT	Compendia rerum iudaicarum ad Novum Testamentum
CSSH	*Comparative Studies in Society and History*
FRLANT	Forschungen zur Religion und Literatur des Alten und Neuen Testaments
HTR	*Harvard Theological Review*
IEJ	*Israel Exploration Journal*
INJ	*Israel Numismatic Journal*
JA	*Jewish Antiquities* of Flavius Josephus,
JBL	*Journal of Biblical Literature*
JJS	*Journal of Jewish Studies*
JQR	*Jewish Quarterly Review*
JR	*Journal of Religion*
JRA	*Journal of Roman Archaeology*
JRS	*Journal of Roman Studies*
JSJ	*Journal for the Study of Judaism*
JSNT	*Journal for the Study of the New Testament*
JSOT	*Journal for the Study of the Old Testament*
JSP	*Journal for the Study of the Pseudepigrapha*
JW	*Jewish War* of Flavius Josephus,
Life	*Life* of Flavius Josephus
MGWJ	*Monatsschrift für Geschichte und Wissenschaft des Judentums*
NEAEHL	*The New Encylopedia of Archeological Excavations in the Holy Land*
NovT	*Novum Testamentum*
NTS	*New Testament Studies*
PEQ	*Palestine Exploration Quarterly*
RelSRev	*Religious Studies Review*
SBLASP	*Society of Biblical Literature Abstracts and Seminar Papers*
SNTSMS	Society for New Testament Studies Monograph Series
TDNT	*Theological Dictionary of the New Testament*, ed. Kittel and Friedrich
TLZ	*Theologische Literaturzeitung*
WUNT	Wissenschaftliche Untersuchungen zum Neuen Testament
ZDPV	*Zeitschrift des deutschen Palästina-Vereins*
ZNW	*Zeitschrift für die neutestamentliche Wissenschaft*

Introduction

Galilean Studies: Problems and Prospects

'Galilee, Galilee, you hate the Torah. In the end you will be victimised by oppressors.' (Johanan ben Zakkai, *y. Shabb.* 16,8; 15d).

'Surely you are not from Galilee. Search the Scriptures and see that no prophet is to arise from Galilee.' (Chief Priests and Pharisees, Jn 7,52).

'With this limited area and although surrounded by such powerful foreign nations the two Galilees have always resisted any hostile invasion, for the inhabitants are from infancy inured to war. . . . Never did the men lack courage nor the country men.' (Josephus, *JW* 3,41–42).

'Every nation called to high destinies ought to be a little world in itself, including opposite poles. . . . It was the same with Judea. Less brilliant in one sense than the development of Jerusalem, that of the north was much more fertile; the greatest achievements of the Jewish people have always proceeded thence. . . . The north has given to the world the simple Shunammite, the humble Canaanite, the impassioned Magdalene, the good foster-father, the Virgin Mary. The North alone has made Christianity: Jerusalem, on the contrary is the true home of that obstinate Judaism which founded by the Pharisees, and fixed by the Talmud, has traversed the middle ages and come down to us.' (Ernest Renan, *The Life of Jesus*, 55 f.)

'Geographically, this northernmost district of Palestine was a little island in the midst of unfriendly sees. . . . Its overwhelming Jewishness was a relatively recent phenomenon.' (Geza Vermes, *Jesus the Jew*, 44).

'What if we let Galilee take its place in the Greco-Roman world? What if the people of Galilee were not isolated from the cultural mix that stimulated thought and produced social experimentation in response to the times? What if the Galileans were fully aware of the cultural forces surging through the Levant? What if we thought that the Galileans were capable of entertaining novel notions of social identity? What then? Why then we would be ready for the story of the people of Q. (Burton Mack, *The Lost Gospel. The Book of Q and Christian Origins*, 68).

The variety of perspectives on Galilee represented by this selection of ancient and modern witnesses underlines both the fascination and the difficulty of providing an accurate account of life in the region during the Hellenistic and Roman periods. With our modern critical awareness it is possible to detect the particular biases of the ancient texts, all expressing the views of Jerusalemite outsiders. Recognising the perspectives that shape modern scholarly construals, including one's own, is a more difficult task. Because of its association with the formative periods of both Rabbinic Judaism and Early Christianity the relative lack of evidence about the region has not inhibited scholars from filling the vacuum with vastly divergent accounts of the ethnic mix and the religio-cultural affiliations of the Galilean populace. The essays collected in this volume represent my ongoing search over the past 20 years for a more adequate understanding of the complexity of Galilean life. They are presented here not as definitive solutions to the many intriguing problems that have emerged through dialogue with the views of other scholars, but rather as a contribution to the ongoing debate about Galilee which currently shows no signs of abating. In particular the many archaeological excavations and surveys in the region are providing new data that call for new hypotheses to be put forward and old certainties to be challenged. In the light of these discoveries Renan's description of the landscape being like a fifth gospel, 'torn but still legible', takes on a significance that even he could scarcely have imagined, as the remains of ancient sites emerge into the light of day across the Galilean countryside.[1]

The Awakening of Scholarly Interest in Galilee

In the earliest accounts of Christian pilgrims visiting the Holy Land one can detect a growing desire to find evidence for the biblical stories in the landscape, but also an idealisation of the countryside and its people.[2] This expression of early Christian piety provides an interesting backdrop for what occurred in the eighteenth century, when western pilgrims 're-discovered the Holy Land' in the wake of the Napoleonic wars.[3] Jerusalem, naturally, was the focus of attention, and Galilee does not seem to feature very much, either in terms of the pilgrims' expectations or actual

---

[1] Renan, *The Life of Jesus,* English translation of *Vie de Jésus* (Paris, 1863; ET Buffalo: Prometheus Books, 1991) 23 f.

[2] Cf. J. Wilkinson, *Egeria's Travels* (London: S. P. C. K. 1971) and *Jerusalem Pilgrims before the Crusades* (Warminster: Aris and Phillips, 1977).

[3] N. Shepherd, *The Zealous Intruders. The Western Rediscovery of Palestine* (London: Collins, 1987).

visits to the region. Thus, as late as 1860 Ernest Renan as leader of a French cartographic expedition to Phoenicia could sit in his hut on the borders of Galilee, admire the landscape and romanticise about its lush vegetation providing the proper setting for the pure religion of Jesus, devoid of both its Jewish aridity and its Christian dogmatism.[4]

Renan's *Life of Jesus* was a best seller in France, even though it was excoriated by the Christian churches. Despite his highly idealised account of Jesus and his religion, Renan was a scholar with an excellent knowledge of the languages and cultures of the Near East. Other liberal lives that dominated the first quest for the historical Jesus, were less interested in the Middle Eastern context of the ministry, especially the Jewish background, given the desire to present Jesus as a teacher of universal ethics that transcended his own immediate background. It was left to scholars of a more pietist persuasion who made Palestine the object of their researches for decades to emulate Renan's efforts. This flood of interest by British, German and French scholars, travellers and missionaries, sometimes in competition with each other, eventually gave rise to the establishment of such foundations as The Palestine Exploration Fund (PEF London, 1865), the Deutscher Palästina-Verein and the Deutsches Evangelisches Institut für Altertumswissenschaft (1887 and 1900 respectively). These organisations ensured a more scholarly approach to the investigation of the Holy Land, but each in its own way was committed to the defence of the Bible from its rationalistic detractors.[5] As well as surveying the countryside intensive attention was also given by German scholars to the ancient sources, especially Josephus and Eusebius, in terms of their geographical information, corresponding to German Jewish scholars' interest in the geography of the Talmud in the same period.[6]

The French, unlike the Germans and the British, did not at first establish nationally supported institutes for the research of Palestine, similar to those that they had established earlier in Athens and Rome. In 1890 a graduate school for the scientific study of the Bible in the context of the Near Eastern cultures was established in Jerusalem by the French Dominican priest and biblical scholar, Père Marie-Joseph Lagrange. Because of its

---

[4] *The Life of Jesus*, 39f.

[5] Shepherd, *Zealous Intruders*, 193–227.

[6] A. Neubauer, *La Géographie du Talmud*, 2 vols. (Paris, 1868), vol. 1, 177–240 on Galilee; S. Klein, *Beiträge zur Geschichte und Geographie Galiläas* (Leipzig, 1909) and *Neue Beiträge zur Geschichte und Geographie Galiläas* (Vienna, 1923); id., 'Hebräische Ortsnamen bei Josephus,' *MGWJ* 59 (1915) 163 f.; E. Klostermann, *Eusebius. Das Onomastikon der Biblischen Ortsnamen* (Leipzig: J. C. Hinrichs, 1904; reprint, Hildesheim: G. Olms 1966); P. Thomsen, 'Palästina nach dem Onomasticon des Eusebius,' *ZDPV* 26 (1903) 97–141 and 145–88; W. Oehler. 'Die Ortschaften und Grenzen Galiläas nach Josephus,' *ZDPV* 28 (1905) 1–26 and 49–74;

scholarly achievements, it was subsequently recognised in 1920 by the French Académie des Belles Lettres as the École Biblique et Archéologiques Française. Due to their political interests in Syria/Lebanon and Egypt the French had, however, engaged in an official mapping exercise of both territories, but this did not include Palestine initially. In 1870, ten years after Renan's 'mission to Phoenicia,' the cartographic work done in the Lebanon was extended to Galilee, but only one map of lower Galilee was actually produced.[7] Individual French scholars such as Victor Guérin, an explorer, and Charles Clermont-Ganneau, an epigrapher, did, however, contribute to the research of Palestine, the latter as a member of the Palestine Exploration Fund for a time. Guérin produced a detailed survey of the whole country between 1863 and 1871, and was the first to record every ruin and village in the countryside, including Galilee, and to attempt an identification of these with biblical sites.[8] He thus prepared the way for the detailed survey by Claude Conder and H. H. Kitchener between 1871 and 1877, the maps of which were published in 1880, together with accompanying reports, including one on Galilee written by Trelawney Saunders.

These efforts by the British and Germans to survey and map the whole of Palestine were continued subsequently east of the Jordan with some success in the Golan and to the south in the old kingdom of Moab. Identification of sites with biblical places on the basis either of Arabic place-names retaining something of the older Semitic ones or of other indications from ancient sources, was not always accurate. Yet these surveys and maps provided the starting point for subsequent research when more scientific methods of surveying, allied to stratified digs at chosen tells, the importance of which had not been previously understood, became the norm. However, it should not be forgotten that both the PEF and the German Evangelical Institute, and to a lesser extent the Deutches Palästina-Verein, were initially motivated by a desire to defend the accuracy of the biblical records against their rationalist detractors. In this they were merely continuing in a more systematic manner the aims of the many travellers, missionaries and surveyors who had visited the Holy Land over the previous century and a half. Among these, the name of Edward Robinson stands out because of his efforts to move beyond the paths well trodden by monks

---

[7] D. Gavish, 'French Cartography of the Holy Land in the Nineteenth Century,' *PEQ* 126 (1994) 24–31.

[8] V. Guérin, *Description géographique, historique et archéologique de la Palestine* (Paris, 1868–80); C. Clermont-Ganneau, *Recueil d'archaeologie orientale*, 5 vols. (Paris, 1903). T. Sanders, *An Introduction to the Survey of Western Palestine* (London: Palestine Exploration Fund, 1881).

and pilgrims and he traversed the whole country consulting with the Arab population of the villages.[9]

Notwithstanding his indefatigable desire for accuracy, Robinson was a man of deep puritan piety, combining the mind of a rationalist with the soul of a mystic. Thus the danger was real that, like other zealous Protestant clergymen of his generation, the details of Palestinian life would be transposed to biblical times in the enthusiasm to explain or illustrate aspects of the biblical narratives. This tendency to idealise the Palestinian landscape, so graphically illustrated in the case of Renan, can be detected in a number of later accounts of Galilee based on the work of the PEF. George Adam Smith's influential *Historical Geography of the Holy Land* (1894) combines an impressive knowledge of both the literary sources and the actual terrain, together with a highly romantic account of the effects of the landscape on Jesus as a growing boy in Nazareth, surrounded with 'a map of Old Testament history.' On the other hand, the study of the 'anthropo-geographical relations' in Galilee by V. Schwöbel (1904), also based on the detailed maps of the PEF, seeks to establish the connections between the physical features of Galilee, its patterns of human settlement, network of roads and trade routes in a highly interesting manner. Nevertheless, the overall effect of the investigation is to contrast the present impoverished situation of Galilee with its previous 'golden age' in biblical times when it was a thriving, populous region, endowed with every gift of nature. The same natural conditions – mountains, hills and plains, climate and springs – obtain now as they did 2000 years ago. Only humans have failed over the centuries, and the remedy which Schwöbel proposes is that the present population be awakened from its lethargy through contact 'with western cultural circles' so that a stable government could repulse 'the evil powers of the desert.'[10]

It would be misleading to suggest that the scientific study of Galilee originated solely in the nineteenth-century search for the historical Jesus and the response of Christian scholars to that challenge. The Enlightenment had lead to the emancipation of European Jewry after centuries of confinement to the ghetto, an occurrence that had deep repercussions within the Jewish community itself. Total assimilation was one response to the new situation in the desire of some Jews to participate fully in the intellectual life of Europe. It was in this climate that the Science for the Study of Judaism (*Wissenschaft des Judentums*) emerged with the aims of

---

[9] E. Robinson, *Biblical Researches in Palestine and the Adjacent Regions. A Journal of Travels in the Years 1838 and 1852 by E. Robinson, E. Smith and Others* (London: J. Murray, 1856); Shepherd, *Zealous Intruders*, 90–95.

[10] V. Schwöbel, 'Galiläa: Die Verkehrswege und Ansiedlungen in ihrer Abhängigkeit von der natürlichen Bedingungen,' *ZDPV* 27 (1904), 1–151, especially 135 ff. and 149.

demonstrating Judaism's ability to examine its own history and tenets
critically, thereby underlining its importance for world culture, while at
the same time maintaining its separate and distinctive identity faced with
what many perceived to be its impending disintegration.[11] There was then
an apologetic impulse to the movement, even when various scholars were
to adopt different stances and saw the tasks differently. Many of the most
outstanding scholars were the products both of the Jewish Seminaries with
their rabbinical training and the major universities such as Berlin, Leipzig,
Vienna and Budapest, where the study of the ancient world (*Altertumswissenschaft*) was a highly developed science.

One significant aspect of the movement was the concern with Jewish
history, based on the recognition that in the past Judaism had been able to
adapt to the various historical situations which confronted it. History
could, therefore, teach lessons for the present, whether that be seen as opportunity or as threat. Thus, for Abraham Geiger (1810–74), a radical reformer, the task of the present for Jewish scholarship was to 'loosen the
fetters of the previous period through the use of Reason and historical investigation, without interrupting the connection with the past.' For his near
contemporary Heinrich Graetz on the other hand, the study of Jewish history would provide roots for a Jewish identity, battered and diminished by
modernity.[12]

Galilee had particular significance within the history of Judaism despite
the negative judgements on the region expressed by Jerusalem scribes such
as Johanan ben Zakkai or the leaders of the Jerusalem council, cited at the
outset. It was there that the Jewish Sanhedrin re-established itself after the
Bar-Cochba war of 132–35 CE. In Galilee the rabbinic schools of Sepphoris and Tiberias had produced such lasting monuments of Jewish life as the
Mishnah and the Palestinian Talmud between the second and the fifth centuries CE and many of the important sages of the period were associated
with various centres of both upper and lower Galilee.[13] It is because of this
historical significance that Galilee figures prominently in the work of several Jewish scholars of the late nineteenth and early twentieth centuries
within the general approach of the *Wissenschaft des Judentums*. In addi-

---

[11] L. Wallach, *Liberty and Letters. The Thoughts of Leopold Zunz* (London: Leo
Baeck Institute, 1959), especially 5–32.

[12] M. Maher, 'The Beginning of *Wissenschaft des Judenthums*' in *The Edward Hincks
Bicentenary Lectures,* ed. K. Cathcart (Dublin: The Department of Near Eastern Languages, University College Dublin, 1994) 138–77, especially 160 f.

[13] A. Kaminka, *Studien zur Geschichte Galiläas* (Berlin, 1890) is an early example of
this interest, combining rabbinic sources and Josephus' writings in dealing with issues
such as the legend of the cleansing of Tiberias and the population mixture in Galilee. Cf.
more recently L. Levine, *The Rabbinic Class of Roman Palestine in Late Antiquity* (Jerusalem: Yad Izhak ben-Zvi, 1989) 33–42.

tion to the geographical studies of Neubauer and Klein already mentioned, this latter also concentrated on the earlier history of Judaism in Galilee, a topic that is still very much to the fore in recent studies of the region, as we shall presently see.[14]

Various studies by A. Büchler (1867–1939) were of particular significance in terms of the social conditions of Jews in Palestine in the early centuries of the Common Era. Trained as a Rabbi at the Jewish seminaries of Breslau and Budapest, he later studied at the university of Leipzig and taught at Vienna for a time, before transferring to Jews' College, London, where he spent most of his academic career. His extensive scholarly output was very much in the spirit of *Wissenschaft des Judentums*, especially its apologetic agenda. His writings covered such topics as the Priesthood in the period prior to the Destruction of the Temple (1895), the Jerusalem Sanhedrin and the *Beth Din* of the Temple (1902), Sin and Atonement (1904), the Economic Conditions of Judea after the Destruction of the Second Temple (1912), the Political and Social Leaders of the Jewish Community of Sepphoris in the Second and Third Century (1914), the *minim* of Sepphoris (1912) and Types of Jewish Palestinian Piety from 70 BCE–70 CE (1922). While all of these studies have Galilee very much in their sights, it was Büchler's 1906 book on the Galilean *'am ha-'aretz* that was most debated and the issues which it raised are still highly significant in current discussions about Galilee.[15]

Büchler was highly critical of German Protestant scholars who had used the distinction between *haver* and *'am ha-'aretz* in the rabbinic sources as a means of explaining Jesus and his movement in terms of his championing of the ordinary people of Galilee (for the most part) who had been despised by the scribal and pharisaic leadership in Jerusalem. To counteract this distortion, as he saw it, of first-century Jewish life under the law, Büchler made a distinction between the *'am ha-'aretz le-mitzwot* and the *'am ha-'aretz le torah*, the latter term applying to anybody who disregarded the directions of the Torah, irrespective of the period or the location. The concept of the *'am ha-'aretz le-mitzwot* on the other hand was, according to Büchler, the product of the rabbis of the Ushan period (i.e. post 135 CE). The regulations covering the *haverim* were, he claimed, addressed only to the Galilean Aaronides, and the disparaging remarks about the *'am ha-'aretz* were not meant for the populace as a whole but only to

---

[14] S. Klein, *Galiläa von der Makkabäerzeit bis 67* (Berlin, 1923); id., *Galilee: Geography and History of Galilee from the Return from Babylonia to the Conclusion of the Talmud, by S. Klein. Completed from the Literary Remains of the Author*, ed. Y. Eltizur (Jerusalem: Translations and Collections in Jewish Studies 20, 1967) [Hebrew].

[15] A. Büchler, *Der Galiläische 'am ha-'aretz des zweiten Jahrhunderts* (reprint, Hildesheim: G. Olms, 1968).

those of priestly background who were lax, and whom the sages sought to
goad into proper observance of the tithing and food laws. This restriction
of the term to a later period and to a specific audience meant that it should
not be used to explain the world of Jesus and his objectives in Galilee, according to Büchler. In this regard Emil Schürer's great work, *Geschichte
des jüdischen Volkes im Zeitalter Jesu Christi* (1886–90) seems to have
particularly attracted Büchler's attention, and Schürer himself responded
vigorously to the charge of having misrepresented the situation.[16]

Later Jewish scholars have also recognised the difficulties with Büchler's handling of the evidence in his apologetic desire to counter the anti-
Jewish trends of some German Christian scholarship, especially when it
came to presenting Jesus in his historical context of Galilee.[17] It must be
said, however, that Schürer's position was also one-sided. In his view,
Galilee had only recently been Judaised, and surrounded by a ring of important Greek cities, the epithet 'Galilee of the gentiles' could be employed as an accurate description of the population mix as late as the first
century BCE. This was only one step away from a thoroughly gentile Galilee as represented by those scholars who were influenced by the History of
Religions approach to the emergence of early Christianity, ultimately leading to the assertion that 'in all probability Jesus was not a Jew,' since Galilee was pagan.[18] This trend among some scholars towards describing Galilee as essentially gentile, and therefore seeing early Christianity as a Hellenistic rather than a Jewish movement from its inception, fitted well with
the tenor of the times, as the Nazi storm clouds gathered over Germany in
the opening decades of the twentieth century, and the towering influence
of Rudolf Bultmann held sway in New Testament studies with the demise
of the first quest for the historical Jesus from the turn of the century.

In such a climate it is important to recall that such scholars as G. Dalman (1855–1941) and A. Alt (1883–1956) were to continue the work of

---

[16] Büchler, *Der Galiläische 'am ha-'aretz,* 1–5 and 126–28; cf. E. Schürer's review of
Büchler's book in *TLZ* 23 (1906) 620. It is interesting to note that the revisers of
Schürer's original work, among whom was the noted Jewish scholar G. Vermes, chose to
change the title of the section from 'Life under the Law' to 'Life and the Law,' and decided not to revise the particular section of the original, since one is faced here 'not so
much with an antiquated account or a faulty historical reconstruction, as with question-
able value judgements.' (*A History of the Jewish People in the Age of Jesus Christ,* revised ed. G. Vermes, F. Millar, M. Black, 3 vols. (Edinburgh: T. & T. Clark, 1973–86),
vol. II, 464, n. 1).

[17] A. Oppenheimer, *The 'Am ha-'aretz. A Study in the Social History of the Jewish
People in the Hellenistic-Roman Period* (Leiden: Brill, 1977), especially 1–18 and 200–
217.

[18] Schürer, *The History of the Jewish People,* vol. 2, 7–10; W. Grundmann, *Jesus der
Galiläer und das Judentum* (Leipzig: Georg Wigand, 1941) 166–75, especially 175. Cf.
'Archaeology and the Historical Jesus,' below pp. 160 ff.

the two German foundations already mentioned. The former's massive 7 volume study of Palestinian customs and manners is still an invaluable resource along the lines of Guérin and others who had found the situation of contemporary Palestine congenial for understanding the world of the Bible. In his *Orte und Wege Jesus* (1924), however, Dalman combined a detailed knowledge of the land – both Galilee and Judea – with an excellent grasp of the literary sources, and this same knowledge was also evident in his study of the languages of Palestine in the first century, especially Aramaic. Alt succeeded Dalman as director of the German Protestant Institute, while maintaining close links with the Palästina-Verein. He had an unparalleled knowledge of ancient sources as well as an intimate acquaintance with the terrain of Palestine, and he also familiarised himself with the results of the early archaeological explorations, thus anticipating more recent developments which seek to utilise the results of both literary and archaeological studies in their reconstructions of the past. In his special contribution to the historical geography of Palestine, Alt's studies of Galilee from a *Territorialgeschichte* perspective have made a unique and lasting contribution to Galilean studies by tracing the impact of different regimes on the administrative and cultural life of Galilee through the different epochs from the Assyrian to the Roman conquests.[19] In general his approach points to continuity of population and allegiance over the centuries to a Jewish way of life in Galilee. This counterbalances to some extent the trend towards a wholesale Hellenisation of Galilee which prevailed in German New Testament scholarship of the Bultmann era, as represented by such scholars as W. Bauer (1926), W. Bertram (1935) and W. Grundmann (1941), following Schürer's earlier lead.[20]

Archaeology and Galilee

This brief sketch of early scholarly interest in Galilee has uncovered two main areas of concern, namely, a better acquaintance with the world of Jesus and its natural conditions and an exploration of the early history of rabbinic Judaism. Both interests were confessionally motivated, but that does not preclude their contributions to our knowledge of the region hav-

---

[19] A. Alt, 'Galiläische Probleme 1937–40,' in *Kleine Schriften zur Geschichte des Volkes Israel,* 3 vols. (Munich: C. H. Beck, 1953–64), vol. 2, 363–435.

[20] W. Bauer, 'Jesus der Galiläer,' in *Festgabe für Adolf Jülicher* (Tübingen, 1927) 16–34, reprinted in *Aufsätze und Kleine Schriften,* ed. G. Strecker (Tübingen: J. C. B. Mohr, 1967) 91–108; W. Bertram, 'Der Hellenismus in der Urheimat des Evangeliums,' *Archiv für Religionswissenschaft* 32 (1935) 265–81; Grundmann, *Jesus der Galiläer und das Judentum.* Cf. however the dissenting voice of A. Oepke, 'Das Bevölkerungsproblem Galiläas,' *Theologisches Literaturblatt* 62 (1941) 201–5.

ing a lasting value. The surveys of the early explorers may be seen as the forerunners of more developed methods of archaeological research, the beginnings of which are usually dated to the work of Flinders Petrie at Tell el-Hesi, with his discovery of the importance of Tells as repositories of accumulated rubble of the centuries and not mere natural mounds (1890). With this discovery it became possible through stratigraphy to date the pottery and thus arrive at tentative dating of the various periods of occupation of a given settlement. These techniques were developed further by William Foxwell Albright at Tell Beit Mirsim (1926–32), and later still by Kathleen Kenyon at Jericho (1951).[21] Despite the more 'scientific' approach, the apologetic nature of Biblical Archaeology as it was developing through the first half of the twentieth century can be seen today, especially in the work of Albright who has sometimes been accused of using archaeology to re-establish confidence in the historical nature of the Bible.

In this context a new interest in Galilee emerged in the search for Israelite origins, a search which could be shared by Jewish and Christian scholars alike. Galilee had featured prominently in the 14th century BCE Amarna letters from Egypt, emerging in the Late Bronze Age as a region of city-states, ruled by local princes as officials of the Egyptians, and often engaged in territorial struggles with each other, such as one between Abimilki of Tyre and Abdi-Tirshi of Hazor.[22] Archaeological investigation of some important northern sites such as Hazor (Y. Yadin), Megiddo (G. Schumacher, Y. Yadin) and Dan (A. Biran) suggested a major change at the end of the Bronze Age/early Iron Age (i.e. 13th century BCE), consisting of destruction, followed by re-settlement on a far lesser scale. Inevitably, these finds seemed to match Albright's discoveries elsewhere, and were seen to confirm the biblical account of the conquest as recorded in *Joshua*. However, a survey by Y. Aharoni (1951–53) in the previously unoccupied, mountainous region of Upper Galilee raised doubts. He discovered some fifteen smaller settlements from the Iron Age, but no city settlements corresponding to the Bronze Age ones in the plains, thus supporting Alt's theory regarding the origins of Israel as a peaceful infiltration of nomadic people into the uninhabited highlands.[23] Further examination of the evidence, as well as new evaluation of the data from the cities has

---

[21] J. R. Bartlett, 'What has Archaeology to do with the Bible – Or Vice Versa?' in *Archaeology and Biblical Interpretation*, ed. J. R. Bartlett (Routledge: London, 1997) 1–19, especially 6 f.

[22] For an excellent summary cf. R. Frankel, 'Galilee: Prehellenistic,' in *The Anchor Bible Dictionary*, ed. D. N. Freedman, 6 vols. (New York: Doubleday, 1992), vol. 2, 879–94, especially 883 f.

[23] Y. Aharoni, 'Galilee, Upper,' in *Encylopedia of Archaeological Excavations in the Holy Land*, ed. M. Avi-Yonah, 4 vols. (London: Oxford University Press, 1976), vol. II, 406–8.

given rise to a third hypothesis as to the origins of Israel, namely, one of internal revolt within the Canaanite city-states leading to the Israelite foundations by disaffected inhabitants of the larger cities.[24] The importance of these discussions in this context is that they are an early illustration of a recurrent pattern in the history of Galilee, namely, the tensions between the cities of the circle (*ha-galil*) and the interior on the one hand, and the difficulties of deciding from the archaeological record alone the ethnographic changes that may have occurred in a region that was caught between competing world powers on an east/west axis.

Another issue of Galilean history to which archaeology can make a notable contribution is that of the effects of the Assyrian conquest of the north on the population mix of the region. Not only can the evidence from Galilee itself shed light on the extent and nature of the conquest, but the sparse biblical accounts can also be supplemented considerably by the discoveries of the pertinent royal archives from Niniveh. Alt had seen the need to differentiate between the campaign of Tiglath-Pileser III in 732 and that of Sargon II against Samaria in 721 on the basis of the biblical record of 2 Kgs 15,29; 17,24. According to his reconstruction Galilee became part of the Assyrian province of Megiddo, which together with Dor and Gilead formed three separate provinces of the conquered territory as far as the great sea, on the basis of the oracle of Is 8,23. The relative importance of Megiddo, Akko and Hazor in the wake of this conquest is important in deciding how the administration of Galilee was organised, and the work at all three sites for the relevant seventh-century strata calls for careful evaluation. There is also the further issue of the extent to which the Assyrians depopulated the north. Again, Alt's opinion, that only a small minority of the ruling elite was removed, has been influential in determining the ethnic and religious affiliations of the Galileans of a later time as discussed below.[25] However, the survey of lower Galilee by Zvi Gal has certainly challenged the position of the old Israelite peasant population remaining undisturbed, however we are to understand the scarcity of inhabited settlements in lower Galilee until the Persian period that he has postulated. Only further detailed investigation of lesser Iron-Age sites

---

[24] I. Finkelstein, *The Archaeology of the Israelite Settlement* (Jerusalem: The Israel Exploration Society, 1988); id. 'Ethnicity and Origin of Iron I Settlers in the Highlands of Canaan: Can the Real Israel Stand Up?' *BA* 59 (1996) 198–212. For the most up-to-date discussion, cf. C. G. Herr, 'The Iron II Period: Emerging Nations,' *BA* 60 (1997) 114–83.

[25] Cf. 'Behind the Names: Galileans, Samaritans, *Ioudaioi*,' below pp. 114 ff.

such as Ain Zippori will finally decide this rather crucial issue of Galilean history and its implications for the ethnography of the region.[26]

These two examples raise the question of the role that archaeology can play in determining the ethnicity of those who inhabit a particular site, an issue that can be solved more readily in the case of synagogue remains, it would seem. Inscriptional and literary evidence have been of fundamental importance in this regard, yet the scarcity of pre–70 CE synagogues, other than that of Gamala, is surprising in view of the literary evidence from Josephus and the gospels. In fact the archaeological survey of Galilean synagogues was first conducted not by a Jewish scholar, imbued with the spirit of *Wissenschaft des Judentums*, but rather by a German art historian, interested in a comparative study of Greek art in the ancient Near East, Carl Watzinger. Accompanied by H. Kohl he surveyed eleven synagogue sites in Galilee, and suggested a common typology based on the Greek basilica style (1905).[27] Subsequent studies by G. Foerster, E. Meyers and others have developed and corrected these insights, the former suggesting other Greco–Roman alternatives as models for the synagogues, and the latter questioning the development of a systematic typology. Subsequently, Jewish scholars have continued to conduct detailed studies of different aspects of the synagogues of Galilee, and the remains of over one hundred buildings have been identified throughout the country, over half of these in Galilee/Golan. Studies range from the art and architecture (Avi–Yonah) to inscriptions (Fine) to furnishings and layout (Meyers) to distribution (Urman and Fletcher), all highlighting in different ways the participation of the synagogue both as building and as institution in the larger social and cultural ethos of the Mediterranean world, while maintaining a distinctive Jewish identity.[28] Thus, while the conclusions of Kohl and Watzinger have been superseded in many respects, the initial insight of participation in the

---

[26] Cf. J. P. Dessel, 'Tel Ein Zippori and the Lower Galilee in the Late Bronze and Iron Ages: A Village Perspective' in *Galilee through the Centuries: Confluence of Cultures*, ed. E. Meyers (Winona Lake: Eisenbrauns, 1999).

[27] H. Kohl and C. Watzinger, *Antike Synagogen in Galiläa* (Leipzig: Wissenschaftliche Veröffentlichung der Deutschen Orient-Gesellschaft, 1916).

[28] L. Levine, ed., *Ancient Synagogues Revealed* (Jerusalem: The Israel Exploration Society, 1981); id., ed., *The Synagogue in Late Antiquity* (Philadelphia: ASOR Publications, 1987); M. Avi-Yonah, *Art in Ancient Palestine. Selected Studies* (Jerusalem: The Magnes Press, 1981); J. Gutman, ed., *Ancient Synagogues. The State of Research,* Brown Judaic Studies 22 (Chico, Ca: Scholars Press, 1981); E. Meyers and J. Strange, eds., *Archaeology, the Rabbis and Early Christianity* (London: SCM Press 1981); D. Urman and P. Fletcher, *Ancient Synagogues. Historical Analysis and Archaeological Discovery,* 2 vols. (Leiden: Brill, 1995); S. Fine, ed., *Sacred Realm. The Emergence of the Synagogue in the Ancient World* (New York: Yeshiva University Museum; Oxford: Oxford University Press, 1996).

larger environment by observant Jewish communities of the Galilee in the Byzantine period has been confirmed.

The work of the Meiron Excavation Project of Duke University, N.C. (1976) under the direction of Eric and Carol Meyers, James Strange and others is particularly noteworthy.[29] This project was conceived in terms of contributing to the regional study of Galilee through a comparison of synagogue remains in upper Galilee/Golan with those of lower Galilee. In addition to surveying various sites, the group engaged in detailed archaeological investigation of four sites, Kh. Shema, Meiron, Gush ha-Lab and Nabratein, providing detailed reports of their discoveries. While there has been some disagreement in terms of the analysis of the results, the effort to locate these buildings within a larger social and cultural network of upper Galilee in late antiquity, marks a new stage in the understanding of the region as a whole.[30]

Closely related to synagogues are other instruments of the Jewish way of life such as ritual baths, special types of household pottery to do with ritual purity and distinctive burial customs, the identification of which can help to establish the extent of the Jewish presence in the region at different periods. Gradually the map of Jewish Galilee and Golan is being drawn with greater precision by the concentration on village sites, combined with more precise surveys on a local basis.[31] Developments in the study of ceramics are particularly significant, as recent scientific methods have made it possible to move beyond the typological comparative study to the analysis of the provenience and distribution of wares from different production sites. David Adan-Bayewitz and Andrea Berlin in particular have done pioneering work in this regard, making it possible to estimate trade patterns and commercial transactions on intra-regional and inter-regional lines.[32]

---

[29] E. Meyers, J. Strange, D. Groh, 'The Meiron Excavation Project: Archaeological Survey in Galilee and Golan, 1976,' *BASOR* 230 (1978) 1–24.

[30] Cf. R. Horsley, *Archaeology, History and Society in Galilee. The Social Context of Jesus and the Rabbis* (Valley Forge: Trinity Press International, 1996).

[31] Cf. Y. Tsafrir, L. Di Segni and J. Green, *Tabula Imperii Romani. Iudaea Palaestina. Maps and Gazetteer* (Jerusalem: Israel Academy of the Sciences and the Humanities, 1994), especially the accompanying map of Ancient Synagogues and Jewish Centres.

[32] D. Adan-Bayewitz, *Common Pottery in Roman Galilee. A Study of Local Trade* (Ramat-Gan: Bar-Ilan University Press, 1993); S. Herbert, ed., *Tel Anafa II,i. The Hellenistic and Roman Pottery.* (Ann Arbor: *JRA* and Kelsey Museum, 1997); A. Berlin, 'The Plain Wares,' in Herbert, *Tel Anafa II,i.,* 1–36; A. Berlin, 'From Monarchy to Markets,' *BASOR* 306 (1997) 75–86.

Galilee, Judaism and Early Christianity

My particular engagement with Galilee over the last 25 years has been concerned with both aspects of Galilean studies, the origins of which we have traced, namely, its role in the history of early Judaism and the quest for the historical Jesus. Even though these topics emerged from quite separate, even opposing interests in the nineteenth century, inevitably they became intertwined, as Büchler's study of *'am ha-'aretz* had demonstrated. Today, Jewish and Christian scholars operate for the most part in a very different climate to that of a century ago, and while confessional interests are still recognisable in some of the discussions, for the most part critical Jewish and Christian scholars are free to co-operate with each other, often sharing membership of the same scholarly societies and publishing in the same journals. Indeed both international conferences on Galilee so far organised, those at Kibbutz Hanaton in Galilee in 1989 and at Duke University in 1996, had a highly representative participation of scholars from both backgrounds.[33]

While it is inevitable that there should be an overlap between the two sets of concerns – since the history of Jesus is (or should be) treated as part of the history of early Judaism – differences of outlook and emphasis were bound to surface, and are as operative today as they were in the nineteenth century. Neither history was a purely innocent reconstruction of the past, as we have seen, and the practitioners in one area were not always aware of the debates occurring in the other. This led to generalisations and unquestioned assumptions to suit particular agendas, as the history of the quest for Jesus has so graphically illustrated. When Professor Martin Hengel first suggested that I might investigate the topic of Galilee in Hellenistic and Roman times, I was aware of the danger of concentrating solely on the background and immediate context of Jesus' ministry. Instead I opted for a broader canvas in *Galilee from Alexander the Great to Hadrian* (1980), examining how some of Professor Hengel's insights in his monumental *Judentum und Hellenismus* (1972) might apply to a particular region over a longer time frame. In this book I avoided any detailed discussion of Jesus and his ministry other than in the context of possible leaders of revolutionary movements in Galilee.[34] It was several years later

---

[33] The Proceedings of the first conference have been published as *The Galilee in Late Antiquity,* ed. L. Levine (New York and Jerusalem: The Jewish Theological Seminary of America, 1992) and those of the Duke meeting as *Galilee through the Centuries: Confluence of Cultures,* ed. E. Meyers (Winona Lake: Eisenbrauns, 1999).

[34] *Galilee from Alexander the Great to Hadrian. A Study of Second-Temple Judaism* (Wilmington and Notre Dame: Glazier and University of Notre Dame Press, 1980; reprint, Edinburgh: T. & T. Clark, 1998) 220–28.

before I attempted to address the question of Jesus, in *Galilee, Jesus and the Gospels* (1988). Already in this work it was necessary to revise some of my earlier views on Galilee in the light of the ongoing archaeological investigations by the Meiron Project and others, the results of which had been published in the meantime.[35] I have found that my studies have brought me into dialogue with two quite different sets of scholars and this selection of essays is arranged to reflect my continued discussion of both issues, Galilee within the context of Jewish history and the quest for Jesus in a Galilean context. They follow, therefore, a thematic rather than a chronological sequence in their presentation.

Galilee and the History of Early Judaism

One of the pioneers of recent archaeology of Galilee, Eric Meyers, has repeatedly decried the fact that archaeology of the Hellenistic and Roman periods had made little impact on the historical and literary studies of the same period, unlike the close collaboration that has occurred between archaeologists and textual scholars for earlier periods.[36] Meyers himself has consistently attempted to bridge the gap in several of his own publications, and most recently through the organisation of the Sepphoris exhibition at the North Carolina State Museum and an interdisciplinary conference at Duke university.[37] His constructive criticism of *Galilee from Alexander the Great to Hadrian* highlighted the need for dialogue with archaeology if a comprehensive account of Galilee was to be accomplished.[38] While not claiming any competence in the discipline, I have subsequently attempted to continue to inform myself of the developments in this area through frequent visits to the key sites, study of the reports and consultations with the many expert field-archaeologists working in the region.

The task of correlating the archaeological and the literary evidence is not an easy one, however. On the one hand we can encounter a diversity of forms in terms of architectural styles, ceramic typologies and other artefactual objects in the material culture which archaeology investigates, while at the same time meeting 'the Galileans' or the *Ioudaioi* in the literary sources, as though we are dealing with a single, monochromic cul-

---

[35] *Galilee, Jesus, and the Gospels. Literary Approaches and Historical Investigations* (Dublin and Minneapolis: Gill & Macmillan and Fortress Press, 1988) 144 f.

[36] Cf. E. Meyers, 'Judaic Studies and Archaeology: the Legacy of Avi-Yonah,' *Eretz Israel 19. Michael Avi-Yonah Memorial Volume* (Jerusalem: The Israel Exploration Society, 1987) 24*–27*; id., 'Early Judaism and Christianity in the Light of Archaeology,' *BA* 51 (1988) 69–79, especially 74 f.

[37] R. Martin Nagy et al., eds., *Sepphoris in Galilee. Crosscurrents of Culture* (Raleigh: North Carolina Museum of Modern Art, 1996).

[38] E. Meyers, 'Galilean Regionalism: A Reappraisal,' in *Approaches to Ancient Judaism*, ed. W. Scott Green vol. 5 (Missoula: Scholars Press, 1978) 115–31.

ture.[39] It would of course be a false supposition to claim that whereas archaeology can provide us with hard data, the literary material is shaped by ideological concerns and must therefore be regarded as secondary or unreliable. Both archaeological data and texts call for interpretation, and the challenge is to discern how each may or may not confirm the picture which the other suggests, and decide on the probabilities when an apparent conflict of evidence appears to occur. Despite these hermeneutical problems, it must be said that the view 'from the ground' which recent archaeology of Galilee can offer has provided an alternative 'text' which goes well beyond anything that Renan had imagined as he contemplated the Galilean landscape. Indeed an understanding of many aspects of ancient society, not represented at all or only incidentally in the literary remains, is one of the major contributions of socio-archaeology, which concerns itself with understanding the data it uncovers within regional and subregional contexts. In the case of Galilee in particular, this emphasis has helped considerably in providing ethnicity markers for Jewish settlements and determining the extent of that presence in the region at different historical periods, as previously mentioned.

In addition to the debate about archaeology's contribution to historical reconstruction, the issue of the utilisation of texts for similar purposes is also hotly debated. The emphasis of the 'new criticism' on the independence of texts from both their circumstances of production and the world to which they refer, challenges the notion that the relevant texts as far as Galilee is concerned – gospels, Josephus's writings or the rabbinic writings – can be treated as windows on that actual world. Jacob Neusner's trenchant criticism of my original use of the rabbinic material might be viewed, partly at least, under this heading. His own discussion of the Mishnah as a utopian document, the product of priestly insights and scribal imagination, certainly casts doubt on the referential quality of the work in terms of Galilean life, though not all share this scepticism.[40] However, Neusner is particularly scathing about the identification of earlier pre–70 traditions on the basis of their attribution to named rabbis, and has devel-

---

[39] R. Vale, 'Literary Sources in Archaeological Description. The Case of Galilee, Galilees and Galileans,' *JSJ* 18 (1987) 210–28; cf. also D. R. Edwards and C. T. McCollough, eds., *Archaeology and the Galilee. Texts and Contexts in the Graeco-Roman and Byzantine Periods,* South Florida Studies in the History of Judaism 143 (Atlanta: Scholars Press, 1997) especially the articles by J. F. Strange, 'First Century Galilee from Archaeology and from Texts,' 39–48 and D. E. Groh, 'The Clash between Literary and Archaeological Models of Provincial Palestine,' 29–38.

[40] J. Neusner, 'Galilee in the Time of Hillel: A Review,' in id., *Formative Judaism. Religious, Historical and Literary Studies,* Brown Judaic Studies 37 (Chico: Scholars Press, 1982); H. Lapin, *Early Rabbinic Civil Law and the Social History of Roman Galilee,* Brown Judaic Studies 307 (Atlanta: Scholars Press, 1995).

oped a methodology of distinguishing earlier from later layers of the tradition through the internal logic of the development of the law in relation to
the pre-Jamnia, Jamnia and post-Bar Cochba periods. In *Galilee, Jesus and
the Gospels* I attempted to address Neusner's strictures, especially in relation to the distinctive Galilean *halakoth* found in the rabbinic writings.[41]
One way out of this seeming impasse is the method of *Lokalkoloritforschung*, as applied to the gospels by Gerd Theissen. When they are read
against the concrete historical circumstances of Galilean social life, many
gospel passages are illuminated in most interesting ways.[42]

Likewise, the critical study of Josephus' different writings has developed considerably over the last 25 years, especially in the recognition of
the different biases of the individual works. In this regard Shaye Cohen's
study, *Josephus in Galilee and Rome. His Vita and Development as a Historian* (1979) was a benchmark, in that it highlighted how his experience
as commander in Galilee coloured considerably his account in *JW*,
whereas his position under the patronage of the Flavians in Rome meant
that *JA* and *Life* had a very different agenda. Cohen's own reconstruction
of Josephus's role in the revolt, namely, that of Zealot leader, has not won
widespread acceptance. Yet by highlighting the motifs and themes of
Josephus' different writings, which are often expressed through the projec-
tion back to earlier times of the situation of his own day, Cohen's study
was the forerunner for many others in developing a critical approach to the
Josephan corpus before using it for historical reconstruction.[43]

The social sciences have played an important role in recent studies of
the Old and New Testaments, but less so in the study of the Second Temple period. However, Richard Horsley's detailed study, *Galilee. History,
Politics, People* (1995), is the most thoroughgoing attempt at such an
analysis. In this work Horsley applies a conflictual model derived from a
combination of Gerhard Lenski's study of advanced agrarian societies and

---

[41] J. Neusner, *Judaism. The Evidence of the Mishnah* (Chicago: University of Chicago
Press, 1981); Freyne, *Galilee, Jesus and the Gospels*, 213–18.

[42] G. Theissen, *The Gospels in Context. Social and Political History in the Synoptic
Tradition* (Edinburgh: T. & T. Clark, 1992).

[43] S. J. D. Cohen, *Josephus in Galilee and Rome. His Vita and Development as an
Historian* (Leiden: Brill, 1979); P. Bilde, *Flavius Josephus between Jerusalem and
Rome. His Life, his Works, and their Importance,* JSP Supplement Series 2 (Sheffield:
Sheffield Academic Press, 1988); F. Pavente and J. Sievers, eds., *Josephus and the His-
tory of the Greco-Roman Period. Essays in Memory of Morton Smith* (Leiden: Brill,
1994); S. Schwartz, 'The "Judaism" of Samaria and Galilee in Josephus' Version of the
Letter of Demetrius I to Jonathan (*Antiquities* 13, 48–57),' *HTR* 82 (1989) 377–91; J.
McLaren, *Turbulent Times? Josephus and Scholarship on Judea in the First Century,*
JSP Supplement Series 29 (Sheffield: Sheffield Academic Press, 1998); S. Mason, ed.,
Understanding Josephus: Seven Perspectives, JSP Supplement Series 32 (Sheffield:
Sheffield Academic Press 1998).

John Kautsky's politics of aristocratic empires to Galilean social life.[44] In reacting to Gerd Theissen's use of a structural functionalist approach to Palestinian society of the first century CE, Horsley claims that this model has engendered a static view of society, thus ignoring historical changes due to the social conflict which the political economic structure itself had brought about.[45] Thus, the agenda for future investigation of Palestinian society should, in his view, focus on dominant interest groups and the attempts to legitimate their positions of privilege through the rituals and religious institutions which the elite produce and promote.

From this perspective Horsley presents a detailed analysis of Galilean society in terms of an ongoing conflict between the Judeans (his understanding of the meaning of *Ioudaioi* in the sources) and the Galileans. The former represent the ruling class of Judea who function as retainers on behalf of Roman imperial interests, whereas the latter are descendants of the old Israelites, who, while sharing certain traditions with the Judeans in the past, had developed their own customs, institutions and ethos, and were resistant to any imposition from the south. Thus, the history of Jewish society in Palestine from the Hasmoneans to the Rabbis was one of conflict and opposition between north and south. Galilee takes on an identity that is neither pagan nor Jewish but Galilean in terms of a distinctive way of life. Central to Horsley's understanding is the idea that the various strands of social life – political, economic, cultural and religious – must be seen as interconnected, and any attempt to separate out one of these, even for analysis, is deemed to be anachronistic and distorting. Yet in accordance with the Marxist bias of the model, it is clear that economic exploitation is at the root of the ongoing conflictual situation. Horsley repeatedly speaks of the embeddedness of religion in ancient societies. However, this can ultimately lead to its invisibility, since in this view religion has no independent social function but is merely an aspect of the superstructure, serving either to compensate for aspects of life that are missing at the infrastructure, or alternatively, to legitimate certain existing aspects by giving them a status within the symbolic universe.

This study of Galilee is both challenging and informative on many issues that I had struggled with in previous studies. Horsley repeatedly challenges my reading of evidence and situations in *Galilee from Alexander*

---

[44] G. Lenski, *Power and Privilege: A Theory of Social Stratification* (New York: McGraw, 1966); J. H. Kautsky, *The Politics of Aristocratic Empires* (Chapel Hill: University of North Carolina Press, 1982).

[45] R. Horsley, *Sociology and the Jesus Movement* (New York: Crossroad, 1989); id., *Galilee. History, Politics, People* (Valley Forge: Trinity Press International, 1995); id., *Archaeology, History and Society in Galilee. The Social Context of Jesus and the Rabbis* (Valley Forge: Trinity Press International, 1996).

the Great to Hadrian, not always taking into account the fact that my views had changed on various issues in the interim. While I learned a considerable amount from his incisive criticisms I still find myself less than convinced by his overall proposal. This dissatisfaction has ultimately to do with the choice and application of the Lenski-Kautsky model which has been chosen because it highlights conflict leading to historical change. Despite Horsley's explicit intention of working back and forth dialectically between the evidence and the model, this does not seem to have been adequately carried through. It is surprising that the evidence of the gospels is not utilised in the subsequent discussion, since the picture of Galilee/Jerusalem relations that they suggest would at least challenge the view being proposed, namely, that of the Galileans as Israelites, and therefore not sharing an attachment to Jerusalem or its institutions. Other evidence that might challenge the hypothesis being proposed is either summarily dismissed or given little weight in the final assessment, so that one has the impression that the model rather than the evidence is determining the picture to an undue degree.

It emerges from this observation that the choice of model is itself a hermeneutical option that calls for both a critical and self-critical examination, before it is allowed to determine the discussion. Lenski's model for agrarian empires is a highly generalised one and allows for endless variations. He himself acknowledges that the priestly class, 'the last but not the least' of the privileged groups within agrarian societies may not always side with the ruling elite. Lenski instances as a specific example of this the Jewish religious tradition, where the insistence on the god of justice can mean that priests stem the flow of resources into the hands of the elite, thereby functioning as 'the preservers of the ancient redistributive ethic.'[46] Equally, Kautsky's rigid distinction between the religion administered by the aristocracy and that of the peasants, a distinction used elsewhere by Horsley also,[47] is open to question in the case of Palestinian Jewish society. The Elijah-Elisha cycle of stories (both northerners, incidentally) combine popular 'shamanistic' and distinctively Yahwistic elements. Yet in their present form these stories are the product of the Jerusalem scribal classes, who have not suppressed their 'popular' elements, but rather ensured their preservation in the national narrative.[48] A more flexible under-

---

[46] Lenski, *Power and Privilege,* 263 f. and 266.

[47] R. Horsley and J. Hanson, *Bandits, Prophets and Messiahs: Popular Movements at the Time of Jesus* (Minneapolis: Winston Press, 1985) 102–10.

[48] Cf. R. Coote, ed., *Elijah and Elisha in Socioliterary Perspective* (Atlanta: Scholars Press, 1992); T. W. Overholt, 'Elijah and Elisha in the Context of Israelite Religion,' in *Prophets and Paradigms. Essays in Honour of Gene M. Tucker* (Sheffield: Sheffield Academic Press, 1996) 94–111.

standing of the role of popular religion is called for, therefore, than that
based on class distinctions. Rather, the rich tapestry of religious beliefs
which can be documented from the 'official' literary texts has many
threads and these reflect all levels in Palestinian Jewish society, so-called
elites and peasants alike. Had Horsley been predisposed to see that society
through the lens of a structural-functionalist model in addition to the conflictual one he has employed, he might well have viewed the social role of
religion in a different and more favourable light. He would have been able
to capture better the centrifugal as well as the centripetal forces at work in
the Hellenistic and Roman periods.

Galilee and the Jesus Movement

As previously mentioned, the Bultmann era of New Testament scholarship
did not encourage research into the Palestinian background of either Jesus
or his movement. Nor indeed did the so-called 'new quest for the historical
Jesus' inaugurated by Ernst Käsemann in his now famous lecture of 1953
generate any particular attention in that direction either.[49] The one full-
scale account of Jesus by a post-Bultmannian, *Jesus of Nazareth* (1960) by
Günther Bornkamm was more interested in the message rather than the
matrix of Jesus' life and ministry. In fact the importance of Galilee in
German New Testament scholarship of the period was associated more
with its symbolic role within the gospel narratives as these were being explored by the *Redaktionsgeschichtliche Methode*. Thus, for Willi Marxsen
Galilee represented the place of the coming Parousia in Mark's gospel,
whereas according to Hans Conzelmann it belonged to the *arche* or 'beginnings' in Luke's two-volume narrative of the Christian salvation-
history.[50] To some extent Ernst Lohmeyer's *Galiläa und Jerusalem* (1937)
had anticipated this approach to the differing perspectives on Galilee of
the evangelists, beginning with the post-resurrection narratives. Lohmeyer's study also raised the further question of a Galilean Christianity
and its distinctive colouring from that of Jerusalem, based both on Jesus'
ministry and those different strands within early Christianity itself that can
be associated with Galilee from later sources. These two issues, the Galilean matrix of Jesus' ministry and the role of Galilee in the emergence of
Christianity are very much alive still in New Testament studies. Indeed as
Lohmeyer himself had seen, the issue of Hellenistic versus Palestinian

---

[49] E. Käsemann, 'Das Problem des historischen Jesus,' *ZTK* 51 (1954) 125–52. An
English version of the article appears in E. Käsemann, *Essays on New Testament Themes*
(London: SCM Press, 1964) 15–47.

[50] W. Marxsen, *Der Evangelist Markus. Studien zur Redaktionsgeschichte des Evangeliums*, FRLANT 49 (Göttingen: Vandenhoeck & Ruprecht, 1959) 35–77; H. Conzelmann, *The Theology of St. Luke* (London: Faber and Faber, 1960) 27–59.

Christianity, as this had been developed from a History of Religions perspective by Wilhelm Bousset and others, ignored the more pressing problem in terms of Christian origins of Galilee/Jerusalem relations as these are reflected in our earliest sources.[51]

Käsemann's article indirectly raised the issue of Galilee, however, once the new quest for Jesus moved beyond the theological parameters of its earliest formulations to a more concrete historical approach. In attempting to formulate a criterion for identifying material within the synoptic tradition that came directly from Jesus himself, Käsemann suggested what has come to be known as the criterion of dissimilarity. According to his terms, 'in only one case do we have more or less safe ground under our feet; when there are no grounds either for deriving a tradition from Judaism or for ascribing it to Christianity, and especially when Jewish Christianity has mitigated or modified the received tradition, as having found it too bold for its taste.' Nevertheless, he goes on to declare that 'we shall not, from this angle of vision, gain any clear view of the connecting link between Jesus, his Palestinian environment and his later community.' What is more important is that 'we gain some insight into what separated him from friends and foe alike.'[52] The limitations of this formulation of an adequate criterion for understanding Jesus have been discussed extensively. What has emerged is the need for a reformulation that would take account of both the continuities and discontinuities of Jesus with his environment.[53] This, however, has raised the issue once more of the Galilean context for Jesus' ministry and how the one may have been shaped by the other.

In the contemporary wave of writing on the topic there are two distinct and clearly discernible trends in describing the Galilean context in relation to Jesus. On the one hand there are the proponents of the Cynic-hypothesis, who call for an urbanised and Hellenised Galilee, represented *par excellence* in the citation of Burton Mack at the beginning of this chapter.[54] On the other hand there are those who insist on a Jewish Galilee,

---

[51] E. Lohmeyer, *Galiläa und Jerusalem,* FRLANT 34 (Göttingen: Vandenhoeck & Ruprecht, 1936).

[52] Käsemann, 'The Problem of the Historical Jesus,' 37.

[53] Cf. G. Theissen, 'Historical Scepticism and the Criteria of Jesus Research. My Attempt to Leap over Lessing's Yawning Gulf,' *SJT* 49 (1996) 146–75, especially 151 note 5 and 162–66; G. Theißen and D. Winter, *Die Kriterienfrage in der Jesusforschung. Vom Differenzkriterium zum Plausibilitätskriterium* (Göttingen: Vandenhoeck & Ruprecht, 1997).

[54] B. Mack, *A Myth of Innocence. Mark and Christian Origins* (Philadelphia: Fortress Press, 1988) 53–77; id., *The Lost Gospel. The Book of Q and Christian Origins* (New York: HarperCollins, 1993) 51–68; J. D. Crossan, *The Historical Jesus. The Life of a Mediterranean Jewish Peasant* (Edinburgh: T. & T. Clark, 1991); L. Vaage, *Galilean Upstarts. Jesus' First Followers according to Q* (Valley Forge: Trinity Press Interna-

represented by the citation from Geza Vermes, though there are also many variations on this picture.[55] A number of underlying questions arise in these differing perspectives, not least the particular hermeneutical stance of the individual authors in their approach to both Judaism and Jesus. In that respect, the debate reflects the old adage *plus ça change, plus la même chose*, despite claims by members of the Jesus Seminar in the U.S.A. that a new and different methodology has been developed.[56] The only change has been that the German liberal Protestant ethos of the first quest has been replaced by the secular North American conditions of the current research. In the end the same universalising and modernising dynamic seems to be at work in both instances. In each case the contemporary culture provides the key to understanding the emerging portraits of Jesus.

A second issue is related to the way in which the study of Galilean culture has been appropriated in the discussions about Jesus. As previously mentioned, the practitioners of one area do not usually operate in the other, at least to the same extent, such are the effects of the increasing specialisation of knowledge within the discipline as a whole. This can lead to over-simplification of complex issues such as the extent and nature of Hellenisation in Galilee or the effects of urbanisation, issues addressed in a number of the articles included in this volume. The understanding of Hellenism that operates in some of these descriptions of Galilee is also dated in that it is seen as being in direct opposition to some form of 'pure' Judaism, despite the fact that Martin Hengel's 1972 study had concluded that 'all of Judaism had been Hellenised from the middle of the second century

---

tional, 1994). Of the many publications of F. G. Downing on the subject of Cynicism and the New Testament, the following are the most relevant to Galilee: 'Cynics and Christians,' *NTS* 30 (1984) 584–93; 'The Social Contexts of Jesus the Teacher: Construction or Reconstruction,' *NTS* 33 (1987) 439–51; *Cynics and Christian Origins* (Edinburgh: T. & T. Clark, 1992) 115–68. For a critique of the Cynic hypothesis cf. H. D. Betz, 'Jesus and the Cynics. Survey and Analysis of a Hypothesis,' *JR* 74 (1994) 453–75.

[55] G. Vermes, *Jesus the Jew* (London: Collins, 1973); B. Meyer, *The Aims of Jesus* (London: 1979); R. Riesner, *Jesus als Lehrer*, WUNT 7 (Tübingen: J. C. B. Mohr, 1981); E. P. Sanders, *Jesus and Judaism* (London: SCM, 1985); Freyne, *Galilee, Jesus and the Gospels*, 219–68; J. Meier, *A Marginal Jew. Rethinking the Historical Jesus*, vol. I (New York: Doubleday, 1991); J. Charlesworth, ed., *Jesus' Jewishness. Exploring the Place of Jesus in Early Judaism* (New York: Crossroad, 1991); R. Horsley, *Jesus and the Spiral of Violence: Popular Jewish Resistance in Roman Palestine* (San Francisco: Harper and Row, 1987); G. Theissen and A. Merz, *The Historical Jesus* (London: SCM, 1998).

[56] Cf. Crossan, *The Historical Jesus*, xxvii–xxxiv; R. Funk and R. Hoover, *The Search for the Authentic Words of Jesus. The Five Gospels* (New York: Macmillan, 1993) and various numbers of the journal *Forum* between 1984–1994.

BCE.'[57] Judaism and Hellenism are thus no longer to be seen as polar opposites. The questions to be addressed concern rather the ways in which the two cultures developed a symbiotic relationship over time, the extent to which older forms were maintained even when appearing in Greek dress, and the impact which the indigenous cultures of the east had on Hellenism itself as a cultural phenomenon.[58] There is also the further complicating factor of the nature of the Hellenistic culture which was mediated by Roman imperialism and how this might have differed from earlier times. Should we in fact speak of Romanisation as well as Hellenisation, and if so, how might the differences be recognised in the material culture?[59]

It is characteristic of our times in a post-Marx era that economic factors have come to be seen as primary in discussions of societies, ancient and modern. Trends in contemporary theology have also contributed to a reading of the Jesus story in materialist rather than religious terms, and hence there is a greater preoccupation with the social world of Galilee than was the case in the past. While this development is to be welcomed in that it highlights the this-world concerns of the 'synoptic Jesus', the danger is that the religious dimension of his message and ministry is minimised or ignored altogether. This same issue arose in the debate with Horsley's emphasis on the nature and extent of the conflict within Galilean Jewish society. Locating the Jesus movement within that tension should not lead to abandoning his religious concerns, and discussion of the extent to which Jewish messianic ideas might have been operative within Galilean as well as Judean society, especially in the light of the new discoveries from Qumran, are both legitimate and necessary.[60] Despite Käsemann's scepticism on the matter, cited above, the issue of Jesus' continuity with both Judaism and early Christianity in Galilee still needs to be addressed.

---

[57] M. Hengel, *Judentum und Hellenismus. Studien zu ihrer Begegnung unter besonderer Berücksichtigung Palästinas zur Mitte des 2. Jh.s v.Chr.* 2nd ed. WUNT 10 (Tübingen: J. C. B. Mohr, 1973), especially 192–95.

[58] Cf. F. Millar, 'The Phoenician Cities. A Case Study of Hellenisation,' *Proceedings of Cambridge Philological Society* 209 (1983) 55–71; id., 'Empire, Community and Culture in the Roman Near East: Greeks, Syrians, Jews and Arabs,' *JJS* 38 (1987) 143–64; 'The Problem of Hellenistic Syria,' in *Hellenism in the East,* ed. A. Kuhrt and S. Sherwin-White (London and Berkeley: University of California Press, 1987) 110–33.

[59] F. Millar, *The Roman Near East, 31 BC– AD 337* (Cambridge: Harvard University Press, 1993); S. Alcock, ed., *The Early Roman Empire and the East* (Oxford: Oxbrow Monographs 95, 1997).

[60] J. J. Collins, *The Scepter and the Star. The Messiahs of the Dead Sea Scrolls and Other Ancient Literature* (New York: Doubleday, 1995); G. Oegma, *The Anointed and his People. Messianic Expectations from the Maccabees to Bar Kochba,* JSP Supplement Series 27 (Sheffield: Sheffield Academic Press, 1998). Cf. below, 'Messiah and Galilee' pp. 230 ff.

Lohmeyer had raised the question of Galilean Christianity, not in opposition to Jerusalem, but as another thread in the variegated tapestry that the new movement displayed from its earliest days. Others too have sought to identify such a movement within the broad chapel of Jewish Christianity, such as the essay by L. E. Elliott-Binns, linking the *Epistle of James* and its echoes of the Jesus sayings-tradition with the region.[61] Both are anxious to point to the continuities between the pre- and post-Easter followers of Jesus in a Galilean setting. The difficulty is that we have so little information for the first century. One has to await the early Byzantine period for the first indisputable traces in the archaeological remains, despite the Herculean efforts of the Franciscan archaeologists at such obvious centres as Nazareth and Capernaum for the earlier period.[62] The search for a *Sitz im Leben* for the various gospels was an element of the Redaction Critical approach. While Galilee has been suggested by various scholars for both Mark and Matthew, the evidence has been far from obvious and the procedure of moving from text to context on the basis of geographical references is regarded as highly problematic.[63] Despite the inconclusive nature of these suggestions, recent trends in *Q* scholarship have given new impetus to the quest for a Galilean setting for the branch of the new movement represented by the tradents of this collection of sayings. In particular the mention of such Galilean centres as Capernaum, Bethsaida and Chorazin (*Q*Lk 10,13–15), suggests to many scholars that a ministry in Galilee, similar to that of Jesus himself, continued there for a time, possibly up to the revolt of 66 CE.[64] Nevertheless, there are very differing views of *Q* and its orientation. Currently the most favoured position, following Kloppenborg's analysis, suggests a multiple redaction of the document. A different

---

[61] L. E. Elliot-Binns. *Galilean Christianity* (London: SCM Press, 1956).

[62] Cf. C. Bottini, L. di Segni, E. Alliata, eds., *Christian Archaeology in the Holy Land. New Discoveries. Essays in Honour of Virgilio C. Corbo,* Studium Biblicum Franciscanum, Collectio Maior 36 (Jerusalem: Franciscan Printing Press, 1990), and F. Manns and E. Alliata, eds., *Early Christianity in Context. Monuments and Documents,* Studium Biblicum Franciscanum, Collectio Maior 38 (Jerusalem: Franciscan Printing Press, 1993).

[63] E. Struthers Malbon, 'Galilee and Jerusalem: History and Literature in Markan Interpretation,' *CBQ* 44 (1982) 242–55; J. R. Donahue, 'Windows and Mirrors'. The Setting of Mark's Gospel' *CBQ* 57 (1995) 1–26.

[64] Cf. in particular the several studies and collections by J. S. Kloppenborg, *The Formation of Q. Trajectories in Ancient Wisdom Collections* (Philadelphia: Fortress Press, 1987); id., ed., *The Shape of Q. Signal Essays on the Sayings Gospel* (Minneapolis: Fortress Press, 1994); id., ed., *Conflict and Invention. Literary, Rhetorical and Social Studies on the Sayings Gospel Q* (Valley Forge: Trinity Press International, 1995); id., 'The Sayings Gospel Q and the Quest for the Historical Jesus,' *HTR* 89 (1996) 307–44; id. with L. Vaage, eds., *Early Christianity, Q and Jesus, Semeia* 55 (Atlanta: Scholars Press, 1991).

approach that may have greater possibilities in the long run is that of examining the local colouring of the sayings on the basis of the archaeological data.[65] Such an approach has the distinct advantage of avoiding the pitfalls of an over-reliance on literary criticism of a hypothetical document, in isolation from other criteria, which can give rise to highly speculative conclusions especially when it is linked to discussions about the Cynic Jesus. However, even if a Galilean provenance for *Q* were to be established, it is not clear how this might change our view of Galilean Christianity as a whole and how the putative *Q* community might be related with the Jewish Christian Nazoreans, intimations of whose presence can be detected in the later literary sources.

Prospects

This brief sketch of scholarly interest in Galilee in the Hellenistic and Roman periods has concentrated on the two main centres of discussion, the study of early Judaism and the quest for the historical Jesus. Undoubtedly these two questions will continue to exercise considerable influence on future study of the region also. Changing fashions in the approach to the main literary sources will undoubtedly play an important role. One suspects that the Jewish sources, especially the Talmud Yerushalmi has many more treasures to yield up, and this in turn may focus more attention on the Byzantine period in the study of the Christian presence in Galilee also.[66]

However, it is to the developments in the archaeological realm that one can reasonably look for the most important advances. In addition to the publication of the results of the surveys conducted on behalf of the Israel Antiquities Authority, dealing with Galilee, we are also awaiting final reports on several sites, most notably that of Sepphoris which has attracted three separate teams dealing with different areas of the city. A clear understanding of the role that this centre played in the heart of lower Galilee in different periods is crucial for an overall judgement of Galilee's contribution both to early Judaism and early Christianity. One hopes that the changing political situation in the Middle East may make it possible for proper surveys of the southern Lebanon including western Hermon, since

---

[65] Theissen, *The Gospels in Context*, 203–34; J. Reed, *Places in Early Christianity: Galilee, Archaeology, Urbanisation, and Q* (Ph.D. Diss., University of California at Claremont, 1994); id., 'The Social Map of Q,' in Kloppenborg, ed., *Conflict and Invention*, 17–36.

[66] Cf. P. Schäfer, ed., *The Talmud Yerushalmi and Graeco-Roman Culture I* Texte und Studien zum Antiken Judentum 71 (Tübingen: J. C. B. Mohr, 1998).

the ethnic patterns in antiquity for this region are still relatively obscure. Yet as the hinterland for the Phoenician cities of Tyre and Sidon it is important for our understanding of their impact on the interior, including also, upper Galilee.

Future studies of Galilee will no doubt concentrate on various aspects of the social and cultural life of the region, supplementing, refining or correcting current positions. In this regard the contribution which the social sciences can make in helping to formulate the correct questions regarding ethnicity, inculturation, regionalism, urbanisation and ancient economics will undoubtedly be crucial in clarifying many issues that are still unclear about historical Galilee and its peoples. My own current emphasis is to study Galilee within a larger regional context, running on an east/west axis from the desert to the Mediterranean, and on a north/south line with Samaria, Judea and Idumea.[67] How did Galilee fare in comparison to other regions and other ethnically controlled territories when faced with the pervasive influence of Hellenism and the increasing presence of Roman imperial power over the centuries? As this survey has suggested, important interests have and still dominate the study of Galilee because of its historical importance for both Judaism and Christianity. For that reason in particular wider regional comparisons and contrasts can assist in broadening the horizons and ensuring that a concentration on Galilee alone does not lead to its being assimilated into our modern preconceptions and images for whatever reason.

---

[67] Cf. S. Freyne, 'Galileans, Phoenicians and Itureans. A Study of Regional Contrasts in the Hellenistic Age' in *Hellenism in the Land of Israel*, ed. J. J. Collins and G. E. Sterling (Notre Dame: University of Notre Dame Press, 2000).

1. The Galileans in the Light of Josephus' *Life*

'With this limited area, and although surrounded by such powerful foreign nations, the two Galilees have always resisted any hostile invasion, for the inhabitants are from infancy inured to war and have at all times been numerous; never did the men lack courage or the country men' (*JW* 3,41 f.). It is surprising how this general characterisation of the Galileans by Josephus has so often found its way into modern writings about Galilee without any detailed study of the *Life*, the one work of his where the Galileans occur more frequently than in all the others together.[1]

This failure to differentiate the terminology of Josephus in his various works has tended to identify the Galileans as revolutionaries, closely associated with, if not positively another name for, Zealots.[2] It is claimed that Galilee was the home of militant nationalism in the first century CE,[3] a conclusion that seems to be corroborated by the fact that Josephus designates the founder of the fourth philosophical sect as Judas the Galilean.[4]

---

[1] Οἱ Γαλιλαῖοι occurs 46 times in *Life*, 20 times in *JW*, 15 in *JA* and once in *Con. Ap.* according to A. Schalit, *Namenswörterbuch zu Flavius Josephus*, Supplement I to *A Complete Concordance to Flavius Josephus*, ed. K. H. Rengstorf (Leiden: Brill, 1968). S. Zeitlin, 'Who were the Galileans? New Light on Josephus' Activities in Galilee,' *JQR* 59 (1973) 189–203, reckons only 34 occurrences in *Life* and therefore does not take account of the following important passages: 66, 84, 143, 190, 198, 302, 311, 350, 368, 383, 391, 398.

[2] Thus A. Schlatter, *Geschichte Israels von Alexander dem Großem bis Hadrian* (reprint, Darmstadt: G. Olms, 1972) 261 and 434 n. 237; F. Jackson and K. Lake, *The Beginnings of Christianity* (London, 1920–30), Part I, vol. I, *Prolegomena*, Appendix A, 'The Zealots,' 421–25, especially 424; R. Bultmann, *The History of the Synoptic Tradition* (Oxford: Blackwell, 1968) 55; S. G. F. Brandon, *Jesus and the Zealots* (Manchester: University Press, 1967) 54 and 65; G. Vermes, *Jesus the Jew* (London: Collins, 1973) 46–48; R. Meyer, *Der Prophet aus Galiläa* (reprint, Darmstadt: G. Olms, 1970) 70 f.

[3] M. Hengel, *The Zealots* (Edinburgh: T. & T. Clark, 1989) especially 56–59, where all the evidence for Galileans as revolutionaries is discussed. Zeitlin, 'Who were the Galileans?'; S. Birnbaum, 'The Zealots: The Case for Revaluation,' *JRS* 61 (1971) 155–70, especially 158, who stresses the links with previous nationalistic revolutionary activity in the province, especially at the time of Herod.

[4] Many scholars identify Judas the Galilean (*JW* 2,118; 432; *JA* 18,23, 20,102; *Ac.* 5,37) with Judas the son of Ezechias (*JW* 2,56). This latter was a Galilean brigand chief who had been put to death by Herod the Great (*JW* I,204 f.; *JA* 14,159.167). Thus e.g., E. Schürer, *The History of the Jewish People in the Age of Jesus Christ* 3 vols. (Revised ed. Edinburgh: T. & T. Clark, 1973–87) II, 600 f.; J. S. Kennard, 'Judas of Galilee and his Clan,' *JQR* 36 (1945) 281–86; Hengel, *The Zealots,* 330–37, and more recently 'Zeloten

Evidence from other Jewish sources as well as early Christian writers is also taken to confirm this picture.[5]

More recently, the Jewish scholar Solomon Zeitlin has re-examined this picture of the Galileans, concentrating for the most part on the *Life*. Yet once again the same conclusion is arrived at: 'I venture to say that the term "Galileans" in the *Life* does not have a geographical connotation, but is an appellative name given to the revolutionaries against Rome and the rulers of Judea who were appointed by Rome.'[6] The following essay also concentrates on the *Life* and comes to a rather different conclusion: the Galileans of the *Life* are not to be identified with revolutionaries, but rather emerge as ardent supporters of Josephus, whose mission it is to preserve peace in Galilee. That two such different conclusions should emerge from a study of such a short, though complex, work like the *Life* may seem surprising. It is the contention of this article that it is only by sifting all the evidence and not just a few texts, which seem to support a particular point of view that a balanced picture emerges. No attempt is made throughout the analysis to pass final judgement on what the real situation in Galilee was, but by way of conclusion certain suggestions are made, based on the presentation of *Life*, which I believe point the way towards a proper understanding of the Galileans' social and religious situations.

---

und Sikarier. Zur Frage nach der Einheit und Vielfalt der jüdischen Befreiungsbewegung 6–74 nach Christus,' in *Josephus-Studien. Festschrift Otto Michel*, ed. O. Betz, K. Haacher and M. Hengel (Göttingen: Vandenhoeck & Ruprecht, 1974) 174–96; M. Black, 'Judas of Galilee and Josephus' Fourth Philosophy,' *Josephus-Studien*, 45–54. However, the identification has been challenged by, e.g., Kirsopp Lake, *Beginnings*, 424, taking Schürer to task; M. Smith, 'Zealots and Sicarii. Their origins and relation,' *HTR* 64 (1971) 1–19; D. Rhoads, *Israel in Revolution 6–74 C.E. A Political History Based on the Writings of Josephus* (Philadelphia: Fortress Press, 1976) 50 f.; G. Baumbach, 'Zeloten und Sikarier,' *TLZ* 40 (1965) 727–40, especially 730 f., considers that the *sicarii* (and not the Zealots) have their origin in Galilee, but this seems to contradict Josephus, who specifically identifies them with the Judean countryside (*JA* 20,185 f.).

[5] *M. Yad* 4:8: a Galilean heretic; Galileans are mentioned in lists of Jewish sects by Justin (*Dialogue with Trypho* 80:2) and Hegesippus (in Eusebius *Hist. Eccl.* IV,22,7). They are also mentioned by Epictetus (Arrian *Diss* 4:7,6) though it is not clear whether this refers to Jewish Christians or not. Galileans are also mentioned in Lk 13,1 and Jesus himself (Mt 26,69; Lk 22,59; 23,60) and his followers (Acts 1,2; 2,7; Mk 14,70 – Peter) are so called, but in these latter references at least the appellation seems to be purely geographical as also in Jn 4,45, where Galilee and Galileans are combined. They also appear in a letter of Bar Cochba from Waddi Murrabba'at, but there is no agreement on the translation of the sentence in question and hence who exactly are intended. Cf. J. T. Milik, 'Notes sur une lettre de Siméon Bar Kokheba,' *Revue biblique* 60 (1953) 276–94; J. J. Rabbinowitz, 'Note sur la lettre de Bar Kokheba,' *Revue biblique* 61 (1954) 191 f.; S. A. Birnbaum, 'Bar Kokhba and Akiba,' *PEQ* 86 (1954) 23–33.

[6] S. Zeitlin, 'Who were the Galileans?' Cf. especially 193, 195 and 202.

Galilee as a General Geographical Term in *Life*

The question of Josephus' authority is the central issue in the *Life*, yet surprisingly we do not find any detailed geographic description of the territory entrusted to him, similar to *JW* 3,35–39. At the same time, the evidence suggests that he has in mind the same geographical territory whose boundaries and dimensions are described in the *JW*. The revolutionary government at Jerusalem, hearing that 'the whole of Galilee' had not yet revolted, sent Josephus and two others there in an attempt to stave off the war (*Life* 28). Twice he speaks of his handling of affairs in Galilee (*Life* 30 and 62) and of Vespasian's arrival there (*Life* 411). We hear also of the distinction of upper and lower Galilee (*Life* 67, 71, 187 f.). More helpful than these general expressions are his references to various places being on the borders of Galilee: Simonias (*Life* 115, 118), Xaloth (*Life* 226) and Dabaritta (*Life* 318). It is a three-day journey from the frontiers of Galilee to Jerusalem (*Life* 269). This frontier is apparently well defined, possibly even defended, as one gathers from several references: Josephus accompanies delegates from Jerusalem to the frontiers (*Life* 270), or dispatches 600 men to guard the roads leading into Galilee (*Life* 240) or to Jerusalem (*Life* 241). On the pretext of guarding the frontier town of Chabolo, he can move his troops around against Placidus who has been sent to ravage the villages around Ptolemais (*Life* 213 f.). People on the frontier with Scythopolis and the Dekapolis are threatened and Josephus can be charged with negligence if he does not go to their aid (*Life* 281, 285).

These details seem to suggest the same outlines for Galilee as those described in the *JW*, where it is said to be bordered by Scythopolis and the Dekapolis, with Xaloth and Chabolo also mentioned as border towns. In particular, both the revolutionary government and Josephus seem to presume that his mandate extends to Tiberias and Tarichaeae even though both these towns and their territories had been given to King Agrippa II by Nero in the year 54 CE (*JW* 2,252 f.; *JA* 20,159), and knowledge of this transfer is presumed in the *Life* (*Life* 34, 38 f.). Yet we find the Jerusalem authorities ordering the dismantling of Herod's palace at Tiberias (*Life* 65) and Josephus actually appointing Silas as στρατηγός of the city (*Life* 89, cf. 272). Even though we hear of him making his quarters at Cana (*Life* 86) or Asochis (*Life* 207, 384), Tarichaeae figures very prominently as both being loyal to him and as his place of residence and refuge, especially in his dealings with Tiberias (*Life* 96, 127, 159, 276, 304, 404). Both cities figure in the list of those fortified by Josephus (*Life* 188).

Sometimes, however, Galilee seems to be particularly associated with the Galileans, so much so in fact that the gentilic 'of the Galileans' can be used interchangeably for the noun Galilee as e.g., at *Life* 190, 214, 398.

This, coupled with other passages to be examined below where the Galileans and 'all Galilee' seem to go together, suggests that Josephus may also use the term Galilee in a non-administrative way to refer to that area where his own loyal supporters come from.[7] This possibility is further strengthened by the fact that the Galileans are sharply distinguished from the inhabitants of the towns especially those that are opposed to Josephus.[8] Before discussing the Galileans as possible revolutionaries it is therefore necessary to follow up this lead suggested by the geographical terms in the *Life* and try to determine more precisely who the Galileans are.

The Galileans

As already mentioned Josephus can use the gentilic τῶν Γαλιλαίων, 'of the Galileans', interchangeably with Γαλιλαία as a general designation of the area under his control (*Life* 190, 214, 398), that is, with a primarily geographic connotation of a general nature. However, our attention is drawn to other instances where the term 'the Galileans' seems to be used in a much more specific sense. They are (a) opposed to the inhabitants of the main cities and (b) from the country regions. We must examine this in detail.

a) The Galileans and the townspeople

Josephus distinguishes the Galileans from the inhabitants of the following towns: Tiberias, Sepphoris and Gabara – the three chief cities of Galilee according to *Life* 123 – and Gischala, the town of his archenemy John.

---

[7] Typical of this more restricted use of the term Galilee is *Life* 240, where Josephus sends a detachment of troops to guard 'the routes from Gabara into Galilee.' Yet elsewhere Gabara is described as one of the leading towns of Galilee (*Life* 123) and could not be described as a border town according to Josephus' own descriptions both in the *Life* and *JW*.

[8] *G. Jossa, 'Chi sono I Galilei nella *Vita* di Flavio Giuseppe,' *Rivista Biblica* 31 (1983) 329–39, while agreeing in general with my analysis considers the distinction I am proposing here too rigid to cover the support that Josephus receives at Tarichaeae e.g., where the Galileans gather twice to support him (*Life* 98f., 303f.). He understands the Galileans in religio-national rather than socio-political terms. For him the Galileans represent a 'group of Jews particularly attached to the ancestral laws, partially at least supporting the positions of the Shammaites and Zealots' (334f.). Cf. further his 'Josephus' Action in Galilee during the Jewish War,' in *Josephus and the History of the Greco-Roman Period. Essays in Memory of Morton Smith*, ed. F. Pavente and J. Sievers (Leiden: Brill, 1994) 265–78. I agree with the emphasis on the religious dimension of the Galileans, but I find little evidence that they are to be understood as a separate group. The fact that they are mainly from the countryside (ἀπὸ τῆς χώρας) does not preclude them coming from the many towns and villages of Galilee.

1) Tiberias. The distinction between Galileans and the people of Tiberias emerges at the very start of the *Life* in the passage already alluded to, where Justus calls on his fellow townsmen for a general revolt in the hope of restoring to his native city its position of prominence. 'Now is the time to take up arms and join hands with the Galileans' (*Life* 39). Yet, this show of solidarity is more apparent than real, for Justus really suggests utilising, for his own selfish intents, the Galileans' resentment of Sepphoris because of its pro-Roman stance. This is clear in the final reference where the distinction occurs, *Life* 391 f. Here Josephus repeats his assertions concerning Justus' real ambitions – he was for war, not because he was a Jewish revolutionary, but because he hoped that in the general upheaval he might obtain the command of Galilee.[9] In this stance Justus was opposed to the majority opinion at Tiberias, which had decided 'to maintain their allegiance to the king and not to revolt from Rome.' However, Josephus comments that there was no possibility of these hopes being fulfilled, since 'the Galileans, resenting the miseries which he had inflicted on them before the war were embittered against the Tiberians and would not tolerate him as their chief' (*Life* 390–92).[10] Clearly then the Galileans are to be distinguished from the Tiberians, and the indications are that the differences are not simply to do with a war stance but are related to much more deeply seated attitudes that were operative at an earlier stage.

This general resentment of the Galileans for their city neighbours is reflected in several other passages of *Life*. On two occasions they have to be

---

[9] According to R. Laqueur, *Der Jüdische Historiker Flavius Josephus* (Gießen, 1929) 7 ff. and 47 ff., *Life* 38 ff. and 391 f. are Josephus' later additions to the *Rechenschaftsbericht* which, he believes, underlies the *Life*. As such they form part of his apologetic against Justus and would not in themselves represent reliable information concerning the situation in Galilee. In using the *Life* for historical purposes, we must certainly take account of its special character, whether or not we accept Laqueur's source-critical analysis. The position of A. Schalit, 'Josephus und Justus. Studien zur *Vita* des Josephus,' *Klio* 26 (1933) 67–95, especially 92, that there is an organic development throughout the whole *Life,* seems to agree better with the general argument of this paper. For him the main *Tendenz* of *Life* is to present Josephus as a mild and considerate person in response to Justus' attack on him. His 'patriarchal' relations with the Galileans should be seen as part of this presentation. Consequently, this picture also stands in need of alternative verification, which can best be done by taking account of any deviations from the overall picture of *Life* and a careful comparison with the picture that emerges in *JW*.

[10] It is difficult to reconstruct the exact circumstances of the Galilean hostility referred to in *Life* 177 f. when the hand of Justus' brother was cut off as a punishment for forging letters. As Schalit, 'Josephus and Justus,' 78, points out, it must have been a political affair of some kind. Josephus himself punishes one of his soldiers in a similar fashion for alleged treason (*Life* 171–73; *JW* 2, 642 f.). According to J. M. Derrett, 'Law in the New Testament: *Si scandalizaverit te manus tua abscide ilium,*' *Revue internationale des droits de l'antiquité* 20 (1973) 11–41, the right hand is used in various legal transactions (cf. Sir. 21,9) and the punishment in question was for the violation of these.

restrained from sacking the town, once at the instigation of the people of Tarichaeae because of the plots on Josephus' life at Tiberias (*Life* 97–100, 123), and once because of the traitorous intentions of the city in sending for help to King Agrippa (*Life* 385–89). Elsewhere Josephus dissociates himself and the Galileans from the revolt of Tiberias against Rome (presumably because he had been accused of being responsible by Justus in his account) and suggests that already under his instigation they had made a bid for independence by attacking the towns of the Syrian Dekapolis, before Josephus ever took over command in Galilee (*Life* 341). Only twice does the distinction we have been suggesting appear to break down and we find Galileans and Tiberians side by side. Some Galileans helped the leader of the rabble of Tiberias, Jesus, in sacking Herod's palace (*Life* 66), and Josephus is aided by a 'large body of Galileans under arms with some from Tiberias' in putting down a revolt at Sepphoris (*Life* 107). Yet, neither example is telling against the overall position. One can readily understand minorities in both groups adopting attitudes different to the dominant trends. The readiness of the more militant of the Galileans to sack Herod's palace is understandable and does not indicate any great sympathy between Galileans and Tiberians, whereas on another occasion Josephus claims to have had some (minority) support at Tiberias (*Life* 99).

2) Sepphoris. The attitude of the Galileans towards Sepphoris is presented in *Life* as being, if anything, more hostile than that shown to Tiberias. This attitude had already emerged before Josephus' arrival in Galilee (*Life* 30), and is attributed to the city's pro-Roman stance, something that is stated more than once in the *Life* (30, 104, 124, 345–48, 373, 394 f.). On that occasion the Galileans had decided to sack the town, but Josephus uses his influence with the crowds and averts the danger (*Life* 31). A large body of Galileans 'under arms' accompany Josephus to Sepphoris as he uncovers their plot against him together with the arch-brigand Jesus, but there is no mention of reprisals on this occasion (*Life* 104–10). However, he was not so successful later and had to resort to a ploy – stating that the Romans had already arrived in the city – in an attempt to put an end to the pillaging of the Galileans who had seized on the opportunity granted them to 'vent their hatred on this city which they detested' (*Life* 273–80).

3) Gischala. This town meets with the ire of the Galileans because of John, one of its chief citizens, whose constant plotting against Josephus, as reported in *Life*, had the purpose of unseating Josephus and gaining the control of Galilee for himself (*Life* 70, 122 f., 189).[11] On two occasions we

---

[11] While John's greed and self-interest are emphasized in both *Life* and *JW*, the characterization in the latter work is much more hostile, as has been noted by Rhoads, *Israel in Revolution,* 122–24. Cf. *JW* 2,585–87 where the term λῃστής is applied to him, and *JW* 2,599 where he is involved at Tarichaeae in a plot against Josephus as a traitor, but is not mentioned in *Life* in the parallel account.

are told of the Galileans desire to destroy the place. The first instance follows immediately on John's intrigues against Josephus at Tiberias. He writes to Josephus proclaiming his innocence in the whole affair: 'The Galileans, many more of whom had again come up in arms from the whole district,' (they had just previously been there to assist him against Tiberias) wanted Josephus to lead them against him 'to exterminate both him and Gischala.' However, Josephus dissuaded them (*Life* 103 f.). Again after the affair with the Jerusalem officials the Galileans asked to be armed and declared their willingness to march against John, the author of all the trouble, but once more Josephus refused to use violence against his archenemy (*Life* 368; cf. *Life* 304, Galilean animosity for John).

4) Gabara. The fourth town that is clearly distinguished is Gabara, according to *Life* 123, one of the three largest cities of Galilee, though subsequently (*Life* 229, 242 f.) as Gabaroth (apparently the same place) it is described as a village. The animosity of the Galileans towards this place seems to stem from its association with John and its consequent acceptance of the Jerusalem delegation. John allegedly had made overtures to Sepphoris, Tiberias and Gabara, but only the latter joined him, due to the instigation of one Simon, a leading citizen, and a friend and associate of John. However, 'the people of Gabara, it is true, did not openly admit their defection; their dread of the Galileans of whose devotion to me they had had frequent experience was too great a deterrent' (*Life* 124 f.).

When we look for a common denominator for this opposition of the Galileans to the four towns in question the only one that suggests itself is the loyalty of the Galileans to Josephus.[12] This point is further emphasised by contrasting these towns with Tarichaeae, which also figures prominently in *Life* as one of the chief cities of Galilee. This town's support for Josephus is in striking contrast to Tiberias, for though on one occasion a plot was formed against him there, its instigators were from Tiberias rather than Tarichaeae and Josephus was able to dissuade the people (*Life* 132–54). It is his constant place of refuge from the plots of Tiberias and the Jerusalem embassy (*Life* 158 f., 174, 276, 304), or even after an accident (*Life* 404). Accordingly, we find the inhabitants of Tarichaeae spreading the word about the plots against Josephus at Tiberias 'throughout all Galilee', and the Galileans responding promptly by coming together in large numbers under arms (*Life* 98 f.). Thus the people of Tarichaeae and the

---

[12] This does not exclude individual reasons for the animosity, many of them predating Josephus' arrival in the province. Yet in the *Life* account it is a common factor: the hostility against Sepphoris is apparently for its pro-Roman stance, but loyalty to Josephus plays a part there also (*Life* 104–10). This same factor operates in their more vehement call against Tiberias (*Life* 99), Gischala (*Life* 103 f.) and Gabara (*Life* 124 f.).

Galileans can make common cause in defence of Josephus. We find a similar combination later also when Josephus, escaping from Tiberias, summons to his aid the leading Galileans at Tarichaeae and they urge him to hesitate no longer, but allow them to exterminate John and the Jerusalem delegate, Jonathan, who was at that time at Tiberias (*Life* 304–06).

b) The Galileans and the country

Since Tiberias, Sepphoris and Gabara are explicitly mentioned by Josephus as the three leading cities of Galilee (Tarichaeae also merits that appellative, *Life* 188) our attention is naturally turned to the background of the Galileans who are so opposed to them. While they can be closely identified in purpose with the people of Tarichaeae, yet they are carefully differentiated from them, as we have seen. Where then do the Galileans come from? Or is the term strictly non-geographical, as Zeitlin asserts?[13]

In several instances a general description is used to indicate the background of the Galileans. Thus we hear that many Galileans come together 'from all quarters' (πανταχόθεν *Life* 99) or 'from the whole country' (ἐκ τῆς χώρας πάσης *Life* 102). Or again the Galileans send messengers 'throughout all Galilee' (εἰς τὴν Γαλιλαίαν ἅπασαν), and large numbers assembled from all quarters (πανταχόθεν), with wives and children (*Life* 206 f.; cf. 384). Perhaps the most instructive passage to answer our question is *Life* 242–44; Josephus sends directions to the Galileans to join him at Gabaroth with their arms and three days' provisions. Next morning he finds the whole plain in front of the village full of armed men who had rallied to his call from Galilee. At the same time 'another large crowd was hurrying in from the villages', who greet Josephus as the saviour of their country (χώρα). On the basis of this passage the Galileans may be identified with the people from the villages, and further, it would seem, 'Galilee' is synonymous with the places which support Josephus. In other words Galilee and Galileans are co-relative expressions, and they refer to the village people who are loyal to the Jerusalemite, Josephus.

The hailing of Josephus as saviour of the country raises the question of whether or not the Galileans may be identified with 'the people of the land' of the rabbinic sources. The term χώρα appears to be used in *Life* in a more juridical sense of 'region' or 'territory', referring to the area under Josephus' official jurisdiction. Thus we hear of Josephus' position as governor of the 'region' being ratified (*Life* 312), or of his intention to quit the 'territory' and return to his native place (πατρίς *Life* 205). On this occasion news of his imminent departure is spread throughout all Galilee by the Galileans, and great crowds including women and children gather in the plains of Asochis where he was then quartered, beseeching him not to

---

[13] Zeitlin, 'Who were the Galileans?' 193 and 195.

leave (*Life* 207). On an earlier occasion young men went to the villages declaring that Josephus intended to betray the country (χώρα) to the Romans because of his desire to return goods stolen from the wife of King Agrippa's overseer. This rumour spread throughout 'all Galilee' (*Life* 129–32) and before the matter is resolved the Galileans have appeared on the scene almost like a chorus in a Greek tragedy (*Life* 142).

In this way Josephus seems to link the land with Galilee proper, and suggests that it is the special concern of the Galileans as well as the sphere of Josephus' influence. Mention of the villages is of particular significance, since these are clearly distinguished from the cities which, as we have seen, were the centres of hostility to Josephus and the object of the Galileans' particular wrath. Indeed, the ambassadors from Jerusalem having been sent to the Galileans (*Life* 198) attempt a tour of the villages, Japha first, and then the others. However, 'unsuccessful in the villages the delegates withdrew to Sepphoris the largest city of Galilee' (*Life* 230–32). Interestingly, the Galileans are not confined to any one place, but may be summoned by Josephus whenever he needs their support, and we find them now at Asochis, now Arbela, or again at Gabaroth or Gischala – that is, spanning the whole territory of Galilee.[14]

From these indications it seems that we can identify the Galileans with the country people of Galilee, living in the many villages scattered throughout the province. It comes as no surprise to hear that they assemble from the whole country at Tarichaeae, for they are truly the country people of this essentially rural province. It is thus that Josephus differentiates them from the city people and suggests two different spheres of organisation and loyalty, but without any hint of laxity in religious matters by the country people, unlike the *'am ha-'aretz* of later times.

Were the Galileans Revolutionaries?

Several times Josephus speaks of the crowd or multitude of Galileans (πλῆθος) an inclusive term that on two occasions at least can include

---

[14] Gabaroth sounds like a Semitic plural ending, possibly indicating a synoecism of several villages. It is called a village whereas Gabara is called a city. Yet the identification or close proximity of the two places seems assured from a reading of the text. The Jerusalem delegates command Josephus to meet them at Gabaroth unarmed (*Life* 229). He replies that he is prepared to meet them in any of the 204 cities and villages of Galilee that they select with the exception of Gabara and Gischala (*Life* 235). At *Life* 240 he puts guards on the roads leading from Gabara to Galilee. He then orders the Galileans to meet him at Gabaroth, and the subsequent scene takes place in the plain in front of the village, without Josephus entering the town or village, whereas the Jerusalem delegation retires to the mansion of Jesus which 'was as imposing as a citadel' (*Life* 240–46).

women and children (*Life* 84 and 210; cf. 198, 262, 302 and 305 f.). Other times he differentiates among the people, speaking of the leaders or authorities of the Galileans, though his terminology may vary slightly. Thus of the οἱ ἐν τέλει, seventy are invited to join him as friends and companions in his travels and as assessors of cases to be tried. Their approbation is sought for sentences passed (*Life* 79).[15] Josephus dines with his friends and the leading men (οἱ πρῶτοι) of Galilee (*Life* 220).[16] Thirty of the Galileans of highest repute (δοκιμώτατοι) are sent to meet the Jerusalem delegation (*Life* 228), and the same designation is used of Galileans who, like the people of Tiberias, have betrayed the country's independence (*Life* 386). That Josephus took the precaution of sending a soldier with each of the thirty sent to meet the Jerusalem delegation, 'to watch them and see that no conversation took place between my emissaries and the other party' (*Life* 228), suggests that for him these Galilean notables are not altogether trustworthy. Yet, he entrusts the presentation of his case to the authorities of Jerusalem to 'a hundred of their (the Galileans) leading men (οἱ πρῶτοι) well advanced in years' (*Life* 266), and after escaping to Tarichaeae from the Jerusalem delegation at Tiberias and John he summons the leading (οἱ πρωτεύοντες) Galileans to plan strategy (*Life* 305).

The picture emerging from these references is that the Galileans have some organisation, however loose, whereby it is possible for Josephus to select certain leading men and delegate to them functions related to his office. It is not clear whether those of highest repute (οἱ δοκιμώτατοι) who later betray their countrymen belong to this circle, nor does Josephus indicate what their rank was or how they came to be chosen. Yet their presence in Galilee right from the start shows that the area was not without its own internal organisation. It comes as no surprise then to find that Josephus convened an assembly (σύνοδος) of the Galileans at Arbela and had their own delegates relate to them how Josephus had been confirmed in his office as governor of Galilee (*Life* 310 f.).[17]

---

[15] In *JW* 2,570 f. the account of this provision is more formal and official in tone: the seventy elders are chosen from the nation (ἐκ τοῦ ἔθνους) and appointed magistrates for the whole of Galilee, as well as seven individuals in each city for petty cases, 'with instructions to refer more important cases to Josephus and the seventy.'

[16] For a discussion of the terminology used here and in the other works of Josephus, cf. W. Buehler, *The Pre-Herodian Civil War and Social Debate* (Basel: Rheinhardtverlag 1974) 20–52. οἱ πρῶτοι is used almost exclusively for men who held positions of authority as rulers of the Jews, and on less than ten occasions for the aristocracy as a whole, but since the form of government was essentially aristocratic this slight fluctuation is understandable. Likewise, οἱ ἐν τέλει can mean eminent persons on four occasions, but generally the term is used as a designation for those who occupy an office such as magistrate or ruler.

[17] This 'assembly' may be the remnant of inner Galilean structures which could go

A constant theme of the *Life* is the loyalty of the Galileans to Josephus. They are more concerned for his safety than for their own and their families' (*Life* 84, 125, 250, 252), and the Jerusalem embassy is asked to ascertain the source of this loyalty (*Life* 198). The Galileans answer his call to arms (*Life* 100, 103, 108, 268) and their anger is not merely towards John of Gischala (*Life* 368) but towards Jerusalem and the Jerusalem representatives as well (*Life* 211, 230, 260, 262). Josephus can rely on them to testify in his favour (*Life* 228, 258). Nor is John able to sow seeds of dissension among them regarding Josephus (*Life* 237). Little wonder that the Galileans can describe him then as 'the saviour of their country' (*Life* 244). Whatever the background and historical veracity of this description, it is clear that for the author of *Life* the Galileans are not irresponsible revolutionaries, but faithful and loyal supporters of him and his policies.[18]

Against this background it seems an unlikely hypothesis to suggest, as Zeitlin does, that 'the Galileans' in the *Life* 'is an appellative name given to the revolutionaries against Rome and the rulers in Judaea who were appointed by Rome.'[19] Nevertheless there is quite an amount of evidence in

---

back to Gabinius' rearrangement of the Jewish territory after Pompey's dismantling of the Hasmonean state. He established the rule of the country as an aristocracy (*JW* 1,169), dividing it into five σύνοδοι, four in Judea proper and one at Sepphoris in Galilee. In *JA* 14,91 they are described as συνέδρια, 'councils', but without any significant difference of meaning (cf. Mt 10,17; Mk 13,9). Such an institution would have undergone changes in the Herodian period, but may well have functioned throughout in a judicial capacity, and its leaders could have been part of Antipas' court (cf. Mk 6,21 οἱ πρῶτοι τῆς Γαλιλαίας). This would explain Josephus' use of the seventy elders as assessors, for he would scarcely have introduced such a new legal concept unless there had been some precedent. Cf. J. S. Kennard, 'The Jewish Provincial Assembly,' *ZNW* 53 (1962) 25–51.

[18] While this overall picture shows a sufficient inner consistency to suggest that it is one of the apologetic motifs of *Life,* as Schalit, 'Josephus and Justus,' 92, and H. Drexler, 'Untersuchung zu Josephus und zur Geschichte des jüdischen Aufstandes, 66–70,' *Klio* 19 (1925) 277–312, especially 296 f. maintain, nevertheless Josephus does not conceal certain attitudes of the Galileans which do not particularly support this apologetic. Attention has already been drawn to those Galileans who joined in the sacking of Agrippa's palace (*Life* 66) and accused Josephus of treachery at Tarichaeae (*Life* 143); he has to send soldiers to accompany the Galilean leaders lest they double deal with the Jerusalem embassy (*Life* 228); the Galileans' real concern is their own safety (*Life* 206 f.), 'influenced I imagine as much by alarm for themselves as by affection for me,' a statement which seems to contradict the rather grandiose opinions expressed in *Life* 84 of their selfless loyalty to him. Perhaps these inconsistencies in the general picture of the Galileans as a willing, pliable mob in need of a leader and saviour are an indication of the real relationship between Josephus and the Galileans: their loyalty was based on self-interest because of exploitation by native elites; when called to defend himself Josephus could point to it, suitably embellished, as indicative of overall reactions to him and his governorship of Galilee.

[19] 'Who were the Galileans?' 193.

the *Life* suggesting that the Galileans are armed and ready for action. Only careful reading of the text can help to clarify the extent and nature of the Galilean revolutionary stance and its significance.

To begin, it is clear that the Galileans are armed. Yet here the circumstances have to be carefully noted. Justus of Tiberias seems to presuppose that the Galileans are already armed when he harangues his townspeople: 'Now is the time to take up arms and join hands with the Galileans' (*Life* 39). At least twice the Galileans arrive already armed when Josephus calls them (*Life* 99, 102). On two other occasions it seems to be presupposed: Josephus brings armed Galileans to Sepphoris (*Life* 107) and orders them to assemble at Gabaroth 'with their arms and three days' provisions' (*Life* 242). Yet this is no undisciplined and unruly mob, for we hear that Josephus has to order them to take up their arms to defend themselves against a possible attack from John and the Jerusalem ambassadors (*Life* 252). Earlier Josephus had yielded to the Galilean entreaties that he stay as their leader, and immediately 'gave orders that 5,000 of them were to join him in arms, bringing their own provisions' (*Life* 212). Corresponding to this situation we hear that 'the Galileans were unanimously of the opinion that I should arm them all, march against him (John) and punish him as the author of all these disturbances' (*Life* 368).

Before passing final judgement on this question, two other sets of facts from the *Life* should be noted. First, Josephus clearly distinguishes between the Galileans and 'the robbers' who are described pejoratively in a number of places throughout the *Life*. They are described as 'evil men' (πονηροί) at *Life* 29 and 151, and the term 'robbers' (ληστής), so frequently employed in the war, occurs in *Life* also.[20] Jesus is an ἀρχιληστής operating on the borders between Ptolemais and Galilee (*Life* 105); λησταί appear as troublemakers at Tarichaeae. It is they who are intent on keeping the disturbances alive after Josephus has appeased first the Tarichaeaens and Galileans, and later even the troublemakers from Tiberias (*Life* 145–47). It is because of the λησταί that Josephus has to conceal his real feelings concerning the war and the power of Rome (*Life* 175). Those who join John are described as 'craving for revolution, by temperament addicted to change and delighting in sedition' (*Life* 87), a description very similar to that of John earlier, except that he is presented as jealous of Josephus and desiring command of Galilee for himself (*Life* 71). That these seditious people are not to be identified with the Galileans appears at *Life* 205 where the latter insist that should Josephus depart their country (χώρα) they would be an easy prey to the λησταί as enemies. This clear separation of Galileans and robbers helps to explain an earlier passage

---

[20] For a discussion of these negative terms as a description of the revolutionaries see Hengel, *The Zealots,* 41–46.

also. Josephus, in accordance with his policy of providing arms in case of an eventual showdown, yet restraining the more rebellious elements (*Life* 28 f.), recognised that he would not be able to disarm the brigands. He adopted the rather unusual tactic of having the people pay them off as mercenaries, 'remarking that it was better to pay them a small sum voluntarily than to submit to raids on their property.' He bound the robbers by oath 'not to enter the district' unless they were called for or their pay was in arrears. And he adds: 'my chief concern was the preservation of peace in Galilee' (*Life* 77–79). One recognises the reasons for the fear of the Galileans in the later passage, and the power of the brigands, to whose presence even Josephus must turn a blind eye, attempting to contain them to the border areas.[21]

A second set of facts arises in conjunction with this episode that helps further to clarify the situations of the Galileans. Apparently it was Josephus' instructions from the revolutionary government to prepare for war in terms of arms and fortifications, but not to provoke it (*Life* 28 f.). We do not hear anything in the *Life* of the strong military force which he seems to have recruited on his arrival in Galilee according to *JW* 2,576 – 100,000 young men 'equipped with old arms collected for the purpose.' However, he does mention in a general way 'the provision of arms', without specifying for whom, in the same context as the reference in *JW* just cited – the erection of fortifications. In *Life* this provisioning may have been of Galileans who, we have seen, are under arms. Alternatively, it may refer to the permanent military organisation that Josephus appears to have around him in *Life*, in addition to the Galileans who are only occasionally summoned. He describes his military tactics against Agrippa's decurion, Aebutius, who had been entrusted with charge of the Great Plain, and on that occasion his army is 2,000 infantry (*Life* 116 f.). Similarly he has only a small force when he decides to engage the Romans who had come to help Sepphoris, and is eventually routed (*Life* 394–97). Yet for his attack on Tiberias his forces seem greater (at least 10,000 men), even though the Galileans are not mentioned as augmenting his army (*Life* 321, 327, 331). At Tarichaeae Josephus feels free to dismiss his troops on the Sabbath,

---

[21] Brigandage was one of the hazards of life in Galilee, as is indicated by the general acclaim for Herod's action in exterminating brigands, *JW* 1,204 f. A good description of the tactics and harassment involved is found at *JA* 15,346 f. Cf. Hengel, *The Zealots*, 25–34 for a general account of brigandage in the ancient world. *Cf. further R. Horsley, 'Josephus and the Bandits,' *JSJ* 10 (1979) 37–63, and 'Ancient Jewish Banditry and the Revolt Against Rome,' *CBQ* 43 (1981) 409–32; S. Freyne, 'Bandits in Galilee: A Contribution to the Study of Social Conditions in First-Century Palestine,' in *The Social World of Formative Christianity and Judaism. Essays in Tribute of Howard Clark Kee*, ed. J. Neusner et al. (Philadelphia: Fortress Press, 1988) 50–69; B. Shaw, 'Tyrants, Bandits and Kings. Personal Power in Josephus,' *JJS* 44 (1993) 176–204.

only retaining a bodyguard of seven (*Life* 159).[22] One suspects that the 5,000 armed Galileans who are allowed to join him for an engagement with Placidus in the region of Ptolemais are not his whole army but rather reinforcements (*Life* 213 f.). He sends James with 200 men to guard the routes to Galilee from Gabara, and Jeremiah with 600 men to watch the roads leading to Jerusalem (*Life* 240 f.). He has an escort of 500 men for his counter-embassy to Jerusalem (*Life* 268 f.) and he can provide a soldier for each of the 30 Galilean leaders whom he sends to discuss with the Jerusalem embassy (*Life* 228). Presumably this permanent, relatively small army which Josephus keeps around himself was also recruited after his arrival in Galilee, but they are never called Galileans and, as already pointed out, the Galileans are quite separate from them.

It is thus apparent that the Galileans are neither to be identified with the λησταί who are eager for trouble and who, at least in the *JW*, are blamed for embroiling the whole nation in war with Rome, nor with the permanent army Josephus keeps. Rather they represent a reserve force whose loyalty to Josephus is unquestioning. The one exception is the incident at Tarichaeae when Josephus had been misrepresented to them as intending to turn the country over to the Romans, but he succeeds in explaining himself successfully and their anger is appeased (*Life* 132–43). Certain militants may come from their ranks like Jesus who seems to have a private army at Jerusalem (*Life* 200) and may or may not be identified with the Jesus employed by the Sepphorites earlier from the region of Ptolemais (*Life* 105 f.), or the Galileans who join with the revolutionary element in Tiberias in burning Herod's palace (*Life* 66). Yet overall they are disciplined and restrained. Ready to answer the call to arms against Josephus' enemies, whether Tiberias, John of Gischala or the ambassadors from Jerusalem (*Life* 306), they do not wish to be identified with the λησταί who are a serious threat to them and their families. They are genuinely patriotic as the one example of their annoyance with Josephus shows. It is not surprising to hear that many Galileans fell in battle as Iotapata and the other fortresses seized by the Romans (*Life* 351), even though some of their more outstanding countrymen had behaved in traitorous fashion (*Life* 386).

Conclusion: Galilee and the Galileans

In the course of this article I have deliberately refrained from making any hypothetical reconstructions of the actual situation in Galilee at the out-

---

[22] That they are dispersed on the Sabbath day at Tarichaeae, not to trouble the populace, may be an indication of their non-Jewish background (*Life* 159). In the *JW* account as well as the Galileans under arms, he had 4,500 mercenaries whom he trusted the most.

break of the first Jewish revolt, attempting rather to allow the text of *Life* speak for itself, since all are agreed that it does represent a unique source of information on the situation there, even allowing for personal biases and the conventions of genre.[23] Before drawing some tentative conclusions from this evidence it is necessary to make a brief comparison of Josephus' use of terminology in his different writings without passing any judgement on the literary relationships between the various works.[24]

The account of the period between Josephus' appointment as governor of Galilee (late November AD 66) and the arrival of Vespasian in the province (May AD 67) – the period covered by *Life* – is greatly curtailed in *JW*. In particular the episode dealing with his attempted removal by the Jerusalem embassy is treated in a summary fashion (*JW* 2,627–31), whereas it occupies the whole centre of *Life* and is most suggestive in terms of inner Galilean tendencies and loyalties.[25] At *JW* 2,622 we hear of Galileans from one town after another (κατὰ πόλεις) 'myriads of men in arms', flocking to Josephus and threatening vengeance on John and his city as the common enemy, because of his plotting against Josephus. This passage should be taken in conjunction with two earlier ones concerning the arming of the Galileans. At *JW* 2,576 it is claimed that Josephus levied 100,000 young men as part of his initial organisation on his arrival in the province. Yet a little later he reduces this very large figure to slightly more acceptable

---

[23] *For more recent discussion of the issues of the dating, sources and audiences of Josephus' writings cf. S. J. D. Cohen, *Josephus in Galilee and Rome. His Vita and Development as an Historian* (Leiden: Brill, 1979); T. Rajak, *Josephus. The Historian and his Society* (London: Duckworth, 1983); P. Bilde, *Flavius Josephus between Jerusalem and Rome. His Life, his Works, and their Importance,* JSP Supplement Series 2 (Sheffield: Sheffield Academic Press, 1988); Pavente and Sievers, eds., *Josephus and the History of Greco-Roman Period.* On the genre of *Life* cf. J. Neyrey, 'Josephus' *Vita* and the Encomium: A Native Model of Personality,' *JSJ* 25 (1994) 177–206.

[24] According to Laqueur, *Der jüdische Historiker*, the official report underlying *Life* is the earlier account. However, Schalit, 'Josephus und Justus,' disagrees with this analysis and regards *Life* as an organic response to the attack of Justus, written after *JW,* which itself was based on an earlier version in Aramaic for τοῖς ἄνω βαρβάροις (*JW* 1, 3). M. Gelzer, 'Die *Vita* des Josephus,' *Hermes* 80 (1952) 67–90, while also disagreeing with Laqueur's suggestion, but for different reasons, sees the *Life* account as earlier than that of *JW* which is a 'straffe Zusammenfassung' (87), written to present himself in heroic manner. *Life* on the other hand was written as a self-defence for the Romans during his two years of captivity at Caesarea (67–69 CE, *JW* 3,409 f.). Recently, S. Zeitlin has discussed the question in a series of articles: 'A survey of Jewish historiography: from the biblical books to the Sefer ha-Kabbalah, with special emphasis on Josephus,' *JQR* 59 (1968) 171–214 and 60 (1969) 37–68. In this latter article he argues that *JW* was the official account corresponding to the revolutionary government's position of being outwardly for the war, whereas *Life* gives the real account, showing Josephus as desirous of peace, and therefore correcting the earlier version.

[25] *Life* 189–335 which contains 21 references to the Galileans.

proportions: he has an army of 60,000 infantry and 350 cavalry ready for action, as well as 4,500 mercenaries and a bodyguard of 600 picked men. The former are easily supported by the towns since only half the number are sent out and the rest kept back to prepare provisions. Despite the use of πόλεις 'cities' in this passage instead of the κώμαι 'villages' and χώρα 'land' of *Life*, it seems that in both works Josephus' main army of reserves was made up of Galilean country people from the many settlements throughout the province, who had to bring their own provisions when summoned by Josephus (cf. *Life* 212, 242). During the incident at Tarichaeae where Josephus is accused of treachery, the Galileans are not explicitly mentioned as in the *Life* account, but their presence is implicit with mention of young men going through the villages by night, slandering Josephus as a traitor (*JW* 2,598). In the sequel there are country people present (οἱ ἀπὸ τῆς χώρας) who are not as easily appeased as the people of Tarichaeae, and apparently it is they who get into an altercation with the Tiberians at the end (*JW* 2,608).

This portrayal of 'the Galileans' continues throughout the subsequent narrative of the war in the province. Sepphoris had abandoned the Galilean cause (*JW* 3,61). Placidus is scouring Galilee, killing helpless Galileans, weak civilians who were exhausted from flight (*JW* 3,110). Josephus considers that should he escape from Iotapata he might be able to gather the Galileans from the country and so divert the Romans from the city (*JW* 3,198 f.). In the siege of this latter city none acted more bravely than two Galilean brothers from the village of Ruma (*JW* 3,233). In the siege of Japha, a town near Iotapata, some Galileans who had ventured out to attack the Romans were excluded by their townspeople as they beat a hasty retreat and were exterminated. The defenders of the town in the ensuing attack are called Galileans, and the final capitulation is described as another calamity for the Galileans (*JW* 3,301.306). Even after Galilee had surrendered the name, 'Galileans' continues to be used for all those who had been at war with the Romans, Gischala included (*JW* 4,1.96.127). Two general references (*JW* 2,232 and 4,127) dealing with the Galileans relations with the Samaritans and the Tyrians might be seen as examples of a more general signification, an allusion to those who dwelt in the region. Yet even in these instances there is a sense of militancy associated with the name, corresponding to the description of the Galilean character given at *JW* 3,41: 'With this limited area (Galilee), and although surrounded by such powerful foreign nations, the two Galilees have always resisted any hostile invasion, for the inhabitants are from infancy inured to war.'

Josephus, it seems, has a particular interest in portraying the Galileans in colours corresponding to his own self-portrayal in both works. In *Life* they support him in his struggle to establish himself in the region and function as his loyal retinue, whereas in *JW* they are militant, independent and prepared to engage the Romans in a noble struggle under his leadership. The sole reference to the Galileans which could be construed as implying a separate group of zealous militants is that which speaks of a σύνταγμα τῶν Γαλιλαίων lead by John of Gischala in Jerusalem that surpassed all others in daring and mischievous deeds (*JW* 4,558). They are portrayed as having escaped with John, leaving the weaker citizens of Gischala to their fate as Titus encircled the city, and on arrival in Jerusalem, they became one of the factions within the civil strife with John as their leader (*JW* 4,106–11 and 121–27). This particular description must, however, be judged in the context of the overall treatment of John in *JW*, where, in contrast to Josephus' own noble performance as a military general in that work, John is described as an unscrupulous intriguer, a brigand intent on war for personal gain. His betrayal of his own townspeople in his final flight from Gischala, accompanied by this group of Galileans, fits perfectly into that particular picture, therefore. It neither corresponds with the picture of John that is given in *Life* nor indeed with that of the Galileans as these emerge in either work.[26]

A perusal of the usage in *JA* on the other hand suggests that it is an essentially geographical sense of the term 'Galilean' that dominates that work: *JA* 5,63: Kedesh is a city of the Galileans; 13,154: Galileans are the inhabitants of Galilee; 14,450: Galileans rebel against the nobles of their own country; 17,318; 18,136: Antipas is tetrarch of the Galileans; 17,254: Galileans are listed among people from other geographical regions who were engaged in disturbances at Jerusalem after Herod's death; 17,288: Varus attacks Galileans, 'those who dwell in the neighbourhood of Ptolemais'; 18,37: Galileans are compelled by Antipas to dwell in Tiberias; 20,118.119.120: Galileans and Samaritans are embroiled in civil strife on the occasion of a pilgrimage. The only references in this list that could be taken as indicating that the Galileans were revolutionaries are 14,450 and 17,254, but neither is decisive. The first refers to a spontaneous reaction against those who had supported Herod, whose governorship of Galilee had weighed heavily on the natives in terms of taxation. In the second instance the hostility of the Galileans is no more marked than that of people from several other regions of the country who have been offended by Roman behaviour during the feast of Pentecost.

From this survey it appears that the primary meaning of the term 'the Galileans' is, as one might expect, geographical: it refers to the inhabitants of Galilee without any distinction of town or country and giving no indication of loyalties or attitudes other than the fact that they are adherents of the Jewish way of life. It is this basic meaning that emerges in *JA*. In *Life*,

---

[26] Rhoads, *Israel in Revolution*, 122–37.

however, a rather distinctive refinement of this basic meaning emerges: the Galileans are the country people as distinct from the inhabitants of the major towns, and they are Josephus' loyal supporters, aggressively nationalistic in terms of the Jewish way of life, but not essentially revolutionary or subversive.[27] As might be expected, *JW*, in line with the overall theme of the work and Josephus' self-portrayal as an outstanding general, depicts the Galileans accordingly. Yet despite these different emphases in the characterisation of the Galileans the underlying contours in both works are similar, namely, the support that Josephus, as a Jerusalem priest was able to muster in the region, despite jealousy from some native aristocrats and the shifting situation of power at the centre.

The primary result of our investigation has been to suggest that the Galileans are not to be identified with revolutionaries, no matter how much of the brunt of the first Roman onslaught they had had to endure.

Secondly, the cause and extent of Galilean animosity towards the larger towns, especially Sepphoris and Tiberias, and to a lesser extent Gabara and Gischala, cannot just be explained by the pro-Roman stance of these towns alone, since with the exception of Sepphoris their pro-Roman attitudes are never explicit or clear-cut. Other, inner Galilean factors must have been at work to explain this situation.

Thirdly, the attitude of the Galileans towards Jerusalem and its authority needs to be explored in greater depth. One suspects that Josephus' account of his support among the Galileans, so strongly emphasised throughout, may have had its own apologetic purpose as part of his response to Justus and his allegations. Yet it cannot simply be apologetic since in this regard at least the accounts in the *JW* and *Life* are at one.

It would seem that the situation of Galilean Judaism is more complex than might appear at first sight. The tensions which emerge in the full light of day under the stress of crisis must have been developing for some time. While Josephus is at pains to stress the idea of ὁμοφυλία, the unity of the nation, throughout *Life* (55, 100, 141, 171, 265, 376 f.), this is wishful thinking, as town and country, province and capital, rich and poor, struggle to assert their own positions just at the moment when the common danger was threatening all alike.

---

[27] *R. Horsley, *Galilee. History, Politics, People* (Valley Forge: Trinity Press International, 1995), comments that this formulation is anachronistic and paints too narrow a picture of what constitutes a revolution in antiquity (348, n. 20). Yet he himself writes in a similar vein: 'The peasants of Lower Galilee seem to have been insurrectionary in two principle ways neither of which involved organised and active revolutionary activity.' (86 f.).

2. Urban-Rural Relations in First-Century Galilee: Some Suggestions from the Literary Sources

Our efforts to understand the culture of Galilee in late antiquity are considerably enhanced by the fact that two major world religions originated in this region. The literature that these religions generated in their formative periods reflects in some way the world of their origins. Thus, the history and culture of the Galilee are, relatively speaking, much more open to recovery than those of almost any other region in antiquity. I say that the Galilee is reflected "in some way" in the literature of early Christianity and formative Judaism since the ways in which these corpora of literature can be used as documentary evidence for life in the Galilee of late antiquity is one of the most hotly debated issues in modern critical studies of both the gospels and rabbinic writings. The fact that so many methodological questions arise in regard to the literary sources should not, however, blind us to the fact that it is not just these sources but also the material remains that require critical interpretation and evaluation. The contrast between hard archaeological facts and biased literary sources is as hermeneutically naive as is the opposite point of view, which uses material remains to validate the Bible or Talmud. Each of us begins from the point at which we are most comfortable in terms of our particular expertise. Nevertheless, we should also include a hermeneutic of suspicion regarding the so-called objective character of the literary and material sources, coupled with a critical awareness of our cultural, academic, and social presuppositions through which the understanding of the past is filtered.

These reflections may help to explain the proposal to draw on an "outside" discipline to provide both a heuristic model and a set of critical criteria for evaluating the evidence for the impact of the Hellenistic urban environment on Galilean life in the first century CE. A modern discipline, if sensitively employed, can provide us with the right framework and the proper set of questions for defining our tasks and articulating the problems to which we seek solutions. The proposed model embraces two different views of society, representative, broadly speaking, of functionalist and conflictual approaches. Thus, since no society is totally homogeneous, and the Galilee in the first century was certainly not, we may hope to uncover rather different aspects of that world, representing the top and bottom levels of the social stratum.

Of the many different topics that suggest themselves as possible probe areas for examining Galilean life in the first century, I have chosen to address the cultural role of the cities. Cities were the main agents for change in the Hellenisation process and in certain circles, in Galilee in particular, the name גליל הגוים / Γαλιλαία ἀλλοφύλων took on a new focus, because of what was perceived by the Jews as the threat of Hellenism (1 Macc 5,15). The accuracy of this perception was borne out almost 200 years later with the anti-Jewish attitudes that surfaced in all the surrounding city territories prior to the First Revolt, most notably in the north of the country, even in such centres of long established Jewish-gentile relations as Scythopolis.

Instead of approaching the problem by attempting to define city (πόλις) and village (κώμη) I shall first summarise the theoretical considerations concerning the cultural role of cities which I propose to apply. Several important distinctions are called for in this regard. Primary is that made by Redfield and Singer[1] between 'the carrying forward into systematic and reflective dimensions of an old culture' (described as the 'orthogenetic' role of the city) and 'the creating of original modes of thought that have authority beyond or in conflict with old cultures and civilisations' (the 'heterogenetic' role of the city). Each gives rise to a different ethos, characteristic type, and relation to the surrounding folk-culture. A further refinement calls for a distinction between primary and secondary urbanisation. The former relates to the development of the surrounding folk-culture into a Great Tradition by the literati, to the virtual exclusion of other elements considered alien or hostile influences. In contrast, the latter occurs when an already existing culture – folk, peasant, or partly urbanised – is perforce brought into contact with wider and divergent cultures either through expansion or by invasion and/or conquest.

The following table delineates some of the more important aspects of these two types of cities and the corresponding stages of social urbanisation to which they give rise. Although by no means exhaustive, it can serve as a helpful framework for interpreting the scattered pieces of literary and material evidence for pre–70 Galilean life.

---

[1] R. Redfield and M. Singer. 'The Cultural Role of Cities,' *Economic Development and Social Change* 3 (1954) 57–73.

	Orthogenetic Cities	Heterogenetic Cities
1. Dominant Social Types	Literati who fashion the Great Tradition;	Businessmen, bureaucrats (mostly foreigners or natives who have been deeply influenced by outside cultural forces); officials; military men; tax collectors
2. Basis for Relationship with Countryside	Common loyalty to a shared worldview; acceptance of the past and its myths, especially as recreated by the literati	Pragmatic, based on mutuality of interests, despite mistrust at the cultural level; attempted myth-making for the future, to cloak cultural differences
3. Economic Patterns	Inequality, cloaked as social necessity or divine arrangement	Openly exploitative, giving rise to resentment
4. Social Unity	Achieved by consensus; dissent perceived as disloyalty	Achieved by coercion; dissent perceived as rebellion

The tendentiousness of two basic sources for this investigation, Josephus' *Life* and the gospels (especially the Synoptics), presents difficulties for the scholar. One must consider to what extent the apologetic purposes of Josephus in *Life*, so ably exposed by S. J. D. Cohen,[2] distort this account of internal social relations, especially since his own relations with the Herodian cities were anything but cordial. Similarly, one must monitor the degree to which later gospel writers may have introduced urban categories on what was the original rural colouring of the Jesus narrative. These considerations should be kept in mind when addressing the question of urban-rural relations in first-century Galilee as portrayed in the sources.

---

[2] S. J. D. Cohen, *Josephus in Galilee and Rome. His Vita and Development as an Historian* (Leiden: Brill, 1979) 101–70.

Dominant Social Types

At first reading, both Josephus and the gospels appear to deal in gen-
eralities. 'The Galileans' (οἱ Γαλιλαῖοι) is the former's constant appellation
for those who rally around the main character, Josephus, whereas 'the
crowd' or 'many' are the evangelist's usual description of those who are
attracted to the wandering teacher-healer, Jesus of Nazareth. The designation 'the Galileans' in Josephus' narrative offers some possibilities for social description, as we shall see, but the latter is much too general to be of
any real assistance. Nevertheless, both narratives offer further insights into
the character of the province because of their dominant social types.

Apart from Josephus, the two main characters in *Life* are John of Gischala and Justus of Tiberias, though their prominence may be more a reflection of the apologetic nature of the work than indicative of the actual
situation. Both may be classed as products of the heterogenetic environment of the Greek cities as far as a Jewish ethos is concerned, but each for
different reasons. Both were obviously Jewish in their basic upbringing.
Josephus presumes that they should accept his authority in the Galilee because of his appointment by the Jerusalem Council. John was ambitious,
unscrupulous, capable of moving with the political tides, and resentful of
those whom he perceived to have bested him, such as Josephus. He may
have had some official status in the Roman administration of the Upper
Galilee. But his power-base was his entrepreneurial skill that made it possible for him to exploit his native village of Gischala as a hinterland supply
centre (of oil and grain) for such Hellenistic-Roman cities as Tyre, Sidon,
and Caesarea Philippi, despite current Jewish-gentile hostilities (*Life* 44;
JW 2,457 f.).[3] However, the countrypeople of Gischala were less than enthusiastic about his show of zealotry and more interested in agricultural
matters (*JW* 4,84). His contacts with the powerful Simon son of Gamaliel
in Jerusalem proved in the end to have been his undoing, since he was bit-
terly disappointed at having been passed over as governor of the Galilee by
the Jerusalem Council.

Justus, on the other hand, had a thorough Greek education and had come
up through the Herodian bureaucracy (*Life* 40).[4] He, too, was an urban type
who found a common link with John (*Life* 88); like his counterpart in the
Upper Galilee, he led attacks on the Greek cities of the Dekapolis although
not openly advocating war with Rome (*Life* 42; 45). His history of Jewish

---

[3] Cf. the studies of U. Rappaport, 'John of Gischala: From Galilee to Jerusalem,' *JJS*
33 (1982) 479–90, and 'John of Gischala in Galilee,' in *The Jerusalem Cathedra*, ed. L.
Levine, 3 vols. (Jerusalem: Yad Izhak Ben-Zvi Institute, 1981–83), vol. 3, 46–57.

[4] Cf. T. Rajak, 'Justus of Tiberias,' *Church Quarterly* 23 (1973) 345–68; A. Barzano,
'Giusto di Tiberiade,' in *ANRW*, II, *Principat*, 20.1, ed. H. Temporini and W. Haase
(Berlin and New York: de Gruyter, 1986) 337–58.

kings from Moses to Agrippa II was clearly an attempt, like that of Josephus, to produce an apologetic account of his people's history in the medium and genre of the Hellenised world in which he had been educated. Like John, he, too, was from the wealthy upper class; Josephus tried to dissociate him from the other Tiberians who owned estates in the countryside (*Life* 32–37; 65). The country Galileans were no more trusting of Justus than they were of John (*Life* 176; 390–92).

Both of these characters represented the type of Jew who was a product of the Hellenistic environment and who was used by Rome to help control this fractious people; both came from the fringes of Galilean life, Gischala being close to the borders of the Phoenician cities, and Tiberias, Herod's new city, with its mixed population.

Josephus' account mentions a number of other similar types such as Agrippa's officers operating either in the king's territory or on its borders, on the Great Plain.[5] The attack by villagers of Dabaritta on the wife of one of these, as she travelled with pomp across the Great Plain protected by an escort of cavalry, may be understood as symptomatic of local resentment of these types (*Life* 126–31). Their ostentatious wealth and other trappings of power made them constant targets of brigandage, which seems to have been a common occurrence. The brigands who recur frequently throughout the work were not a unified social movement, but were partly the result of the emergence of soldiering as a profession in the Hellenistic period and partly the outcome of the particular socio-political circumstances.[6] In the former category we can include leaders of organised armies such as Jesus of Galilee, who operated on the borders of Ptolemais and was hired by the Sepphorians to protect them from Josephus (*Life* 104–11) Later we find him in Jerusalem employed by the authorities to accompany the delegation they were sending to oust Josephus (*Life* 200). Josephus, for his part, had also availed himself of the services of other brigands in his efforts to assemble an army and employed them as mercenaries (*Life* 77 f.; 175; 206).

From these differing profiles we can capture something of the Hellenistic ethos of Galilee under Roman and Herodian rule. The first two types represent the second phase of the urbanisation process – native Jews who, at one level, shared the folk-culture but who, for one reason or another, had availed themselves of the commercial, educational, and pro-

---

[5] *Life* 46 (Philip ben Jacimus); 61 (Modius); 116 (Aebutius); 120 (Neapolitanus); 126 (Ptolemy).

[6] Cf. R. Horsley, 'Ancient Jewish Banditry and the Revolt Against Rome,' *CBQ* 43 (1981) 409–32; S. Freyne, 'Bandits in Galilee. A Contribution to the Study of Social Conditions in First-Century Palestine,' in *The Social World of Formative Christianity and Judaism. Essays in Tribute of Howard Clark Kee*, ed. J. Neusner et al. (Philadelphia: Fortress Press, 1988) 50–69.

fessional opportunities of the times. This stance left them in an ambivalent position at a period of internal crisis such as that covered by *Life*: they were to some extent aliens in their own culture, as is evident in the attitude which the Galileans 'from the country' adopted towards them.[7] The brigands-mercenaries were no befrienders of the powerless in view of their undiscriminating tactics (*Life* 77; 206); neither John nor Justus was able to muster sufficient support to oust their archrival Josephus, who seems to have intentionally cultivated the countrypeople on the basis of his Jerusalem and priestly connections. It is in the villages, not in the cities, that we find him constantly billeted: in Bethmaus, Cana, Simonias, Chabulon, Japhia, Asochis, Gabaroth, and Garis.[8] Only Taricheaeae seems to have broken that pattern, but this city had a much more clearly defined Jewish ethos than Tiberias, as it also served as a refugee centre for the countrypeople. The unpopularity of Justus must have been directly related to the hostility of Galileans towards his native place, which was regarded as alien and unfriendly to deep-seated Jewish sensibilities from the outset (*JA* 18,38), and it is no surprise to find some Galileans involved in the destruction of Herod's palace there (*Life* 66). Gischala never generated quite the same opposition, since it was isolated from the more densely populated areas of the Lower Galilee. Even the inhabitants of his own town clearly did not trust John; Gabara, one of the three major cities that had sided with him, according to Josephus, was extremely cautious because of the animosity of the Galilean countrypeople (*Life* 123; 125).

On the basis of this particular criterion from our model of dominant social types, urbanisation of the heterogenetic type had by no means 'taken over' in terms of the cultural affiliations of the people of the Galilee. Josephus and his colleagues were Jerusalemites who apparently claimed the tithes on the basis of their priestly status (*Life* 77). Likewise, the composition of the delegation sent to oust Josephus had a decidedly religious status, implying that only those who publicly adhered to the Jewish way of life could have been expected to have had any influence among the countrypeople (*Life* 197). Nor are 'the Galileans' to be regarded as unskilled or unlettered 'down and outs.' Repeatedly we hear of the Galileans assembling with their women and children, expressing ties of kinship with a strongly Jewish and rural value system; they provisioned themselves and served as temporary militia to support Josephus. They may be compared to the hoplites, landed peasantry of Greek society on whom the city depended and around whom landowning policy developed, who could afford the arms necessary for infantry engagements.[9] The Babylonian Jews from

---

[7] Cf. S. Freyne, 'The Galileans in the Light of Josephus' *Life,*' above pp. 27 ff.

[8] *Life* 64; 86; 115; 213; 230, 233; 242; 395, respectively.

[9] T. F. Carney, *The Shape of the Past, Models and Antiquity* (Lawrence, KS: Coronado Press, 1975) 236–42.

Batanea mentioned in *Life* give us insight into earlier Herodian policy in this regard: they had well-stocked villages and could be relied upon to support central authority while maintaining their deep religious convictions (*Life* 58; *JA* 17,26 f.).

Thus, insofar as any urban centre dominated the cultural life of Galilee, it would seem that it was Jerusalem, not the Herodian cities, that had the controlling influence over the majority of the population. The gospels confirm this picture. On the one hand, 'tax collectors' are identified as 'sinners', i.e., unacceptable outsiders, but in socio-economic terms they represent the heterogenetic influence on the city. On the other hand, the literati (scribes) of the Great Tradition came from Jerusalem in order to ensure that no deviant trends predominated (Mk 3,22; 7,1).[10] The concern for orthodoxy among the scribes was not always appreciated in its finer points by the peasants, the primary bearers of the folk-tradition who could combine such deviance as sorcery and magic with a more enlightened religious belief (*Life* 149), without necessarily seeing any contradiction between the two. With the exception of Luke (8,1–3; 13,33), the Herodian court and its ethos imposed itself only minimally on the gospel narratives; the Herodians were opponents of the Jesus movement in all the accounts (Mk 3,6; 12,13). While the precise identity of the Herodians is debatable, the part they played points to genuine social divisions in the Galilee between centres of power and affluence on the one hand and a populist religious movement on the other.[11] Both Mark and Josephus mention the οἱ πρῶτοι τῆς Γαλιλαίας but Mark (6,21.27) locates them at the Herodian court on the occasion of Herod's birthday, together with the military men (χιλίαρχοι) 'government official' (σπεκουλάτωρ) and 'the great ones' (μεγιστᾶνες). The precise distinction between the οἱ πρῶτοι and the οἱ μεγιστᾶνες is unclear, but the evangelist differentiates between them by his use of the definite article before each. In *Life* the latter term refers to the non-Jewish noblemen closely associated with the king who came from Trachonitis as refugees (*Life* 112; 149), whereas the former were Jewish leaders, '*aristocratie du pays.*' This would seem to fit Mark's usage also. Given Herodian pressure on the native Galileans to inhabit Tiberias (*JA* 18,35–38), the presence of 'the leading men of Galilee' at the king's birthday need not conflict with their social role in *Life*, where they appear supportive of Josephus' position in the region.

---

[10] The episode concerning Johanan b. Zakkai's stay at Arav (*y. Shabbat* 16, 8, 15d) may be legendary, as J. Neusner, *A Life of Rabban Yohanan ben Zakkai, ca. 1–80 C.E.* (Leiden: Brill, 1962) 27–28, has ably argued, yet it should be seen as typical of the concern of Jerusalem scribes with regard to Galilee generally.

[11] H. Hoehner, *Herod Antipas, A Contemporary of Jesus Christ*, SNTSMS 17 (Cambridge: Cambridge University Press, 1972) 331–42.

Relationships between City and Countryside

We shall first attempt to sketch the overall picture. Both Josephus and Mark distinguish between city and country and describe the links between the two. The evangelist describes Jesus' visits to the territory of Gadara, the borders of Tyre and the villages of Caesarea Philippi (Mk 5,1; 7,24.31; 8,27) but not to any of the cities. One suspects a hint at two very different environments, at least as far as the rural-based prophet and his followers were concerned, but who, incidentally, like others of his ilk, such as Jesus ben Hananiah (*JW* 6,300–309), did not hesitate to go to Jerusalem and proclaim his message there.[12] Josephus helps us to fill out this picture. All ancient cities had their own territories, which were comprised of a network of villages where those who worked the land, either as crop sharers, free landowners or tenants of absentee landlords lived, while the landowning aristocracy, like Crispus of Tiberias, were often city dwellers (*Life* 33).

It is certain that such a situation existed in Galilee. Sepphoris, according to Josephus, could have withstood a Roman siege because it was 'surrounded by numerous villages' (*Life* 346; *JW* 1,304). Similarly, Tiberias and Tarichaeae had their own χώρα or territory (*JW* 2,252 f.; *Life* 155) and the same was true for such surrounding cities as Scythopolis, Hippos, Gadara, and Gamala (*JW* 3,37; *Life* 42, 58).

To suggest that the relationship between the Galileans from the land and these cities was uniformly hostile is a generalisation, and ignores particular circumstances operative in individual instances. The hostility toward Sepphoris, for example, was based on its alleged pro-Roman stance, whereas the attitude toward Tiberias may have been partly due to the social division resulting from the comparative opulence of the Herodian court and partly the result of the constraints on Galileans to join this new city against their will. Yet, when all this is taken into account, there can be no doubt that the rural animosities toward the cities were deep-seated and permanent. Galilean hatred of Sepphoris, Tiberias, and Gabara, the three cities of the Galilee, according to Josephus, is a distinct theme in *Life*.

It may be argued that this is simply part of the apologetic rhetoric of the document or that the immediate pre-war period was exceptional. Yet a perusal of the Jesus tradition, with its strongly rural colouring, especially in the parables, points to a similar pattern of relationships. In Jesus' praise of the rustic John the Baptist we can imagine the chasm that existed in social and cultural terms between the two environments: 'What did you go out

---

[12] *For a discussion of this and other aspects of Jesus' career in the Galilee, cf. my study, *Galilee, Jesus and the Gospels. Literary Approaches and Historical Investigations* (Dublin and Philadelphia: Gill & Macmillan and Fortress Press, 1988) 219–68.

into the desert to see? . . . A man clothed in fine linen? Behold, those who are dressed in fine linen are in the houses of kings' (Mt 11,8; cf. Mk 1,6). In a saying such as this we capture something of the social and cultural differences between city and country as perceived from a rural perspective.

There is little in this emerging picture that is surprising in the light of urban-rural relations generally in antiquity. What specifically concerns us, however, is whether and to what extent heterogenetic factors as suggested by our model could explain the particular tensions in Galilee. The ethos of the Greek cities was deemed hostile, despite the presence of Jewish minorities in Scythopolis, Caesarea Philippi, and other places. The Herodian centres on the other hand boasted many of the trappings of the Greek way of life, such as the stadium at Tiberias, the hippodrome at Tarichaeae, and the theatre at Sepphoris, that were unacceptable in theory in conservative Jewish circles. Yet, this statement calls for qualification since these places were by no means monochromic in their cultural affiliations. Tarichaeae was the place where xenophobic tendencies surfaced, yet it had a hippodrome and its Greek name suggests some outside influence there. The Jewish firebrand, Jesus son of Sapphias, became the leader of the city council of Tiberias for a while, despite its Herodian ethos. In Sepphoris animosity was caused by the city's failure to support the national struggle, when the opposite should have been the case there.

We cannot simply assume, therefore, that Galilean hostility to these places was because they were centres of Greek culture. Jews had learned to accommodate themselves to such an environment while retaining their distinct identity, even in Galilee, as the examples of Scythopolis and Caesarea Philippi indicate. The opposition, even hostility, must have had another basis and motivation; the evidence of the texts we are examining suggests that it was due to a considerable extent to the orthogenetic role of Jerusalem vis-à-vis Jewish culture in Galilee. The prophetic lament for Jerusalem by the Jesus movement, stemming from the *Q* source and therefore dating to pre–70, suggests an emotional attachment to the holy city (Mt 23,37; Lk 13,34 f.). According to all accounts of the trial, a charge made before the high priests that Jesus was about to destroy the Jerusalem Temple was instrumental in his rejection by the pilgrimage crowd (Mk 14,58). Equally, Josephus could chide Sepphoris for not supporting 'the Temple that is common to us all' (*Life* 348 f.), and the suggestion that using the booty which the highwaymen of Dabaritta had confiscated to repair the walls of Jerusalem could exonerate him of the charge of treachery (*Life* 128). The Galileans allegedly honoured the priestly status of Josephus and his colleagues with the tithes that they claimed (*Life* 63, 81), and the delegation sent to unseat Josephus was unsuccessful in the villages of Galilee despite its priestly and Pharisaic composition (*Life* 232).

While Galilean peasant loyalties appear to have been firmly anchored in Jerusalem, the literati, or scribes, attempted to mould that loyalty along particular lines. They attributed the healing powers of the rural prophet, Jesus, to Beelzebub, the prince of demons, in an obvious attempt to denigrate any alternative claims among the ordinary populace (Mk 3,22). While this attempt appears to have had little impact in Galilee, the charge about destroying the Temple had much more serious consequences and succeeded in removing the crowd's support in Jerusalem.

Our evidence shows that two rather different forces were exerted on the village people of Galilee throughout the first century, therefore. The fact that many of the villages were economically controlled by the Herodian cities of the Lower Galilee did not in any way destroy the much older and deeper loyalties to Jerusalem and its cult centre. Regardless of the amount of shared material culture that archaeology has uncovered, there is little evidence of any alternative myth emanating from the Greek cities that might have successfully competed for the loyalties of the villagers. Architectural styles, artefacts, and even language patterns are not the ultimate indicators of cultural affinity, as attested by Cestius Gallus' burning of the Jewish village of Chabulon – despite his admiration for its houses built in the Phoenician style (*JW* 2,502).

Economic Patterns

Cities were obviously the centres of wealth in the ancient world, in terms of both wealth-generating and wealth-amassing activities. According to Josephus, the dispute between Sepphoris and Tiberias was over the fact that the former city contained the royal bank (τράπεζα) and archives (ἀρχεῖα). Both institutions were part of the redistributive exchange system which indicated a thriving market situation, with moneylending and the storing of coinage at the discretion of the wealthy. Little wonder that Sepphoris was reluctant to break with Rome.

It is worth noting that in several instances reported by Josephus where rural opposition to the cities erupted, wealth, in one form or another, was directly involved. The Galileans decided to pillage Sepphoris, allegedly because of its pro-Roman stance, but in fact because of its wealth (*Life* 30). The destruction of Herod's palace at Tiberias by some Galileans, together with the city's destitute classes, raised expectations of gaining considerable booty. Among the items that Josephus claims to have recovered were a large supply of unminted coin and some palace furnishings (*Life* 66–68). Similarly, the affair of the highwaymen of Dabaritta revealed rural resentment of ruling class opulence: four mules laden with apparel and other goods as well as a large supply of silver and 500 pieces of gold (*Life* 128). In addition to these references to the wealth of the Herodian cities, we hear of the imperial granaries of the Upper Galilee coveted by John which served to increase his wealth. Heretofore he had amassed a fortune by the inflation of oil prices in the region. This, too, led to resentment of Gischala by the countrypeople (*Life* 71, 75, 103 f.). In addition, Josephus sequestered for himself corn from the royal estates of the Lower Galilee (*Life* 76).

Wealth was in the hands of the urban-based elites and gave rise to resentment, despite the fact that the Galileans who supported Josephus were apparently not poor, as attested by the fact that they armed themselves and provided for the army's needs (*Life* 210, 242–44). We hear of a destitute class only in Tiberias (*Life* 76). However, in sharp contrast with their resentment of Herodian wealth, the Galileans are apparently willing to pay the tithes to Josephus and his colleagues. While we are undoubtedly dealing with one of Josephus' apologetic motifs in *Life*, wherein he refuses to accept the tithes due to him, as a sign of his own magnanimity and generosity, the fact that the tithes are mentioned and assumed to be owed indicates that in his relationship with the Galileans he adopted the role of a Jerusalem priest. Thus, we encounter rather different attitudes towards social inequality arising from the distribution of wealth. There is a genuine resentment of the inequality represented by Herodian opulence, while there is no hostility concerning the payment of religious dues connected with the Jerusalem Temple. Once again, the orthogenetic and heterogenetic dimensions of the different cities would appear to stand out clearly.

The Jesus movement adopted a rather different strategy regarding social inequality. The situation presumed by many of the sayings is not one of penury, but rather of possessions and greed. Advice such as 'Lay not up for yourselves treasures on earth where moths destroy and thieves break through and steal' (Mt 6,19), presupposes a situation that is similar to that which befell the Herodian lady at the hands of the brigands of Dabaritta. The injunctions to the disciples not to be concerned about money or possessions as they travel from town to town (Mk 6,8–10) propose a totally different value system with regard to wealth than that that reflected in *Life*. It is not a question of giving up a tithe for religious dues, but rather of letting go of all that one has. True, the question of debt looms very large on the horizon, and sayings about violence, reconciliation with neighbours, etc., reflect a world in which the harsh realities of life cause much injustice at a local level. Jesus calls for a transformation of human relations not on a global or even national scale at first, but within the village life of Galilee.[13]

---

[13] Cf. R. Horsley, 'Ethics and Exegesis: "Love Your Enemies" and the Doctrine of Non-Violence,' *Journal of the American Academy of Religion* 54 (1985) 3–31.

The gospel evidence confirms the picture drawn by *Life* and offers a more radical solution to the problem. The wealth-distributing mechanisms of Jewish law, such as the poor man's tithe, did not ultimately challenge the inequalities that Herodian-Roman rule perpetuated through lifestyle, apparel or buildings. The value system of the Jesus movement, had it been adopted, would have proposed an ideal in the name of the God of Israel that was the antithesis of prevailing norms, in religious as well as social terms. From this perspective, both Herodian and Jerusalem values were under attack and both were regarded as distorting and alienating.

Recently it has been suggested that this worldview was Cynic-inspired and that it reflected the 'urbanised' situation of all the Lower Galilee.[14] In terms of our model, heterogenetic cities supposedly provided new mythic patterns that were forward-looking and alternative; undoubtedly the Cynic movement was an urban phenomenon that is attested for nearby Gadara and Tyre. On closer examination, however, there are distinct differences between the Jesus sayings and typical Cynic instructions, particularly in the matter of purse, staff, and begging. Indeed, as Horsley points out, the Pauline letters reflect Cynic attitudes much more obviously than does the Jesus tradition.[15] It would be a mistake, though, both methodologically and factually, to transpose later Pauline, urban Christianity back onto the Palestinian Jesus movement and thereby infer an urbanised Galilee, despite similarities in external form with other counter-cultural movements. The inspiration of the Jesus movement was scriptural and rooted in the Israelite tradition, as indicated by the selection of the core group of the Twelve, symbolising the league of the twelve tribes. It therefore cannot be considered a product of the urban environment, even when its universalist outlook seems to correspond to the *Zeitgeist* of the Hellenistic age.

Social Unity and Dissent

The final element of the model deals with the different ways in which our two contrasting city-types view the issue of social unity and dissent. As the representative of the Jerusalem hierocracy, and therefore acting as an agent of the orthogenetic city, Josephus emphasises loyalty in his dealings in the Galilee. While serving the Josephan rhetoric of self-defence and self-exoneration, it nonetheless indicates that this was the strategy which he

---

[14] A. Overman, 'Who Were the First Urban Christians? Urbanization in Galilee in the First Century,' and D. A. Edwards, 'First Century Urban/Rural Relations in Lower Galilee: Exploring the Archaeological and Literary Evidence,' in *SBLASP 1988*, ed. D. Lull (Atlanta: Scholars Press, 1988) 160–68 and 169–82 respectively.

[15] R. Horsley, *Sociology and the Jesus Movement* (New York: Crossroad, 1989) 116–21.

and others employed. Kinship / ὁμοφυλία is a key term denoting the shared worldview and lineage of all Jews (*Life* 55, 100, 171), and the absence of this basic quality was the greatest indictment of his opponents. An assembly (σύνοδος) of Galileans was called on one occasion (*Life* 310f.) and Josephus also set up a legal institution of seventy Galilean elders to try cases based on the Mosaic model (*JW* 2,570f.; *Life* 79; cf. *JA* 4,214 and 7,287). The term 'traitor' is repeatedly applied to Josephus, to Sepphoris, to Justus, and to all those who were deemed not to share in the common point of view. The action of Jesus, the revolutionary leader in Tiberias who brandished the law of Moses and called on the populace of Tarichaeae to reject Josephus, is a strident example of this theme of loyalty and betrayal, a typical feature of the Jewish ethos of the period when faced with political and cultural threat.

I have repeatedly contended that the Jesus movement was rurally based. Even allowing for the evangelists' later interests, it seems to have attained, initially at least, a widespread popularity among the countrypeople. However, the reasons for this enthusiasm and subsequent rejection should be examined carefully before concluding that this movement does not fit into our model also. As already noted, the literati of the Great Tradition sought to discredit Jesus by claiming that his mighty deeds were evilly inspired. This charge points to the very source of his popularity, namely, that he was a charismatic healer who fulfilled a social need for the countrypeople. Charges of magic by the enlightened are not always appreciated within a folk culture. Instead, it was the charge made in Jerusalem of destroying the Temple that eventually turned the crowds, including presumably his fellow-Galilean pilgrims, against Jesus. The common Great Tradition could tolerate a certain deviance, especially at the periphery, provided it did not strike at the very core of the religious establishment, and in the case of first-century Judaism, this was represented by Jerusalem and the Temple.

On the other hand, the Herodian and Greek cities were, from the view of the countrypeople, the base of military power from whence destruction could come at any moment. Hence, mistrust and hostility were always part of the relationship. A Roman army advancing from Ptolemais pillaged Galilean villages as a matter of course (*Life* 213), while a Herodian stronghold like Tiberias could be dangerous for the villages belonging to other city territories (*Life* 42). A precarious relationship such as this, based solely on power and control and without any built-in corrective in terms of shared worldview, was not likely to generate trust or transform cities, even Herodian ones, into orthogenetic centres for the Galileans. Both Josephus' portrayal of the Galileans and Jesus' avoidance of all cities, especially the Herodian ones of the Lower Galilee, are strong indications that these centres were less than fully integrated into their rural hinterland.

Conclusion

On all four points of our model – dominant social types, relationships between city and countryside, economic patterns, and social unity – we have found considerable evidence that both the Greek and Herodian cities of first-century Galilee were heterogenetic in terms of cultural interchange. This was due to the older and more pervasive relationship with Jerusalem, the orthogenetic city-type, which had been shared by many of the inhabitants of the region – 'the Galileans' of our literary sources.

In formulating such a conclusion we must remember that sociological models always operate according to ideal types; however, when dealing with the real world historical occurrences can blur our academic distinctions. In our discussion we have often pointed to Josephus as a representative of the orthogenetic city of Jerusalem, yet he was also a product of the Hellenistic world in his style, position, and outlook. It was his role as a Jerusalemite priest that he exploited to the fullest in his dealings with the countrypeople. Similarly, the fact that Sepphoris emerges as heterogenetic on the basis of our model may appear surprising in view of its earlier Jewish character (*m. 'Arak.* 9,6). This merely points to the gradual process of secondary urbanisation, in which accommodation to the dominant cultural pattern may have begun already with its refurbishment by Antipas. Material remains attesting to the later period have uncovered ritual baths and Dionysiac mosaics in very close proximity to one another, indicating that the process was considerably accentuated in later centuries.

However, when all due allowances are made for the various shades of Hellenistic influences operating within all branches of Judaism, including Palestinian Judaism, the fact remains that two quite distinctive environments in close proximity to each other can be discerned in Roman-period Galilee. Each had its own identity, values, and norms, despite a degree of shared influences – Jewish and Greek – in which all participated. The task of the historian of antiquity is to find appropriate tools to evaluate those differences and to be sensitive to the compromises and choices made by people struggling to maintain their social and ethnic identity in Galilee so long ago.

3. Town and Country Once More: The Case of Roman Galilee

The work of Professor James Strange has contributed greatly to our knowledge of first-century Galilee, not just as a member of the Meiron Expedition investigating the synagogues of Upper Galilee, but more recently for his ongoing work at Sepphoris. His most recent publication on the location of Shikhin (probably to be identified with Asochis of Josephus) raises the important question of town and country, a question that is crucial for understanding Greco-Roman society.[1] For those interested in the historical Jesus and his movement this question has come centre stage, raising issues about the background of Jesus' audiences and their religious and cultural affiliations, the nature and impact of the Herodian presence on Jesus' movement and message as well as the currency of Cynic ideas in the Galilee. All these questions are currently under continuous scrutiny with different scholars adopting different stances. The vexed question of the choice and use of sociological models is also part of the debate. All of this makes Galilean studies today a showcase of the best in contemporary academic investigation of ancient society, calling on the diverse skills of literary, archaeological, linguistic and sociological expertise of the various clienteles interested in the Galilee of the Roman period.

Within this barrage of often conflicting voices, Strange's work has for me always sounded a note of good sense, bringing to his undoubted skills as a field archaeologist a real understanding of life as it was lived within the everyday experience of people struggling to cope with their environment. This has inevitably meant moving away from main street Sepphoris, and thinking seriously about how life as it was lived in that quarter impacted on the wider environment of the many villages/towns whose remains, like those of Shikhin, dot the landscape of Lower Galilee.

This same topic has also been of central concern to my own study of the Galilee. It was difficult to move beyond fairly general observations when working mainly with literary sources, however, since the texts themselves only illuminated those aspects of the society that interested their authors, and then always with particular interests in view. The terminology em-

---

[1] J. Strange, D. Groh, and T. Longstaff, 'Excavations at Sepphoris: The Location and Identification of Shikhin,' Part I, *IEJ* 44 (1994) 216–27, and Part II, *IEJ* 45 (1995) 171–87.

ployed by different authors admittedly raised interesting questions: why
does Mark (1,38) use the rare κωμοπόλεις on one occasion to describe locations visited by Jesus? Both Luke and Josephus appear to have a highly
flexible use of the term πόλις, the former calling such places as Nazareth
and Capernaum by that designation (Lk 1,26; 4,31), and the latter applying
it to a place which he elsewhere calls κώμη (*JW* 3,129; *Life* 395). The Jewish sources seem to have a more varied terminology – e.g., *kerakh, 'ir, kefar*.[2] Does this mean that the Jewish mode of settlement was different to
that which obtained in other parts of Greco-Roman society, and if so what
were the factors that brought that about?

In Search of a Model

In an earlier study I distinguished two phases of urbanisation with very
different impact on Galilean life, because in my view they were very different in character.[3] The first phase, that of the Ptolemaic/Seleucid period,
took place in the outer circle or *galil* and was thoroughly Greek in its inspiration and intention; the second was Herodian and touched the interior
of Galilee itself in the cities of Sepphoris and Tiberias. While I would still
want to maintain the difference between these two phases, under the influence of archaeological evidence I now see the need to recognise another
element in the settlement of Galilee, namely, those places which can be
attributed to the Hasmonean expansion in the late Hellenistic period, i.e.
late second and early first century BCE. These foundations arguably had a
more profound and lasting impact on the overall ethos of Galilee than had
either of the other two phases. At least, as we shall see, that is one of the
major issues at stake in this debate.

That study, which was completed in 1978, but which for circumstances
beyond my control did not appear until 1980, did not include the important
survey of Galilee and the Golan of the Meiron Excavation Project.[4] In ret-
rospect what shaped my thinking most profoundly, if implicitly, was my
experience of having grown up in the rural West of Ireland that was dotted
with towns of various size and importance, ranging from villages (usually
a number of dwellings grouped around a church and/or a school) to larger
market and county towns, with one or two places that could have been de-

---

[2] M. Goodman, *State and Society in Roman Galilee, A.D. 132–212* (Totowa, NJ:
Rowman and Allenheld, 1983) 27–31.

[3] S. Freyne, *Galilee from Alexander the Great to Hadrian. A Study of Second Temple
Judaism,* (reprint, Edinburgh, T. & T. Clark, 1998) 101–56.

[4] E. Meyers, J. Strange, and D. Groh, 'The Meiron Excavation Project: Archaeological Survey in Galilee and the Golan, 1976,' *BASOR* 230 (1978) 1–24.

scribed as cities. This environment gave me a life-long appreciation of the subtle but real differences that can exist not just between town and country, but also between various villages despite their proximity, with the next hill, stream or valley providing the social as well as the physical boundary between various townlands. A sense of local pride, ranging from esteem earned through displays of prowess by certain individuals (even in faction fighting among different villages) to acquired skills, manual or otherwise (such as those of the seanachai, or story-teller), gave rise to differentiation between villages, even though all shared a sense of relative deprivation by comparison with the inhabitants of even the medium sized towns around. These were visited on market-days, for sports meetings or other events, but there was always a sense of reserve, even suspicion among the peasants with regard to the townspeople. The social boundaries between one village and another arose and were maintained for apparently intangible reasons to do with loyalties expressed at times of political or physical crises (e.g., the bitter, post-revolution civil war of 1922–23, or the great famine of the last century), which were deeply engrained in the folk memory. Other factors, such as economic stratification in terms of the quality of land, or blood relations etc. all played their part in this highly complex network of social relations. Despite these very real divisions there was a shared sense of solidarity of these peasants, if that is what we must call them. They maintained their rootedness to the land, even to unproductive holdings, often eking out a meagre existence through subsistence farming of their own few acres, combined with seasonal labour elsewhere through harvesting as hired workers on larger estates elsewhere, mostly in England. In particular, I am impressed by the ways in which through song, story and seasonal rituals, they were able to maintain their social and cultural identity and ancestral values, even when for extraneous reasons, the tongue of the coloniser had become the *lingua franca*. It was this pattern of cultural resistance, despite the attractions of outside influences that gave rise to the description of 'the bog Irish', with their strong group and weak grid identity.[5]

Far from disqualifying my hunches about Galilee, I now realise that I was operating with an implicit model that was just as feasible as any other drawn from Mediterranean cultures today in terms of a working hypothesis for discussing Galilean life. All that was missing was a critical apparatus to test the resulting picture in terms of its 'fit' with historical Galilee and in particular the archaeological and literary evidence pertaining to the region. In subsequent publications I have applied models drawn from the social sciences dealing with the cultural role of cities and ancient econo-

---

[5] M. Douglas, *Natural Symbols. Explorations in Cosmology* (New York: Pantheon, 1982) 59–76.

mies, which, though based on ideal types, have proved useful in understanding the cultural role of the Herodian cities and their impact on the hinterland.[6] The conclusions were that both Sepphoris and Tiberias functioned heterogenetically as far as Galilean peasants were concerned, not because they were gentile enclaves in a Jewish hinterland (and in this they differed markedly from the Greek cities in the circle), but because, as Herodian centres, they represented an intrusion in a more traditional way of life, by a new type of Hellenised (or Romanised) Jew who was prepared to collaborate with an alien Roman system as its power-brokers.

An Urban Overlay?

This picture is undoubtedly overdrawn, as all pictures based on ideal types must perforce be. There is also the clear bias of Josephus' account to be considered and evaluated. Yet the question remains as to the possible truth of such a depiction. It is here that James Strange's interest in urban/rural relations from an archaeological point of view has proved a challenge for testing, refining or rejecting previous positions. In a recent article that is highly pertinent to the present discussion he speaks of 'an urban overlay' as a way of describing the clear signs of Roman imperial presence, which, at least on the basis of Sepphoris, reached down to the very domestic level of Jewish life in the city.[7] Comparisons with other important sites such as Caesarea Maritima, Ptolemais/Akko and Scythopolis/ Beth Shean suggest to Strange that in its architectural remains Sepphoris was part of a wider pattern in which the city, conceived as model, can be seen as 'a conceptual artefact' of the culture as a whole. Through its buildings and other visual expressions it represents the way in which people living in that place, 'the locals', viewed the world and gave expression to those views in stone. This architectural symbolism can then be used as a gauge or yardstick to measure the degree to which Roman ideas had blended together to make a comprehensive statement within the larger framework of Roman imperial ideology, as mediated within Galilee by Herod Antipas.

In developing his argument Strange does acknowledge the possible clash of Roman and Jewish cultures, and the ways in which this will express itself through the different art and architectural forms – theatre, baths, hippodrome, aqueduct for the Romans, and temple and synagogue for the Jews. Nevertheless, he does not see any serious clash between the

---

[6] Cf. 'Urban-Rural Relations in First Century Galilee,' above pp. 45 ff.

[7] J. Strange, 'Some Implications of Archaeology for New Testament Studies,' in *What has Archaeology to do with Faith?* ed. J. Charlesworth (Valley Forge: Trinity Press International, 1992) 23–59.

two; 'strangeness' inhibiting the graft between them is the nearest he comes to positing any real opposition. It is a matter of focusing or centring of the different symbolic expressions rather than establishing any rigid boundaries between them. Insofar as it is permissible to speak of boundaries it is the symbolically neutral zone where forms and symbols have a more generalised meaning and are not specific to either culture. This absence of conflict between Roman and Jewish cultures in Galilee was due to the fact that Hellenism had prepared the way for both, on the one hand providing the Romans with a suitable repertoire of symbols for its purposes, and on the other preparing the Jewish culture for its encounter with Rome. The process of grafting that can be perceived at Sepphoris was not confined to the city but had extended itself well outside that setting so that it is possible to detect it in the earliest strata of the Jesus tradition as these are represented in *Q* and Mark, where a strong urban overlay can also be detected in the imagery and language.

Strange's account differs most pointedly from mine in that he sees a real similarity between Sepphoris and other Greco-Roman towns in Palestine on the one hand, and on the other he posits a continuity between it and the rest of Galilee in terms not just of the material culture but also the symbolic impact of its forms. He understands my work as espousing an isolationist Galilee, one that being free of Hellenisation is also free of urbanisation, since the two go hand in hand.[8] Leaving aside the possibility that we are both misreading each other, how might one adjudicate between the two accounts and methodologically, where is the difference between us located?

Taking a Cue from the Literary Evidence

A first answer is that we both have different starting points, he with the archaeological remains and I with the literary texts. In itself this should not lead to such a different assessment of the overall picture provided each is open to the other's perspective, as would seem to be the case. Another difference concerns the time spans within which each discipline operates. Archaeologists speak of early, middle and late Roman periods, each having as much as 100 years duration, which is not sufficiently precise for the historian seeking to differentiate between the period of Jesus in the thirties and Mark's reporting of this in the sixties. In this regard it is noteworthy that James Strange and Eric Meyers differ in their dating of the theatre at Sepphoris, the former attributing it to the period of Antipas and the latter

---

[8] 'Some Implications,' 27 and 53, n. 40.

to later in the first century, possibly even post–70.[9] This is not to suggest that the two disciplines should not seek to dialogue with each other. Strange proposes a useful model for such a conversation, each discipline performing its own tasks before entering into dialogue with the other. The temptation is for each to seek a complete picture (insofar as this is ever attainable) without having all the pieces in place or all the perspectives of the texts fully examined and articulated. Some interaction and mutual correction should be possible even as the separate tasks are being conducted, however. How might such a critical co-relation be achieved?

On the literary side, too little attention has perhaps been given to what can be learned from the Jewish sources, especially Mishnah and Tosefa. The fact that in their present form these are late compilations has made scholars cautious in using them for pre–70 historical reconstruction, especially following the strictures of Jacob Neusner about uncritical use by scholars, Jewish and Christian, of rabbinical sources. When all due allowance is made for Neusner's pioneering work in deciphering the individual statement of each of these works understood as a literary production, there is no good reason for not taking seriously their description of social *realia* as being actual, rather than fictional, especially the size and nature of settlements. The designations *kerakh*, *'ir*, and *kefar*, as well as many variations on these, were inherited, not invented by the Tannaim, no matter how much they used them to explain various *halakoth* dealing with spatial matters.[10] A more realistic starting point for archaeologists and literary historians alike would be to accept that both the New Testament and Josephus are limited in the available Greek terminology, leaving us to fit various types and sizes of settlements into one of only two possible categories – city or village – on the basis of such different criteria as size, capacity for defence, population numbers, administrative role etc. In our post-industrial world, a village has the slightly pejorative connotation of a place that did not have the resources or capacity to 'make it' to the status of town, and is therefore, backward, primitive and uncultured.

This picture of the village is quite inappropriate in terms of pre-industrial society. According to *t. Mak* 3,8 a distinction was made between cities of medium size and villages. This may be reflected also in Josephus' description of a 'a village not inferior to a city' (Batanea, *JA* 17,23, and Lydda, *JA* 20,130), and in Mark's unusual κωμοπόλεις (Mk 1,38). Elsewhere, different plans for cities are described: rectangle, circle, semi-

---

[9] J. Strange, 'Six Campaigns at Sepphoris: The University of South Florida Excavations, 1983–1989,' and E. Meyers, 'Roman Sepphoris in Light of New Archaeological Evidence and Recent Research,' in *The Galilee in Late Antiquity*, ed. L. Levine (New York: The Jewish Theological Seminary, 1992) 339–56 and 321–38 respectively.

[10] C. Dauphin, 'Les *komai* de Palestine,' *Proche Orient Chrétien* 37 (1987) 251–67.

circle, gamma shaped, long on one side and short on the other (t. *'Erub.* 4,4 f.) While this passage may have been produced in order to work out all possible permutations for fulfilling *Shabbat* requirements, the fact that such patterns have been detected at various excavated sites suggests that it is at least based on reality and not a purely fictional creation. Many aspects of life within the cities can be gleaned from other references: a distinction is made between private and public buildings (t. *Sheb.* 8,2; t. *B. Qam.* 4,3; t. *Ned.* 5,5); fortification was important (t. *'Arak.* 5,12; t. *'Erub.* 10,30); the location of various installations such as oil presses and tanneries as well as the burial place is stipulated (t. *B. Bat.* 2,8–9; 4,7–8). In addition, threshing floors, granaries and wells are all mentioned.[11]

Even this cursory glance at village life from the literary texts suggests a place of some self-sufficiency as far as domestic and communal life was concerned. It is a picture that has been corroborated by many different surveys and excavations at various Jewish sites both in Galilee – Meiron, Kh. Shema, Nabratein,[12] Chorazin and Kefar Hanania,[13] and in the Golan, Qatzrin,[14] Kefar Naffakh, Na'aran, Farj and Er Ramthaniyye.[15] Not dissimilar patterns of village life have been reported from the Hauran (Auranitis) for the Hellenistic and Roman periods.[16]

Unfortunately archaeology in Egypt has, for various reasons, not been systematically conducted, even in the larger urban sites, such is the embarrassment of riches in papyri, temples and tombs. There is, however, some information from the Fayum region which dates from the early Hellenistic period when many of the villages originated as settlements for Greek and Macedonian military colonisers, and so would correspond with the expansion of settlements in Galilee in the Hellenistic period. The papyri are invaluable in terms of understanding the organisation and self-sufficiency of village life. Those from Keranis (one of the few Egyptian villages excavated in any detail) suggest that the inhabitants of these villages were

---

[11] For a full discussion see Z. Safrai, *The Economy of Roman Palestine* (New York and London: Routledge, 1994) 17–103.

[12] Meyers, Strange and Groh, 'The Meiron Excavation 1976.'

[13] D. Adan-Bayewitz, 'Kefar Hananya,' *IEJ* 37 (1986) 178–79, and 39 (1989) 98–99.

[14] Z. Ma'oz, 'The Golan: Hellenistic Period to the Middle Ages,' in *NEAEHL* 2, 234–46.

[15] C. Dauphin and J. Schonfield, 'Settlements of the Roman and Byzantine Periods on the Golan Heights,' *IEJ* 33 (1983) 189–206; C. Dauphin and S. Gibson, 'Ancient Settlements and their Landscapes: The Results of Ten Years of Survey on the Golan Heights (1978–88),' *Bulletin of the Anglo-Israel Archaeological Society* 12 (1992/93) 7–31.

[16] F. Villeneuve, 'L'économie rurale et la vie des campagnes dans le Hauran Antique,' in *Recherches Archéologiques sur la Syrie du Sud a l'Époque Hellenistique et Romaine: Hauran I,* ed. J.-M. Dentzer (Paris: Librairie Orientaliste Paul Gauthier, 1986) 63–129.

farmers owning their own plots of ground, and the buildings, other than houses, seem to confirm this – granaries, threshing floors, bakeries, potteries and a pigeon house. Almost half of those inhabitants who could be estimated on the basis of tax records owned plots of between 10 and 39 arouras, i.e. subsistence or just above subsistence levels, and a small percentage owned larger plots of above 70 arouras requiring slave or hired labour in order to run the farm. Activities other than farming were largely of the service variety. Second-century Keranis had an oil maker, a baker, retailers of wine, fish and vegetables, though these also owned land. There were also 16 people engaged in the fabric industry, everything from carding and weaving to sack making. There is very little evidence of any production of luxury items or trades to do with care of the body. As regards local government, because of the nature of the evidence one could easily get the impression of a highly bureaucratic system, but that would be to overdraw the picture since there is a striking absence of any imperial official. Nevertheless, the evidence suggests a well-ordered community life, with the ubiquitous tax collectors predominating. The *komarchs* had considerable powers, not just in terms of naming there own successors but also in distributing the various liturgies to be performed on behalf of the community, with almost half of the male population involved in some kind of public duty. There is also evidence of inter-village movement on several levels, not least through inter-marriage, and movement outside the district was not infrequent, mainly for official reasons when a visit to the nome capital was called for.[17]

While this picture is based on the specific conditions of fourth-century CE Egypt and due allowance has to be made for the many changes that had occurred in imperial policy and government, nevertheless, many elements are recognisable in terms of what we know of first-century Palestinian village life, not least from the recently published Babatha archive.[18] If anything the picture of village life from an earlier period shows a greater degree of prosperity and diversity of activity.[19] In the end what may have distinguished village life (at least in the larger ones) was the permanent relationship to the land and with it the maintenance of traditional values. Insofar as we can judge, the Herodian land policy did not favour the large estates on the basis of the evidence both from Batanea and Gaba (*JA* 15,294; 17,24) This meant that side by side with the propagation of impe-

---

[17] R. Bagnall, *Egypt in Late Antiquity* (Princeton: Princeton University Press, 1993) 110–47.

[18] B. Isaac, 'The Babatha Archive. A Review Article,' *IEJ* 42 (1992) 62–75.

[19] G. McLean Harper, 'Village Administration in the Roman Province of Syria,' *Yale Classical Studies* 1 (1928) 107–68.

rial ideology in the founding of Greek-style cities at carefully chosen sites, other patterns of settlement and land distribution were also maintained that did not disrupt earlier colonising patterns established both by the Hellenistic monarchies and the Hasmoneans. Sepphoris and Tiberias seem to have fallen somewhere between these two, because of the ambitions of Antipas, but also on account of the limitations of his political position.

Judaisation or Urbanisation?

This brings us back to Strange's urban overlay in Galilee and how we are to assess its symbolic significance. If the suggestion that the majority of the settlements of Galilee are better understood in terms of the Hebrew rather than the Greek nomenclature has any merit, then the question of the urbanisation of Galilee becomes the question of its Judaisation, not, at least in the first instance, of its Hellenisation! As is well known this is a controversial issue with various views supported more on the basis of the authority of modern scholarship than on an examination of the hard evidence. Suggestions of the remnants of the old Israelite population,[20] the forced circumcision of the Itureans,[21] or Hasmonean colonisation,[22] have all had their supporters. In *Galilee from Alexander the Great to Hadrian*, I supported Alt's position and may have consequently 'ruralised' Galilee more than was warranted, since my own experiences suggested that it was among such people living in a peasant ethos that folk memories, such as one might associate with an old Israelite presence continuing through the centuries, endured longer. The archaeological evidence, however, seems to point to the Hasmonean expansion/conquest as the most likely hypothesis. The Meiron Expedition Survey (1976) of a limited number of sites postulated a rapid expansion in the late Hellenistic period for Upper Galilee, within a hitherto sparsely populated area. However, preliminary indications from Galilee of the Archaeological Survey of Israel by M. Aviam and others, which is much more far reaching in scope, suggests a profile of a gradual upward curve in the number of settlements – from 93 in Hellenistic times to 138 in the Roman period to 162 in Byzantine times. There are two further pertinent conclusions emerging from this survey, namely,

---

[20] A. Alt, 'Galiläische Probleme 1937–40,' in *Kleine Schriften zur Geschichte des Volkes Israels* (Munich: C. H. Beck, 1953–64), vol 2, 363–435. See below 'Behind the Names: Galileans, Samaritans, *Ioudaioi*,' pp. 114 ff.

[21] E. Schürer, *The History of the Jewish People in the Age of Jesus Christ*, 3 vols., revised by G. Vermes, F. Miller, and M. Black (Edinburgh: T. & T. Clark, 1973–84), vol. 2, 7–14.

[22] M. Aviam, 'Galilee: the Hellenistic to Byzantine Periods,' in *NEAEHL* 2, 452–58.

on the one hand, the abandonment of certain Hellenistic sites, e.g., Har Mizpe Yamim, where clear signs of Pagan worship were discovered,[23] and on the other the emergence of new settlements, not previously inhabited, which on the basis of the coin finds, appear to be Hasmonean foundations. All students of Galilee in antiquity await with anticipation the detailed publication of this survey, but on the basis of the evidence thus far available, it seems to point unmistakably to an aggressive Jewish colonisation of the Galilee by the Hasmoneans in line with what we know from Josephus of their approach at Samaria and Scythopolis. Yet it would seem that this development was able to build on a previously existing Hellenistic presence in the region.

How does such a profile fit with the urban overlay hypothesis? On the one hand, Strange is correct in seeing the grafting of a Jewish culture onto a previously existing Hellenistic one. However, the Hellenisation of the Hasmoneans is known enough from the literary sources to see how they could combine architectural, political and military aspects of Greek culture with a strongly religio-nationalistic ideology.[24] Strange's hypothesis raises the question of whether or not the remnants of that mix were sufficiently potent to resist the Roman overlay in its symbolic intentions of celebrating Roma Aeterna, while of course adopting without demur certain aspects of that presence at the material, everyday level. In other words, my major difficulty is not with the Roman overlay in terms of Galilean life, but with the understanding of what that was saying at a symbolic level to country Galileans. Here I am considering my own experience of how West of Ireland peasants resisted colonising influences, and transformed those dimensions they did absorb. If one were to change the metaphor from the architectural to the anatomical, the question I want to ask is: was there an underbelly of resistance, and if so where was it located? How did it organise itself and what resources – religious, and cultural – did it draw on? What memories inspired it and where did it find its symbolic and ritual expressions?

Architectural Symbolism

This list of questions takes us well beyond the scope of this article. However, it does seem to me that, as stated, Strange's case needs to be nuanced somewhat. These stones do not speak; it is we who give them voice. But is

---

[23] R. Frankel, 'Har Mispe Yamim, 1988/9,' *Excavations and Surveys in Israel, 1988/89* (Jerusalem: The Israel Exploration Society) 9 (1989) 100–102; R. Frankel and R. Ventura, 'The Mispe Yamim Bronzes,' *BASOR* 311 (1998) 39–55.

[24] D. Mendels, *The Rise and Fall of Jewish Nationalism* (New York: Doubleday, 1992) 55–73.

our voice the same as those who originally spoke through them? The more pertinent question, perhaps, is how were these symbolic statements received? There were, and always are more than one 'local' voice. I agree fully that the building of Sepphoris and Tiberias were aggressive acts of Romanisation by Antipas. Even if we allow that the theatre at Sepphoris belongs to the earliest phase of Antipas' refurbishment of that site in order to be 'the ornament of all Galilee', there are still some notable absentees in terms of Greco-Roman architectural statements from those centres. Thus far at least, there are no pagan temples, no altar to Roma Aeterna, no large public statues as distinct from private figurines. Can archaeology tell us what images were visible in the agora at Sepphoris in the first century? Despite its different, more cosmopolitan character by contrast with nearby Iotapata or Gamala, I still remain to be convinced that it made the same bold statement that Caesarea Maritima, Caesarea Philippi/Banias, Scythopolis/Beth Shean or Samaria/Sebaste achieved in terms of Roman power and presence. By those standards it seems to my ear to be making a considerably more muted statement. Why, I wonder? Is it because the past history of the Herods in Galilee, including Sepphoris itself (*JA* 17,289), meant that one had to tread cautiously, no matter how much one wished to celebrate Rome?

If, therefore, reservation is called for in affirming a continuity of symbolic statement between Sepphoris and some of the other Greco-Roman cities of Palestine, what of the continuity between Sepphoris and its hinterland in Lower Galilee? I defer to the expertise of the archaeologists in terms of the actual evidence, but personal experience as well as social theory causes me to query any idea of a cultural continuum being established just because the peasants may find outlets for their produce at urban centres, or continue some, at least, of the urban architectural styles at lesser settlements (e.g., Chabulon, *JW* 2,503 f.). My own experience has taught me that even in the case of language itself, the most basic of all cultural expressions, changes forced by commercial or administrative circumstances do not entail adoption of the cultural assumptions associated with the language in other contexts. Rather, native idioms give a new vitality to the alien tongue and can transform it, as anybody familiar with the poetry of W. B. Yeats or the plays of J. M. Synge can attest. Both drew much of their inspiration from the landscape and people of Western Ireland. Social anthropologists have pointed to the salient fact that not all aspects of any culture are internalised by any individual, much less any sub-group. Many features remain at the cliché level as far as the ideal culture is concerned. Motivational theory, as employed in Cultural Anthropology suggests that there is a far greater variety within any given cultural matrix than any of our generalised labels such as urbanisation, inculturation or even urban

overlay can capture.[25] All cultures are a complex network of factors coalescing to form certain general patterns of behaviour, attitudes, life-styles
and values. The process of sifting, selecting or rejecting and internalising
is itself also highly complex. To infer the acceptance of all aspects of the
dominant culture from the fact that building or decorative habits conform
to an urban typology, or that certain styles of pottery, glass ware or other
items of everyday requirement at rural sites are part of a cultural continuum between town and country, is to go well beyond the evidence. On reflection it does not conform to our own experiences within the global culture of contemporary mass media communications.

Back to the Literary Evidence

This raises once again the importance of texts for historical reconstruction.
It is fashionable today to point to the perspectives of all texts as tellings,
not showings, from particular points of view. Yet the role of hermeneutic
suspicion in uncovering such biases can be of interest to the social historian in terms of the factors that gave rise to those biases in the first instance. The recognition that different literary genres are themselves based
on social conventions is also highly significant as far as social historians
are concerned, since literary works especially in antiquity are intended as
oral communicative exercises that depend on their verisimilitude in order
to achieve their desired effect.

As already mentioned, the study of Josephus' *Life* made it clear to me
that both Sepphoris and Tiberias are presented as heterogenetic as far as
Galileans 'from the land' are concerned. However, one might be rightly
suspicious of this depiction, in that it conforms to Josephus' own concern
to vilify Justus and other Galilean leaders and to present himself as the
agent of moderation in an otherwise volatile situation.[26] As part of his
strategy, Josephus deliberately portrays the Galileans as his loyal supporters, ready to vent their anger on the two Herodian centres, for religious as
well as social reasons, thereby aligning themselves with the Jerusalem perspective of the author. Does this mean that we must dismiss this whole account as pure fabrication, or does it in any sense conform to reality, even if
Josephus has highlighted certain aspects for his own purposes? Before
jumping to the 'obvious' conclusion of a total fabrication, Josephus' self-
characterisation and his relations with various factions in Galilee have to

---

[25] R. D'Andrade and C. Strauss, *Human Motives and Cultural Models* (Cambridge:
Cambridge University Press, 1992).

[26] S. J. D. Cohen, *Josephus in Galilee and Rome. His Vita and Development as a Historian* (Leiden: Brill, 1979).

be evaluated from the point of view of the encomiastic nature of the work as a whole.[27] Josephus seeks to uphold the pivotal value of honour, not just with regard to his own conduct of affairs, but also in relation to the stance of Sepphoris, in that it maintained its πίστις or trust with Rome by refusing to join the revolt, unlike Justus' native place, Tiberias, which betrayed its trust to King Agrippa (*Life* 30, 103, 346). This is something Josephus admires despite his own rejection by the city (*Life* 104–10). At the same time he is critical of its refusal to support Jerusalem and tells of the Galileans' anger in attacking it, causing the chief citizens to flee to the acropolis, an action that corresponds to the complicity of some Galileans in the sack of Herod's palace in Tiberias (*Life* 66, 273–80, 348 f.). It thus would appear that once the *Life* is read in terms of the prevailing conventions, especially those to do with honour/shame, its statements and characterisations of the various personalities cannot be so lightly dismissed as mere Josephan fabrication.

Interesting confirmation of this conclusion might be gleaned from the Jesus tradition. Strange rightly points to the urban as well as the rural imagery in the earliest strata of that tradition. The really pertinent question, however, is how does the imagery function within that setting? It is true that such urban characters as the merchant, the judge and the wealthy landowner (usually an urban resident) can function as personalities in some parables, side by side with farmers, shepherds and tenant farmers. But this does not amount to espousing the values of the urban elites. The consistent criticism of wealth as well as the rejection of the Herodian court life-style point unmistakably to a distancing from that world, both physically and emotionally. Jesus is not critical of the city, just as he does not romanticise rural life, but I do believe that the silence about a visit to Sepphoris or Tiberias is not accidental. His opposition is not to places as such, but to certain values that are associated with city dwellers, especially among the elites who shaped and dominated their ethos, especially as this was viewed from the distance of the peasant.

Thus in the Jesus tradition dating from the thirties to the sixties of the first century and in the *Life* of Josephus, though written in the nineties, but purporting to describe the situation in the sixties, there appears to be a converging picture from the literary sources of ongoing tensions between town and country in first-century Galilee, not because such hostility was inevitable, but because the Herodian foundations of Galilee represented alien values as far as 'country' Jews were concerned, that is, the Jewish population of the Galilee living in towns and villages, whose loyalties to Jerusalem and the symbolic world represented by its cult-centre were suf-

---

[27] J. Neyrey, 'Josephus' *Vita* and the Encomium: A Native Model of Personality,' *JSJ* 25 (1994) 177–206.

ficiently intact, despite the distance, social and physical that separated them from that centre. The urban overlay, detectable in their environment did not, it seems to me, represent any capitulation on that score. The very fact of the revolt, however disorganised the Galilean phase was, must be seen as the failure of imperial propaganda as far as some of the inhabitants were concerned. In summary, in my view the archaeological evidence does not disconfirm the literary evidence and can itself be understood without recourse to the idea of an 'urbanised' Galilee, in the sense that some of the proponents of that idea have wished to maintain.

Conclusion

James Strange's article called for a genuine dialogue between spade and text, and in this brief response I have sought to address the challenge. For me the exercise has been more than worthwhile in forcing me to take a critical look at my own methodological assumptions and my choice and use of evidence. The conversation with the archaeological work that I have sought to conduct has been for me a most fruitful encounter with another view of how that world was, reminding me that all our worlds are constructions in constant need of revision. I hope that this contribution, offered in appreciation of James Strange and his work will lead to further fruitful dialogue between the proponents of spade and pen, archaeology and text. We can surely learn a lot from each other.

4. Galilee-Jerusalem Relations According to Josephus' *Life*

Josephus' *Life* raises many important literary and historical questions that are not easily resolved. This may explain why, for the most part, it has been ignored by New Testament scholars, despite the fact that it is the only extant writing from the first century that bears directly on Galilean life and culture and was written by somebody with immediate experience of that location.[1] Its tendentious character has been ably exposed by Shaye Cohen's study, *Josephus in Galilee and Rome. His Vita and Development as an Historian* (1979). Yet it can still yield invaluable information on social relations within the province, provided we approach it in the proper critical fashion, framing our questions carefully and being attentive to the presuppositions of the author.

This paper will concentrate on one of the more important questions about Galilee for the historian of early Christianity interested in reconstructing either the history of Jesus or that of a possible Galilean Christianity.[2] The focus will be on the issue of the relation between Galilee and Jerusalem as this comes to expression in the work. In their different ways this complex relationship is also central to the narrative about Jesus in all the gospels. Whether one treats this as a purely literary creation (Struthers-Malbon), or as the product of early Christian theologising (e.g., Lohmeyer, Marxsen, Kelber, Meeks), it does call for examination within the wider pattern of relationships operative in first-century CE Palestinian Judaism.[3]

---

[1] An interesting exception to this is Walter Bauer's 1927 article, 'Jesus der Galiläer,' in *Festgabe für Adolf Jülicher* (Tübingen, 1927) 16–34, reprinted in *Aufsätze und Kleine Schriften*, ed. G. Strecker (Tübingen: J. C. B. Mohr, 1967) 91–108.

[2] Cf. S. Freyne, *Galilee from Alexander the Great to Hadrian. A Study of Second Temple Judaism* (Wilmington: Glazier; University of Notre Dame Press, 1980; reprint, Edinburgh: T & T Clark, 1988), especially section II with ample bibliography. M. Goodman, *State and Society in Roman Galilee, A. D. 132–212*, Oxford Centre for Post-Graduate Hebrew Studies (Totowa: Rowman and Allenheld, 1983), combining Rabbinic documentation with archaeological evidence corroborates this account for the later period. For the most complete archaeological account cf. E. Meyers, 'The Cultural Setting of Galilee: The Case of Regionalism and Early Judaism,' in *ANRW* II 19,1, ed. W. Haase (Berlin and New York: de Gruyter, 1979) 686–702. For recent bibliographical data on the archaeology of Galilee, cf. 'Archaeology and the Historical Jesus,' below pp. 160 ff.

[3] E. Struthers Malbon, 'Galilee and Jerusalem: History and Literature in Markan Interpretation,' *CBQ* 44 (1982) 242–55; G. Theißen, 'Die Tempelweissagung Jesu. Prophe-

The Mishnah and Talmuds, though reflecting later conditions, also witness to distinctive Galilean attitudes and customs.[4] All kinds of factors, ranging from the geo-physical to the historico-cultural, make such regional differences between an outlying province and its religious capital plausible. Thus, the possibilities that this situation has to offer in exploring the social worlds of both Jesus and the first Christians are highly intriguing.

Josephus' Appointment and the Range of Authority of the Jerusalem Council

There seems to be no good reason for doubting that Josephus' appointment to Galilee in 66 CE was considered to be official by the newly constituted revolutionary council in Jerusalem. While *Life* varies the terminology somewhat with its use of the following descriptions: οἱ τῶν Ἱεροσολυμιτῶν πρῶτοι (310), τὸ κοινὸν τῶν Ἱεροσολυμιτῶν (65, 72, 190, 254, 267, 309, 341, 393), τὸ συνέδριον τῶν Ἱεροσολυμιτῶν (62), Josephus is at pains to stress the official status of those responsible for his appointment. His role is likewise described in various ways: ἀρχή (190, 302, 310), προστασία (312, 324, 343), στρατηγός (176, 194, 341), πρόνοιαν ποιεῖσθαι (62), ἐξουσία τῶν πραγμάτων (72). Since both sets of terms occur interchangeably, often in the same context, we should not attach any particular importance to the differing usages beyond the fact that the author is presupposing an official assembly at Jerusalem with supreme authority in matters of Jewish affairs throughout the country.[5] Even if Josephus' insistence on this point raises suspicion about his apologetic intentions (that he was not a usurper in Galilee), we should note that this very circumstance makes his assumptions about the nature and extent of the Jerusalem council's control all the more significant. In any self-defence a plausibility factor comes into play, especially when the issue is a public

---

tie in Spannungsfeld zwischen Tempel und Land,' *Theologische Zeitschrift* 32 (1967) 144–58; E. Lohmeyer, *Galiläa und Jerusalem,* FRLANT 34, (Göttingen: Vandenhoeck & Ruprecht, 1936); W. Kelber, *The Kingdom in Mark* (Philadelphia: Fortress Press, 1974); W. Meeks, 'Galilee and Judea in the Fourth Gospel,' *JBL* 85 (1966) 159–69.

[4] Differences in weights and measures: *m. Keth* 5,9; *m. Hul.* 11,2; customs relating to Passover and the Day of Atonement: *m. Pesah.* 4,5; *m. Hul.* 5,3; funeral rites and customs *y. Mo'ed Qatan* 3,5; *Sem.* 3,6; 10,16; marriage laws and divorce *m. Keth* 1,5; 4,2.

[5] In an unpublished dissertation at Duke University, *Galilean Judaism in the Writings of Josephus* (1975), F. Malinowski argues for a consistently distinctive meaning for the terms συνέδριον, βουλή, κοινόν as used by Josephus (199). However, the attempt is somewhat forced and pays insufficient attention to the contexts in which the various terms occur.

one. Others as well as the immediate protagonists know the circumstances. Josephus often exaggerates, but he rarely tells downright falsehoods.

The *JW* account has an even more formal tone, though with a different focus from that of *Life*. The revolutionary council appointed generals to all the different regions of the country after the defeat of Cestius Gallus, and Josephus was assigned to the two Galilees and Gamala (*JW* 2,566–68). The terminology employed in this account of his appointment (ἡγεμών and στρατηγία) underlines the military bias of that work, as well as the author's desire to portray himself as a wise and knowledgeable general, well versed in the art of war.[6] Yet despite this colouring and the historical questions that the report as stated raises, its underlying drift is the same as that of *Life*, namely, that Josephus' appointment to Galilee was officially sanctioned at Jerusalem (cf. *JW* 2,626–31).

The first question that needs to be addressed, therefore, is the actual role of the Jerusalem assembly at this time.[7] Are we, as *JW* suggests, dealing with an exceptional set of circumstances in which the council had been taken over by a militant group? If so, the whole episode of Josephus' appointment could scarcely be regarded as typical for any time other than the confused situation of the immediate pre-war period. It should, however, be noted that Josephus presumes a similar control for the Jerusalem Sanhedrin during the rise of the young Herod to power, when he was summoned from Galilee to answer charges of having murdered Hezekiah, the native brigand-chief, 'in violation of our law' (*JA* 14,167.170 f.179 f.). Furthermore, this legal control over Galilean internal affairs on the part of the Jerusalem council is assumed, despite the fact that the Romans had only recently set up provincial councils, including one at Sepphoris in Galilee, as part of their dismantling of the Hasmonean state (*JA* 14,91).[8]

Apart from this specific incident, which could be attributed to the serious nature of the crime involved, there is good reason to accept the authenticity of the *Life* version of the circumstances and intentions surrounding Josephus' appointment to Galilee, including the sending of two companions, who are not mentioned at all in the *JW* account. In *JW* there is a tendency to bring together events that are likely to have been quite separate both in time and intention, as, for example, the attacks on Jews in the surrounding Hellenistic cities. This gives an artificial character to the ac-

---

[6] As noted above the term στρατηγός also occurs at *Life* (176, 341), even though the military prowess is not so pronounced in that work. The two references listed do occur in the context of Josephus' military exploits, however.

[7] Cf. C. Roth, 'The Constitution of the Jewish Republic, 66–70,' *JSS* 9 (1964) 295–319.

[8] J. Spencer-Kennard, 'The Jewish Provincial Assembly,' *ZNW* 53 (1962) 25–51, especially 28, claims that these councils had been dismantled by Caesar, but without giving any evidence for the assertion.

counts and it could be argued that at least some of the generals of various regions are Josephus' invention as a way of heightening the importance of his own appointment.[9] In addition, the *JW* account does not adequately explain how and why the council was so effectively taken over by rebels later without any continuity of outlook and membership. It is more likely, then, that under the leadership of Ananus and others Josephus' appointment was merely the extension by the council of its authority in religious matters to other spheres of life with the temporary collapse of Roman authority after the defeat and retreat of Cestius Gallus. In that case we must conclude that the appointment was not the result of the special circumstances of the time, but was based on older and more firmly established claims on Galilean life on the part of the Jerusalem council.[10]

For the purposes of this essay there is no need to adjudicate between the two different accounts of his commission which Josephus gives – to prepare for war (*JW*), or to contain the situation (*Life*). Both are tendentious in their different ways, and the probability must be, pace Cohen, that his role was less clearly defined, but with the emphasis on avoiding open confrontation. More significant for the aim of this study is the need to explore the background to Josephus' appointment and its scope once he was established in the province.

Josephus was of priestly and aristocratic stock, and by his own admission consorted with the chief priests and the leading Pharisees (*Life* 1–3, 22). Before his appointment to Galilee he had undertaken a successful mission to the imperial court on behalf of other priests whom Felix had sent to Rome on a 'slight and trifling charge' (*Life* 13).[11] There seems little doubt that this pedigree was vital for his appointment to the Galilean command. As already mentioned, Ananus and his ilk had continued to control Jerusalem affairs (cf. *JW* 5,647–51), whether by astuteness or, as

---

[9] S. Cohen, *Josephus in Galilee. His Vita and Development as an Historian* (Leiden: Brill, 1979) 91 and 197.

[10] Kennard, 'The Jewish Provincial Assembly,' 44 f., points to Josephus' description (*JA* 20,251) of the Jewish government after the deposition of Archelaus as being aristocratic with the high priest entrusted with the dominion of the nation. As long as Antipas lived this arrangement did not apply to Galilee, but Josephus certainly assumes that it applied there afterward. However, there is no good evidence that this aristocratic council was replaced by a revolutionary one in 66 CE. It seems better, therefore, to accept the internal logic of events after the defeat of Cestius and recognise with Cohen, *Josephus in Galilee,* 195–99, the increasing pressure that came on the aristocracy from the revolutionaries.

[11] Cohen, *Josephus in Galilee,* 61, argues that this phrase, which also occurs at *JA* 20,215, is a cover for revolutionary activity, since in this latter context it is associated with the appearance of robbers in the land. Thus, its use in *Life* would lend support to Cohen's overall thesis that Josephus was a revolutionary which he carefully attempts to conceal, especially in this work.

Cohen argues, by sharing the revolutionary ideals, despite the initial take-over by the extremists.[12] The combination of chief priests and Pharisees concerned about relations with Rome appears in the gospels also (cf. Jn 11,46), but, as will be argued below, in all probability Josephus' appoint-ment was due more to his priestly origins than to his alleged association with Pharisees. In this regard the fact that *JW* 2,562 mentions that the de-cision to send him to Galilee was taken when the council leaders were meeting in the temple may be significant.[13] The symbolic claims of the temple, and therefore by association of the priesthood, on the loyalty of the country people at large must be carefully weighed, despite the un-doubted fact that in the first century CE the priesthood had become in-creasingly politicised and in the process may have lost some of its claims to legitimate authority over the temple state.[14] This observation is under-scored by the report in *Life* that Josephus and his colleagues claimed tithes as their due in Galilee (*Life* 63, 80), suggesting that in establishing their authority within the province they had recourse to their priestly back-ground and the claims that could be made for support from the people in the name of the Jerusalem temple (cf. *Life* 29). To underscore the point Josephus chides the inhabitants of Sepphoris for not sending assistance 'when the temple that is common to us all was in danger of falling into the

---

[12] *The issue of Josephus' own stance with regard to the revolt is a matter of ongoing debate. Cohen's position (cf. previous note) has recently been argued forcibly by M. Vo-gel, 'Vita 64–69, das Bilderverbot und die Galiläapolitik des Josephus,' *JSJ* 30 (1999) 65–79. On the other hand R. Horsley, *Galilee. History, Politics, People* (Valley Forge: Trinity Press International, 1995) 72–75 argues for understanding Josephus' mission in Galilee against the background of the role of native aristocracies within the Roman em-pire, who were expected to moderate situations of conflict and maintain order on behalf of their Roman overlords in return for the privileges they enjoyed under imperial rule. Cf. also, Freyne, *Galilee from Alexander the Great to Hadrian*, 241–45.

[13] In this regard it is interesting to note with Cohen, *Josephus in Galilee,* 190, the priestly pedigree of all the provincial generals and the absence of anybody of known Pharisaic background among those named by Josephus.

[14] *Horsley, *Galilee. History, Politics, People,* 136 f., sees this lack of legitimacy as indicative of the isolation of the priesthood from the people, and therefore, the repressive nature of the Judean attempts to control Galilee. He regards my claim (*Galilee from Alexander the Great to Hadrian,* 287–97) that the Galileans were loyal to Jerusalem de-spite the vicissitudes of history as an 'unwarranted assumption' (315, n.22). The most recent archaeological evidence from Sepphoris, Iotapata and Gamala gives considerable support to my view, however (Cf. 'Archaeology and the Historical Jesus,' below pp. 160 ff.). Symbolic systems have a power to generate long-lasting moods and attachments that can ignore or transcend what to outsiders appear as blatant social inequality or even repression. In this regard people are slow to accept that the meaning they have come to attach to such systems as an expression of 'the really real' is in fact groundless. Cf. C. Geertz, 'Religion as a Cultural System,' in *Anthropological Approaches to the Study of Religion*, ed. M. Banton, (ASA Monograph series 3, London, 1966) 1–46.

enemy's hand' (*Life* 348). Though the intention is to embarrass Justus about the rebelliousness of his native Tiberias in contrast to the pacifism of Sepphoris, it is even more impressive testimony to the presumed sphere of influence of the temple and the loyalty it could be expected to evoke in a Galilean setting (cf. *Life* 128).

This point also helps to clarify the intense rivalry between John of Gischala and Josephus. It is not just a matter of native Galilean resentment of an outsider from Jerusalem who claimed control over Upper Galilee as well, even though John would appear to have held some official role there, possibly in charge of an eparchy (*Life* 72 f.). One could easily be misled by Josephus' vilification of John in *JW* and thus overlook the similarity of background of the two men. John too believed in the temple and its indestructibility as the house of God (*JW* 6,99). Perhaps the failure, or more likely, the refusal of the Jerusalem delegation to install John as governor of Galilee was the reason for his joining the Zealots rather than the aristocrats when he finally went to Jerusalem.[15] It is significant that John's friendship was with the Pharisee, Simon, and not with the high priestly aristocracy, and Simon is not explicitly described as an actual member of the council, despite his influence in the city (*Life* 193; cf. 309). John's contacts were in the end not as influential as those of the Jerusalem priest, Josephus, with whose attitudes he had so much in common, since according to the admission of *Life* 43 f., John, like Josephus, had tried to restrain the enthusiasm for revolt of his fellow-townsmen at Gischala.[16]

Within the range of issues which Josephus' commission was intended to cover, the non-military aspects are the ones of greatest interest for the present discussion, since these are more likely to be typical of the general situation. While Josephus was certainly prepared to take initiatives in dealing with affairs in Galilee, he felt obliged at the outset to report by letter to the Jerusalem council asking for instructions. It comes as some surprise that one of the orders of a council, supposedly concerned with the peace of Galilee, is the destruction of Herod's palace with its animal representations that were declared to be contrary to Jewish law (*Life* 66). This order had not been prepared for in the previous narrative with the rather general advice to Josephus on his departure from Jerusalem 'to take precautions for Galilee.'[17] However we are to understand the account, the territorial

---

[15] U. Rappaport, 'John of Gischala: From Galilee to Jerusalem,' *JJS* 33 (1982) 479–90, especially 488 f., treats suggestively of John's break with the moderates in Jerusalem.

[16] U. Rappaport, 'John of Gischala in Galilee,' in *The Jerusalem Cathedra*, ed. L. Levine, vol. 3 (Jerusalem, Yad Izhak Ben-Zvi Institute, 1983) 46–57, argues this case convincingly.

[17] A. Schalit, 'Josephus und Justus. Studien zur *Vita* des Josephus,' *Klio* 26 (1933) 67–95, especially 71–77, sees Josephus' description of his dealing with Tiberias as the direct

assumptions which the narrator makes are highly significant. As the appointee of the Jerusalem council Josephus is expected to implement a religious policy of strict adherence to the laws of the Jews, even in an area where the council did not have political control, namely within the city of Tiberias which had its own βουλή and belonged to the jurisdiction of Agrippa II (*Life* 38). Accordingly, the narrator is careful to note that Josephus' meeting with the leading men of the city council took place outside the city confines. The Jerusalem council had urged him and his fellow-priests to destroy the offending palace, and 'I exhorted them (the Tiberians) to allow us to accomplish this speedily,' thereby acknowledging the city council's rights in the matter. After some deliberation, Josephus and his colleagues succeeded in having their way, only to be anticipated by Jesus, son of Sapphias, the revolutionary leader within Tiberias (*Life* 64–66). The significance of this account, then, would seem to be that the Jerusalem council assumed responsibility for the enforcement of Jewish law even beyond the territory over which it could claim political control (cf. Acts 9,2).

Another aspect of the broader picture concerns the administration of justice. The *Life* account of the arrangement in this regard seems more realistic than the idealistic version of *JW*, which represents Josephus as establishing a juridical system for Galilee, similar to that of Moses – councils of seven men in each city, with an overall council of seventy (*JW* 2,570 f.; cf. *JA* 4,213.287).[18] In *Life* 79 the arrangement is for a council of seventy to accompany Josephus on his travels to assist and approve his judgements. Thus his authority extends to civil as well as religious cases, which are to be judged by Jewish law, and while there would appear to be some effort to placate local feeling, the judicial system is represented as being in 'in accordance with our laws' (cf. *Life* 128).

---

result of Justus' attack on him, and hence apologetically motivated. *Vogel, 'Das Bilderverbot,' 72–76, sees the failure to mention this event in *BJ*, as well as the apparent inconsistency in the *Life* account between the alleged pacifism of his mission and his subsequent involvement in actions such as this destruction, as indicative of Josephus' real anti-Roman attitude, in line with other such burnings by the radicals which had taken place in Jerusalem in this period (*JW* 2,426.430 f.). Thus, according to Vogel, the justifying remark that animal representations were contrary 'to our laws' should be deemed part of the self-portrait of the *Antiquities/Life* account in which Josephus adopts a rigorist attitude towards the Pentateuchal prohibition on images.

[18] Cohen, *Josephus in Galilee,* 92, n. 26.

Galilean Religious Loyalties and Jerusalem

Up to this point the question of Jerusalem's control of Galilean affairs as this is exemplified in the appointment of Josephus has been the focus of attention. More than once it emerged that these were based on certain assumptions by the author of *Life* about religious loyalties in Galilee. It now seems appropriate to explore the document more thoroughly in order to catch further important glimpses into the assumed religious situation of first-century Galilee according to this work.

At the outset it is significant to note that we are presented with a Jewish Galilee in terms of its religious loyalties, but that is only to be expected given the perspective of the author and his apologetic intentions. Gentiles rarely intrude on the picture, and when they do, as in the case of the noblemen of Tarichaeae who had fled from the territory of the king, they are only acceptable to the people if they undergo circumcision. Unlike the case of the burning of Herod's palace which was justified on the basis of 'our laws', Josephus on this occasion, partly at least in order to impress a Roman readership, presents himself as having adopted a more liberal attitude, claiming that everyone should be free 'to worship according to his conscience' (*Life* 112 f.). Of course the acceptance of strangers was enshrined in Jewish law also, and while they and the Israelites are to live under the one law (Ex 12,49; Nm 15,16), circumcision is never explicitly mentioned, even though various other regulations are specified (Lv 16,29; 17,10; 24,16; Nm 9,14). Thus, in this instance, Josephus could scarcely be accused of violation of the ancestral laws, and indeed his regret at having to send the strangers back to the king's territory seems motivated by the sense of not having been able to observe properly the custom of hospitality to strangers (*Life* 148–54).

What is most significant about the episode is that those who demand the circumcision of the noblemen are described not as Galileans or even Tarichaeaens, but as Ἰουδαῖοι. Why then does Josephus depart from his usual designation of the Galileans in this instance? Is this his way of suggesting a particularly rigorist attitude, untypical of the population as a whole, since he can scarcely be suggesting that the Galileans or the inhabitants of Tarichaeae, or indeed he himself were not also Jews in the broad sense of adherents to the Jewish way of life.[19] One possible avenue is to

---

[19] J. Ashton, 'The Identity and Function of the Ἰουδαῖοι in the Fourth Gospel,' *NovT* 27 (1985) 40–75, especially 53–56. *Horsley, *Galilee. History, Politics, People*, surprisingly does not develop this usage in support of his overall view that Ἰουδαῖοι means Judeans as distinct from Galileans, when it might appear to support such a claim (154 and 318, n. 43). He sees the incident as an example of an Israelite (covenantal) ob-

see this episode within the larger context of Josephus' attitude to the conversion of foreigners to Judaism. While proselytes were welcomed, the evidence seems to be lacking for seeing Judaism as a missionary religion, at least in a manner similar to early Christianity.[20] The story of the full conversion of the royal house of Adiabene as a climax of *JA* (20,17–96) is particularly striking, therefore. In this episode we encounter Eleazar who is described as coming from Galilee and who had a 'reputation for being extremely strict when it came to the ancestral laws' admonishing Izates, the king of Adiabene and a Jewish sympathiser, that he should be circumcised, despite the possible political consequences of such a move (*JA* 20,43).[21] Eleazar too is called a Ἰουδαῖος, not a Γαλιλαῖος, similar to those who were insisting on the circumcision of the noblemen at Tarichaeae, but unlike the former, the latter attempted to impose circumcision forcibly. Thus in at least these two instances, Josephus would appear to be using the term in a highly specialised sense of rigorists in terms of observance of the Jewish laws. Yet he could not possibly be seen to support forcible conversion. Hence he represents himself as having dealt with the situation impeccably, if somewhat improbably, in returning the noblemen safely to their homeland where they were subsequently pardoned by Agrippa (*Life* 154).

This still does not explain why the term Ἰουδαῖος is used in this instance. *Life* does indicate that there were other pockets of rigorist attitudes, especially in Tiberias, Jesus, son of Sapphias being the outstanding example. Brandishing the Law of Moses in his hand, he accused Josephus of being about to betray his country's laws by handing over his city to the Romans (*Life* 135). As we have seen, he was responsible for having Herod's palace with the offending images demolished. While some Galileans were involved in this act, they are unrepresentative of Galileans generally as portrayed in this work, nor is Jesus typical either, even of Tiberian attitudes. It would be unwarranted, therefore, to generalise from any

---

ligation that had 'deep roots in Galilee, prior to the arrival of the Torah as the law and/or scripture of the temple state.'

[20] *S. D. Cohen, 'Crossing the Boundary and becoming a Jew,' *HTR* 82 (1989) 13–33; M. Goodman, *Mission and Conversion. Proselytizing in the Religious History of the Roman Empire* (Oxford: Clarendon, 1994).

[21] *S. Mason, 'Should Any Wish to Enquire Further (*Ant* 1,25): The Aim and Audience of Josephus' *Judean Antiquities/Life*,' in *Understanding Josephus. Seven Perspectives*, ed. S. Mason (Sheffield: Sheffield Academic Press, 1998) 64–103, especially 90–95, discusses the significance of this story as a climax to *Antiquities/Life* in presenting the ideal that God rewards those who recognise the goodness of Judaism and embrace it wholly. Goodman, *Mission and Conversion*, is more cautious in regard to proselytising attitudes in Judaism generally, and in regard to the Adiabene story notes that Eleazar did not go to the court specifically to proselytise but to pay his respects.

of these incidents to a more widely based, rigorist Torah-observance in Galilee as a whole, such as that represented in the *18 Halakhot* and associated with the Shammaites and Zealots.[22]

Our question remains therefore, as to how we are to characterise the prevalent form(s) of Judaism in Galilee on the basis of this text. In contrast to others such as John of Gischala (*Life* 74–76), and the Jerusalem delegation (*Life* 275–91, 295, 302), who are represented as riding roughshod over Jewish religious sensibilities, Josephus is at pains throughout the work to present himself as a meticulously observant Jew, sensitive to the religious feelings of the native Galileans. He does not wish them to be disturbed on the Sabbath (*Life* 159, 161), and he carefully observes the prohibition against killing or injuring a fellow-Jew (*Life* 27, 128, 171, 377). He never makes a direct claim to having been a Pharisee, but he does say that he governed his life by their rules and associated with leading Pharisees (*Life* 12, 21), foremost among whom was Simon, an old friend of John of Gischala but for whom Josephus also has admiration (*Life* 192). Cohen attributes this emphasis in both *Life* and *JA* as distinct from *JW* to the circumstances of writing of the two works in the nineties when the successors of the Pharisees were the most influential group in the Jewish religious world.[23] Yet he has to admit that there is nothing distinctly Pharisaic about Josephus' conduct even when he claims to have respect for the ancestral laws. The question remains, therefore, as to the nature of the Galileans religious affiliations, especially in view of their alleged attachment to Josephus.

One passage which could help to shed some light on our question is *Life* 187 f., which describes the composition of the Jerusalem delegation sent to

---

[22] Cf. M. Hengel, *The Zealots. Investigation into the Jewish Freedom Movement in the Period from Herod I until 70 A.D.* (Edinburgh: T. & T. Clark, 1989) 200–206. Earlier (56–59) Hengel has cautiously espoused the view that the Zealots were called Galileans on the basis that the founder of the Fourth Philosophy was called Judas the Galilean, as well as scattered references in later writers to the Galileans as a separate sect. However, the identification of the Fourth Philosophy with the Zealots has been seriously challenged in more recent scholarship, and hence the characterisation of the Galileans likewise is weakened.

[23] *Josephus in Galilee,* 144–51. However, cf. D. Schwartz, 'Josephus and Nicolaus on the Pharisees,' *JSJ* 14 (1983) 157–71, who argues that Josephus' treatment of the Pharisees in both *Life* and *JA* is more historical than that in *JW* which was written much closer to the revolt, and therefore extremely careful to avoid any suggestion of political involvement on the part of the Pharisees. In that view the references to Pharisees in *Life* and their role in the revolt may be quite factual. *For a recent thorough discussion of Josephus' Pharisaism and the role of the Pharisees in his writings cf. Z. Rodgers, *Josephus: Patriot, Priest, Politician. His Vita and Contra Apionem as a Witness to his Concerns for Jews and Judaism,* Doctoral Dissertation, Trinity College, Dublin 1997 (Forthcoming, Leiden: Brill, 2000) 81–86.

unseat Josephus, as well as the instructions which the members were given by the Jerusalem council. Two aspects of the account call for special attention, namely, the social and religious background of the delegation and the list of possible reasons for the continued loyalty of the Galileans for Josephus which they are ordered to explore.

The delegation had a balanced blend both socially and religiously. Two members are described as δημότικοι, that is, of the rank of the people, and were also Pharisees. Elsewhere Josephus tells us that the Pharisees were popular with the townspeople (δῆμοι *JA* 18,15), and this particular designation for members of the delegation causes no surprise, therefore. A third member was also a Pharisee, but of a priestly family, which in the context can only mean that he was an aristocrat in contrast to the two plebeian Pharisees. The fourth member, Simon, was from the high priests and therefore also an aristocrat. One is struck by the strong Pharisaic presence on the delegation. This is not too surprising since in the first place the initiative came from John of Gischala through his friend, the influential Pharisee, Simon son of Gamaliel, but also because the base of Josephus' support may have been in the many smaller towns of Galilee, of which there were many according to *JW* 3,43.[24] Nevertheless, it must be recognised that this colouring of the delegation's make-up suited Josephus' interest in stressing his own Pharisaic leanings in this work, already alluded to. Accordingly, in exploring Galilean religious attitudes it is better to focus our attention on the possible reasons given for Josephus' popularity in the province.[25]

Three possible reasons are listed – the fact that he was from Jerusalem, his accurate knowledge of their laws and his priestly office. Since the second of these relates to his Pharisaism, we will do well to concentrate on the other two. Cohen has stressed the fact that once it had arrived in the

---

[24] *The extent of the Pharisaic presence in Galilee is not easy to assess, given the nature of all the literary sources in which they are mentioned – gospels, Josephus and Rabbinic texts. Cf. J. Neusner, *The Rabbinic Traditions about the Pharisees before 70*, 3 vols. (Leiden: Brill, 1971); Freyne, *Galilee from Alexander the Great to Hadrian*, 309–29; R. Wild, 'The Encounter between Pharisaic and Christian Judaism: Some Early Gospel Evidence,' *NovT* 27 (1985) 105–24; A. Saldarini, *Pharisees, Scribes and Sadducees in Palestinian Society* (Edinburgh: T. & T. Clark, 1988) especially 291–96 on the Pharisees in Galilee; S. Mason, *Flavius Josephus on the Pharisees: A Compositional-Critical Study* (Leiden: Brill, 1991); Horsley, *Galilee. History, Politics, People*, 149–52; R. Deines, *Jüdische Steingefässe und pharisäische Frömmigkeit*, WUNT 52 (Tübingen: J. C. B. Mohr, 1993). Recent archaeological evidence from Sepphoris, Iotapata and Gamala suggests the presence from the early Roman period of people who had a special concern with the purity regulations; cf. above n. 14.

[25] *JW* 2,268 makes no mention of the Pharisaism of the group, but this could be explained in terms of the time of writing and his desire to dissociate them from any involvement in the revolt.

province the delegation made no effort to install John and the choice of the Galileans was between itself and Josephus. As a provincial John could not compete with those who claimed the allegiance of the country people on the basis of the fact that they had come from the capital, Jerusalem, especially when, as in the case of Josephus, the sacral character of the city could be appealed to by stressing his own priestly origins. While I agree with Cohen that the Pharisaic way of life seems to have made little inroads into Galilee in the first century CE, I would attribute the failure of the Jerusalem delegation to oust Josephus, not to its Pharisaic make-up, as he does,[26] but rather to the astuteness of the priestly aristocrat. Josephus had exploited his Jerusalem origins and his priesthood to the full in order to consolidate his political position within the province before the arrival of the delegation. John had not been able to compete with such a pedigree and the delegation arrived too late.

This conclusion corresponds to that which I arrived at in a more general way in *Galilee from Alexander the Great to Hadrian*, namely that an old and deep-seated attachment to Jerusalem and its temple, demonstrated particularly in fidelity to the pilgrimage, was capable of overcoming the social and economic tensions that existed between rural peasants from an outlying province and a ruling Jerusalem aristocracy who owned the better land and controlled the markets.[27] In a word, a shared symbolic worldview, of which the Jerusalem temple was the central focal point, compensated for the sense of alienation that was otherwise experienced by Galileans in a social world that was dominated by their religious leaders. Social scientists alert us to the fact that peasants do not form a class by themselves but are defined only in terms of the larger social world of which they are a part,[28] and in the case of the Galilean Jewish peasants that was determined by the claims and assumptions of a priestly aristocracy and the temple which they served.

---

[26] *Josephus in Galilee*, 226 f.

[27] Cf. especially 293–97. *Horsley, *Galilee. History, Politics, People,* 144–7 is dubious of the claim that Galileans took part in the pilgrimage to Jerusalem in any significant numbers. However, his own reading of the evidence is problematic in view of the fundamental claim of his study which colours all his handling of the evidence, namely that Galileans and Judeans are opposed to each other. He must, therefore, minimise the significance of the indications for Galilean-Jerusalem relations that are in the literary sources and ignore the fact that nowhere is there any suggestion of a positive hostility of Galileans to Jerusalem or its temple.

[28] Cf. in particular the various theoretical discussions on the nature of peasantry in *Peasants and Peasant Societies,* ed. T. Shanin (Penguin Modern Sociology Readings, 1971) and M. Kearney, *Reconceptualizing the Peasantry. Anthropology in Global Perspective* (London and Boulder: Westview Press, 1996).

In this paper I have focused on just one aspect of the social life of Galilee in the first century, namely, the nature of its relationship to Jerusalem, in terms both of administration and religious affiliations. In confining the discussion to Josephus' *Life* it has been possible both to describe the relationship that the narrator assumes and to test at various points the plausibility of that picture. The relationship was reciprocal, it was argued. The Jerusalem council could claim authority over Galilee, and Galileans, at least in this work, are presented as an integral part of the ἔθνος τῶν Ἰουδαίων in the land of Israel. In support of its claim the Jerusalem council could point to its privileged position as the temple city with the pivotal role of the priestly aristocracy supported by Pentateuchal law. The Galileans, for their part, remained attached to that city as the symbolic centre of their beliefs, even when such loyalty was sorely tested by an uncaring, even venal aristocracy. The fact that local 'big men' such as John of Gischala and Justus of Tiberias had to yield to the Jerusalemite, Josephus, is a clear indication of the strength of such attachment.

The relevance of this picture for a better understanding of Jesus and his movement within Second Temple Judaism should be obvious. It is best illustrated by the report of Josephus on the attitude of the Jerusalem aristocracy on the occasion of Galilean pilgrims being attacked by the Samaritans as they journeyed to Jerusalem. The rulers of the city urged the populace to desist from avenging the blood of the Galilean who had been murdered, declaring that their act would bring down the wrath of the Romans on the city. Rather, they should take pity on their country and the sanctuary, 'since all these were threatened for the object of avenging the blood of a single Galilean' (*JW* 2,237; *JA* 20,123). This sentiment of the Jerusalem aristocracy is similar to that attributed to the high priest and the Pharisees in regard to Jesus the Galilean at Jn 11,47–51. Jesus was not just another Galilean pilgrim, however, but one whose claims about God's rule and presence subverted the centrality of the holy place on which Jerusalem's authority depended. It comes as no surprise, therefore, to find that in all the accounts of the trial it is the Jerusalem aristocracy, priestly and lay, that is instrumental in having him removed, just as later they were opposed to Jesus son of Ananias, the rude peasant who uttered his woes against the people, the temple and the city (*JW* 6,300–310).

5. Herodian Economics in Galilee. Searching for a Suitable Model

One of the occupational hazards of ancient historians must surely be the temptation to draw a complete picture of whatever segment of life interests them, irrespective of the adequacy of their data for such a task. Few of us are happy to acknowledge the many gaps in our knowledge of the ancient world, no matter how sophisticated the modern retrieval systems are. This dilemma, the need to present a coherent hypothesis (often disguised as the definitive description) despite the absence of sufficient information, poses important hermeneutical questions which scholars are sometimes reluctant to address. For instance, when I reread my own previous work on Galilee I find myself repeatedly asking why precisely I had opted for a particular understanding of the data. The answer, one hopes, is because the evidence pointed in that direction, even when other possible interpretations had been considered. The question becomes more acute still on comparing one's own views with those of others writing about the same topic. Why is Martin Goodman's description of Galilee very like my own – a predominantly peasant Jewish village culture? Why is it that D. Edwards, A. Overman and J. Strange can all speak so confidently about the urbanisation of Galilee, particularly lower Galilee, with all the attendant consequences for social and religious life in the region?[1] Is this due to the bias of the sources which may be selectively chosen, or are there deeper methodological or even ideological issues at play and how might one rationally adjudicate among the competing views?

One important new tool in the repertoire of the ancient historian is the use of the social sciences, whose critical application can mean an end to what has been described as 'the intuitivist approach', with its 'hit or miss' aspect. By carefully choosing an appropriate model and applying it as rig-

---

[1] M. Goodman, *State and Society in Roman Galilee A.D. 132–212* (Totowa, NJ: Rowman and Allenheld, 1983); D. Edwards, 'First-Century Urban/Rural Relations in Lower Galilee, Exploring the Archaeological and Literary Evidence,' and A. Overman, 'Who were the first urban Christians? Urbanisation in first-century Galilee,' in *SBLASP 1988*, ed. D. Lull (Atlanta: Scholars Press, 1988) 169–82 and 160–68 respectively; J. Strange, 'Some implications of archaeology for New Testament studies,' in *What has Archaeology to do with Faith?* ed. J. H. Charlesworth (Valley Forge: Trinity Press International, 1992) 23–59.

orously as possible many mistakes can be avoided and it becomes possible to assess the validity of one's initial intuitions and to compare the results with those of others in a more critical and rational manner. In a previous essay I attempted to develop and apply a model to do with the cultural role of cities to Galilean social life basing myself primarily on the writings of Josephus.[2] Though reasonably pleased with the exercise another challenge emerged, namely, how best to integrate the findings of the rapidly growing corpus of archaeological work on the region with the literary evidence. How is one to bring spade and text together in view of the fact that the one (texts) are tellings, not showings, whereas the other (archaeological data) are showings in need of tellings which are largely dependent on those very texts? Unlike the earlier concentration on isolated sites or on particular types of buildings such as synagogues, the more recent archaeological work is informed by insights from landscape, ethno- and socio- archaeology, as findings at individual sites are being integrated with the results of regional and inter-regional surveys. In these developing branches of the new archaeology, there is considerable input from the social sciences also, as researchers attempt to develop adequate models for understanding and interpreting the data so painstakingly acquired.[3]

Models will not of course obviate the need for ongoing critical assessment of one's procedures, nor will they fill in the gaps in our information where these exist. There is the initial task of choosing a model appropriate for the task to which one wishes to put it. Even then models can never encapsulate the whole of life in all its complexity, but rather select and highlight certain key aspects, which after careful reflection, are deemed to be crucial in understanding the whole. Inevitably, therefore, there is an element of personal judgement involved as one attempts to match the model based on typical features with the particular aspects of a given society. Despite this subjective dimension, the value of model building is that it assists in making one's presuppositions explicit. There will be less likelihood that essential aspects will be overlooked and such abstract notions as power, elites etc. can be dissected analytically by asking more detailed questions like: to whom? For what purpose? In whose interest? Who de-

---

[2] 'Urban-Rural Relations in First-Century Galilee: Some Suggestions from the Literary Sources,' above pp. 45 ff.

[3] E. Meyers, J. Strange, D. Groh, 'The Meiron Excavation Project: Archaeological Survey in Galilee and Golan, 1976,' *BASOR* 230 (1978) 1–24; D. Urman, *The Golan. A Profile of a Region during the Roman and Byzantine Periods* (Oxford: BAR International Series 269, 1985); G. Barker and J. Lloyd, eds., *Roman Landscapes. Archaeological Surveys in the Mediterranean Region* Archaeological Monographs of the British School at Rome 2 (London: British School at Rome, 1991); J. Rich and A. Wallace-Hadrill, eds., *City and Country in the Ancient World* (London: Routledge, 1991).

cides what the problems are?[4] Finally, the application of a model helps in assembling and organising the scattered pieces of data at our disposal and in uncovering the missing links. Thus within the overall frame of reference which the model represents it is possible to predict the direction which changes are likely to take by having a clearer perception of the role which individual items play within the whole system

Modelling an Economic System

There are few serious analytical studies of ancient economies by biblical scholars. In this respect the discipline contrasts unfavourably with that of ancient history where much more attention has been given to the question by historians of Greece and Rome. The omission is all the more surprising in view of the fact that economic issues figure so prominently in the recorded sayings of Jesus. There have been various attempts to describe the economic realities of first-century Palestine and the gospels,[5] but with rare exceptions the question of how deeply economic issues were at the heart of Jesus' own experience and ministry, as well as that of the early Christians, has not been adequately addressed.[6] There are undoubtedly many reasons for such an oversight. The fact that economic issues in antiquity are seen as embedded in, and therefore inseparable from political ones is certainly a factor. However, this should not be overstated. While it is true that abstract thinking on economics as we know it today is a product of the industrial revolution, this does not mean that 'rational' economic thinking never occurred in pre-industrial societies. There is enough evidence ranging from fifth-century BCE Athens to fourth-century CE Egypt to indicate that there was a general awareness of issues such as the maximising of resources, the need to keep production costs low and the possibility of manipulating market demand in order to achieve higher prices.[7]

---

[4] T. F. Carney, *The Shape of the Past. Models and Antiquity* (Lawrence, KS: Coronado Press, 1975); J. Elliott, 'Social-Scientific Criticism of the New Testament: More on Models and Methods,' *Semeia* 32 (1986) 1–33; *What is Social-Scientific Criticism?* (Minneapolis: Fortress Press, 1993).

[5] F. C. Grant, *The Economic Background of the Gospels* (Oxford: Clarendon Press, 1926).

[6] D. Oakman, *Jesus and the Economic Question of his Day* (Lewiston, NY: The Edwin Mellen Press, 1986); H. Moxnes, *The Economy of the Kingdom. Social Conflict and Economic Relations in Luke's Gospel* (Philadelphia: Fortress Press, 1988); G. Hamel, *Poverty and Charity in Roman Palestine, First Three Centuries C.E.* (Berkeley: University of California Press, 1990).

[7] D. Rathbone, *Economic Rationalism and Rural Society in Third-Century A.D. Egypt. The Heroninos Archive and the Appianus Estate* (Cambridge: Cambridge Univer-

Among ancient historians the work of Moses Finley has dominated much of the recent discussion. His theory of the ancient city being parasitic on the countryside in a highly exploitative way set a very definite landmark that is only gradually being modified, but which is never likely to be entirely abandoned.[8] Finley's model, like that of Weber on which it was based, sharply contrasted the ancient 'consumer' city with its medieval 'producer' counterpart. It stressed the inequality of the relationship between town and country by maintaining that control of the land, the most important ancient resource, was essentially in the hands of a wealthy elite, who for political reasons dwelt in cities and had little interest in reinvesting into the economy of the countryside, provided their own relatively luxurious life-style was maintained. The resulting stagnation meant the increased impoverishment of and pressure on the remaining small landowners, as well as precluding the emergence of an urban merchant or entrepreneurial class. In this view of the city as the village 'writ large' in terms of economic realities, relating to its hinterland in the way that a village relates to its fields, the wealthy landowner shares the peasant's passion for self-sufficiency, without any qualitatively different view of the possibilities of greater production.[9] Little account is taken of the manufacturing and commercial potential of ancient cities in terms of the production of goods such as household wares which are not directly related to agriculture. On this understanding, therefore, ancient cities are primarily administrative centres where the wealthy landowners reside and play a full part in the civic and political life of the *polis*. It is the honour and prestige attached to such activities rather than the maximising of resources in commercial enterprises that determine their conduct of affairs.

Several modifications of these ideas have been suggested, particularly in view of the fact that in the wake of Alexander's conquests, the city itself as institution had been transformed from the freestanding entity of the classical period, the main focus of Finley's typology. It was now put to the service of the commercial, cultural and administrative policies of the Hellenistic monarchies and later the Roman Empire. In particular, the opening up of new and lucrative trade routes changed the whole commercial balance of the middle eastern world, several of which touched directly on Galilee. Both local and international trade developed in a manner and scale never before experienced as the demands for goods and services increased among the wealthy elites of the west. In this changed climate it has been

---

sity Press, 1991); R. Osborne, 'Pride and Prejudice, Sense and Subsistence: Exchange and Society in the Greek City,' in Rich and Wallace-Hadrill, *City and Country,* 119–46.

[8] M. Finley, *The Ancient Economy,* 2nd ed. (London: Chatto and Windus, 1977); id., 'The Ancient City from Fustel de Coulanges to Max Weber,' *CSSH* 19 (1977) 305–27.

[9] Osborne, 'Pride and Prejudice,' 120.

suggested that cities and towns were 'organisers' of the countryside in that they paid for their consumption needs through profits from the increased trade that they were engaged in. Thus, it is claimed, cities should be seen as production centres, giving rise to a commercial class who were able to pay the rural population for their produce, thereby enabling the peasants to pay their taxes in money rather than in kind.[10] Archaeological evidence is seen as crucial in establishing this changed picture. On the one hand it is argued that the evidence from Pompeii and even Rome itself suggests a much greater diversity of commercial activity, even in the elite residential areas, than might have been expected.[11] In support of Finley, however, it has been claimed that coinage is relatively scarce in the countryside until the third century CE and the evidence on the ground from Roman Britain and elsewhere in the western provinces does not support the notion of cities as manufacturing centres.[12] Of course this debate is by no means settled and there is every reason to suppose that local circumstances may have prevailed in different contexts. A lot seems to hinge on what size town is being discussed, whether upwardly towards the πόλις / *civitas* end of the spectrum or downwardly towards the κώμη / *vicus* end. This is a large topic which cannot be dealt with adequately here. What the debate highlights, however, is the need for a model that will encompass economic issues dealing with manufacture, exploitation, and redistribution of wealth. We must not reduce the undoubted urban/rural differences as these were perceived in antiquity to a meaningless tautology, yet we must equally avoid setting up rigid oppositions that fail to capture, however imperfectly, the many-faceted dimensions of that relationship.

This leads us back to Galilee, and more specifically to the Galilee of Antipas. I am particularly interested in the impact of all these changes on life in that whole northern region of Palestine at that particular period. For it is possible to detect a pattern of change in terms of the development of urban settlements, not only in Galilee but also in Perea as well as in the territory of Antipas' brother, Herod Philip (*JA* 18,26–28). These developments were not merely concerned with the honouring of their Roman patrons in terms of the names given to the new foundations and the fact that Josephus mentions them in the context of the new arrangements taking place in Judea on the deposition of Archelaus in 6 CE. The proposal of this

[10] K. Hopkins, 'Taxes and Trade in the Roman Empire. (200BC–400AD),' *JRS* 70 (1980) 101–25; id., 'Economic Growth and Towns in Classical Antiquity,' in *Towns in Societies: Essays in Economic History and Historical Sociology*, ed. P. Abrams and E. Wrigley (Cambridge: Cambridge University Press, 1980) 35–77.

[11] A. Wallace-Hadrill, 'Elites and Trade in the Roman Town,' in Rich and Wallace-Hadrill, *City and Country in the Ancient World*, 241–72.

[12] C. R. Whittaker, 'The Consumer City Revisited: the *Vicus* and the City,' *JRA* 3 (1990) 110–18.

paper is that some further far-reaching and rapid forms of change were occurring that had a strong economic component built into them. This would provide the immediate context in which to understand the ministry of Jesus also, with its emphasis on wealth and poverty, money lending, wages, debts etc. and the value system related to such matters. Of course these realities were not new on the Palestinian landscape, but the conjunction of the proposed developments for Galilee in the reign of Antipas and the concern of the Jesus movement with such issues just at that time points to a growing preoccupation that would explain many features of the gospel narratives, not least the total silence with regard to Sepphoris and Tiberias among the places in which Jesus conducted his ministry.

To verify (or falsify) such a suggestion an appropriate model is required, one that could register and highlight rapid economic change, for this is the claim that needs to be tested. T. F. Carney's study, *The Shape of the Past. Models in Antiquity* (1975), has proved to be a helpful resource for others engaged in this task of model-building to study various aspects of the ancient world, since it displays an unusual historical sense of both the ancient world and social scientific theory. Carney contrasts the different procedures involved in profiling a stable economy on the one hand, and, on the other, plotting change within a situation of rapid development. In the former instance it is simply a matter of capturing a 'still life' view of the various component parts of the total system and presenting them in a manner which portrays their interrelationships (Figure 1). Profiling change is a more complex task, however. Here according to Carney, the challenge is one of selecting and highlighting key elements or 'probe zones', as he terms them, which are essential for rapid change to occur. These elements affect 1) the relations between production and distribution (i.e., the market itself); 2) the social structures and institutions controlling the market, and 3) the values and decision-making processes which determine what the dominant priorities are. In each of these crucial areas it is necessary to concentrate on certain aspects which act as spurs for change within the total system. These are attitudinal changes with regard to production and consumption, leading to increased specialisation within the productive sector. This in turn calls for a more sophisticated exchange mechanism associated with the more widespread use of money. When there are clear signs of all three elements – attitudinal changes, specialisation and monetisation – occurring simultaneously, then, according to the model's underlying assumptions, rapid changes are taking place throughout the whole system. These call for the steering political control group to handle carefully the adaptation of the institutions to meet the new situation, maintenance of the stability of the social order through the military, law-courts, policing etc. It includes the integration of the new insights in

THE MARKET

Resources	*Natural*	*Human*
	Land, water, minerals	Skilled and unskilled labor
Supply – Production		
	Agricultural produce: grain, olives, vines	Manufacturing: pottery, oil and wine, fish products
Distribution	*Roads*	*Ports*
	Beasts of burden	Shipping
Needs and Demands	*Subsistence*	*Elite*
	Food, clothing, shelter	Luxury items: glass ware; ornaments; spices

MODES OF EXCHANGE

Types	*Barter*	*Redistribution*	*Markets*	*Mobilization*
	Non-organised	Centralised	Free Trading	State controlled
Personnel	Peasants; day labourers	Estate managers	*Negotiatores; navicularii*	*Agoranomoi*; tax collectors
Modes of Exchange	In kind	Corvee: share cropping	Money (accounting / banking)	Tribute in kind and in cash
Social Types	Village and clan leaders; elders, householders	Military personnel and religious hierarchy	Entrepreneurs, money lenders and bankers	Herodian client kings and their retainers

VALUES AND ATTITUDES

Dominant Systems	*Internal*	*External*
	Jerusalem Religious System	Roman Imperial Ideology
Key Values	Kinship; Sharing limited goods	Political control of production and supply; Appeal to patrimonial values for support
Institutions	Household, clan, village; Temple and pilgrimage	The polis institutions; patron-client relations; gymnasia
Behavioural Patterns	Petty feuds; violence; Social discrimination on purity grounds	Ostentatious life-style and lack of concern for lower strata

Figure One: A Cross-Sectional Model of Socio-Economic Factors in Roman Galilee (following T. F. Carney) technology, values etc. through education and other means of dissemination of ideas. Thus, the changes need to be politically inspired, controlled and channelled if the body politic is to survive and social chaos avoided.

The stimuli for change are both external and internal, but since no political system exists in isolation, the external factors are inevitably seen to be the more important, especially in dealing with a merely regional situation such as Galilee. The external factors that Carney lists can certainly be shown to have been operative throughout the whole Mediterranean world, and not least in Palestine, in view of Herod the Great's active propagation of the values of 'the new age' of peace.[13] The temple of Roma and Augustus, set on a high podium overlooking his harbour, Caesarea Maritima (*JA* 15,339), was a symbol of Herod's intentions as King of the Jews to introduce a new climate of thought, new international alliances of power and new technology into his kingdom. Inevitably these factors were to percolate downwards to the whole of Palestinian society as the building programme developed, calling for specialisation of labour, a more widespread use of money and changes in attitudes with regard to traditional values, despite his best attempts to placate Jewish religious opinion. Thus, in applying the model to Galilee, the main focus of attention will be on the internal changes there, always keeping in mind the backdrop of the wider, international changes of which these were a symptom (Figure 2).

Applying the Model to Galilee

Antipas inherited a territory which had been grossly over-taxed in order to support the many projects of his father, Herod the Great, both at home and abroad. This situation emerges clearly from the delegation sent to Rome to complain to Augustus on Herod's death, as well as by Archelaus' withdrawal of some of the taxes (*JA* 17,204–5.304–8). Sober evaluation of Herod's reign has, however, come to acknowledge the good aspects of his domestic policies as far as stimulating the economy, particularly his many building projects. He could also show himself to be a benign dictator, imitating his Roman masters in providing for a supply of corn from Egypt on the occasion of a famine.[14] The development of the port of Caesarea as a rival to the more northerly Phoenician cities of Tyre and Sidon shows his

---

[13] P. Zanker, *The Power of Images in the Age of Augustus* (Ann Arbor: University of Michigan Press, 1988).

[14] A. Schalit, *König Herodes. Der Mann und sein Werk* (Berlin: de Gruyter, 1969) 259–97; M. Stern, 'The Reign of Herod and the Herodian Dynasty,' in *The Jewish People in the First Century*, ed. S. Safrai and M. Stern, CRINT I (Assen: van Gorcum, 1974) 216–307, especially 270–77.

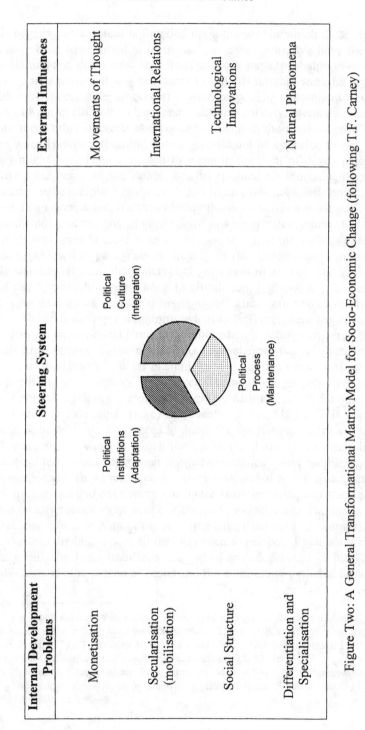

Figure Two: A General Transformational Matrix Model for Socio-Economic Change (following T.F. Carney)

grasp of the value of having direct access to a larger foreign market as well as to the income derived from tariffs and similar charges. This achievement in forward economic planning can be contrasted with the reluctance of both Augustus and Tiberius to build a proper port at Ostia for the grain imports to Rome, a task only completed at enormous expense by the emperor Claudius.[15] Roads were developed and hitherto underoccupied agricultural lands were planted with veterans from his own army (Gaba in the Great Plain) or with Babylonian and Idumean settlers (Batanea and Trachonitis). It is against this background – easily documented from both literary and archaeological evidence – of a rapidly developing economy already under Herod the Great that we should evaluate the performance of Antipas in this regard, especially in view of the fact that Herod seems to have concentrated most of his energies in the south and in the territories of the pagan cities. In a real sense it was only with Antipas that the full effects of the Romanisation of the Augustan age were felt directly in Galilee.

1. The Market

Carney describes the market as an exchange arena wherein goods and services are bartered in order to maximise the returns to buyers and sellers alike. This description calls to mind the agora or market place which was so central in the layout of Roman towns. This public space was, however, only a sign of the larger and more complex arena where supply and demand meet to the mutual benefit of buyers and sellers. Using the aid of the model, the question is whether the reign of Antipas represented a particularly significant moment for Galilee in the development of this demand/supply network which had received a major boost with the emergence of the Principate after the civil wars of the previous half-century.

What had Galilee to offer? In the sixth century BCE the prophet Ezekiel was aware of its role as supplier of agricultural produce to Tyre.[16] The plain of Gennesareth was extolled by Josephus for its rich and varied fertility (*JW* 3,35–38), and both Strabo and Pliny describe the natural resources of the Lake. Galilee was relatively better endowed than other regions in terms of soil and moisture, thus ensuring good annual yields – wheat in the rich alluvial valleys running in an east/west direction in lower Galilee and olives and vines in upper Galilee and in the Carmel region.[17] In terms of the model, it was well positioned, therefore, to be developed, when demand for basic products called for greater exploitation of resources. Nor did it lack the human resources in terms of population, even

---

[15] Carney, *The Shape of the Past*, 285–306 on Claudius and the grain trade.

[16] I. M. Diakonoff, 'The Naval Power and Trade of Tyre,' *IEJ* 42 (1992) 168–93.

[17] M. Avi-Yonah, *The Holy Land from the Persian to the Arab Conquest* (Grand Rapids: Baker Books, 1966) 201–6; Goodman, *State and Society*, 16–24.

though the figures of Josephus are generally accepted to have been exaggerated.[18] His mention of 204 settlements in his own day (*Life* 235) can be corroborated to some extent from the findings of recent regional surveys, which suggest an increase in the number of settlements from the Hellenistic to the Roman periods.[19]

Peter Garnsey has documented the repeated food crises which were endemic to Roman society throughout the Republican period. The causes were complex, but essentially stemmed from the fact that the Italian peninsula was not able to produce sufficient grain to meet the needs of a rapidly expanding city population, largely dependent on wheat for its staple diet.[20] Piracy at sea, fluctuations in terms of yields from one year to another due to human inefficiency and natural causes, all contributed to the unstable situation, not to mention the increased demands to supply the various armies that had to be maintained. Pompey had succeeded in stabilising the situation, especially with his victory over the sea pirates, but it was only during the reign of Augustus when Egypt emerged as a major supply centre that the situation was finally regulated with the *lex Iulia de annona*. This measure whereby the state guaranteed an annual corn dole to the citizens of Rome itself, effectively meant a state mobilisation of the exchange in terms of the model in figure one, since 'the grain that found its way to Rome was, in the first place, state grain, coming in the form of taxes in kind from tribute-paying provinces, or of rents in kind from tenants of the *ager publicus* or of imperial estates.'[21] It is not absolutely clear to what extent this provision and the arrangements that had to be put in place to support it allowed for the free market of grain to continue. In all probability it was greatly restricted. The absence of a state fleet meant however that private ship-owners were encouraged to ply the routes between Alexandria and Puteoli and on to Ostia. The presumption must be that these *navicularii* were also *negotiatores*, or middlemen merchants, who could make a handsome profit from the grain trade with prices guaranteed by the state and with protection against shipwreck and other hazards of transport.

While Galilee could certainly not compete in terms of grain production with Egypt or Syria as a major supplier for Rome and Italy, the fact that these latter sources were likely to have been fully stretched to meet impe-

---

[18] H. Hoehner, *Herod Antipas*, SNTSMS 17 (Cambridge: Cambridge University Press, 1973) 291–97; A. Byatt, 'Josephus and Population Numbers in First-Century Palestine,' *PEQ* 105 (1973) 51–60

[19] M. Aviam, 'Galilee: the Hellenistic to Byzantine Periods,' in *NEAEHL* 2, 452–58.

[20] P. Garnsey, *Famine and Food Supply in the Greco-Roman World* (Cambridge: Cambridge University Press, 1988).

[21] P. Garnsey, 'Grain for Rome,' in P. Garnsey, K. Hopkins, C. R. Whittaker, *Trade in the Ancient Economy* (Cambridge: Cambridge University Press, 1983) 118–30, especially 120.

rial demands only meant that lesser suppliers had the opportunity to meet more local needs. The exact amount of tribute in land and poll tax that Antipas had to pay to Rome is not known, even though Josephus does inform us that he was allowed 200 talents in personal income from his combined territories. The wording of Caesar's decree would seem to suggest that a payment in kind had been stipulated: ' . . . and that in the second year they shall pay the tribute at Sidon, consisting of one fourth of the produce sown, and in addition they shall pay tithes to Hyrcanus and his sons, just as they paid to their forefathers' (*JA* 14,203). Despite the well-known problem of how the reference to the second year is to be understood, the general tenor of this decree assumes a payment in kind, similar to the Jewish religious system. There is no evidence that this was changed subsequently under the Principate and in this instance the argument from silence would seem to support the view that it was not.

This would merely bring the situation in Galilee into line with that which obtained elsewhere as cited above from Garnsey, namely, that in order to meet the needs of the *annona* in Rome the imperial administrators were happy to receive payment in kind in terms of the grain produce of the various provinces. This would also explain the term τὸν Καίσαρος σῖτον, the imperial corn, used by Josephus for the corn stored in the villages of upper Galilee, which John of Gischala had hoped to confiscate (*Life* 71). On the other hand Josephus also mentions explicitly corn stored at Besara (in lower Galilee) collected from the neighbouring villages which belonged to Queen Berenice, the wife of Agrippa II. Since this area of lower Galilee was not in the king's territory at that time it must mean that the Herodian house retained private estates in this region, close to Gaba where Herod the Great had settled some veterans, as previously mentioned (*Life* 118–19). Admittedly, this evidence comes from some thirty years after Antipas' reign, but it does give us some insights into the situation with regard to wheat production in Herodian Galilee. The surplus corn would have been used both to pay the tribute to Rome in accordance with the decrees of Caesar, which were still operative, and presumably also to supply market needs for the personal income of the Herodian family. Their agents would have functioned as estate managers and *negotiatores*, ensuring that whatever surplus could be obtained would reach the most lucrative markets either in Rome itself or nearer still in the Phoenician cities. The fact that seafaring operated close to the coast (an example is Paul's journey to Rome in Acts 27,1–3) meant that a considerable amount of trading was done at intermediate rather than long-distance range.[22] As we shall see,

---

[22] R. Duncan-Jones, *Structure and Scale in the Roman Economy* (Cambridge: Cambridge University Press, 1990) 48–58.

there are very good reasons for thinking that the pattern of trading with Tyre suggested by Ezekiel was maintained into the Roman period.

According to the proposed model increased international pressure inevitably leads to internal changes as well. In an agrarian economy specialisation would mean a shift in landowning patterns from small, family run farms to larger estates in which the tenants work the estate, often for an absentee landowner under a manager,' receiving a subsistence living in return for their labour. In a developing economy where surplus production is necessary in order to maximise profits, such estates make it possible to have increased production and specialisation in various crops and to develop a rational and monetised economy.[23] It is difficult to be definitive on landowning patterns on the basis of the evidence available. The Jewish ideal of private ownership in small holdings as expressed in such texts from the Persian and Hellenistic periods as Neh 5,1–11 and 1 Macc 14,10 seems to have persisted into the Roman period despite pressures to the contrary, which can be documented for Galilee as early as the third century BCE from the Zenon papyri.[24] The problem is that there is no way of distinguishing between private and lease holdings even when settlement patterns from archaeological surveys suggests nucleated villages rather than the centralised villa-style settlements, some of which have been identified in Samaria.[25] A recently excavated site near Caesarea Maritima (Byzantine over Roman period) would appear to be typical of the kind of settlement which the Mishnah describes as an *'ir* (*m. B. Bat.* 4,7). Here the remains of water cisterns, wine and olive presses, a threshing floor and residential quarters for as many as 100 people suggest a more intense form of production than that of the family-run farm of 6–9 acres which has been estimated as the average size.[26]

On the basis of the evidence from Egypt and elsewhere it is reasonable to find the two types of ownership and the two modes of production side by side in Galilee as well. The better land would belong to the wealthy elite, either through forcible expropriation or default in payments of taxes by small holders, and in some cases also through bequests of larger tracts of land by the central administration. Such a picture would fit in well with Herodian landowning patterns already alluded to: the settlement of veter-

---

[23] Rathbone, *Economic Rationalism and Rural Society,* 116–49 and 318–30.

[24] S. Freyne, *Galilee from Alexander the Great to Hadrian. A Study of Second Temple Judaism* (reprint, Edinburgh: T. & T. Clark, 1998) 156–59.

[25] S. Dar, *Landscape and Pattern. An Archaeological Survey of Samaria 800 B.C.E.- 636 C.E.* (Oxford: BAR International Series 308 i, 1986), with historical commentary by S. Applebaum, 257–69.

[26] D. Fiensy, *The Social History of Palestine in the Herodian Period* (Lewiston, NY: The Edwin Mellen Press, 1991) 92–95; Y. Hirschfeld and R. Birger-Calderon, 'Early Roman and Byzantine Estates near Caesarea,' *IEJ* 41 (1991) 81–111.

ans in Gaba and Babylonian Jews in Batanea, Trachonitis and Auranitis by
Herod the Great, as well as the ownership of private estates in the great
plain and presumably also in the better lands of lower and upper Galilee.

We must await detailed publication of survey findings before the archaeological evidence can be adduced as confirmation of the landowning
patterns and the consequent styles of agricultural production. Nevertheless, the refurbishment of Sepphoris and the founding of Tiberias in a short
space of time by Antipas surely point in this direction. In the case of Tiberias allotments of land were granted in return for residence in the new city
(*JA* 18,36–38). Later in the first century when Josephus is describing the
social classes in the city, he mentions a certain Crispus among several of
the leading class having the *praenomen* Herod. He happened to be absent
on his estates across the Jordan when the city revolted against Josephus,
thus pointing to the pattern of residence in the city while owning property
in the country, typical of urban elites everywhere in antiquity (*Life* 33). In
the case of Sepphoris, Josephus can chide it for its pro-Roman stance at
the outbreak of the revolt, alleging that had it so wished, it could have
made a brave stand against the Romans, 'surrounded as it was by many
villages' (*Life* 346). The reliance of the people of Sepphoris on these outlying villages for provisions presumably indicates a similar ownership pattern to that of Tiberias for the fertile land of the Netofa valley, since elsewhere we hear of the Galileans (i.e. the independent landowning class)
showing hostility to the inhabitants of Sepphoris, storming the city and
forcing the leading citizens to flee to the acropolis (*Life* 372–78). Nothing
that archaeology has so far uncovered at either site goes against the suggestion that these foundations of Antipas fit into a pattern of Herodian
landownership which was concerned with maximising production, and
some of the finds point positively in that direction. Apart from the many
underground storage silos at Sepphoris, an inscribed lead weight found
there mentions two named ἀγορανομοί or market inspectors, and another
ostracon has the Hebrew letters '*pmlsls* which has been interpreted as a
transliteration of the Greek word ἐπιμελητής or manager inscribed on it.[27]
Equally, two lead weights from Tiberias have been published with the
names of ἀγορανομοί and the rulers, Antipas and Agrippa II, the one dating from 29/30 CE and the other from 61/62 CE. According to the editor it
is quite unusual to have the names of both rulers and managers on these
weights, possibly linking the Herodian rulers with the market in a special
way, or at least suggesting their tight control of the institution.[28]

---

[27] R. Martin Nagy et al., eds., *Sepphoris in Galilee. Crosscurrents of Culture* (Raleigh: North Carolina Museum of Art, 1996) 170 and 201.

[28] S. Qedar, 'Two Lead Weights of Herod Antipas and Herod Agrippa I and the History of Tiberias,' *INJ* 9 (1986/87) 29–35.

Thus far we have concentrated on changing landownership patterns associated with Antipas' two foundations as symptomatic of economic changes in Galilee. There are also other significant indicators which can be positively evaluated in the light of the model. In particular Galilee is famed in the rabbinic sources for its olives.[29] Climatic and soil conditions in upper Galilee seem to have been particularly suited for their cultivation, though they were cultivated in lower Galilee also. While the notorious incident of John of Gischala availing of the higher prices for oil among the Jewish community in Caesarea is used by Josephus to vilify his opponent (*Life* 74–76), it does in fact indicate a ready market among the observant Jews in Syria and beyond for this product, so essential for cooking in the Mediterranean culture generally and therefore so integral to Roman trading patterns.[30] Thus the association of the olive oil industry with Galilee can already be dated to the first century. The many discoveries of olive presses at various sites is ample archaeological testimony to corroborate the literary evidence. What is most significant for our present purpose, however, is the concentration of various types of olive presses with various subregions of Galilee.[31] In particular the fact that in western lower Galilee a type characteristic of the Phoenician littoral is consistently found, while in eastern Galilee and the Golan typological affinities with Judea can be demonstrated, is a significant indicator of trading links also. The Phoenician cities must have provided the natural market for much of the oil produced in its immediate hinterland, irrespective of cultural or religious diversity that may have existed between town and rural hinterland.

Land was not the only natural endowment of Galilee. The pagan writers and Josephus are all conscious of the lake and the fertility of its environs, features that are at least implied in the gospels. In describing the lake Josephus mentions a special type of fish, the *coracin*, that otherwise was only found in the Nile (*JW* 3,506–8.520). This may well point to the development of the fish industry as early as the Ptolemaic period. Both Bethsaida and Migdal Nun (Magdala) have been associated with fishing on the basis of their names. The latter has been identified with Tarichaeae of the Hellenistic period, a name which is believed to be associated with the salting of fish. This technique was itself symptomatic of the market economy, allowing for export of Galilean produce to centres as far away as Rome. Closely associated with this industry was the production of various fish sauces, especially one called *garum*, which was very popular in Rome and which would have required jars or amphorae if in fact it was produced at the fish-

---

[29] Avi-Yonah, *The Holy Land,* 202f.

[30] D. Mattingly, 'Oil for Export? A Comparison of Libyan, Spanish and Tunisian Olive Oil Production in the Roman Empire,' *JRA* 1 (1988) 33–56.

[31] R. Frankel, 'Some Oil Presses from Western Galilee,' *BASOR* 286 (1992) 39–71.

ing centres of Galilee also.[32] Archaeological surveys around the lake have uncovered the remains of many breakwaters, anchorages, harbours, storage pools and the like from the Roman period, not to mention the famous 'Galilean boat', all confirming the high level of commercial activity that went on.[33] The fact that Jesus recruited his first followers from those who were engaged in such an enterprise shows that his message was not addressed solely to the peasant farmers in the villages, something that needs to be borne in mind in evaluating its alternative value system, as we shall see. It is surely significant that in leaving their nets, families and hired servants, the first followers of Jesus were actually rejecting the values of the market economy as these operated in Galilee then and that they were highly commended for so doing.

Discussion of oil and fish products inevitably turns attention to the pottery industry which of late has been receiving special consideration due to the scientific analysis of David Adan-Bayewitz in particular. Guided by the literary evidence he has sought to identify the sources of supply and the range of distribution of the common household wares found at various northern sites from the Hellenistic to the Byzantine period, using modern techniques of chemical analysis of sherds recovered from various sites. Six types of standard wares (with a number of sub-types) have been identified and tentatively dated to different periods. What is most significant for our purposes is that two important production centres in Galilee, Kefar Hanania on the borders between upper and lower Galilee and Shikhin near Sepphoris, have been identified, each with their own specialisation, the former in household wares and the latter in storage jars and different household wares. The extent of the distribution of the Kefar Hanania pottery is significant as well. This centre provided all the household wares in use at important sites in the Galilee, especially Sepphoris, and a considerable percentage of that in use in a number of Golan sites sampled, as well as being represented in the wares of Akko/Ptolemais on the coast and Susita/Hippos in the Dekapolis.[34]

This pattern of considerable specialisation at various centres based on the locally available raw material (black clay mentioned in the rabbinic

---

[32] D. P. S. Peacock and D. F. Williams, *Amphorae and the Roman Economy* (London and New York: Longman, 1986) 35–37.

[33] M. Nun, *Ancient Anchorages and Harbours around the Sea of Galilee* (Kibbutz Ein Gev: Kinnereth Sailing, 1988); S. Wachsmann, *The Excavation of an Ancient Boat in the Sea of Galilee, Atiqot* 19 (Jerusalem: The Israel Antiquities Authority, 1990). *K. C. Hanson, 'The Galilean Fishing Economy and the Jesus Tradition,' *Biblical Theology Bulletin* 27 (1997) 99–111.

[34] D. Adan-Bayewitz, *Common Pottery in Roman Galilee. A Study of Local Trade* (Ramat-Gan: Bar-Ilan University Press, 1993); D. Adan-Bayewitz and I. Perlman, 'The Local Trade of Sepphoris in the Roman Period,' *IEJ* 40 (1990) 153–72.

sources) or produce (as in the case of the fish industry) confirms the impression that larger market conditions rather than purely local needs were operative in Galilee, and that many Galileans, not just the inhabitants of the two main Herodian centres, had adapted to the changes. It is important not to exaggerate the extent of the pottery industry which was on the whole confined and could not be compared with the African Red Slip ware e.g., which was widely distributed. Apart from the two sites mentioned whose wares have been studied in detail there is archaeological evidence for other pottery manufacturing centres in Galilee.[35] In particular the oil trade and the fish industry would have required the manufacture of amphorae in order to realise their potential for export. Thus the pottery industry has been described as parasitic and dependent on routes established for other purposes. This makes Adan-Bayewitz' findings all the more significant in terms of our model, since it suggests trading was being conducted within a limited wider region than political Galilee, while at the same time corresponding to the general pattern in the ancient world, namely, that with a few notable exceptions, long distance trade was not highly significant factor in the economy.[36]

In applying the first element in our model to Herodian Galilee the focus of attention has been on specialisation in production as an indicator of increased market awareness. Inevitably the discussion has touched on other aspects of the model also, particularly the modes of exchange and the emergence of personnel, exchange centres etc. that would have been necessary to implement such a development. In using the archaeological evidence it is difficult to be precise to the point of being able to date developments to the reign of Antipas, even when dealing with sites such as Sepphoris. Nevertheless, the changes to the economic conditions involved in the building of two new centres such as Sepphoris and Tiberias should not be underestimated, since these projects involved demand for labour, materials, development of roads, water systems and the introduction of some skilled craftsmen into the region. These in turn must have acted as further spurs for attitudinal changes. The new settlements increased the demands for basic food supplies for their inhabitants, thereby stimulating the rural economy also. It remains to be seen how all these changes affected different strata of the population and who stood to benefit from the changes. In terms of the earlier discussion of the consumer/producer city debate there is nothing in the evidence from Galilee so far examined to challenge the basic assumption of Finley's model, however. The increased activity among the village culture both in production and manufacture

---

[35] F. Vitto, 'A Look into the Workshop of a late Roman Galilean Potter,' *Bulletin of the Anglo-Israel Archaeological Society* 3 (1983/84) 19–22.

[36] Duncan-Jones, *Structure and Scale in the Roman Economy*, 48–58.

does not of itself imply escaping the net of patronage, control of resources and channelling of profits. Perhaps the exploration of other probe zones from Carney's model may help in deciding how far those changes which we have been able to document were for the benefit of the few or the many in Galilee.

2. Monetisation

Various types of exchange, ranging from reciprocal (i.e. barter) to redistribution (state controlled) were operative in antiquity, often side by side within the same region. This has given rise to the question of how far it is proper to speak of a free market, especially under the Principate. Certainly the *annona* was an outstanding example of state intervention, but it should be recalled that this operated only in regard to corn and only for the city of Rome. The absence of a state fleet meant that there was a reliance on *navicularii* and *negotiatores*, as we have seen, so that it is a moot point as to whether these are to be regarded as private traders or agents of the state. It is scarcely adequate therefore, to consider, as some have done, that free market exchange was confined to very local trading, irrespective of the amount of political control that operated in all ancient economies.[37] Admittedly, in the case of long-distance trading there are problems in distinguishing between what is free and what is state controlled, since both will follow the same distribution patterns. On the basis of all the available evidence, however, it does seem more probable that some free trading did occur, at least on an inter-regional basis, and that the emergence of the Principate was a considerable stimulus to more long-distance trading also.

This suggestion raises the issue of the diffusion of money throughout the empire. The proposal has been made that increased long-term trade meant a much greater diffusion of coins by the central imperial administration, giving rise to 'a single monetary economy', with the resulting insistence on payment of taxes in cash rather than in kind.[38] However, as noted above, this conclusion has been challenged on the basis of insufficient evidence apart from the indirect taxes levied on the monetised elements of the economy, such as the traders.[39] The use of money for paying the army was still the primary method of diffusion of the imperial, as distinct from city, coinage, and that occasioned by inter-regional and long-term trade was never great. At first sight this might appear to put Galilee of Antipas' day at a distinct disadvantage in terms of cash flow, since at that time there was no Roman division stationed there, unlike Judea to the south where a procuratorial guard was present, or Syria to the north, where the

---

[37] Peacock and Williams, *Amphorae and the Roman Economy*, 59–63.
[38] Hopkins, 'Economic Growth and the Towns,' 45.
[39] Duncan-Jones, *Structure and Scale in the Roman Economy*, 187–98.

nearest Roman legion was stationed. The mention of *chiliarchs* among the guests at Antipas' birthday party (Mk 6,21) reminds us, however, that he must have maintained some standing army, especially in view of his troubles with the Nabateans and that these would have had to be paid.

Why is monetisation so important in terms of a developing economy? According to Carney, money can be defined as 'any type of object that has generalised value allowing for goods and services.'[40] It is vital for the development of the market economy since it functions as a legitimate and recognised unit of value which can be stored. It can also be used subsequently in the purchase of goods or services as required from a supplier other than the person with whom the original transaction took place. It thus allows for a far a greater range of exchange possibilities than would be feasible if one were dependent on repayment in kind, as in a reciprocal exchange system. Since the wealth that is generated can be stored in a nonperishable form of coinage, payment can be deferred, provided an accounting system is in operation whereby debts and other promises are recorded. Meanwhile, goods and services can be availed of and used to generate further wealth, before repayment takes place and money itself can be used to gain more money by lending at a price, thus becoming an end in itself. Such developments obviously benefited those who owned the wealth generating resources and who could protect their income against thieves if required, either through policing or well protected residences. Inevitably also, there were major shifts in values as the wealthy were in a position to increase their status through the acquisition of luxury goods, often in an alienating fashion that radically changed the ways in which people interacted in home, village and region.

As a medium of exchange, money had been used in Palestine at least since the Persian period, as is evidenced by the famous *yehud* coins. Succeeding overlords, Ptolemaic and Seleucid, as well as the Hasmonean rulers had struck their own coins. This was partly for personal propaganda reasons, but also to facilitate intra- as well as inter-regional exchange. While the ban on human representation may have somewhat inhibited the former aspect, Jews, like other peoples, certainly availed of the trading possibilities that money offered. In addition, cities such as Tyre, Ptolemais and Scythopolis struck their own coins from the Hellenistic age and these were also current in Palestine. The large Jewish Diaspora in Egypt, Mesopotamia, Syria, Asia Minor and the western Mediterranean cities meant that there was bound to be a steady flow of people to and from the homeland, requiring goods and services, inevitably contributing to a greater supply of money in the economy generally. As already noted, John of Gischala showed his entrepreneurial spirit by availing of the much better price

---

[40] Carney, *The Shape of the Past*, 142.

for oil among fellow Jews in Caesarea than in his home town. He was scarcely an exception among a certain class of Jewish inhabitants in the land in first-century Palestine.

As the national cult-centre the Jerusalem temple was undoubtedly a source of foreign revenue for the Palestinian economy generally with the various rituals of pilgrimage, offerings and festivals, all requiring service from caravaneers, innkeepers, and moneychangers. In particular the half-shekel offering which every adult male Jew was expected to pay annually for the upkeep of the temple meant a steady inflow of the much sought after Tyrian coinage to Palestine. No greater tribute could be paid to the stability of this currency than the fact that, despite bearing the image of Melqart/Heracles, it was described as the 'coin of the sanctuary' according to a later halachic decree.[41] The city of Jerusalem undoubtedly profited most directly from this source of revenue, yet given the difficulties of overland travel many Galilean centres must also have benefited from those travelling along the more important routes, especially those from the east who would require shelter and sustenance on their journey.

The internal monetary situation in Antipas' Galilee must also be explored, even when coin finds are not as useful as pottery sherds in tracing commercial transactions. Not enough is known about the numbers of coins minted at various centres to allow definite conclusions to be drawn about trading patterns on the basis of coin finds at different sites. Since coins are an extremely portable item and since in the ancient world in particular they remained in circulation for a long time after their issue, their intermediate usage cannot be determined, but only their point of origin and final deposit.[42] Despite these reservations some things can definitely be asserted about the monetary situation in Galilee that are relevant to the present discussion. Neither Tiberias nor Sepphoris struck their own coins until much later, thus indicating their inferior status in comparison with other nearby cities that were 'free and autonomous.' They both functioned within the overall constraints of the regional economy, thus underlining their retainer status within an overall situation of an agrarian empire. This does not mean that they played an insignificant role locally, however. Justus of Tiberias bemoans the fact that with the transfer of his native city to the territory of Agrippa II by Nero, it had lost its status as capital of Galilee, which had reverted to Sepphoris. This meant that the royal bank and the archives were now located in that city (*Life* 38). This complaint is revealing in that it points directly to a situation in which money could be stored, and presumably borrowed also, and where records of such transactions were kept.

---

[41] A. Ben David, *Jerusalem und Tyros. Ein Beitrag zur palästinensischen Münz- und Wirtschaftsgeschichte* (Basel: Kyklos-Verlag, 1969) 5–9.

[42] Adan-Bayewitz, *Common Pottery in Roman Galilee*, 247 f.

The fact that Justus sees the loss of this facility as damaging to his native city suggests that for him and his ilk control of banking offered possibilities for the generation of wealth, presumably by charging of interest on loans. This also provides the context for the action of the destitute class of Tiberias who, together with some Galileans, stormed Herod's palace, ostensively for religious reasons, and confiscated luxury items together with a considerable amount of unminted silver (*Life* 68).

It must be remembered that Antipas himself operated under constraints in terms of his fiscal policy. Not even Herod the Great was allowed to strike silver coins, presumably because of the greater financial independence this would have given him. Only three strikings of Antipas' coinage can so far be documented: one for the year 19/20 CE, another for 26/27 CE and a third for 38/39 CE. All three strikings were minted at Tiberias, bear his name as ethnarch and are of a large denomination (c. 16 grams). They have no human or animal representation, unlike the palace at Tiberias (*Life* 65), but have various decorations of a palm branch or a reed, a wreath and on the final striking a bundle of dates as well. These latter also have the inscription: 'To Gaius Caesar Germanicus' – ironically, in view of the fact that it was this emperor who deposed him in that very year.[43] One can detect in these coins somebody who is caught between the religious conservatism of his largely Jewish population and his subordination to imperial fiscal policy, and who nonetheless is anxious to honour his patron, make a personal statement and facilitate small-scale local trade, possibly between the two diverse parts of his territory.

In view of these signs of the development of the internal market under Antipas, it is striking but not altogether surprising that according to the archaeological finds Tyrian coins had the widest currency in Galilee. The evidence for upper Galilee is clear and is in line with what we might expect in light of the literary sources already mentioned. Apart from Hasmonean coins which were of smaller denomination than the Tyrian didrachma and therefore, presumably, used for smaller transactions on a local basis, coins from Tyre represent the largest percentage of all coins found at Meiron (4.7% compared with 1.9% of Herodian – mainly of Herod the Great). A similar percentage is reported for other upper Galilean sites – Kh. Shema (3.5) and Gush Halav (4.5). Even more surprising is the fact that a similar percentage of Tyrian coins (4.5) is reported for Sepphoris as compared with only 0.5 Herodian coins for the same site.[44] While

---

[43] Y. Meshorer, *Jewish Coins of the Second Temple Period* (Tel Aviv: Am Hasefer Publications, 1967) numbers 63, 64 and 65.

[44] R. Hanson, *Tyrian Influence in Upper Galilee* (Cambridge, MA: ASOR Publications, 1980) 51–54; J. Raynor and Y. Meshorer, *The Coins of Ancient Meiron* (Winona Lake: Eisenbrauns, 1988) 83–85.

this figure is based on earlier excavations and does not take account of recent and ongoing digs at this site, it is nonetheless quite significant. It certainly points to the importance of trade with Tyre for all of Galilee and could be seen to confirm our suggestion concerning the subordinate role of Sepphoris within the total economy of the northern region, despite its preeminence internally in Galilee. This situation is confirmed by the fact that very few coins from Tiberias have been found in the Upper Galilean sites. By contrast Tyrian coins predominate in hoards found in Lower Galilee. Thus in the Migdal hoard of coins dating from Titus to Elagabulus, 74 of a total of 188 bronze coins were from Tyre. This has been explained by the fact that the mint at Tyre produced many more coins than those from other competing mints.[45] Perhaps more significant, in view of the latest date (52/53 CE), is the Isfija-hoard of almost 5000 Tyrian silver coins of various denominations found in 1960 in the Carmel range. Several theories as to the significance of such a large find have been suggested, none totally convincing.[46] Whatever the circumstances in which they came to be hidden, it is clear that they indicate the continued dominance of Tyre as the major trading centre for the lower as well as upper Galilee, despite the development of Caesarea to the south as a possible rival port.

In their different ways the Synoptic gospels testify to the fact that money was widely used in everyday transactions, even by the poor. This would point to the fact that the use of money had penetrated right through the society and was now the standard form of exchange even among the day-labourers, widows and other marginalised people. Did the fact that all male Jews had to make an annual contribution of a half-shekel to the temple mean a higher degree of monetisation in that culture than in similar societies in antiquity? In this regard it should be noted that according to *m. Sheq.* 1,3 tables for money changers were set up outside Jerusalem before the great feasts in order to facilitate the pilgrims. Likewise, Josephus' colleagues from Jerusalem are said to have 'amassed a large sum of money' from the tithes owing to them as priests from the Galilean country people before returning to Jerusalem (*Life* 62). It is interesting also to note that apart from one *Q* saying (*QLk* 6,38; Mt 7,2) about the measure one gives determining the measure one receives and the parable of the unjust manager (Lk 16,1–9), there is not a hint of barter exchange in any of the sayings of the Jesus tradition. People are presumed to have money for purchasing necessities or to meet other emergencies (Mk 6,36–38; Lk 10,35).

---

[45] H. Hamburger, 'A Hoard of Syrian Tetradrachms from Tiberias' *Atiqot* 2 (Jerusalem: Israel Antiquities Authority, 1959) 133–45; Y. Meshorer, 'A Hoard of Coins from Migdal' *Atiqot* 11 (Jerusalem Antiquities Authority, 1968) 54–71; D. Barag, 'Tyrian Currency in Galilee,' *INJ* 6/7 (1982/83) 7–13.

[46] Ben David, *Jerusalem und Tyros,* 33–36.

However, Jesus' own attitude towards money would appear to have been one of suspicion, if not of downright hostility. The practice of hoarding is described as futile; the disciples are not to rely on money in their travels and the tables of the moneychangers were overturned. We can enquire about the reasons for this attitude in view of the fact that Jesus and his followers accept the reality of money. Nevertheless, this question brings us to the third element in the model, that of changing values and institutions. The results of the present probe, however, point firmly toward a monetised economy which is dominated by trading links with Tyre, even though local trading within Galilee and with the Golan region was also thriving.

3. Institutions and Values

Carney insists that for rapid change to occur leading to a full blown market economy a change of values also had to take place. This would affect the existing institutions and give rise to new values – influencing kinship and family, entrepreneurship, status maintenance and other determinants of honour and shame, those two pivotal Mediterranean values. Elsewhere he speaks of this as a process of secularisation, whereby the masses are no longer controlled by the dominant belief-system, but have to be persuaded or coerced (mobilised) to achieve public goals.[47] Sectional interests surface as more individualistic modes of thinking emerge. Thus in fifth-century BCE Athens, the rise of rationalistic and 'atheistic' thinking went hand in hand with monetisation and the development of markets, which were subsequently made to serve the interests of the redistributive/mobilised economies of the Hellenistic monarchies. A similar pattern can be seen with the rise of the Principate in the first century CE, putting an end to rationalistic debates among the elites of late Republican times and leading to a growth in superstition, re-enforcement of traditional values and the promulgation of a new ideology, namely the victory of Rome and the Emperor that ushered in the age of peace. Herodian policies in Palestine have to be evaluated in the light of these developments. With the aid of both the multivariate, matrix model (which should help in seeing all the factors that were operative within the situation) and the transformational one (which suggests where and how rapid change can affect the whole system), we shall attempt to explore the extent to which the ethos of Galilee was undergoing dramatic changes in the early first century CE.

It would be wrong to suggest that prior to the aggressive Romanisation process of the Herodians, Palestinian society had not experienced the effects of rapid economic changes and their related attitudinal shifts. The Zenon papyri give us some insights into these changes for Galilee as well

---

[47] Carney, *The Shape of the Past*, 149–52 and 334 f.

as for other regions in the Ptolemaic period.[48] The process appears to have been accelerated under the Seleucids with the emergence of the extreme Hellenisers at the time of Antiochus Epiphanes, who are described as being lawless men, and who complained that traditional Jewish isolationism precluded them from availing of the economic advantages of the new era (1 Macc 1,11). It was no accident that these ideas were beginning to be expressed at a time when a Greek-style gymnasium had been established in Jerusalem. Despite their appeal to ancestral pieties in re-establishing the cult and legitimating the conquest of the land, the Hasmoneans did nothing to reverse the social trends that had been occurring for centuries, as some recent archaeological evidence for the first century BCE from Samaria clearly suggests.[49] The extreme pressure on traditional values may be seen in the fact that such levelling mechanisms as the Jubilee and Sabbatical Year were increasingly employed as images for the eschatological future in the literature of the period, rather than as currently functioning institutions. True, the *prosbul* arrangement points to a situation in which the need for a cash flow was recognised as being essential in order to maintain the stability of the society, and hence the stipulation of cancellation of all debts every seventh year could not be adhered to. In addition the Pentateuchal and prophetic ideal for Israel of 'every man under his own olive or fig tree', i.e., individual ownership of land in traditional holdings (1 Kgs 5,5; Mic 4,4; Zech 3,10), was at least part of Hasmonean ideology also (1 Macc 14,10). Even Herod the Great's land policy comprised of smaller lots for his veterans side by side with the development of royal estates. It was in the interests of the Hasmoneans to maintain such a pattern since the system of tithes and pilgrimages was in effect a functioning mobilisation exchange system, legitimated by shared religious values, but which could be both punitive and exploitative as far as the country people were concerned (*JA* 20,181.206 f.; *Life* 63). This ambivalence caused the political rebellion against Rome to be turned into a full-scale social revolution in 66 CE when the country peasants of Judea joined with the lesser clergy in Jerusalem in ousting those who had lived the double standard and established in their place an egalitarian alternative (*JW* 2,242–47; 4,147–48).

During the ministry of Jesus, however, matters had not yet come to such a pass. The emergence of the Herodians and the alliance established between them and the retainers of the Jerusalem priestly aristocracy, the Pharisees (Mk 3,5; 12,18), must, however, have helped in unmasking the inequalities of the situation. While the latter could use religious categories based on the purity system as a way of maintaining their social elitism, the

---

[48] V. Tcherikover, *Palestine under the Ptolemies. A Contribution to the Study of the Zenon Papyri* (Mizraim, vols. IV-V, New York: G. E. Stechert, 1937).

[49] Dar, *Landscape and Pattern,* especially 230–55 on a royal estate.

former had no such inhibitions. An ostentatiously luxurious life-style is hinted at in Jesus' encomium on John the Baptist (*Q*Mt 11,9; Lk 7,25; *Gos. Thom.* 78), giving rise to a sense of alienation and resentment on the part of the ordinary people (*Life* 67, 118 f.; cf. Mk 12,7). The emergency of banditry as a social phenomenon is another consequence of such an ethos in which inequalities are no longer disguised, and people have a heightened awareness of being unfairly treated.[50] Indeed Josephus' as distinct from the Gospels' account of the death of John the Baptist hints at the fact that it was his critique of the lifestyle of the affluent, particularly his call for the practice of justice to one another, that had caused Antipas to have him removed from the scene because of the danger of a revolution (*JA* 18,118).[51] This makes the relative freedom of Jesus even more surprising, though it may explain his strategy, as we shall presently see.

Carney argues that the institution which is central to the redistributive system but which is wholly unsuited to the market economy is the extended family. It operates on and is held together by values that are not suited to the needs of a market situation. The specialised skills required are not necessarily available within the family unit and bonding is for reasons other than the maximisation of profits from the available resources. Accordingly, the market worked in favour of the privileges of the few rather than to the advantage of the many, and maintenance of status became a primary concern for those who controlled the resources. Nor was there any incentive or motivation to improve the lot of the peasants or lower classes. Thus the market economy, far from bringing about an improved situation for all was highly exploitative in a way that lead to social stratification and fragmentation. In a system based on kinship this could be disguised more easily through the shared acceptance of other, non-economic values which shielded those less able to compete.

In such a situation traditional institutions invariably come under severe pressure and the values that have held them together are easily eroded. In this regard it is noteworthy that Josephus repeatedly appeals to the value of ὁμοφυλία, kinship, as a way of maintaining harmony among the various factions in Galilee during his sojourn there. Justus of Tiberias is charged with violating these bonds by acts of violence on the Galileans (*Life* 302) and Sepphoris is blamed for its refusal to support the temple 'which is common to us all' (*Life* 348) when it was in danger. Such appeals high-

---

[50] R. Horsley and J. Hanson, *Bandits, Prophets and Messiahs. Popular Movements at the Time of Jesus* (Minneapolis: Winston Press, 1985) 48–87; S. Freyne, 'Bandits in Galilee. A Contribution to the Study of Social Conditions in First-Century Palestine,' in *The Social World of Formative Christianity and Judaism. Essays in Tribute of Howard Clark Kee*, ed. J. Neusner et al. (Philadelphia: Fortress Press, 1988) 50–69.

[51] Hoehner, *Herod Antipas*, 136–46.

light the ambivalent situation that Josephus found himself in as governor of Galilee. As a wealthy Jerusalem landowner he undoubtedly shared the economic values of the wealthy Galileans, including the Herodians of Tiberias such as Justus, whose education in the Greek manner he acknowledges, and one suspects, admires also (*Life* 40). Yet the native nobility resented his appointment as governor in their own territory. In this situation Josephus needed the support of the peasants and played on their loyalty to Jerusalem and their hostility towards the aristocratic elites within the region. At the same time he had no desire to foment a full scale social revolution against those elites, such as occurred in Jerusalem, as was noted earlier. The fact that he was able to maintain his position successfully prior to the Roman advance speaks volumes both for the strength of the peasants' religious convictions and their loyalty to the Jerusalem cult-centre, and his ability to mobilise them for his own purpose.[52]

Such were the competing values and loyalties in Galilee at the outbreak of the first revolt. It was not a new situation then, nor had it emerged overnight. We must surmise that some thirty years earlier this situation was beginning to surface, as both Sepphoris in its refurbished state and Tiberias were recent establishments. What was new about them was that they had introduced into the heart of lower Galilee in a relatively short space of time people whose values clashed directly with those on which the Jewish peasants' lives had operated. It was not a question of their encountering these values for the first time, but now in their midst these values had received visible expression in stone and an institutionalised presence, often in the person of fellow Jews. It was this complex of factors that generated the tensions which surface so clearly thirty years after Jesus.

Jesus' Message and Herodian Economics

The situation of rapid change in basic values symbolised in the two new foundations helps to explain both the values and the strategy of Jesus. A critical correlation between his stance and the demands of the new situation appears both possible and plausible. Both Sepphoris and Tiberias were avoided not necessarily because Jesus shared the alienation of the peasants towards those centres, but because he rejected the value system on which their position of power was based. The treatment of the Baptist undoubtedly also cast its own shadow. Jesus' ministry was rurally based, but did not exclude the lesser officials, such as the tax collectors in the villages, who were positively welcomed. Thus, the Jesus movement was not one other protest movement, venting its anger on the elites in violent ac-

---

[52] Cf. 'Galilee-Jerusalem Relations according to Josephus' *Life,*' above pp. 73 ff.

tions. Neither did it espouse the kind of social and personal withdrawal that were associated with various forms of Cynicism which have recently found favour as the most suitable analogue in some contemporary studies of Jesus.[53] He proposed an alternative way of life that both adopted and adapted the kinship and familial values being eroded in the larger culture represented by Antipas' foundations. Drawing on the ethical insights of the prophetic motif of the restoration of Israel, and combining these with common wisdom, he sought to give these values concrete expression in a new style of community living. Family feuds must have occurred as the direct result of the social changes taking place and the invitation to join an alternative family would have resonated particularly with those who had become alienated or excluded in the prevailing social upheaval.

The proposal is that Jesus and his renewal movement are best understood as offering another set of values in addition to the two competing ones which we have seen within the social world of Antipas' Galilee. Insofar as it might be expected to have had a widespread appeal in that particular setting, it was potentially threatening to both. The very radical nature of its social programme was a challenge to the values that the Herodian market economy espoused, and the revision of the traditional religious categories of temple, Torah and land which it called for would have undermined the centrality of Jerusalem and the unqualified loyalty that it was able to foster among its rural adherents. The fact that in the end it proved more threatening to the latter than to the former is perhaps indicative of the reserve with which the Galilean peasantry viewed its radical social agenda, despite the sense of alienation from the dominant system that must have been experienced, and the seeming inability or unwillingness of the cult-based system to halt the drift towards penury. The wandering charismatic/healer/holy man, Jesus, may well have fulfilled a definite social need in the Galilean villages, but in a climate in which people clung precariously to some things, though all was in danger of being lost, his call to abandon everything would appear to have been too demanding and too utopian. That same message propagated by the tradents of the *Q* tradition, albeit adapted in the light of new experiences, would appear to have still been equally unattractive to the fishermen and farmers of Capernaum, Bethsaida and Chorazin some decades later.[54] If Josephus is to be trusted they found it less disruptive to support Jerusalem and its temple while venting their anger against the Herodian centres than to follow the millen-

---

[53] E.g., J. D. Crossan, *The Historical Jesus. The Life of a Mediterranean Jewish Peasant* . (Edinburgh: T. & T. Clark, 1991); B. Mack, *The Lost Gospel. The Book of Q and Christian Origins* (New York: HarperCollins, 1993).

[54] J. Kloppenborg, 'Literary Convention, Self-Evidence and the Social History of the Q People,' *Semeia* 55 (1991) 77–102.

nial dream. Thus when he took over as governor there in 66 CE the two systems, Herodian and theocratic, were still firmly in place and to an extent competing with each other, while forming an alliance of convenience in order to maintain their privileges. Nowhere can we detect any trace of the Jesus movement or its agenda in the social world of *Life*. Instead that movement and its alternative value system had found more fertile soil in the cities of the Mediterranean world, where its appeal for many, though muted because of the political realities, was still based on the challenge it posed to the mobilised economy that was Rome.

Conclusion

In applying the model to the Galilee of Antipas' day I have concentrated on those elements which Carney has suggested should be selected and highlighted for special treatment, namely attitudinal changes in production and consumption, increased organisational specialisation and monetisation of transactions. Under all three headings we have been able to identify clear signs of such movement within the society of Jesus' day. The values of a market economy with all the attendant signs of exploitation of the weak and ostentatious living of the wealthy are easily documented; specialisations in terms of more intensive harvesting of produce both from the land and lake, as well as production of goods for inter-regional trade in addition to domestic use were occurring; and there are clear signs of the extension of monetisation as a means of exchange with the production of native Galilean coins for the first time, however subordinate these remained to the Tyrian money. It seems possible to link these developments with Antipas' foundations of Sepphoris and Tiberias, as symptomatic of the more complex changes occurring within the whole region. It is not a case that with Antipas these developments occurred for the first time, but rather that his attempts to emulate his father and his desire to convince Augustus of his right to kingship, meant that there was a particular intensification in Galilee of processes that had been in train in Palestine in general for a considerable time.

Thus, the use of Carney's model seems to have more than justified itself. Not only has it assisted in clarifying the changes that were taking place, but it has also brought into sharper focus the most immediate historical context for the rise of the one Galilean renewal movement known to us from the first century CE and the reason for the particular set of values which that movement espoused.

6. Behind the Names: Galileans, Samaritans, *Ioudaioi*

The fact that this is the second congress of Galilean Studies is indicative of the importance of the region in recent discussions of Second Temple Judaism and Early Christianity. This focus of attention on Galilee is in no small measure due to the initiative and industry of Eric Meyers over the last twenty-five or so years. He was in fact the first to speak of the need to see Galilee within a larger regional context, pointing to the cultural continuities with the Golan on the one hand and the differences between Upper and Lower Galilee on the other.[1] The two recent books of Richard Horsley have also indirectly highlighted the issue of regionalism by positing tensions between the Judeans on the one hand and the Galilean Israelites on the other.[2] Perhaps the time has come for a consideration of Galilee, not in isolation but in relation to other regions within first-century Palestine. Such an undertaking would constitute a useful hermeneutical exercise, refining the various hypotheses about Galilean society that have been proposed over the years. There are plenty of 'surface' indicators – everything from geography to winemaking techniques – to suggest a rich cultural diversity within the borders of this relatively small territory, and our literary sources for the period are aware of such diversity.

This paper focuses not directly on Judea, but rather on the in-between world of Samaria, which had fraught relations with both Galilee and Judea in our period. Samaria has been neglected in discussion of Galilee. Yet two incidents, both with a strong religious colouring from the first century CE highlight the tensions in Galilean/Samarian relations. Luke states that Samaritan villages rejected the emissaries of Jesus, 'because his face was set toward Jerusalem' (Lk 9,52). Josephus twice reports the civic turmoil occasioned by an attack on Galilean pilgrims to Jerusalem by Samaritans from the village of Ginae (*JA* 20,118–36; *JW* 2,234–46). It is possible to interpret Luke's report as the construct of the evangelist in the light of his portrayal of Jesus and the early Christian missionary activity, but the episode reported by Josephus cannot be so lightly dismissed despite the dis-

---

[1] E. Meyers, 'Galilean Regionalism as a Factor in Historical Reconstruction,' *BASOR* 221 (1976) 93–101.

[2] R. A. Horsley, *Galilee. History, Politics, People* (Valley Forge: Trinity Press International, 1995) and *Archaeology, History and Society in Galilee* (Valley Forge: Trinity Press International, 1996).

crepancies between the two accounts. Tacitus also knows of these disturbances which took place in the procuratorship of Cumanus (*Ann.* XII, 54).[3]

The fact that both incidents occur in the context of the pilgrimage to Jerusalem is significant. Yet, as Horsley repeatedly reminds us, religion was
embedded in the real factors for conflict in agrarian societies, namely, the
political, economic and social dynamics. It is easy to suggest economic
reasons for the Samaritan resentment of Galilean pilgrims bringing their
produce to Jerusalem rather than to Gerizim. Pilgrims were a boost to the
local economy in the ancient no less than the modern world. However, the
Gerizim temple was in ruins at this time, not having been rebuilt after its
destruction by John Hyrcanus, over 150 years earlier.[4] Thus the economic
explanation loses some of its cogency and raises other questions: why did
the Galileans prefer Jerusalem? What circumstances lead to their bypass-
ing their natural cult centre, if, as 'Israelites' (in Horsley's view), the Galileans shared a common heritage with 'the Israelites of Argarizein'? What
does his tell us about the Galileans and the Judeans?

A survey of contemporary scholarship on Samaria and the Samaritans
reveals two separate but cumulative explanations given for their separate-
ness from both Galilee and Judea: the Galileans and the Samarians suffered different fates at the hands of the Assyrians in the eighth century and
these marked their relationships afterwards[5]; and secondly, the building of
a temple on Mt Gerizim and the process of Hellenisation represent two
stages of the so-called Samaritan schism, whereby a final wedge was
driven between Samarians and the adherents of the Jerusalem temple, including, presumably, the Galileans. The following discussion re-examines
critically these two explanations, conscious that they have both entered
recent scholarship via the anti-Samaritan polemic of the Jerusalem priest
Josephus as expressed particularly in his *Jewish Antiquities.*[6] This is not
the most reliable source in these circumstances.

---

[3] S. Freyne, *Galilee from Alexander the Great to Hadrian* (reprint, Edinburgh: T. &
T. Clark, 1998) 73 f.

[4] R. J. Bull, 'An Archaeological Footnote to "Our Fathers worshiped on this Mountain",' *NTS* 23 (1977) 460–62.

[5] I propose to use the term Samarian (Σαμάρεις) for the inhabitants of the region, irrespective of their religious affiliation and to reserve Samaritan (Σαμαρεῖται) for the
adherents of the Gerizim cult. There is good Josephan warrant for this since he uses the
former at *JA* 9,125 when speaking of the reign of Jehu. However, he uses Σαμαρεῖται
after the fall of the Northern Kingdom, since, in his biased view it is proper to date the
origins of the Samaritan cult of his own day back to that moment (*JA* 9,290).

[6] R. J. Coggins, 'The Samaritans in Josephus,' in *Josephus, Judaism and Christianity,*
ed. L. H. Feldman and G. Hata (Leiden: Brill, 1987) 257–73. *For another account, also
with a more nuanced treatment of the literary sources, cf. M. Mor, 'Samaritan History:
the Persian, Hellenistic and Hasmonean Period,' in *The Samaritans,* ed. A. Crown
(Tübingen: J. C. B. Mohr, 1989) 1–18. Cf. also, J. D. Purvis, 'The Samaritans and Juda-

The Assyrian Experience

Albrecht Alt in particular, drawing on the biblical account (2 Kgs 15,29; 17,23) as well as the Assyrian Annals, proposes that whereas the majority of the Galilean peasantry was left undisturbed when Tiglath-Pileser conquered the north in 733 BCE, Samaria suffered a very different fate twelve years later under Salmanasar I (721 BCE). The ruling aristocracy was taken into exile and replaced by people of non-Israelite stock. Galilee was now administered from Megiddo, the capital of one of three new provinces established by Tiglath-Pileser and treated subsequently as a 'kingsland.' Samaria with its own new governing elite and a cultic centre was treated as a temple state within larger imperial structures which continued into the Persian and Greek periods. This new elite, while worshipping the god of the land never fully inculturated with the peasantry in Samaria, who eventually felt more drawn to the Jerusalem temple than to the one established on Gerazim.[7]

To this administrative-historical argument, Horsley has added a socio-economic component as required by the materialist bias of his macro-model of agrarian empires.[8] In his view, Galilee was deprived of its local ruling officials and craftsmen (some of whom may not even have been of Israelite extraction) and it was now ruled from Megiddo by imperial officials. Denuded of a native aristocracy, the Galilean Israelites were left free to conduct their own village affairs according to ancestral custom. By contrast, Samaria did have a 'native' elite (presumably of non-Israelite stock) who, when ousted from the capital in the fourth century, resettled at Shechem and established a temple on Mt Gerizim. Thus, unlike Galilee, the changes in Samaria meant a ruling secular elite and a priestly and scribal retainer class. This latter was eventually to provide a legitimating version of the Torah that was intended to counter the Jerusalem hegemonic claims after the destruction of the Gerizim temple. The Galileans had no such luck, or misfortune, depending on your point of view, maintaining their traditions orally. Yet, they were resistant to any imposition of the laws of

---

ism,' in *Early Judaism and its Modern Interpreters*, ed. R. A. Kraft and G. Nickelsburg (Atlanta: Scholars Press, 1986) 81–98; A. D. Crown, 'Another Look at Samaritan Origins,' in *Essays in Honour of G. D. Sixdenier. New Samaritan Studies of the Societé D'Études Samaritaines*, ed. A. D. Crown and L. Davey, University of Sydney Studies in Judaica 5 (Sydney: Mandelbaum Publishing, 1995) 133–56.

[7] A. Alt, 'Die Assyrische Provinz Megiddo und ihr späteres Schicksal,' in *Galiläische Probleme 2, Kleine Schriften zur Geschichte des Volkes Israels*, 3 vols. (Munich: C. H. Beck 1953–64) 374–84.

[8] Horsley, *Galilee*, 8–9.

the Judeans, despite their common roots in Israelite tradition.[9] Several observations can be made about these reconstructions with respect to our question concerning the causes of later Galilean/Samaritan hostility.

The available evidence makes this reconstruction of the different experiences of Galileans and Samarians under the Assyrians problematic. Unless the findings of Zvi Gal's survey are disproved by detailed excavations, the evidence he provides for the depopulation of lower Galilee in the sixth century BCE must be taken into any account of the region's history, pace Horsley's dismissal.[10] However, even the literary sources do not support this scenario. The places listed in the Assyrian annals – Gabara, Hinatuma, Qana, Iatbite, Irruna – can all be confidently located in lower Galilee. They neatly flesh out the more general statement of 2 Kgs 15,29 that lists 'Galilee, all the land of Naphtali' as part of the devastated territory together with such upper Galilean strongholds as Ijon, Kedesh, and Hazor.[11] Indeed, if Alt is correct in reading the oracle of Is 8,23 as addressed to the three new Assyrian provinces of the north – Megiddo (including Galilee), Dor and Gilead – it would seem to refute his own suggestion elsewhere that Galilee, as such, escaped the ravages of Tiglath-Pileser's conquest.[12] Where does that leave the Galilean Israelites? Moreover, if they existed, why do they not make common cause with their Samarian peasant counterparts?

Even if the Alt/Horsley version of the events be accepted, an additional question concerns the very notion of separate Israelite traditions being maintained by peasants over centuries. I also once held that position, but have come to see its inherent improbability.[13] Morton Smith had long ago found plenty of evidence in the literary sources for what he calls 'the syncretistic cult of Yahweh' throughout the whole country.[14] A study by John S. Holladay, Jr., of the archaeological evidence distinguishes between what he describes as state cult centres and popular domestic religion in the

---

[9] Ibid., 25–29.

[10] Z. Gal, *Lower Galilee During the Iron Age,* ASORDS 8 (Winona Lake: Eisenbrauns, 1992); Horsley, *Galilee. History, Politics, People,* 290, n. 13.

[11] Cf. H. Tadmor, *The Inscriptions of Tiglath-Pileser III King of Assyria* (Jerusalem: Israel Academy of the Sciences and Humanities, 1994). For a recent discussion of the evidence cf. K. Lawson Younger Jr., 'The Deportation of the Israelites,' *JBL* 117 (1998) 201–27.

[12] A. Alt, 'Jesaja 8,23–9,6. Befreiungsnacht und Krönungstag,' *Kleine Schriften, vol. 2,* 206–25.

[13] Freyne, *Galilee,* 23–26, but cf. S. Freyne, *Galilee, Jesus and the Gospels* (Dublin and Philadelphia: Gill & Macmillan and Fortress, 1988) 169–70.

[14] M. Smith, *Palestinian Parties and Politics that Shaped the Old Testament* (New York: 1971, reprint, London: SCM Press, 1987) 62–74.

divided monarchy and comes up similar conclusions.[15] Working on the hypothesis that one of the major goals of state religious cult in antiquity was to promote national unity and a feeling of distinctiveness *vis à vis* neighbouring states, Holladay looks at the evidence for cultic activity from eight different sites, north and south. He uses various criteria for distinguishing between conformist and tolerated nonconformist religious activities – these latter addressing the needs of excluded minorities or dealing with aspects of the divine world not adequately represented in the state, or conformist, cult. Of the Northern sites examined, Dan represents a national or regional cult centre, Megiddo a conformist neighbourhood shrine while Hazor represents a domestic nonconformist profile. Samaria on the other hand is a nonconformist shrine, situated outside the walls and containing a significant number of small figurines and other objects. However, it lacks the incense altars associated with the establishment sites. The evidence of domestic religious objects of a nonconformist type from Stratum V at Hazor (i.e. eighth century BCE) shows a marked increase over strata representing earlier periods, suggesting an intensification of such activity at periods of crisis such as that of the Assyrian onslaught. On the basis of this analysis of the evidence, it would appear that in situations in which the national cult was perceived to have failed, Galileans would have been more likely to turn to nonconformist religious practices in domestic settings which were not specific to the conformist Israelite cult.

Galilean Israelites might alternatively have been expected to frequent a national or local shrine where a sense of separate identity could continue to be fostered. Depending on its previous character, Dan might have provided such a centre, at least until the arrival of the god Pan to nearby Banias in the Seleucid period. There is evidence of at least two stages of building in the temenos area during the Hellenistic period and in addition there is the tantalising bilingual inscription 'to the God who is in Dan.'[16] Or, if the tradition of the priest from Bethel instructing the new arrivals in the worship of the god of the land has any substance, then some form of Yahwistic worship must have continued in Samaria (2 Kgs 17,28). Certainly, accounts from the Persian period assume the presence of Yahweh worshippers in Samaria whose overtures of help to Jerusalem were rejected (Ez 4,1–5; *JA* 11,85–88). Presumably, one of the reasons why these

---

[15] J. S. Holladay, Jr., 'Religion in Israel and Judah Under the Monarchy: An Explicitly Archaeological Approach,' in *Ancient Israelite Religion*, ed. P. D. Miller, P. D. Hanson and S. D. McBride (Philadelphia: Fortress Press, 1987) 249–302.

[16] A. Biran, 'To the God who is in Dan,' in *Temples and High Places in Biblical Times*, ed. A. Biran (Jerusalem: HUC-JIR Publications, 1981) 142–51; V. Tzaferis, 'The "God who is in Dan" and the Cult of Pan at Banias in the Hellenistic and Roman Periods,' *Eretz Israel* vol. 23, *A. Biran Volume* (Jerusalem: The Israel Exploration Society, 1991) 128*-135*.

possibilities are not explored by modern scholars is the common understanding that in Samaria in particular, a new, syncretistic form of worship
was thought to have been emerging that would have been inimical to Israelite Yahwism (see below). Or perhaps we are in danger of unconsciously
imposing a far too rigid notion of Yahwism as it was propagated later in
the Deuteronomic reform on to an earlier, more fluid situation. Holladay's
remark that 'the uneasy thought that actual religious practice in ancient
Israel might not have mirrored our texts in any recognisable fashion has
disturbed many a scholar's ponderings' may sound somewhat dramatic.
However, scholars such as William Dever and P. Kyle McCarter suggest
that the understanding of Israelite religion needs to be broadened considerably in the wake of Kuntillet 'Ajrud and other discoveries, despite the
ideological claims of the literary texts.[17]

The point of the argument so far is that a reconsideration of the circumstances of the Assyrian conquest of the North does not support the suggestion that later Galilean/Samaritan hostility had its roots in that experience.
On the contrary our putative Galilean Israelites should have been drawn to
link up with their Samarian co-religionists – not just for religious reasons,
but because they can both be presumed to have suffered similarly under
the foreign overlord in terms of economic and social pressures on their
traditional way of life. To be sure, the imperial principle of 'dividing and
ruling' can be seen to be operative in the establishment of different provinces for the continued subjugation of conquered territories. Such a policy
may have inhibited alliances between Israelite remnants in both Galilee
and Samaria, but there is certainly no reason to suppose that Galilean and
Samarian Israelites who survived the conquests should have regarded each
other as enemies. Indeed, the fact that they were administered by new elites from Samaria and Megiddo should have strengthened the bonds between them. Perhaps modern scholarship has been unconsciously influenced by Josephus' anti-Samaritan handling of this episode, highlighting
their foreign 'Cuthean' origins and their devious and unfaithful character
as expressed in their religious rites 'up to this day' (*JA* 11,290).

The Temple on Gerizim and Hellenisation

A virtual consensus seems to have emerged among the most influential
scholars of the Second Temple period that the building of the Samaritan
temple on Gerizim should be linked to the arrival of Alexander and the

---

[17] P. Kyle McCarter, Jr., 'Aspects of Religion in the Israelite Monarchy: Biblical and
Epigraphic Data,' in *Ancient Israelite Religion*, 137–56; W. Dever, 'Will the Real Israel
Please Stand Up? Archaeology and the Religions of Israel,' *BASOR* 298 (1996) 37–58.

Macedonians as Josephus indicates (*JA* 11,303–8).[18] According to this consensus the establishment of a Macedonian colony in the capital Samaria either by Alexander or his governor, Perdicas, led to the dispersal of the ruling aristocracy, who re-established the previously abandoned ancient site at Shechem. Styling themselves the 'Sidonians at Shechem' they set up their own sanctuary at Gerizim, without any support from Jerusalem. This dating is thought to be supported by both the Wadi Daliyeh Samaritan papyri and the excavations at Shechem (Tel Balatah).[19] Though Yahweh-worshippers, their Cuthean origins and the possible presence of Greek trading elements in their midst made them prey to the Hellenisation process to the point that they voluntarily requested Antiochus Epiphanes to establish the cult of Zeus at their sanctuary in the second century BCE.

In view of the most recent findings, however, there are serious problems with this construal. It is unlikely that the Macedonians would have permitted the building of a fortified city at Shechem by the ousted Samarians. This is even less likely if the charred remains of over 300 people in the caves at Wadi Daliyeh are, as Frank Moore Cross has suggested, those of Samarians fleeing from the Greeks.[20] One dissenting voice to the consensus was that of Richard Coggins who believed that the archaeological evidence from Tel Balatah was too imprecise to date its re-foundation to the time of Alexander. In addition he considered the linking of the Gerizim temple with Alexander as part of Josephus' anti-Samaritan bias of his own day, and hence lacking historical credibility.[21]

Recently, Yitzhak Magen has proposed a different account of Samaritan origins based on his archaeological work on Mt Gerizim since 1990.[22] What has been uncovered is not just a temple but also a fortified city and a sacred precinct at its centre, both built at the same time. While there is evidence of habitation at the site from the Ptolemaic period, Magen summarises his findings to the effect that 'the architectural, ceramic and numismatic evidence indicates that the Hellenistic city on Mt Gerizim and the sacred precincts were established during the reign of Antiochus III

---

[18] E. Bickerman, *From Ezra to the Last of the Maccabees* (New York: Shocken Books, 1962) 43–44; M. Hengel, *Jews, Greeks and Barbarians* (London: SCM Press, 1980) 8 f.; J. Purvis, 'The Samaritans,' in *The Cambridge History of Judaism. Vol. 2. The Hellenistic Age*, ed. W. D. Davies and L. Finkelstein (London: Cambridge University Press, 1989) 591–693, especially 602.

[19] G. E. Wright, 'The Samaritans at Shechem,' *HTR* 55 (1962) 357–66.

[20] F. Moore Cross, 'Aspects of Samaritan and Jewish History in the late Persian and Hellenistic Times,' *HTR* 59 (1966) 201–11.

[21] R. J. Coggins, *Samaritans and Jews. The Origins of Samaritanism Reconsidered* (Oxford: Blackwell, 1985) 96 f., 103–6.

[22] Y. Magen, 'Mount Gerizim and the Samaritans,' in *Early Christianity in Context*, ed. F. Manns and E. Alliata (Jerusalem: Franciscan Publications, 1993) 91–147.

(early 2nd century BCE).'[23] Magen is aware that none of the literary sources mentions a city at Gerizim, but he attributes this silence to its destruction in less than a hundred years by John Hyrcanus; as a result, only the sacred character of the mountain was remembered. Apart from the evidence of the material remains, the suitable political circumstances for such a foundation need to be considered. It is unlikely that the inhabitants of the restored Shechem, whoever they may have been, built another city on Gerizim, let alone a temple. In fact, Magen believes that the restored Shechem was a Macedonian fortress, built to guard an important pass, and not the seat of the ousted Samarians. Antiochus III's well-known favourable treatment of the Jerusalem Jews (*JA* 12,138–53) appears to have extended itself to Samarian Yahweh-worshippers also, since the sacred precincts have been modelled on the Jerusalem sanctuary, and in addition the material remains all suggest a similar form of worship to that in Jerusalem.

What is particularly suggestive about these considerations, hypothetical though Magen's reconstruction of the history may be at present, is the very different profile of the Samaritans and their Temple that results. This was not the building of ousted Samarians of Cuthean extraction whose religious affiliations were dubious at best as in later Jewish estimation. It was, rather, the foundation of Yahweh worshippers with strong Israelite connections. Josephus, despite all his anti-Samaritan bias, acknowledges that the Gerizim temple was modelled on that in Jerusalem (*JA* 11,310; 13,235), something that Magen's discoveries seem to confirm.[24] That there were Yahweh-worshipers in Samaria in the Persian period is amply documented from the books of Ezra and Nehemiah. It is to them, rather than to any possible syncretistic Samarians, that the foundations of Samaritanism as a discrete cultic community are to be attributed. The fact that Yahweh temples, other than the Jerusalem one, can be documented throughout the Second Temple Period demonstrates that the description 'schismatic' for the Gerizim foundation is an anachronistic label.[25] Equally, the emergence of the Samaritan Pentateuch, the beginnings of which have been convincingly dated to the period following John Hyrcanus' destruction of their temple, should not be seen as the sign of an obdurate sect who refused to accept the full and authentic canon of Jewish Scriptures. This picture ignores the fluid state of the canonical process generally as well as the debates in later rabbinic circles as to the relative importance of various sec-

---

[23] Ibid., 135.

[24] Ibid., 102–3 and see p. 139 for a description of the northern gate in line with the description in the *Temple Scroll* from Qumran, as well as other finds suggesting that 'the sacred precinct was built according to the same sacred precinct of the Jerusalem temple which Josephus describes'.

[25] Smith, *Palestinian Parties*, 69 f.

tions of Tanakh, with the Prophets and Writings existing for the sole purpose of leading people back to the knowledge of the Torah.[26] Indeed other
archaeological evidence in the Samarian region develops this trajectory
further. The remains of Samaritan synagogues as well as domestic and
communal *mikwaoth* at various sites point to developments similar to
those that occurred among Judean Yahweh-worshippers.[27] In addition, literary evidence from Josephus indicates a wider dispersal of Samaritans to
Transjordan (*JA* 13,253–56; *JW* 1,62), as well as to Egypt (*JA* 12,10;
13,74–76). More surprising still in the light of the usual stereotype of a
beleaguered community around Gerizim, is the second-century BCE evidence from the island of Delos, in which we read of 'the Israelites who
make offerings to hallowed (ἱερὸν ἅγιον) Argarizein.'[28]

This evidence points to a profile of the Samaritans as observant, loyal
Yahweh-worshipers who availed of the first political opportunity to build
their own temple. Furthermore, having been spurned for political rather
than religious reasons by their Jerusalem co-religionists, they maintained
their separate religious identity even after their temple was destroyed by
the political leader of the Judeans. The reconstruction faces, however, the
serious objection that, according to Josephus (*JA* 12,257–64), these Yahweh-worshipers were prepared within a very brief period of time to abandon their convictions, appealing directly to Antiochus IV to convert their
worship into that of Zeus, the friend of strangers, and being prepared to
abandon their Sabbath and other observances. This account differs from
that of 2 Macc 6,2, where it is stated that worship of Zeus was imposed on
both Gerizim and Jerusalem by Antiochus Epiphanes. It is only Josephus
who describes them as 'the Sidonians at Shechem,' a description that has
most often been taken to refer to a colony of traders who were present
there as also at Marissa in Idumea. Magen reports the remains of imported
pottery at Tel Balatah, thus supporting the presence of such foreign trad-

---

[26] R. Boid (M. N. Saraf), 'Use, Authority, and Exegesis of Mikra in Samaritan Tradi-
tion,' in *Mikra. Text, Translation, Reading and Interpretation of the Hebrew Bible in
Ancient Judaism and Early Christianity*, ed. Martin Jan Mulder, CRINT 2/1 (Assen: Van
Gorcum; Philadelphia: Fortress Press, 1988) 595–633.

[27] R. Pummer, 'Samaritan Material Remains and Archaeology,' in Crown, *The Samaritans*, 135–77; Y. Magen, 'Qedumim – A Samaritan Site of the Roman-Byzantine
Period,'; 'The Ritual Baths (*miqva'oth*) at Qedumim and the Observance of Ritual Purity
among the Samaritans' and 'Samaritan Synagogues,' in *Early Christianity in Context*,
167–80, 181–92 and 193–230; *J. Zangenberg, *Frühes Christentum in Samarien. Topographische und traditionsgeschichtliche Studien zu den Samarientexten im Johannesevangelium* (Tübingen: Franke Verlag, 1998) 10–57 has the most recent account of the archaeological discoveries in Samaria for the Hellenistic and Roman periods.

[28] A. T. Kraabel, 'New Evidence of the Samaritan Diaspora has been Found on
Delos,' *BA* 47 (1984) 44–46. P. Bruneau, 'Les Israelites de Délos et la Juivrie Délienne,'
Bulletin de correspondance hellénique 106 (1982) 465–504.

ers, whose views need not have been shared by all at Gerizim – anymore than were the views of Jason and his followers shared by all in Jerusalem at the same time. Coggins, on the other hand, once again views the Josephan modifications of 2 Macc as a sign of his Jerusalemite, anti-Samaritan bias, an attitude that he was by no means the first to portray, as can be seen from Sir 50,26, with its reference to 'the foolish people who live in Shechem.' Josephus has earlier indicated that the Samaritans refer to themselves as Sidonians (*JA* 11,344) by way of dissociating themselves from the Jews – a constant ploy of theirs, according to him, when faced with a foreign threat. Thus, Coggins prefers a rhetorical rather than an historical referent to the description, especially in view of the fact that 'Sidonian' is also used as a highly derogatory term already in Is 23,2–3.[29]

Whichever explanation be accepted, it does not seem necessary to abandon the proposal for a revised understanding of the Samaritans as descendants of Yahweh worshipers in the region generally, and not just the successors of the non-Israelite elite from the capital city. Their understanding of Yahwism did not preclude worship outside Jerusalem, but that did not necessarily make them syncretists or any less committed to their Israelite heritage, as their arrogation of the name 'Israelite' makes clear. They may not have accepted the Deuteronomic ideal of the 'Yahweh alone' party in terms of worship only in Jerusalem. Yet they had a Deuteronomic warrant for their choice of sacred site (Dt 27,11–26; cf. 11,29–30). This choice could be discussed by the sages of the Mishnah later (*Sotah* 7,5) without any animosity towards the Samaritans of their own day, unlike the Josephan treatment we have encountered more than once.

This conclusion merely highlights the paradox of the Galilean/Samaritan animosity more forcibly. Far from finding the Gerizim cult centre a threat, Galilean Israelites, as depicted by Horsley, should have been attracted to it, given this revised understanding of its social as well as its religious matrix among the older Samarian village community. Furthermore, the picture that emerges from Shimon Dar's survey of Western Samaria is that of a village, peasant culture, consisting of small, family-sized farms of 5–25 *dunams* (20–100 acres), either freeholdings or leaseholdings. In all probability there was a mixed landowning pattern in Samaria as in Galilee.[30] The presence of more than a thousand field towers dating from the

---

[29] Magen, 'Mount Gerizim and the Samaritans,' 141f.; Coggins, 'The Samaritans in Josephus,' in, *Josephus, Judaism and Christianity*, 265f.

[30] S. Dar, *Landscape and Pattern. An Archaeological Survey of Samaria 800 B.C.E.–636 C.E.* (Oxford: BAR International Series 308 i, 1986) with commentary by S. Applebaum, 'The Settlement Pattern of Western Samaria from Hellenistic to Byzantine Times: A Historical Commentary,' i, 257–69; D. Fiensy, *The Social History of Palestine in the Herodian Period* (Lewiston, NY: The Edwin Mellen Press, 1991) 31–43.

Ptolemaic to the Herodian periods in the area surveyed suggests a more organised pattern of cultivation, and probably indicates a trend towards larger estates. This development was intensified further in the Herodian period as Dar's study of Qarawat bene Hassan and its environs typifies. A large, Herodian-style building has been identified and a number of local place-names still echo the region's Herodian connection. The village consisted of close to 200 family holdings, with individual plots marked off to an area of 2500 acres and an extra 500 acres for pasturage. In all probability the large building served as the residence of the estate manager and other building complexes in the vicinity may have served as granaries.[31] Just east of this site is the modern village of Haris which has been identified as Josephus' Arus, where one of Herod the Great's associates, Ptolemy of Rhodes, owned a village as his private κτῆμα (*JA* 17,189; *JW* 1,473), probably acquired as a grant from the king. In addition we hear that Herod planted six thousand veterans in the territory of Sebaste (*JA* 15,296; *JW* 1,403), presumably in this instance in smaller allotments similar to the foundation at Gaba on the borders of Galilee (*JA* 15,294).

Social conditions for the Samarian peasantry may, if anything, have been worse than for their Galilean counterparts. It should also be remembered that the effects of urbanisation came to Samaria earlier than to Galilee with the presence of the Macedonian colony in the capital from the early Hellenistic age. Herod the Great's establishment of Sebaste at this site continued the trend on a scale that was far greater than Antipas could have attempted with Sepphoris or Tiberias, even when these foundations put further pressure on the traditional Galilean way of life. In these circumstances, common politico-economic as well as socio-cultural factors, together with shared traditional values of a similar provenance, should have made for a coalition of Galileans and Samaritans – at least those who continued to claim legitimation for that way of life from the Israelite memory. It might be hypothesised that the very intensity of the animosity which our sources indicate is due to the fact that, at least in the eyes of the Samaritans, Galileans were being deeply disloyal in not supporting them rather than the Judean/Jerusalem centre, when social and religious experiences might have been presumed to have dictated differently. Such a conclusion sharpens further the focus of our initial question: why did the Galileans turn to Jerusalem? What role did Judea and Jerusalem play in determining relations within this interregional network of Yahweh-worshippers with very different historical experiences? How were the rival claims and their embodiment in competing cultic centres legitimated through appeals to a shared religious story?

---

[31] Dar, *Landscape and Pattern*, 230–54.

Galileans, Samaritans and the *Ioudaioi*

Of all the literary sources from the first century, the Fourth Gospel expresses the competing religious claims of the Samaritans and the Jews most sharply. The Samaritan woman is surprised that Jesus, a Jew, should ask her, a woman of Samaria, for a drink of water. Later she moves from water to worship, declaring: 'our ancestors worshiped on this mountain, but you say that Jerusalem is the place where people must worship.' In reply, Jesus makes the definitive statement: 'salvation is from the Jews' (Jn 4,9.20.22). By contrast, Josephus, despite all his anti-Samaritan bias which we have noted, is not as definitive on the matter. Samaritans may have been disloyal, and they may have had dubious origins, but the Hasmoneans did not require them, unlike the Idumeans and the Itureans, to be circumcised in order to be included in the Jerusalem cultic community; their illegitimate Temple had merely to be destroyed. Whereas the expulsion of Christians from the synagogue may explain the sharpness of the Johannine portrayal, the Jerusalem priest, Josephus, writing *JA* in the nineties at a time when the one centre that mattered for him lay in ruins, seems anxious not to exclude any strand of Jew from the larger family.

For our purposes of attempting to understand the complexity of these tangled relationships of Galileans, Samaritans and *Ioudaioi*, Josephus' account of events in the Jewish community in Egypt during the reign of Ptolemy Philometer (180–145 BCE), is quite significant.[32] Firstly, the ousted Jewish priest, Onias IV, petitioned the king to be allowed to build a temple resembling the one in Jerusalem for his co-religionists, 'because they are ill-disposed to one another, as is also the case with the Egyptians, because of the multitude of their temples and their varying opinions about the forms of worship' (*JA* 13,66). The message is clear: a multiplicity of places of worship creates social upheaval. Whatever the success of Onias' temple in other respects, it was unable to heal the divisions between Egyptian Jews on the issue of the competing temples in the homeland. Jews and Samaritans appear before the king in the very next episode, debating as to whether the offerings should be sent to Jerusalem or Gerizim as the authentic Mosaic shrine (*JA* 13,74; cf. *JA* 12,10). Once again the proponents of Jerusalem win out and the defenders of Gerizim's claims are executed. The same message is delivered: adherence to the Jerusalem temple alone can create national unity; anything else will cause destruction. Nevertheless, in the treatment of the Samaritans in this episode nothing of the bias displayed elsewhere occurs: neither their dubious origins nor their disloy-

---

[32] S. Schwartz, 'The "Judaism" of Samaria and Galilee in Josephus' Version of the Letter of Demetrius I to Jonathan (*Antiquities* 13,48–57),' *HTR* 82 (1989) 377–91, especially 385 f.; Coggins, 'The Samaritans in Josephus,' 263 f.

alty are even mentioned. They, too, are Yahweh-worshipers, following the Mosaic dispensation, but their temple lacks the legitimacy they claim for it. In other respects they are potential *Ioudaioi* (cf. *JA* 11,85–88).[33]

That this was Josephus' view is confirmed by his treatment of the offer by the Seleucid pretender, Demetrius, as reported in 1 Maccabees. In order to win the favour of the Jews in his struggle for power with Alexander Balas, Demetrius offers to cede to Jonathan three border districts in Samaria (1 Macc 10,29–30). Josephus, however, transforms this into an offer of the three toparchies of Samaria, Galilee and Perea, that is, the whole Jewish territory as viewed later in Herodian times and as Josephus himself describes it prior to the great revolt (*JW* 3,35–58). Furthermore, Demetrius is made to declare that 'it shall be the concern of the High Priest that not a single 'Ιουδαῖος shall have a temple to worship other than that at Jerusalem (*JA* 13,50.53). The irony that it was a Jerusalem Jewish leader, John Hyrcanus, not Demetrius, who achieved this goal was surely not lost on Josephus, yet he merely mentions its destruction in passing, unlike his detailed, gloating account of the fall of Samaria itself (*JA* 13,257.281).

In his recent detailed study of Galilee, Horsley consistently translates οἱ 'Ιουδαῖοι as 'the Judeans.' He thus confines its meaning solely to its geographical-political reference of the Judean Temple State, and does not acknowledge its more extended, religious significance in terms of worshiper at the Jerusalem temple, irrespective of one's native district.[34] This restricted understanding then plays a major part in Horsley's treatment of the ongoing opposition between the Galilean Israelites and the Judean Jews in accordance with his conflictual model, based on political-social-economic factors. The remarks of John Ashton with regard to a similar interpretative attempt in respect of the 'Ιουδαῖοι in the Fourth Gospel, seem apposite

---

[33] L. Feldman, 'Josephus' Attitude towards the Samaritans. A Study in Ambivalence,' in L. Feldman, *Studies in Hellenistic Judaism* (Leiden: Brill, 1996) 114–36, acknowledges Josephus' apparent ambivalence, but finds no appreciable difference between the treatment in *JA* and *JW*, despite the former's more strident anti-Samaritanism. In this regard, he claims, Josephus' is not dissimilar to the Rabbinic attitude.

[34] Horsley (*Galilee*, 45 and *passim*) stresses Josephus' use of the term ἔθνος τῶν Γαλιλαίων in support of his theory of a radical separation of Galileans and Judeans in Josephus's mind, so that the former were never fully integrated into the Hasmonean-Judean temple state. Ironically, such a contention does not sit easily with Horsley's desire to see the Galileans as Israelites, since as Feldman has argued, the vast majority of Josephus' uses of the term ἔθνος refer either to the Jewish nation as a whole or to other surrounding peoples who are ethnically not Jews ('Josephus' Attitude Towards the Samaritans,' 117f.). In fact Horsley can slip from Galileans as Israelites to Galileans as Itureans rather easily, since on the one hand he seems to support the idea of forcible Judaisation of Itureans similar to the treatment of the Idumeans, but on the other hand he is anxious to maintain the predominance of the Israelite connection (41f.).

here.[35] A term such as ᾿Ιουδαῖος does indeed continue to retain something of its geographic connotation, even when it is applied to people who no longer live in Judea, or indeed may never have done so themselves. When one speaks of the Poles in Britain or the Irish in America, for example, while their place of origin (or their ancestors) is acknowledged, so it is also affirming that however long the group in question may have lived elsewhere, 'they can still be singled out by the customs they share with the "folks back home."' Furthermore, those customs especially include religious customs, as the examples of the Poles and the Irish testify so well.

Significantly, Josephus himself seems to be aware that ᾿Ιουδαῖος is not just a geographical term: 'This name which they have been called from the time when they went up from Babylon, is derived from the tribe of Judah; as this tribe was the first to come to those parts, both the people themselves and the country have taken their name from it' (*JA* 11,173). Presumably, the processes were slow and by no means uniform whereby this group of returning exiles from Babylon were able to impose their understanding of the national sanctuary, as the struggles with the Samarian Yahweh-worshipers and the Judean *'am ha-'aretz* make clear. Thus, to restrict ᾿Ιουδαῖος to a geographical-political meaning, without attending to the very definite associations of the term with worship in the Jerusalem temple and acceptance of the customs, rituals and practices associated with that worship, is to ignore the powerful impetus that religious belief and practice can give in transcending intolerable social and economic factors, which from a secular post-Marxist perspective may be judged as being thoroughly alienating. While agreeing with Horsley that 'religion' as a discrete and separable aspect of life is a construct of the Enlightenment, in dealing with the ancient world I prefer to speak of religious beliefs and practices, especially Jewish ones, not just as being *embedded* but also as *embodying* the social and economic realities of that culture.[36]

---

[35] J. Ashton, 'The Identity and Function of the ᾿ΙΟΥΔΑΙΟΙ in the Fourth Gospel,' *NovT* 27 (1985) 40–75. *Cf. further the several discussions of S. D. Cohen: 'Crossing the Boundary and Becoming a Jew,' *HTR* 82 (1989) 13–33; ' Religion, Ethnicity and Hellenism in the Emergence of Jewish Identity in Maccabean Palestine,' in *Religion and Religious Practice in the Seleucid Kingdom*, ed. P. Bilde et al. (Aarhus: University Press, 1990) 204–23; ᾿Ιουδαῖος τὸ γένος and Related Expressions in Josephus,' in *Josephus and the History of the Greco-Roman Period*, ed. F. Pavente and J. Sievers (Leiden: Brill, 1994) 22–38; 'Ioudaios: "Judean" and "Jew" in Susanna, First Maccabees and Second Maccabees,' in *Geschichte – Tradition – Reflexion. Festschrift für Martin Hengel zum 70 Geburtstag*, ed. H. Cancik, H. Lichtenberger, P. Schäfer, 3 vols. (Tübingen: J. C. B. Mohr, 1996), vol 1, 211–20. For a discussion of the inscriptional evidence cf. M. Williams, 'The Meaning and Function of *Ioudaios* in Greco-Roman Inscriptions,' *Zeitschrift für Papyrologie und Epigraphik* 116 (1997) 249–62. .

[36] Horsley, *Galilee*, 12, 129 and *passim*. In contrast see J. Neusner, *The Social Study of Judaism. Essays and Reflections*, vol. I, Brown Judaic Studies 160 (Atlanta: Scholars Press, 1988) especially 3–23.

The Samaritans are of course never called ᾿Ιουδαῖοι by Josephus. They also seem to have continued to call themselves Israelites in continuity with the name of the Northern Kingdom. Yet, by the logic of Josephus' own position they could, indeed ought to have been capable of being so designated, if only they had not behaved so obstinately with regard to their place of worship. The actual reality was quite different. Not all inhabitants of Samaria were Yahweh-worshipers and presumably not all Yahweh-worshipers there were of old Israelite stock. They refused, however, to accept the ideology of only one place of worship espoused by the Judeans. The establishment of their own centre of worship on Gerizim gave them a separate social, economic, and religious identity, however, that continued beyond the destruction of their temple. The memory of that act of destruction by a Judean leader ensured that no reconciliation was possible between them and the Judeans – or those who, though geographically not Judeans, still espoused the cause of their temple as ᾿Ιουδαῖοι. This memory also ensured that they could not participate in the struggle for political freedom from the Romans that was inspired by allegiance to the claims of Jerusalem, even when they themselves may have harboured similarly motivated aspirations (*JA* 18,85–89; *JW* 3,307–15). Undoubtedly, interests other than religious ones were operative in these tensions. It was, however, the differences about the proper understanding of the same religious tradition which ultimately gave rise to the emergence of two different political entities, recognition of which had to be made by various imperial ruling powers subsequently. Even when social and cultural patterns within the two communities were very similar indeed, these crystallised differently around the conflicting religious issues and no rapprochement was possible.

This understanding of Samaritan/᾿Ιουδαῖοι tensions already points the way for an adequate explanation of these Samaritan/Galilean tensions mentioned. These were not based on events in the Assyrian period. There is no warrant in the relevant accounts when critically examined and correlated with the archaeological evidence to suggest serious social or religious differences emerging at that time. Rather, the tensions belong to more recent events. It is only with the Hellenistic age and with the Hasmonean expansion in particular that Galilee as such comes into view in the literary sources. Even then Josephus is singularly lacking in information on how the expansion occurred in Galilee, in contrast to his treatment of Samaria and Perea. Is this silence merely because of a lack of sources or a lack of anything of note to report?[37] The hypothesis of enforced Judaisa-

---

[37] Cf. Schwartz, 'The "Judaism" of Samaria and Galilee,' 384, n.17, who suggests that the standard account of the all-conquering Hasmoneans based on Josephus and enshrined in Schürer-Vermes, is in need of revision. In this regard Horsley's search for a

tion of the Itureans has been developed by modern scholars to fill the gap, but without sufficient basis either in the literary or archaeological evidence.[38] Archaeology, not generalised macro-sociological models, will have to answer this question, independently of the literary sources. Quite a lot is at stake ideologically both for the author of 1 Maccabees and for Josephus in their portrayals of the Hasmoneans and their exploits.

The reports of various surveys suggesting a steady increase in settlements in Galilee from the Hellenistic to the Byzantine period point to a more gradual expansion than the model of a sudden, violent take-over based on a military campaign would suggest.[39] Furthermore, as more information on the nature of those settlements emerges, their social role can be more adequately interpreted. The evidence so far available does not support Horsley's claim that the settlements have the nature of military outposts. Even if there is evidence that Gush Halav was fortified, it was on the border with Tyre, as Horsley himself recognises. Its role as a military outpost, if it was such, was therefore more likely to have been defensive against invaders rather than as protection against recalcitrant elements of the older native population. In this regard the absence of the round towers which were such a feature for the same period for western Samaria may be significant in assessing the Galilean situation.[40] In other words, if a colonisation of Galilee is to be posited for this period, is it correct to see it as an

---

more comprehensive category than conversion (*Galilee*, 46–52), is highly significant. However, his conflictual model encompassing resistant Galileans and exploiting Judeans seems to preclude the possibility of genuine inculturation, even though that seems to be the logic of such statements as: 'their shared roots in Israelite traditions provided a basis for the incorporation of Galileans under the Judean temple-state' (51).

[38] Archaeological evidence for the Iturean expansion shows very little signs of either so-called Iturean ware or their characteristic style of habitation in Galilee, similar to those found in the Golan. See M. Hartel, 'Kh. Zemel, 1985/86,' *IEJ* 37 (1987) 270–72 and *Northern Golan Heights: The Archaeological Survey as Source of Local History* (Qatzrin: Israel Department of Antiquities and Museums, 1989) [Hebrew].

[39] M. Aviam, 'Galilee: the Hellenistic to Byzantine Periods,' in *NEAEHL*, ed. E. Stern, 4 vols. (Jerusalem: The Israel Exploration Society, 1993), vol. 2, 452–58.

[40] R. Horsley, 'Archaeology and the Villages of Upper Galilee. A Dialogue with Archaeologists,' *BASOR* 297 (1995) 5–15, especially 7 f., regards Gush Halav as the site of a Hasmonean-Herodian fortress similar to Iotapata and Sepphoris, based on *m. Arak.* 9,6. But see E. Meyers' response: 'An Archaeological Response to a New Testament Scholar,' *ibid.* 17–25. For Iotapata cf. D. Adan-Bayewitz and M. Aviam, 'Iotapata, Josephus and the Siege of 67: Preliminary Report on the 1992–94 seasons,' *JRA* 10 (1997) 131–65, who suggest a considerable expansion of the site down the slopes of the hill and onto the southern plateau in the early Roman period (i.e. late first century BCE/early first century CE). The uncovered structures indicate domestic and light industrial usage. This would suggest that irrespective of the character of the original site it should not be described as a 'fortress' in the Roman period, even though the enlarged city had fortifications also, like several comparable sites in Roman Galilee.

imposition on an older, resistant native population giving rise to internal hostilities and the need for defensive arrangements for the new arrivals? What would the archaeological remains of such a process look like? In fact, the pattern of such Hellenistic-style colonisation going back to Alexander was one of encouragement to inculturate with the older population through inter-marriage, adoption of local language, customs and the like. Even the Herodians appear to have respected local sensibilities. Herod the Great's subsequent establishment of a colony of veterans at Gaba in the great plain and of Babylonian Jews in Batanea took the form, not of military outposts, but of village settlements, comprised of small landowners – in all probability not dissimilar in layout to Qarawat bene Hassan, but as far as we can tell, without the field towers.

Unlike his treatment of the Samaritans, Josephus can call the inhabitants of Galilee 'Ιουδαῖοι, even though his most frequent designation is Γαλιλαῖοι. Important for the argument here is *JW* 2,232, the episode in which the Samaritans attacked the Galilean pilgrims on their way to Jerusalem: 'a Galilean, one of a large company of 'Ιουδαῖοι on their way up to the festival, was murdered.'[41] This is precisely the extended meaning already discussed: Galileans, insofar as they share in the customs – especially relating to worship in the single temple in Jerusalem – are naturally designated 'Ιουδαῖοι. Similarly, during another festival, it is reported that people from Galilee, Idumea, Jericho and Perea were gathered in Jerusalem, together with a great multitude from Judea itself (αὐτῶν τε 'Ιουδαίων πλῆθος). A bitter confrontation arose between these and the Roman troops. As Josephus relates the ensuing battle, he speaks simply of οἱ 'Ιουδαῖοι, assuming that all who had gathered from regions other than Judea could still be designated 'Ιουδαῖοι since they shared common assumptions about the Temple and its sacredness (*JA* 17,254–58).

Several scholars have attempted to give a special meaning to the use of Γαλιλαῖος in *Life*, effectively identifying it with the alleged Zealot party opposed to Roman rule. The term is used virtually devoid of any geographical connotations, except insofar as the Galileans in particular were regarded as violently anti-Roman.[42] This stereotype of the Galileans is due to Josephus' description of the people he was sent to command, as part of his self-glorification in *JW* (cf. 3,41 f.). Furthermore, the use of the term *zealot* to cover all shades of Jewish nationalism in the first century CE is

---

[41] The significance of this juxtaposition of Γαλιλαίων and 'Ιουδαίων seems to have been missed or overlooked by Horsley (*Galilee*, 146). While the account in *JA* 20,118 ff. diverges at several points from that of *JW*, nevertheless, it clearly assumes that Galileans can call on 'Ιουδαῖοι for their support in vindicating the murder of their kinsmen.

[42] Cf. 'The Galileans in the Light of Josephus' *Life*,' above 27 ff.; L. Feldman, 'The Term "Galileans" in Josephus,' in *Studies in Hellenistic Judaism*, 111–13.

no longer admissible. Yet, a case can be made for a very special use of the term Γαλιλαῖος in *Life,* namely to refer to the mainly village people who, Josephus claims, supported him against his local rivals for the command of Galilee, notably John of Gischala and Justus of Tiberias.[43] Several times they are designated as being ἀπὸ τῆς χώρας 'from the land,' to distinguish them from the urban elites. This can also be interpreted in terms of urban-rural tensions in the region in the wake of growing Herodian urbanisation.[44] What cannot be doubted is that at least from Josephus' point of view these Galileans are Ἰουδαῖοι in the sense discussed here. This is true even when this epithet is used to represent the strictly observant residents of Tarichaeae who insisted on the refugee, pagan noblemen being circumcised before they could be allowed to stay among them (*Life* 112–13).

The evidence that suggests that this picture of a Jewish Galilee is more than just Josephan rhetorical propaganda will not be re-examined here, though of course it is that also. Suffice it to say I see no reason to change my overall views about a Jewish Galilee from at least the Early Roman Period, despite Horsley's critique. One of the reasons Horsley does not find any literary evidence to support my contention of Galilean pilgrims in Jerusalem may be that he virtually excludes the gospels as sources for reconstructing Galilean life in the period, even though they may well be our best literary evidence for Jewish practices in the first century, despite all their well-established *Tendenzen.*[45] Such a view appears to be supported by the results of the present enquiry, namely, that first-century Galilean Israelites seem to be missing at those very times and places where they would be expected to show up, while Galilean Jews have left very clear traces of their presence in the archaeological as well as the literary evidence.

---

[43] G. Jossa, 'Chi sono I Galilei nella *Vita* di Flavio Giuseppe?' *Rivista Biblica* 31 (1983) 329–39, while essentially agreeing with my conclusion that Josephus uses the term Γαλιλαῖος for his own supporters in Galilee, wants to extend its range to the citizens of the major towns also. The opposition, in his view is not between urban and rural, but between traditionalists (Shammaites and Zealots) and *neoteristai,* that is, those who were prepared to compromise the ancestral customs for the Greek way. However, there is no basis in the *Life* for characterising the vast majority of Galileans in this way.

[44] S. Freyne, 'Urban-Rural Relations in First Century Galilee. Some Suggestions from the Literary Sources,' and 'Herodian Economics in Galilee. Searching for a Suitable Model,' above pp. 45 ff. and 86 ff. respectively.

[45] Horsley, *Galilee. History, Politics, People,* 144–47. See his remarks on the use of the gospels (14). As M. Goodman has suggested (personal communication), there is no great evidence for pilgrimage on a grand scale prior to Herod the Great. It may be that Herod encouraged pilgrims from the Diaspora as well as the homeland for economic reasons, in view of the vast expenditure involved in extending the Temple Mount and refurbishing the Temple itself. In any case, not simply the gospels but also Josephus attests to the Galileans making the pilgrimage in the first century CE.

7. Hanina Ben Dosa, A Galilean Charismatic

The 'rediscovery' of Hanina ben Dosa by Geza Vermes may not have had the same repercussions in the study of Second Temple Judaism and early Christianity as those other discoveries of our times have had, in the elucidation of which Professor Vermes has played a notable part. Nevertheless, by drawing attention to this little known 'Galilean saint' the question of the immediate context of the ministry of Jesus of Nazareth and his social role within Galilean life have been raised in a new and provocative manner.[1] In this present essay I do not intend to address myself directly to Vermes' thesis as this has been set out in his book *Jesus the Jew* (1973). Instead I wish to suggest an alternative approach to the evaluation of the Hanina traditions on which the argument of that study is based. In brief we shall be less concerned with finding data in the Hanina traditions which parallel those of Jesus, and more interested in discovering the role those traditions played in Jewish life and faith during the Tannaitic and Amoraic periods. The reasons for this rather different focus will emerge as we proceed, though it is possible to state at the outset that it seems to be the only valid option, given the nature of the material to be examined. If Bultmann and many other New Testament scholars after him have had 'to make virtue out of necessity' and abandon the detailed quest for the historical Jesus, even a fleeting glance at the Hanina traditions must convince us that this applies with even greater force in his case.[2]

---

[1] Two articles by Professor Vermes, 'Hanina ben Dosa. A Controversial Galilean Saint from the First Century of the Christian Era,' *JJS* 23 (1972) 28–50 and *JJS* 24 (1973) 51–64 (hereafter 'Hanina ben Dosa I,' and 'Hanina ben Dosa II,') formed the essential background for his book *Jesus the Jew. A Historian's Reading of the Gospels* (London: Collins, 1973). *Subsequently, Professor Vermes has published two further books, *Jesus and the World of Judaism* (London: SCM Press, 1983) and *The Religion of Jesus the Jew* (London: SCM Press, 1993). Both works, but particularly the latter, explore the understanding of Jesus' Jewish religious experience on the basis of the earlier study of the charismatic typology. However, this general approach to the historical Jesus has been criticised on the basis that the evidence does not permit a description of his inner consciousness and experience. Cf. further 'Jesus and the Urban Culture of Galilee,' below pp. 183 ff., where the approach to Jesus is through his public socio-religious stance in the particular conditions of the Galilean ministry.

[2] See W. Scott Green, 'What's in a Name? – The Problematic of Rabbinic "Biography",' in *Approaches to Ancient Judaism: Theory and Practice*, ed. W. Scott Green, Brown Judaic Series 1 (Missoula: Scholars Press, 1978) 77–96. The concluding sentence summarises a position shared by many scholars adopting Jacob Neusner's approach to

Fortunately, this scepticism does not make our task a negative one from the outset. We do have Hanina traditions, and Vermes' study of them, though at times lacking the methodological rigor of the Neusner school, has, nevertheless, been extremely helpful in isolating and classifying the relevant data. Accordingly, even if the historical Hanina lies shrouded in the mists of rabbinical polemics and legendary accretions, the discovery of the different tendencies in the traditions about him has much to tell about the role of the חסיד hasid and/or charismatic miracle worker within the developing Judaism of the period. In this way our study may make some contribution to the overall theme of ideal types in ancient Judaism, since types can be literary as well as historical and play a real social role. This is true especially when we are dealing with literature that has been developed within and is addressed to the live concerns of a believing community.

The Hasid and the Man of Deed: Defining a Role

Before examining the Hanina traditions it will be useful to attempt to define his functional identity as the sources themselves present it. Though he is consistently called Rabbi and his disciples (תלמידים thalmidim) are mentioned once at t. Ber. 3,20, it seems very improbable that Hanina ever functioned as a Rabbi in the restricted sense of propounder of halachic teaching – the normal meaning of the title after 70 CE. This does not rule out its use in an honorific though more general sense in the earlier period, but we shall do well to prescind from such a possibility in attempting to discover Hanina's role and function, at least initially.[3]

The most characteristic designation in our sources for Hanina is 'man of deed' (איש מעשה 'ish ma'aseh), and it is assumed by many that this is equivalent to hasid. In fact Hanina is described by this latter term only twice, and both ascriptions are late,[4] whereas at m. Sota 9,15, as a 'man of

---

the study of Rabbinic sources: 'The basic problematic of rabbinic "biography" is not the recovery of the life or mind of a given master, but the study of how and if his traditions change and develop across documents and through time' (90). See below, notes 20 and 21 for Neusner's own position.

[3] Vermes, *Jesus the Jew*, 111–21, has attempted to establish that *mar(i)*, 'lord' ('my lord,' but without any suggestion of a personal relationship) was the more usual designation for a Palestinian miracle-worker, and that when *mar(i)* and *rabbi* are used in close conjunction, the former is always the more honorific. However, the linguistic evidence he adduces is mostly much later Babylonian evidence, which does not inspire confidence with regard to pre–70 CE Galilean usage. Cf. J. Fitzmyer, *A Wandering Aramaean. Collected Aramaic Essays* (Missoula: Scholars Press, 1979), especially 115–42, for the Semitic background to the title κύριος, where he takes issue with Vermes at several points.

[4] At y. Sota 23b his name is accidentally added to the list of *hasidim* of m. Sota 9,15, even though the distinction of the Mishnah verse is retained at 24c of the same Talmud. *ARN*a ch. 8 also lists him as one of the חסידים הראשונים *hasidim ha-ri'shonim*, but this is a late development (cf. below, note 34).

deed', he is explicitly differentiated from the *hasidim*. Even when a close relationship between these two terms is assumed there is no consensus on the precise meaning of the former expression – miracle-worker or performer of deeds, conforming to certain norms of piety. Thus, at the outset some terminological clarity seems called for, if we are to evaluate correctly the traditions ascribed to Hanina in the name of both designations.

In his desire to differentiate between the *hasidim* and the Essenes, A. Büchler argued that the expression 'man of deed' applied to Hanina at *m. Sota* 9,15 (and parallels) does not involve miracle working. By insisting that the term *ma'aseh* refers to deeds of loving kindness and the like, Büchler saw Hanina as a man of practical action whose piety expressed itself in activity rather than in study of the Torah.[5] At the same time he recognised that the tradition distinguished Hanina from the *hasidim*, citing *t. Sota* 15,5 (and parallels) which places Hanina among the ranks of the *'anshe ma'aseh* and Aba Jose ben Ketonith among those of the *hasidim*.[6] More recently S. Safrai has also argued that 'man of deed' refers to somebody engaged in works of a philanthropic nature rather than miracle working. In doing so he equates 'men of deeds' with *hasidim*, to whom he ascribes a special halakhah that distinguished them from being merely strict observers of general rabbinic teaching.[7] In support of his identification Safrai cites *m. Suk* 5,4: 'the *hasidim* and the men of action used to dance before them', referring to the festal dance for the pilgrims mentioned at Dt 16,14f. The commentaries on this notice are more explicit, giving the chants of the various groups without clearly distinguishing between them, and it is on this that Safrai bases his case for the identification.[8] However,

---

[5] A. Büchler, *Types of Jewish Palestinian Piety from 70 B.C.E.–70 C.E. The Ancient Pious Man* (London: Jewish College Publications, no. 8, London 1922) 81–96.

[6] *Types*, 100 n.1, where he points out that because the ancient pious man's attitude towards prayer (cf. *m. Ber.* 5,1) is illustrated at *t. Ber.* 3,20 and *y. Ber.* 9a by an example of Hanina (whereas the parallel baraita, *b. Ber.* 32b attributes the attitude to an *hasid*), the identification of Hanina as a *hasid* was accepted by such scholars of his day as Weiss and Kohler. It would seem that this is now true of Vermes also who repeatedly uses the term for Hanina throughout the articles and in his book. For a similar phenomenon in the tradition regarding Honi, cf. below, note 15.

[7] S. Safrai, 'Teaching of the Pietists in Mishnaic Literature,' *JJS* 16 (1965) 15–31, especially 18 f. and 25 ff., where such expressions as *misnat hasidim* (*ARN*a ch. 27) and *megillath hasidim* (*y. Ber.* and *ARN*b ch. 26) are examined.

[8] Safrai, 'Teaching,' 16 f., note 11, interprets 'men of action' and 'penitents' in *t. Suk* 5,2; *y. Suk* 55b as two subgroups of the *hasidim*, each with its own chant. Büchler, *Types*, 79 f. had also noted the parallels, but pointed to *b. Suk* 53a where *hasidim* and 'men of deed' are identified by attributing only one chant to both groups. Even if we accept Safrai's interpretation of the two former passages (it is also possible that they are sub-groups of both the main categories, *hasidim* and 'men of deed'), it seems clear from

this turns out to be a rather tenuous argument, since apart from the obscurity in the passages in question, it was a general tendency in Graeco-Roman religious circles of late antiquity to identify roles that were originally quite separate.[9] Consequently, it would be a methodologically unsound procedure to read such later identification back on to earlier levels of the tradition in this case also, especially since, as we shall presently suggest, there are good reasons for keeping them separate.

In his treatment of Hanina, Vermes rejects both Büchler's and Safrai's position and points instead to the overwhelming weight of the tradition which regards Hanina primarily, 'not as a social worker or promoter of public welfare . . . but as the most celebrated miracle-worker in Rabbinic Judaism.' However, Vermes then assumes that Hanina is also a *hasid*, and throughout his articles there are frequent allusions to Hanina's hasidic piety.[10] Recently, this assumption has been seriously challenged by Dennis Berman who points to the methodological weakness of adopting the most outstanding feature of the tradition about one individual, namely Hanina's miracle-working capacity, and using this as the criterion for what constitutes a *hasid*.[11] Berman presents considerable evidence to suggest that the primary traditions about *hasidim* and *hasidut* point consistently in a different direction, namely of the *hasid* as 'the ideal of the active life, distinguished by his radicalism, spiritual fervour and zeal for the law.'[12]

It must be admitted, as Berman does, that individuals can play several different roles, and later tradition suggests that there was nothing inherently incompatible between the *hasid*, understood in the sense just defined, and the miracle-worker in Judaism. This observation causes no great surprise in light of the general trend in late antiquity already referred to, of producing a synthetic figure that is at once philosopher, sage and thaumaturge. Nevertheless, we cannot assume that the lines between these types were always blurred, especially in Judaism, as recent studies of the *theios aner* figure make clear. In the Hellenistic world generally it was the heroes of moral virtue from the philosophical schools, not the popular miracle

---

the *b. Suk* reference that there is a development in the tradition, whereby two groups, originally separate, came to be gradually identified. Our investigations will hopefully confirm that this is a general tendency.

[9] Cf. the studies cited in notes 13 and 15 below.

[10] 'Hanina ben Dosa, I,' 48, 50 and 'Hanina ben Dosa, II,' 54.

[11] D. Berman, *'Hasidim* in Rabbinic Tradition,' in *SBLASP*, ed. P. Achtemeier, 2 vols. (Missoula: Scholars Press, 1979), vol. 2, 15–33, here 17. This article is based on his doctoral dissertation, which, unfortunately, I have not been able to consult. His copious notes give ample and convincing evidence from the primary sources of the positions he has espoused, although it is not clear from this summary what critical stance he has adopted towards the rabbinic sources in terms of historical reconstruction.

[12] 'Hasidim,' 20.

workers, that formed the most clearly defined stream of traditions about the divine man.[13] Thus, in Judaism, Hellenistic Jewish writers generally downplayed the miraculous elements in their presentation of the heroes of the past, stressing rather their moral and exemplary attributes.[14] Undoubtedly the emphasis varied with the different levels of society, and in approaching the traditions about Hanina we shall do well to distinguish at least in theory between those which portray him as *hasid* and those which stress his miracle-working activity.

This working hypothesis receives considerable support from a recent study of the Honi traditions, which Vermes has also appealed to as a further example of his Galilean *hasid*-type.[15] At *m. Ta'an.* 3,8 a rain-making miracle is attributed to Honi, whereas in the 'parallel account, *t. Ta'an.* 2,13, the same miracle is attributed to an *hasid*. Naturally the tendency has been to conflate the two versions and regard Honi as another example of the *hasid*-type. However, a detailed examination of the structure of the two accounts shows that the latter is not a simple abridgement of the former, but a deliberate adaptation in which the *hasid*'s prayer is answered directly, and is not the result of a magico-superstitious act.[16] Furthermore, any suggestion of lack of trust in the Lord of the Heavens by praying for the rains to cease is removed in the Tosefta version by an allusion to the promise of Gn 9,11 that Yahweh would never again bring a flood upon the earth. We are justified then in seeing here a miracle story with magical elements being deliberately toned down and made to conform to the con-

---

[13] D. L. Tiede, *The Charismatic Figure as Miracle Worker*, SBLDS 1 (Missoula: Scholars Press, 1972) has a detailed discussion of the relevant data, both from the Hellenistic and the Jewish-Hellenistic spheres. Cf. 98–100 and 238–40 for useful summaries.

[14] Carl H. Holladay, *Theios Aner in Hellenistic Judaism*, SBLDS 40 (Missoula: Scholars Press, 1977) has carried forward the research of Tiede (previous note) focusing in particular on Hellenistic Judaism. For summaries of findings relevant to the present point cf. 100–102; 194–98; 231 f.; 234 f.

[15] In his articles Vermes does not stress the Honi material, making only a passing reference when dealing with the rain-miracle which he has in common with Hanina, and a brief reference to a charismatic type to which Jesus, Honi and Hanina belong, and of which Elijah is the prototype, opposed to rabbinic orthodoxy in the first-century Judaism ('Hanina ben Dosa, I,' 40 and 'Hanina ben Dosa, II,' 54 f.). This last point is developed more fully in *Jesus the Jew*, 69–72, 80–81, 90, 94, where all three figures are seen to be opposed to rabbinic orthodoxy in first-century Judaism. On p. 72 the possibility of Honi being a Galilean is raised but the evidence is too tenuous for any argument to be developed. Yet to suggest the possibility could be misleading. For a detailed discussion of the Honi traditions, but with sharper critical focus cf. W. Scott Green, 'Palestinian Holy Men: Charismatic Leadership and Rabbinic Tradition,' in *ANRW* II, *Principat*, 19, 2, ed. H. Temporini and W. Haase (Berlin and New York: Walter de Gruyter, 1979) 619–47.

[16] Green, 'Palestinian Holy Men,' especially 634 f. with indications concerning the magical nature of the circle and the intimacy with God in the account.

ventions of hasidic piety.[17] There is at least an a priori probability that the Hanina traditions have been adapted in a similar fashion, and that is what we must determine in our next section.

The Hanina Traditions: A Re-Examination

Basing himself on three references to Hanina in the Mishnah Vermes conveniently distributes the traditions under three headings: i) the healer (*m. Ber.* 5,5); ii) the miracle worker (*m. Sota* 9,15); and iii) the teacher (*m. 'Abot* 3,9–10). To these he adds a fourth category, 'Hanina's praises', which consists of references to the great man in exegetical and later Amoraic writings.[18] The distribution, though convenient, is of course artificial, and could even be misleading. Categories i) and ii) are closely related at least formally (cf. sub-section (i) below), and besides the distribution gives no clue as to the relative amount of material in the different categories. Thus category iii) has only a few general sayings and some exegetical comments that scarcely merit the epithet 'teacher' for their author without a good deal of what can only be described as biographic license. In fact this principle of arrangement can easily lead to treating the material as potentially biographical, a trap Vermes falls into only too often in his apparent desire to establish good parallels between the historical Jesus and the historical Hanina. This is unfortunate, since the historicising tendency vitiates what is otherwise a most able analysis from a form-critical point of view of the Hanina traditions that are preserved in our literary sources.

A more nuanced methodology for the application of form-critical insights to these traditions is that pioneered by Jacob Neusner and successfully demonstrated by a number of his students.[19] As mentioned in the in-

---

[17] Green, 'Palestinian Holy Men,' 631 f., for a synoptic comparison of the two versions of the miracle.

[18] 'Hanina ben Dosa, I,' 28 f.

[19] For a statement of his evolving methodology in regard to the use of rabbinic texts for historical reconstruction. cf. J. Neusner, *Method and Meaning in Ancient Judaism*, Brown Judaic Series 10 (Missoula: Scholars Press, 1979) especially 41–58, For the application of the methodology in question by several of Neusner's students, cf. W. Scott Green, ed., *Persons and Institutions in Early Rabbinic Judaism*, Brown Judaic Studies 3 (Missoula: Scholars Press, 1977). *In the interim since this note was written in 1981, Jacob Neusner's output has been little short of phenomenal, not just in quantity, but in the quality of his sustained concern to develop a critical methodology for the proper study of the Rabbinic corpus. My sense of his present position is that, having completed his detailed analysis of the various discrete elements of that corpus as independent literary works and having described the Judaisms which they embody, his attention has reverted to more historical concerns of the social and religious circumstances of the late antique world in which these documents must be understood and which they themselves mirror.

troduction, this approach is not burdened by the impossible task of determining how the traditions relate to the historical person, and so can concentrate on what they have to say to the situation to which they are addressed in their present form. After isolating and classifying the units of
tradition the goal is to tabulate the available data in terms of the sources in
which they occur, recognising at the same time their nature as legal, exegetical or anecdotal. In this way it is possible to recognise where the pre-
ponderances in the tradition lie, at what stratum of the tradition they occur
and which types of material are either scantily represented or not at all at
various levels. It is thus possible to establish a more reliable trajectory of
the tradition as a whole. The hermeneutical task is to attempt to explain
this in terms of the known concerns of Tannaitic and Amoraic times. Vermes is not the type of Talmudic historiographer so roundly castigated by
Neusner. He is well aware of the methodology here outlined, as his remark
about the absence of Hanina material in the Palestinian Talmud (hence-
forth PT) being a pointer to Galilean Jewish-Christian concerns of a later
age, makes clear.[20] However, his search for the 'historical' Hanina has not
allowed him to carry out his whole investigation along similar lines. What
follows is an attempt to suggest how this might be accomplished.

(i) The Miracle Story Tradition

The largest single body of items associated with Hanina falls under the
category of what can loosely be described as miracle stories. On closer inspection a number of different tendencies can be detected in these stories
in the different sources and it is on these aspects of the tradition that we
must focus our attention. Vermes attempts to distinguish two levels in this
material. First there are 'the healing stories' which he regards as containing the earliest traditions, and then 'the miracle stories' which he terms
'mostly later elaborations.'[21] One ground for this distinction is apparently
the fact that the former are allegedly found in both Talmuds whereas with
one exception the latter are found only in the Babylonian Talmud (hence-
forth BT). However, there are two reasons for seeing this classification as
unsatisfactory. In the first place two stories which Vermes puts in his sec-

---

[20] 'Hanina ben Dosa, II,' 64. On examination, only one story, the cure of Gamaliel's
son, *b. Ber.* 34b has any close formal or thematic similarity to the Jesus stories, and PT
does have a version of that particular episode, while none of the stories of Vermes' second category has any close resemblance to gospel records, yet all are missing from PT.

[21] 'Hanina ben Dosa I,' 29–46; cf. in particular 39. Language does not seem to play
any important role in his methodology since he can accept either the Hebrew or the Aramaic section of different stories as more original with only passing reference to its significance for their dating. Cf. e.g., 40 and 42.

ond category belong formally with those of his first grouping in that they all reflect Hanina's powers of prayer. Secondly, in both his categories, and not just the second one, there is a scarcity of this type of material in PT, something we must seek to explain in a more convincing way than does Vermes, who suggests that it may be due to embarrassment among Palestinian Jews because of its similarity with the gospel stories about Jesus.[22]

It seems that a more satisfactory classification of the material could be suggested taking account of each item's tendencies while also acknowledging that not all the items to be attributed to any one class necessarily come from the same level of the tradition. Table one attempts to lay out this distribution more clearly. A number of general features stand out in our table and should be noted. Of the eighteen items listed, twelve are found in BT, whereas only three are in PT. Even more significant is the fact that of these three items in PT, one illustrates Hanina's concentration in reciting one of the official prayers of Judaism, the Tefillah,[23] and a second is used to illustrate his meticulous attitudes towards tithing. This story is particularly significant in that PT also tells of Hanina's scrupulous observance of the Sabbath commencement (*y. Ber.* 7c). The third item is a parallel to BT's account of the cure of Gamaliel's son. However, PT's version of it significantly omits any mention of the fluidity of Hanina's prayer, which is the centre of the BT story, highlighting instead his personal gift of intimacy with the divine will through prayer. In short, PT shows no interest in Hanina's miraculous activity. When it does include any material that can be so classified, it is for reasons that have nothing to do with extolling Hanina's miracle-working capacity.

In the following table,

* Denotes parallel account in other source

( ) Denotes parallel account in same source

---

[22] Cf. above note 20.

[23] One detects a concern with the story in PT when compared with the Tosefta version. In the former his disciples ask a question which allows Hanina to disclaim any heroism in his act of praying, since he did not even feel the snake. Another comment suggests that it was his speed in getting to the water first, not any special power, that killed the snake. There follows what Vermes calls 'a compensating re-assertion of the miraculous,' which explains that Hanina was able to outdistance the snake through a special gift from the Almighty ('Hanina ben Dosa, I,' 35 f.). By contrast the BT version has no such problems with the story.

Table One: The Deeds of Hanina

	M./T.	BT	PT	Later Sources
1. Nature of Hanina's prayer	(i) *m. Ber.* 5,5			
2. Miracles illustrating the power of prayer		*(i) *b. Ber.* 34b (Gamaliel's son) (ii) *b. Ber.* 34b (Johanan's son) (iii) *b. B. Qam.* 50a (*b. Yeb* 121b (Nehuniah's daughter) (iv) *b. Ta'an.* 24b (Rain Miracle) (v) *b. Ta'an.* 25a (Golden Table Leg	(i) *y. Ber.* 7d	
3. Miracle displaying attitude at prayer (cf. *m. Ber.* 5,1)	*(i) *t. Ber.* 3,20 (Snake dies while he prays Tefillah)		*(i) *y. Ber.* 7a	
4. Miracle illustrating Halachic attitude re. tithing (cf. *y. Ber.* 7c on his scrupulosity re. The Sabbath)			(i) *y. Dem* 22a (Heavenly warning about untithed food	(ii) *ARNa* ch. 8 (Hanina's donkey refuses untithed food and returns home)

	M./T.	BT	PT	Later Sources
5. Miracles of a Thaumatur-gic Nature		*(i) *b. Ber.* 33a (Snake killed) (ii) *b. Ta'an.* 25a (Ikku's House) (iii) *b. Ta'an.* 25a (Sabbath lamp) (iv) *b. Ta'an.* 25a (Hanina's goats) (v) *b. Ta'an.* 24a-25b (Sabbath bread) (vi) *b. Ta'an.* 25a (Neighbour's hens) (vii) *b. Pesah.* 112b (demoness Agrath)		

The material in BT is fairly evenly distributed between items that illustrate Hanina's powers of prayer and what we have called thaumaturgic reports. In view of our contention that 'man of deed' was the earliest designation for him in relation to his miracle-working capacity it comes as some surprise to find no such item reported in the Mishnah and only one in the Tosefta. Vermes overcomes this difficulty by claiming that the BT *baraitot* represent earlier strands of the tradition, which the saying about Hanina's prayer being fluid on his lips (*m. Ber.* 5,5) presupposes rather than evokes.[24] This may well be so, but even then it would appear that not all the stories about his prayer in these *baraitot* reflect the same stage of development. Thus in 2(iii) there is no explicit mention of Hanina praying at all, but simply of his threefold exit and entrance and the final assurance 'she has now come out', referring to Nehuniah's daughter who had fallen into a pit. In 2(i) it is explicitly stated that he withdrew and prayed, and on being questioned as to the source of his knowledge of the cure he makes his statement about prayer being fluent on his lips which is the statement cited in *m. Ber.* 5,5 also. In 2(ii) on the other hand Hanina actually prays in the presence of the petitioner (in this case R. Johanan ben Zakkai) and his prayer is heard. In 2(iv) we are given a sample of Hanina's prayer to the Lord of the Universe, recalling the story of Honi's rain-making prayer at *m. Ta'an.* 3,8, but lacking any of the quasi-magical elements of that account such as the swearing of an oath and the making of the circle.[25] Instead, the Hanina story is simple and performed in favour of the miracle worker himself, at least in the first instance. An appended comment by

---

[24] 'Hanina ben Dosa, I,' 30 f.
[25] Cf. above note 15.

Rav Yoseph rather ironically contrasts Hanina's powers with those of the official high priest in time of drought. Thus the Hanina rain-making story belongs to a later theological stratum when, as we shall see, the person of Hanina is being developed theologically. Finally 2(v) appears to be a further legendary development in which Hanina uses his praying powers in a rather cavalier way to satisfy the whims of a nagging wife.

Attempting to suggest a history of the development of this set of stories is obviously a hazardous undertaking, Yet it does seem that the differences noted between (i), (ii) and (iii) (which fall in Vermes' first category) are substantial and cannot all be treated as early or authentic in the same way. It seems safe to suggest that a constant underlying recollection is that of Hanina's reputation for powerful prayer of a mysterious nature which at least in the first instance 2(iii) suggests intimate knowledge of the divine action rather than miraculous powers which he himself possessed. The continuation of this story with the query 'Are you a prophet?' and Hanina's denial with the words of Amos (Am 7,14) links the end of the story to 2(i), where the same words are repeated. The recollection of Amos, the country prophet opposed to the official priesthood of Bethel, is scarcely unintentional. It seems to suggest that Hanina's powers were regarded as a threat to the established religion, something that is clearly spelled out in the remark appended to the later rain-making miracle 2(iv): 'what is the use of the high priests' prayer against that of Hanina ben Dosa?' – the irony of which, one suspects, the Babylonian tradent rather approved.

The tensions between the country 'prophet' and the temple establishment may well be a genuine pre–70 recollection of the tradition, however, especially in view of its more explicit expression in the Honi story, and the likelihood that Nehuniah in the Hanina story 2(iii) was a temple official.[26] What is interesting, however, is that Hanina is also juxtaposed to two rabbinic figures, Gamaliel and Johanan ben Zakkai, both of whose children are cured through his prayer. Abstracting from any biographical information that these stories might be thought to contain and focusing rather on their functional intention, it seems that they reflect a conscious coming together of both strands of Jewish life, the institutional and the charismatic. Gamaliel sent a message to Hanina who does not hesitate to use his powers on behalf of the Jerusalem-based sage, or more probably, his grandson who became head of the Jamnia school. He in turn acknowledged the source of Hanina's power.[27] The Johanan story has Hanina as

---

[26] A certain Nehuniah, with the same occupation as that of the principal in the story is mentioned at *m. Shek* 5,1 in a list of temple officials.

[27] The problem of the identity of Gamaliel is related to the dating of Hanina's career. Vermes opts for the pre–70 period, and consequently favours Gamaliel the elder, but points out that the tradition would normally have used *ha-zaken*, not *rabban* in that case

one of the famous Rabbi's pupils yet acknowledged to have closer intimacy with the Almighty than his master. Nor is the impression changed by the ending where Johanan's chagrin at his wife's taunt is reported and he compares himself and Hanina's relations to God as those of a prince and servant before the king.[28] In other words, while both stories, especially the latter, reflect a certain uneasiness in the relationship between the figure of Hanina and the Rabbis, they both serve to smooth out the relationship rather than to accentuate differences. This insight will be of particular importance in our next section when we shall attempt to situate the development of the tradition in the context of Palestinian religious life.

Turning finally to the material we have grouped under row 5 in our table as thaumaturgic reports, we can note first of all that apart from 5(i), they all occur in the tractate *Ta'anit* of BT. Though we are not necessarily suggesting that this material originated in Babylonia, it is still noteworthy that there was a special interest in collecting and preserving it there. We must examine the data with an eye for possible tendencies that could help in locating the special interest in this aspect of Hanina's career. Already 5(i) may point the way since it seems to be another version of the story found in 4(i) in the Tosefta and PT about Hanina's concentration at prayer in illustration of the ancient hasidic attitude as described at *m. Ber.* 5,1. However, BT omits any mention of prayer in its version, concentrating simply on Hanina's powers which make him immune to the snake's bite even when he exposes his heel to him. Hanina in contravention of the purity laws takes the snake's carcass to the school house and delivers a moralising lesson on the theme of sin, based on Gn 3 – a theme that is also reflected in his sayings (*m. 'Abot* 3,9–10) and was popular among the early *hasidim*. Noteworthy is the fact that this version shows no interest in the prayer of Hanina, as does Tosefta and PT where he is the model of official piety – the recitation of the Tefillah – and the BT version shows no concern with his ignoring of the purity laws.[29] Rather, he has a school of piety

---

('Hanina ben Dosa, II,' 59 f.). While not denying the probability of a pre–70 career for Hanina, the approach to the story here suggested, which abstracts from the biographical issue, strongly suggests R. Gamaliel II, R. Johanan's successor at Jamnia as the more likely candidate.

[28] The question of Johanan's wife and his response could well be a later addition to the story, using the theme of the nagging wife, to make the theologically relevant point that though beholden to the charismatic the Rabbi was his superior. For the possible date of such concerns see below section III.

[29] Cf. *b. Hul.* 127a, based on Lv 11,29. The question of the *hasidim* ignoring the ritual purity laws as elaborated by the later Rabbis, has been noted both by Vermes, 'Hanina ben Dosa, I,' 36 f., and Safrai, 'Teachings,' 25 f., 36, but the former does not develop the point in terms of the history of the tradition, and the latter attempts to minimise the problem even though he cites (24) *b. Shab* 121b which states that 'the spirit of the sages is

whose concerns are those of the *hasidim ha-ri'shonim*.[30] We are justified then in seeing here a relatively early story, yet its interest for the Babylonian tradent may be explained, partially at least, by 5(iv), the story about Hanina's goats, ownership of which is also in direct contravention of the prescriptions of the *haburot* in Palestine according to *m. Dem* 2,3. A highly legendary story about goats being turned into bears is used to raise the question of Hanina's non-observance of such regulations and no satisfactory answer is given. The explicit introduction of this issue appears to reflect the עם הארץ \ חברים *'am ha-'aretz / haberim* debates of second-century Galilee of the Ushan period, which never had the same intensity in Babylonia as in Palestine itself, and where the attitudes towards the *'am ha-'aretz* were considerably softened from the third century onwards.[31]

Is Hanina then being regarded as an example of *'am ha-'aretz* attitudes in this collection of *baraitot*? Stories 5(iii) and 5(v) (sabbath lamp and sabbath bread) touch on subjects that could be of concern to the strict observant of the prescriptions of the *haberim*, especially since, as noted, item 3(i) explicitly uses a miracle story for this purpose and also refers to his careful observance of the beginning of the sabbath (*y. Ber.* 7c). Yet in fact neither story is developed in that direction by BT but rather his miraculous

---

not edified by them' (i.e. those *hasidim* who did not kill snakes or scorpions on the Sabbath). Cf. succeeding note and below Section III.

[30] The precise meaning of this expression is debated, though Safrai is probably correct in applying it to certain figures of the immediate pre–70 period, rather than to the time of the Hasmoneans on the basis of the parallel expression 'the first sages' (*t. Yad* 2,16), meaning those of the immediately previous generation. ('Teaching,' 20, cf. also Büchler, *Types*, 78 f., note 2). These earlier pious men, whom the later tradition still remembered, do appear to have had a distinctive set of teachings: *m. Ber.* 5,1 (prayer attitudes); *t. Ned.* 1,1 (anxiety regarding sin offerings, as the expression '*asam hasidim*', *t. Ker* 4,4, suggests); *Sem.* 12,5 (precedence for funerals over weddings); *t. B. Qam.* 2,6 (care in regard to damaging another); *b. Nid. 38a.b.* (avoidance of sexual intercourse on Sabbath); *b. Menah. 41a* (care with the fringes of their garments). On the basis of this and other evidence (above note 8) Safrai holds for a special group with its own distinctive halakhah, which is best preserved at *m. Ber.* 5. However, as Berman, 'Hasidim in Rabbinic Tradition,' 18, points out, there is nothing either in the name or the details to suggest an organized group of pietists from the earlier period, though he does suggest the names of Bava ben Buti and Yose ben Yoezer from the 1st and 2nd Centuries BCE as examples. In this regard such passages as *m. 'Abot* 5,10–14, which praise the attitudes of the *hasidim*, can be seen as a further example of this older material, which we find reflected in the Hanina sayings of the same tractate. Note that *b. B. Qam.* 30a suggests to a later generation that anyone wishing to implement the piety of the *hasidim* should follow 'the ethics of the fathers' or alternatively the tractate on 'blessings'.

[31] A. Oppenheimer, *The 'Am ha-'aretz. A Study of the Social History of the Jewish People in the Hellenistic-Roman Period* (Leiden, Brill: 1977) especially 113 f.; R. Meyer, 'Der 'Am ha-'ares. Ein Beitrag zur Religionssoziologie Palästinas in ersten und zweiten Jahrhundert,' *Judaica* 5 (1947) 169–99, especially 196 f.

powers are transferred to his daughter and his wife. This miraculous power is also portrayed in the story of Ikku's house that is joined together merely by his word, 5(ii), but the later concluding remark of Pelimo, while wishing to authenticate the remarkable miracle, attributes it to Hanina's prayer.[32] This addition might seem to run counter to the point made earlier about BT showing no interest in Hanina's prayer in the snake story. However, in that instance it was a question of his praying the official Tefillah prayer as distinct from his own highly charismatic 'fluid' form. Consequently, if we are to see in Pelimo's intervention a local Galilean interest in Hanina's miracle (as Vermes thinks[33]), we can recognise that in the second century there was still a lively memory of his independent miracle-working activity in the province. Rabbinic orthodoxy had been forced to deal with this activity in the way suggested earlier in our consideration of the function of the Johanan and Gamaliel stories, but it was not able to suppress this memory entirely.

The fact that Hanina's miracle-working activity is also reflected in Amoraic tradition in BT shows that a lively interest was maintained in this aspect of his life. When we examine these two pieces of evidence, 5(vi) and (vii), we see that they appear to retain the concerns of the *baraitot* already examined. Thus 5(vi), the story of how Hanina miraculously happened to own goats, is introduced as a direct answer to one of the objections raised against him at the end of the previous story in *b. Ber.* 25a, 5(iv), which we have called 'Hanina's goats' – the goats were not acquired but miraculously produced from a neighbour's hens. On the other hand, story 5(vii), *b. Pesah.* 112b, has Hanina abroad at night in further contravention of a rabbinic prescription, a trend we saw in stories 5(i) and (iv) also, and which was queried but now answered in the latter instance. However, this aspect of his action causes no concern in story 5(vii). Instead, it is his power of curtailing the demons that is stressed. Hanina and his teaching have received a heavenly commendation according to Agrath, the princess of demons. He in turn calls on the esteem that has been granted to him in heaven to curtail her influence in the world. While Vermes deals with this story in treating of Hanina's praises, logically it belongs rather to the miracle story tradition which highlights his powers for different pur-

---

[32] Vermes, 'Hanina ben Dosa, I,' 40, accepts that the comment of Pelimo verifying the miracle and attributing it to Hanina's prayer was part of the original story. Yet the fact that the narrative of the incident is in Aramaic and the two comments appended to it (one being that of Pelimo) are in Hebrew would strongly suggest two different stages of the tradition of the story – an original unit of a decidedly thaumaturgic nature, and a subsequent rehabilitation of the story in terms of Hanina's power of prayer.

[33] 'Hanina ben Dosa, I,' 41.

poses. It is the final stage of the development of the Hanina tradition, and we shall discuss its significance in section three below.[34]

(ii) Sayings and Exegetical Material

As already mentioned, the amount of sayings attributed to Hanina in the tradition is minimal and despite the ascription to him of the title Rabbi, the absence of any legal rulings in his name must be decisive. He never was considered to have been a teacher and this observation could cast doubts on the authenticity of even those few sayings that do appear in his name. Certainly the distribution of the material in two very different strata of the tradition – Mishnah and the late Midrash, *Pirqe de R. Eliezer* – as well as their very different form and inspiration does not engender confidence that we are dealing with tradition that has played a significant part in the formation of the Hanina legend, despite Vermes' high valuation of its autobiographical value.[35]

There are two features of the later tradition of the Hanina sayings from *m. 'Abot* that are pointers to their place in the tradition. Firstly in *Aboth de R. Nathan* Ch. 56, the first two of the sayings are combined with some sayings of Johanan ben Zakkai, the latter serving as a critical comment on the former. Whereas Hanina had extolled fear of sin and deeds over wisdom Johanan compared wisdom and fear of sin to a craftsman and his tools: the latter are useless if the necessary knowledge is lacking. Since there is no evidence of the tradition that made Hanina a pupil of Johanan in the passage we can only assume that this editorial activity was a conscious effort to downplay the particular kind of piety espoused in the Hanina sayings which, when taken in isolation, are tantamount to a rejection of the piety of the *thalmide hakhamin*.[36] Further support for this conclusion

---

[34] The story of Hanina's donkey miraculously returning 4(ii) is clearly a legendary development, which reflects a trend similar to that of stories 5 (iii) and (v) where his miraculous powers are extended to his daughter and wife. However, we have placed this story in category 4 since it clearly reflects the desire to make Hanina a *hasid* par excellence, and he is compared to Abraham as one of the 'first *hasidim*', in that both their animals showed a meticulous observance of rabbinic law about idols and tithes, as an extension of their owners attitudes. The designation of Hanina as 'first *hasid*' is not then the same as that outlined in note 30 above, since in this instance he is an example of the piety of the sages, not that which was distinctive of the pre–70 pious men, and the expression is probably prompted because of the comparison with Abraham.

[35] In 'Hanina ben Dosa I,' 48, he writes: 'Taken together the three sayings define religion as inspired by gentle devotion and kindness towards one's fellows. As in the stories, he appears not as an austere ascetic, but as a warm-hearted lover of men, a true *hasid*'. Again: 'if the first three . . . sayings are accepted as genuine they echo not only the voice of a remarkable personality living in first century Palestine . . .' (50).

[36] On the anxiety of the Jamnia period concerning the role and importance of study, see Oppenheimer, *The 'Am ha-'aretz*, 97–106.

can be found already in the famous saying of Hillel recorded at *m. 'Abot* 2,6 which declared that no unlearned person could be sin-fearing, nor a member of the *'am ha-'aretz a hasid*.[37] Hanina and Hillel are made to espouse two different approaches to piety and the former puts action before study, something that was unacceptable to the sages at all times and positively resisted by them in the Jamnia period. It is perhaps a measure of the popularity of Hanina and his lifestyle that the greatest sage of the period, Johanan ben Zakkai, is introduced to counteract his position. We have seen a similar linking of the two men in the miracle-story tradition, and we shall have reason to posit below the Ushan period as the more likely time for that particular rapprochement. In the sayings material on the other hand we appear to be in the early Jamnia situation when Hanina has not been as yet transformed into the *hasid* he was later to become, for example in the miracle stories of PT.

A second feature of the transmission of the Hanina sayings points in a similar direction. The third logion attributed to him at *m. 'Abot* 3,10 is combined with his sayings about prayer being fluid on his lips (*m. Ber.* 5,5), and they are both attributed to R. Akiba at *t. Ber.* 3,3. Vermes notes this transfer, but because he has already committed himself on the authenticity of Hanina's sayings he is content to comment that 'there was a danger that his teaching would be taken over by more famous Rabbis.'[38] The question surely is why this should be the case. Our contention in regard to the processes at work in regard to the two logia of *m. 'Abot* 3,9 would seem to apply here also. This third logion attributed to Akiba does not have the works/wisdom opposition of the earlier ones but equates dealings with one's fellow man and one's relation with God. Consequently, this saying is acceptable to Jamnia piety and could be ascribed to one of the great figures of the later period, whereas the issue of the earlier statements was hotly debated. In this regard a *baraita* that appears in a number of different sources is illuminating, telling of a debate at Lydda as to whether

---

[37] Oppenheimer, *The 'Am ha-'aretz*, 103–5, argues against attributing this saying to the first century Hillel and instead ascribes it to R. Hillel, a third century Amora. Apart from some textual evidence from the MSS, one of his main arguments is the fact that the contents of the saying are not very appropriate for Hillel the elder since according to the tradition he was a sage, not a 'first *hasid*' or 'a man of deed'. However, this argument is not at all conclusive should it be considered that Hillel is being made the proponent of what constitutes a *hasid*, for the purposes of the Jamnia generation. Thus Oppenheimer's second objection, namely that the *'am ha-'aretz* is being condemned not for failing to be a *thalmid hakhamim* but rather a *hasid*, is unimportant, since *hasid* and *hakham* have been identified in the person of Hillel, the most famous sage of the pre–70 period. The expression at Jn 7,49, 'this people who know not the law are accursed,' seems to support the early expression of the sentiments in question.

[38] 'Hanina ben Dosa I,' 49.

study or deed was more important. R. Tarfon declared himself in favour of the former and R. Akiba for the latter, but after some discussion they all agreed that study was the more important since it leads to the practice of deeds (*b. Qidd* 40b; *Cant R.* 2,14; *Sifre Dt* 41,71b; *y. Hag* I, 76c).

It would seem then that we can detect an uneasiness in the Jamnia period with the piety that had been espoused by or was attributed to Hanina. Various attempts were made to counteract the latent tendencies of such views. The exegetical material attributed to Hanina in *Pirqe de R. Eliezer* shows no such concerns on the other hand. Indeed the fact that exegetical material can be attributed to him so readily shows how far his rabbinisation had progressed. In Ch. 31 the figure of the ram from the Aqedah story is allegorically interpreted, with different parts being made to apply to rites and persons that were sacred in later Israel: the Day of Atonement sacrifice, David's lyre, Elijah, the giving of the law on Mt Sinai, the advent of the coming age. Vermes recognises that the linking of the Aqedah story with the rites of the Day of Atonement was late,[39] but in fact the whole passage is a clear reflection of the development whereby the merit of the sacrifice was transferred from Abraham to Isaac and then to the ram that was sacrificed in Isaac's place, whose ashes thereby became sacred.[40] This development is to be found in the later Midrashim, and consequently all the passage can tell us is the continued vitality of the Hanina image once had had been accepted within the rabbinic fold.

(iii) In Praise of Hanina

The data that Vermes assembles under this heading are found at three different strata in our sources, and are set out in table two below. Our table clearly shows that the praise of Hanina was developed particularly among the Babylonian *Amoraim*. This corresponds with the pattern seen also in the miracle stories, since even though we ascribed these at first to the *baraitot* of BT rather than to the *Amoraim*, they clearly continued to have relevance in that period also, and we did see two Amoraic stories about Hanina from the later period. However, our table also shows that Hanina's greatness was positively affirmed earlier, so that the later development can be seen as a natural outgrowth of such recognition.

---

[39] 'Hanina ben Dosa I,' 50, note 68.

[40] E. E. Urbach, *The Sages. Their Concepts and Beliefs*, 2 vols. (Jerusalem: Magnes Press, 1975) I, 500–504, and II, nn. 87 and 88.

Table Two: In Praise of Hanina

	M./T.	BT	PT	Anoraim
1. Man of Deeds	*(i) *m. Sota* 9,15 / *t. Sota* 15,5	*(i) *b. Sota* 49b	*(i) *y. Sota* 24c	
2. Man of Truth				(i) *Mek. R. Ish- mael* Ex 18,21
3. *Bath Qol*		(i) *b. Ta'an.* 24b (*b. Ber.* 17b; *b. Hul.* 86a)		
4. His generation favoured in Hea- ven because of him		(i) *b. Hag* 14a (*b. Pesah.* 112b)		
5. World to Come Created for him		(i) *b. Ber.* 61b (*b. Ber.* 17b; *b. Ta'an.* 24b		

We have already discussed the significance of the attribution 'man of deed' to Hanina and its possible significance. Here we are more concerned with what its place in the tradition can tell us about later concerns. The statement 'when R. Hanina died, men of deeds ceased', occurs in a list of famous rabbinic personalities from the Jamnia and Ushan periods that follows a set pattern: 'when R. X died, virtue Y ceased.' In its present form the list appears to be a late compilation since R. Judah the prince (c. 200 CE) is included, though it is possible that additions have been made to an earlier list.[41] If we were correct earlier in arguing that 'man of deed' should be differentiated from *hasid*, and that in regard to Hanina the tendency was to assimilate the two roles, then the retention of the epithet in this list might appear to create difficulty. However, this objection is not as telling as appears at first sight, since the expression 'man of deed' was capable of a quite acceptable interpretation in terms of the performance of pious acts, provided these originated in and were inspired by the study of the Torah. Besides, the fact that even PT retains some miracles of Hanina shows that there was no objection in principle to the miracle-worker, once

---

[41] J. Neusner, *Development of a Legend. Studies on the Traditions of Yohanan ben Zakkai*, 2nd ed. (Leiden: Brill, 1970) 51.

he could be portrayed not in opposition to but as an observant of rabbinic halakhah and his miracles could be seen to aid him towards this end.

The expression 'man of truth' is applied to Hanina in the *Mekilta* commentary to Ex 18,21 in the course of a discussion of the qualities that Moses would require from those to be appointed judges and helpers in the land of Israel. As the whole context makes clear there were differences of opinion on such questions among the Jamnia rabbis as a result of the loss of confidence in all the national institutions in the wake of the Roman conquest. The appearance of Hanina's name in such a discussion is a clear indication of how thoroughly acceptable he had become. Yet in view of the underlying concerns of the debate, it would be rash to attempt to complete this description with other expressions of hasidic piety such as Vermes attempts as part of his composite picture of the historical Hanina.[42] R. Eleazar of Modi'im who introduces Hanina as an example of a man of truth goes on to require that the appointees be not only free from economic stress but that they also be 'such as occupy themselves with the study of the Torah.' Clearly the moral attributes of the judge in this picture are not based on hasidic piety of detachment, as Vermes would have it, but rather are inspired by such passages as *m. Meg.* 1,3, where we read of 'men of leisure' who occupy important places in the community because of their wealth, and consequently would be ideally suited as judges since they have no need to accept bribes.[43] In addition however, they must be men who study the Torah, and since the traditional picture of Hanina was that of a poor man, this can only mean that in R. Eleazar's eyes he is indeed a *thalmid hakhamim* par excellence. It is in this sense that he is 'a man of truth.' Thus we see once again how his picture has been thoroughly transformed in the wake of the Jamnia reorganisation, and this passage reflects the end of the development we were able to uncover at an earlier stage when discussing his sayings.

The remaining passages in praise of Hanina are to be attributed to the Amoraic period according to Vermes.[44] He is the recipient of a *bath qol* which declares that the whole world is sustained on his behalf, 3(i); his generation is favoured in heaven because of him 3(ii) and the world to come was made on his account, 3(iii). All three statements reflect a conscious theologising of the person of Hanina, similar to that of the miracle stories of BT, especially those from the Amoraic period. Thus 3(i), the gift of the heavenly voice is a reassurance of his 'cosmic' role, despite his hu-

---

[42] 'Hanina ben Dosa II,' 51 f.

[43] Cf. G. Alon, *Jews, Judaism and the Classical World* (Jerusalem: The Magnes Press, 1977), 'Those Appointed for Money,' 374–435, especially 391–93; Oppenheimer, *The 'Am ha-'aretz*, 107.

[44] 'Hanina ben Dosa, II,' 52–55.

mility, and 3(ii) simply applies that understanding to his own generation, as for example in the rain-making miracle (2(iv) in table one above). In the final statement the doctrine of the two worlds is introduced: the world to come has been made on behalf of Hanina as against the present evil age which belongs to Ahab, who was, significantly, Elijah's adversary. Story 4(vii) already intimated that Hanina had some control even over the present age because of his being especially favoured in heaven. Vermes sees the figure of Elijah behind these praises, to whom many different end-time functions were attributed in later Rabbinic sources.[45] This is altogether probable in view of the earlier miracle-story tradition, which shows traces of being deliberately styled on the Elijah cycle of 1 Kgs.[46]

The reasons for this development must be attributed to the Babylonian context of the Amoraic period within which it took place. The social role of the Rabbi had become extremely elevated to the point that various kinds of supernatural powers were attributed to him because of his superior knowledge of the Torah.[47] In Hanina's case, though his rabbinisation had been progressively developing, it had never been completely carried through to the point that halachic teaching could be attributed to him. His assimilation to and gradual identification with the hasidic strand at an earlier period was not able to remove completely those traces of independence, even to the point of betraying characteristics of the *'am ha-'aretz*, that had become associated with his name in Palestinian circles, and which PT had attempted to counteract.[48] However, if Hanina could not be attributed supernatural powers for the same reasons as the Rabbis, there was still enough material at hand from earlier strata of the tradition to ensure that he could be endowed with Elijah-like qualities. The *bath qol* was not accepted unreservedly in Rabbinic circles,[49] yet for the Babylonian Amo-

---

[45] 'Hanina ben Dosa, II,' 54. Cf. J. Jeremias' article Ἡλίας *TDNT* 2, 928–41.

[46] Compare in particular the praying posture – head between the knees – story 2(iv) above, and 1 Kgs 18,42.

[47] J. Neusner, *A History of the Jews in Babylonia*, 5 vols. (Leiden: Brill, 1968–70) vol. IV, 297–402.

[48] BT does not accept all the Hanina material unreservedly either. Vermes has pointed out at least two instances where a fourth century Babylonian Amora, R. Aha, attempts to counteract Hanina's miracle working-activity. In the PT account of the cure of Gamaliel's son he interjects that Hanina was praying the eighteen benedictions; and at *b. B. Qam.* 50a (the account of the rescue of Nehuniah's daughter) he rather ungraciously remarks: 'all the same she died anyhow'. In the same story the girl attributes her deliverance to the ram of Aqedah. Clearly not everyone in Babylonia and Palestine was happy with the Hanina stories.

[49] Urbach, *The Sages*, 118 f. Cf. *b. Pesah.* 114a: 'we pay no heed to a heavenly voice'; *b. Yeb* 102a: 'if Elijah were to come and say . . . he would not be listened to.' Contrast *b. B. Qam.* 59b: 'Thereupon a heavenly voice came forth and said: 'why do you dispute with R. Eliezer (himself not an uncontroversial figure) for the halakhah accords with his view in all matters'.

raim, to whom we are indebted for preserving, if not actually creating, most of the Hanina traditions, it was the high point of their acclamation of this figure from the distant past. He had come to them through the filter of the *hasid*-figure, but this had not been able to obliterate all traces of another and independent persona.

The Hanina Traditions in the Context of History

This account of the development of the Hanina traditions and their concerns suggests a rather different trajectory to that of Vermes. It remains to examine this within the history of Palestinian, and more specifically Galilean developments of the first three centuries CE. Should the stages we have suggested on tradition-critical grounds correspond with what can be known from a wider perspective about the religious ethos within which the development took place, there would be significant corroboration of the analysis conducted. Perhaps more significantly for our present purposes such a correspondence could suggest the way in which Judaism perceived such types as the charismatic 'man of deed' and the *hasid* within the changing character of its own orthodoxy.[50]

We have made no attempt to date the historical Hanina, though the pre–70 period suggested by both Vermes and Neusner does seem to be a more plausible context for his activity as a man of deed.[51] Recent theoretical discussions from sociological and anthropological perspectives have focused

---

[50] *B. Bokser, 'Wonder-Working and the Rabbinic Tradition: the Case of Hanina ben Dosa,' *JSJ* 16 (1985) 42–92, initiates a fresh study of the Hanina traditions, confirming at several points the analysis of this study. However, drawing on the work of Peter Brown and others, he extends the discussion significantly in terms of general trends in late antique piety, pointing out that what was at stake was not just the issue of authority between charismatic and institutional religion, but also the question of attitudes towards the way in which the divine manifests itself, and the need for Jews to stress a type of piety that was available to all, particularly in the wake of the destruction of the temple. These considerations help to explain more precisely the differences between the Tannaitic and Amoraic sources on the one hand and likewise the differing emphases between the Babylonian and Palestinian Talmuds in their handling of the Hanina materials. Cf. further, G. Anderson, *Sage, Saint and Sophist. Holy Men and their Associates in the Early Roman Empire* (London and New York: Routledge, 1994).

[51] ' Hanina ben Dosa II,' 59f. based essentially on the circumstantial evidence that all significant traditions presuppose that he belonged to the pre–70 temple period, something that is reflected in the late account of stones for the temple also, *Qoh R.* 1,1. Cf. also Neusner, *A Life of Rabban Johanan ben Zakkai*, 47, who dates Johanan's sojourn in Galilee to the years 20–40 CE, which would also mean that Hanina belonged to that epoch, should there be some historical basis for the tradition that links the two men.

on the relational rather than the personal aspects of the charismatic's role, that is, as both embodying and evoking the desires and aspirations of those attracted by his ministry.[52] We have no evidence that Hanina evoked a response from a particular group of intimate followers, or that he engaged in a wandering charismatic healing ministry, like Jesus of Nazareth and his followers. Consequently, we cannot postulate for Hanina the same social role as that suggested by G. Theissen and others in recent discussions of the Jesus movement and its milieu.[53] Given the apocalyptic tenor of almost all Jewish groupings in the immediate pre–70 period it is unlikely that Hanina's deeds could have been perceived as anything other than the signs of the new age that all eagerly awaited.[54] Yet in the absence of any significant evidence[55] we cannot attribute to Hanina ideas of gathering together the community of the end-time such as the Jesus movement and the Essenes, for example, claimed for themselves. We shall consequently have to look for another niche for him and his deeds within Galilean life of the time. Fortunately, one seems ready to hand.

Galilee's rejection of, or at least lack of involvement with the halakhah of the Pharisaic sages of the pre–70 era can be readily documented from the New Testament as well as from Josephus and Rabbinic sources. In all probability Johanan ben Zakkai's apparently unsuccessful visit to the province was to conduct a scribal mission similar to those we hear about at Mk 3,22; 7,1, as well as from Josephus' *Life* (192–98). It has sometimes been suggested that the province was the seed-bed of apocalyptic beliefs, and consequently many assume that the Zealot movement found its ideological base within the social conditions prevalent there prior to the revolt of 66 CE. In a recent study of Galilee in Second Temple times I have attempted to show the unfounded nature of these generalised assumptions, and to suggest instead a peasant ethos where life was lived close to the land in the scattered hamlets by small landowners, tenant farmers and

---

[52] J. Gager, *Kingdom and Community. The Social World of Early Christianity* (Englewood Cliffs: Prentice Hall, 1975) 28 f., citing the studies of P. Worsley, *The Trumpet Shall Sound. A Study of "Cargo" Cults in Melanesia* (New York: Schocken, 1968); and K. L. Burridge *New Heaven, New Earth* (Oxford: Blackwell, 1969).

[53] G. Theissen, *The Sociology of Palestinian Christianity* (Philadelphia: Fortress Press, 1977).

[54] Thus H. Clark Kee, *Community of the New Age. Studies in Mark's Gospel* (Philadelphia: Westminster Press, 1977) 79–87, stresses that apocalyptic reassurance rather than miracle stories of divine men is the correct conceptual framework within which the gospel stories should be understood.

[55] When Hanina is accredited with followers, as at *y. Ber.* 7a (*thalmidim*) and *Mekilta de R. Ishmael*, Ex 18,21 (*haberim*), they appear in contexts where his rabbinisation is clearly reflected and so the followers are also couched in rabbinic categories as the terminology suggests. Most of the stories presuppose no such associations, however.

share-croppers.[56] Nothing typifies the overall mood better than Josephus'
report about the peasants of the Gischala region being anxious for peace
because of the arrival of the harvest, when faced with the possibility of
confronting the Roman army in the end-time apocalyptic struggle (*JW*
4,84). Yet there was a genuine attachment to the Jerusalem temple as can
be seen from the loyalty to the pilgrimage and even the tithing system, despite the fact that Pharisaic halakhah in these matters was not always rig-
orously adhered to.[57] In these circumstances of what may justifiably be described as a 'pilgrimage religion', the Pharisaic movement that was de-
signed to bridge the gap between the temple and the everyday, but particularly adapted to meet the needs of townspeople rather than the rural population,[58] was likely to have little appeal in rural Galilee.[59] Consequently,
the 'man of deed' had a definite religious function of bringing the power
and presence associated with the temple into the lives and needs of country
people. In this regard the casting of Hanina in the figure of the northern
prophet Elijah, but in his role of charismatic healer and rain-maker rather
than that of eschatological bringer of salvation, has a very definite social
setting and is likely to be the earliest stratum of the tradition. The world of
the Hanina stories has a rural and peasant ring about it – inquisitive or in-
credulous neighbours, the need for rain and sun with the changing seasons,
trespassing goats and wandering donkeys and hens. Even though the stories as transmitted are demonstrably addressed to later concerns, there can
be little doubt that behind them lies a Galilean figure of some stature
among his contemporaries because he fulfilled a real need in their lives.[60]

---

[56] Cf. S. Freyne, *Galilee from Alexander the Great to Hadrian. A Study of Second
Temple Judaism* (Wilmington: Glazier; University of Notre Dame Press, 1980; reprint,
Edinburgh: T. & T. Clark, 1998), 194–200 on the peasant society and 208–47 on the
revolutionary ethos.

[57] Freyne, *Galilee from Alexander the Great to Hadrian*, 275–93.

[58] While disagreeing with some aspects of his presentation, I am indebted to E.
Rivkin, 'The Internal City: Judaism and Urbanisation,' *Journal for the Scientific Study of
Religion* 5 (1966) 225–40 for this profile of the social significance of the Pharisaic
movement. Cf. *Galilee from Alexander the Great to Hadrian*, 335, n. 2.

[59] *Cf. however, 'Archaeology and the Historical Jesus,' below pp. 160 ff. where the
evidence for the Jewishness of Galilee is discussed in the light of more recent archaeological evidence from such centres as Sepphoris, Iotapata and Gamala.

[60] J. Z. Smith, 'The Magician and the Temple' in *God's Christ and His Bible. Studies
in Honour of Nils Alstrup Dahl*, ed. W. Meeks and J. Jervell (Bergen: Universitetsvorlaget, 1977) 233–47, especially 237 f. Cf. also C. Geertz, 'Religion as a Cultural System'
in *Anthropological Approaches to the Study of Religion*, ed. M. Banton, ASA Monograph
Series 3 (London: Tavistock, 1966) 1–46, especially 24–34, on the need to bridge the gap
between the moods engendered by the cult and everyday life if the symbol system is to
remain vital for the lives of people. This would apply *a fortiori* to the Galilean situation
where the pilgrimage created a very special cultic situation that was altogether different
from the usual conditions of life.

It is important to recognise that in the social role we are positing for Hanina he was not in opposition to the temple, but rather an extension of its symbolic function for the lives of rural people. However, the balance was a fine one, and any ostentatious display of independence over against the cultic authorities could easily have been fatal to his future within the tradition.[61] We have suggested an early assimilation of the 'man of deed' and the *hasid*, as reflected in the sayings from *m. 'Abot*. This process may have been accentuated by the desire to smooth out the tensions we detected in the earlier strata of the miracle stories between country charismatic and temple officials. The sayings attributed to Hanina, especially the concern about fear of sin, are closely related to the sentiments of those who later came to be called the *hasidim ha-ri'shonim*, even though the single attribution of that epithet to Hanina showed other interests.[62] The first *hasidim* were particularly devoted to bringing sin-offerings to the temple according to several relatively early traditions,[63] and so the assimilation of Hanina the 'man of deed' with this display of temple piety strongly suggests a desire to show him totally in tune with the temple religion and its sphere of influence. Thus we can posit the combination to a pre–70 date with some confidence.

We have also seen that the corrective, if not the implied criticism of the Hanina sayings made in the name of R. Johanan ben Zakkai, as well as the contrast with the piety espoused in the name of Hillel, betrayed some early concern with the piety being espoused in the name of Hanina. It is highly probable that this type of corrective in which the person of Hanina has not yet been totally transformed into the *hasid* belongs to the early Jamnia period. No doubt the process continued in a more positive vein, so that Hanina, as a student of Torah becomes the 'man of truth', who would be to-

---

[61] It is interesting in this regard to contrast the figure of Honi, whose much more daring activity is seen in the account of his rain-making miracle *m. Ta'an.* 3,8, and who is openly criticized by a leading Pharisaic sage, Simeon ben Shetah, at an early stage of the tradition. (Cf. Green, 'Palestinian Holy Men,' 636 f.). The fact that already Josephus had a story of his violent end (*JA* 14,22–25) suggests that Honi may well have posed a much greater threat to 'the establishment' of his day, and it could well be that this is reflected in the later traditions about him, both in their relative scarcity by comparison with Hanina, and in their more conscious and deliberate rabbinisation (cf. e.g., *b. Ta'an.* 23, and Green, art. cit., 641–46). By contrast the criticism of Hanina is more subtle, allowing further for stories that betray '*am ha-'aretz* tendencies. It is by transforming him into a *hasid* following the norms of rabbinic piety, and not the outstanding teacher of his day that the process of his acceptance is effected.

[62] Above note 32.

[63] Büchler, *Types*, 73–78. Cf. especially *t. Ned.* 1,1: R. Jehudah (*b. Ilai*) says: 'The ancient pious men desired to bring a sin-offering, because God did not bring an offence into their hands.'

tally acceptable as judge in Israel. From what we know of the circumstance of the time it is possible to suggest a very plausible reason why the
figure of Hanina night have received special attention in the Jamnia period. He was a Galilean from a province that had not been noted for its interest in the Pharisaic scribes of the pre–70 period, and now their heirs and
successors were making fresh efforts to win the region over to their own
halachic point of view.[64] One way of achieving this was to transform a representative of their rural piety into a faithful student of the sages and, in
his recitation of the Tefillah, the model of the piety of the synagogue,
which now had replaced the temple as the holy place within Jewish life.[65]

After the failure of the Bar Cochba revolt the Jamnia rabbis were forced
to move to Usha in Galilee. We then hear of an invitation from their leaders to the elders of Galilee to come and teach if they had previously
learned Torah, or alternatively, to come now and learn (*Cant R.* 2,5). This
suggests a conciliatory approach, but it also indicates that there were many
different views still operating in Galilee. The way of Torah of the Jamnia
sages had not been totally successful. Several of the tendencies we uncovered in our discussion of the Hanina traditions would appear to address
the circumstances now operative. The miracle stories that present Hanina
performing favours on behalf of the two outstanding Rabbis of the Jamnia
period clearly reflect a desire for a genuine rapprochement, with the initiative coming from the rabbinical side. At the same time we saw two rather
different uses of the Hanina traditions represented in the *baraitot* of PT
and BT, the former using them to indicate care with the tithing laws,
whereas the latter has a number of stories which show no such concerns,
appearing in fact to ignore deliberately certain rabbinic prescriptions about
the purity laws. Without agreeing with the thesis of A. Büchler, there
seems little doubt that the Ushan period witnessed an intensification of the
problems concerning the *haberim* and the *'am ha-'aretz*, as is clear from
the debates of R. Meir and R. Judah on this issue.[66] It is to these discussions that we must attribute the stories in question. The interesting feature
here is that Hanina is being used on both sides of the debate: he is both the
model of the *hasid* who has become *haber*, and he is the champion of an
independent piety that refused to succumb to rabbinic pressure.

---

[64] Freyne, *Galilee from Alexander the Great to Hadrian,* 323–29.

[65] Synagogue worship was a real concern of the early Jamnia period. Cf. J. Neusner
'Studies in the *Taqqanoth* of Yavneh,' HTR 63 (1970) 183–98. These concerns were also
reflected in Galilee as we learn from *m. Ta'an.* 2,5; *b. Ta'an.* 16a; *b. Ros Has* 27a.

[66] A. Büchler, *Der Galiläische 'am ha-'aretz des Zweiten Jahrhunderts* (reprint, Hildesheim: G. Olms, 1968). For a discussion and critique of his thesis, cf. Oppenheimer
The 'Am ha-'aretz, and Freyne, *Galilee from Alexander the Great to Hadrian,* 305–09.

This use of the Hanina traditions on both sides of an intense, sometimes bitter debate is a measure of the stature he had acquired as a Galilean who had first come to prominence as a 'man of deed', but who had become a propaganda figure in the struggle to impose a definite religious point of view on his native province a century and a half later. This helps to explain the final stage of the development in which his person can be invested with all the praise that rabbinic orthodoxy bestowed on figures it most admired because they had been made the bearers of a piety that was in conformity with its own ideals. Those stories which at an earlier stage may have been used against those very ideals lost some of their polemical significance in the changed climate of later centuries, especially in Babylonia. Hanina's powers as a 'man of deed' are now no longer any threat to the way of the Torah, but rather can function as its validation and support within the larger synthesis of which they are a small but significant part.

A Charismatic Type?

This study has focussed on the development of the Hanina traditions and has attempted to situate them within the developing history of rabbinic Judaism. A final question reverts to a point made at the beginning of this paper, namely, to what extent Hanina in his charismatic activity as a 'man of deed' can be regarded as a type of Jewish piety in the period. To establish the existence of a well-defined type, it would be necessary to discover over a period of time and through changing circumstances a number of individuals whose lives had been cast in a similar mould because they had been perceived to be similar, and whose social roles could be clearly distinguished, even in the popular mind from other related types whose activity had evoked its own kind of response at different levels of society.

Vermes has argued for the inclusion of Jesus, Hanina and Honi in the one type, and regards the figure of Elijah as providing the necessary prototype by means of which the lives and activities of the three men in question were perceived. Other names could be added to this list, such as R. Phineas ben Yair (*y. Dem.* 22a) or Jacob the *min* from Kefar Sekaniah (*t. Hul.* 2,22–24). Insofar as they engaged in a charismatic healing activity the disciples of Jesus might also be included, as well as the unnamed exorcist of Mk 9,38 f. These examples would range from the first century BCE to the second century CE. However, when all the material that might conceivably be included in the production of a suitable profile has been considered, it seems that we would still have to query the possibility of the charismatic being in itself a viable type within the overall religious context of Palestinian life in the early centuries of our era.

This negative assessment is founded upon the way in which these characters have been transmitted to us in our literary sources. We have focussed on Hanina and discovered that from an early stage, probably even before the Jamnia period, it was necessary to link his miracle-working activity with other acceptable aspects of Jewish piety. The subsequent development did not exclude the charismatic activity entirely, merely subsuming it to serve other interests and concerns. Even in the final stage of the process when Hanina's teaching ministry could not be appealed to and his memory might have been expected to wane in the light of developments concerning the image of the Rabbi, he still retained his individuality and importance as the recipient of the *bath qol*. In this way his image remained vital within an acceptable, if extraordinary theological framework.

Recent studies of the gospel genre point to a similar development of the Jesus traditions, even if there is as yet no agreement on the various phases or circumstances that gave rise to them.[67] In this process the canonical gospels stand apart from the apocryphal ones as well as from the various Acts of the Apostles that were soon in circulation, highlighting the miracle-working activity of Jesus and his apostles. The former were received by the orthodox believing community, whereas the latter were regarded as the product of groups considered to be either heretical or peripheral, and have left little impact on the creedal, as distinct from the popular devotional life of the church.[68] What is significant about this process of selection in the name of orthodoxy is that even the canonical gospels have preserved a portrait of Jesus the miracle-worker, within a larger framework either of teacher (Matthew, Luke) or revealer (John, Mark). This corresponds to what we have discovered in detail for the Hanina traditions, and a comparison of the ways in which the traditions about the two men had been transmitted would have been a more scientifically acceptable focus for Vermes' study. However, such a comparison would reveal that despite the real similarities and overlapping of interests in the process of transmission, major differences exist between the end products. The memories of the miracle-working activity of the two men have been put to rather different uses within the larger portrait that has been developed. Even more significantly still, the Jesus traditions are part of an independent corpus, behind which stands the person of Jesus and the community gathered around

---

[67] Cf. e.g., such studies as R. Fortna, *The Gospel of Signs. A Reconstruction of the Narrative Source Underlying the Fourth Gospel*, SNTSMS 11 (Cambridge: Cambridge University Press, 1970); T. Weeden *Mark: Traditions in Conflict*: (Philadelphia: Fortress Press, 1971); Kee, *Community of the New Age*, especially 17, 32–38.

[68] Cf. H. Koester, 'One Jesus and Four Primitive Gospels,' in J. M. Robinson and H. Koester, *Trajectories through Early Christianity* (Philadelphia: Fortress Press, 1971) 158–205, especially 157–93.

his memory, whereas the Hanina traditions have been incorporated into a much larger whole within which he can only claim to play a relatively minor role in comparison to the chief figures within that corpus, namely, the sages or teachers of the different epochs. The ultimate reason for this difference in the way in which later tradition perceived the two men must surely go back to the fact that at the earliest stage of the tradition they were perceived to have played different social roles. Lest this statement be regarded as special pleading, it should be noted that even within the rabbinic corpus itself the figure of Elijah who is the alleged prototype of the charismatic is presented in different roles,[69] and significant differences between the Hanina and Honi traditions can also be suggested.[70]

The fact that the miracle-working image has been muted in all three figures raises the question of why this transformation was considered necessary. In view of the later interest of both Judaism and Christianity it cannot be that they both regarded the idea of miracle as unacceptable in itself. The most plausible reason would seem to be that behind the figure of the miracle-worker lurks the sinister presence of the magician and no self-respecting community or group could officially accept the burden of such an image, even if there are many examples of popular accommodation in both traditions. Morton Smith's recent book has at least alerted us to images of Jesus less favourable than those to which we have been accustomed.[71] One wonders if Hanina merited similar attention from his detractors. Unfortunately we have no way of knowing, but perhaps this too points to some essential differences between the two men.

---

[69] Cf. above note 45 and below, 'Messiah and Galilee,' pp. 230 ff.

[70] Cf. above, note 61.

[71] M. Smith, *Jesus the Magician* (New York: Harper and Row, 1978). *The Historical Jesus and the Rejected Gospels*, C. W. Hedrick, ed., *Semeia* 44 (1988); *The Apocryphal Jesus and Christian Origins*, R. Cameron, ed., *Semeia* 49 (1990); H. Koester, *Ancient Christian Gospels: Their History and Development* (Philadelphia: Trinity Press International, 1990); M. Franzman, *Jesus in the Nag Hammadi Writings* (Edinburgh: T. & T. Clark, 1996).

8. Archaeology and the Historical Jesus

It is sometimes suggested that the current wave of interest in the historical Jesus is due to the recent archaeological findings from Roman Palestine. There is little concrete evidence to support the claim, however, beyond the sometimes over-enthusiastic comparisons made between the Dead Sea Scrolls and Jesus. In this regard little has changed from the origins of the quest for Jesus in the nineteenth century. Browsing today through those lives and their discussion of sources, one is indeed struck by the virtual total silence about aspects of the material culture, apart from the highly romanticised notions of the landscape.[1] Surveys of the early explorers came too late, were not known or were considered irrelevant to the tasks of those engaged in the 'first quest' for the historical Jesus.[2] Earlier in this century scholars such as Dalman and Alt did focus on aspects of the material culture in dealing with the ministry of Jesus, but their efforts made little or no impression on mainline research about Jesus.[3] Biblical Archaeology had already acquired a conservative, apologetic image (which it has not wholly shed even today), and as long as Bultmannian and post-Bultmannian trends dominated 'the new quest' for the historical Jesus it was not likely to receive much of a hearing. Many liberal scholars, operating mainly from the literary sources, still find little of importance to attract them to archaeology. This ignores that, due largely to developments in the discipline, we are now in a position to write Renan's 'fifth gospel' in ways and in details that he could never have imagined. Many of the recent 'third wave' of historical Jesus studies have little or no serious engagement with the archaeological data dealing with conditions in first-century Palestine that are now available. For other scholars, still under the impression of its apologetic, rather than exploratory nature, the mention of

---

[1] Thus e.g., E. Renan, *Vie de Jésus* (Paris: 1863; ET Buffalo: Prometheus Books, 1991), speaks of the landscape of Palestine as being like 'a fifth gospel, torn but still legible,' (23) which he came to know intimately and romanticise during his mission to explore ancient Phoenicia during the years 1860 and 1861.

[2] V. Guérin, *Description géographique, historique et archéologique de la Palestine* (Paris: 1868–80); C. R. Conder and A. H. Kitchener, *The Survey of Western Palestine I. Sheets I–VI, Galilee* (London: Palestine Exploration Fund, 1981); T. Saunders, *An Introduction to the Survey of Western Palestine* (London: Palestine Exploration Fund, 1881).

[3] G. Dalman, *Orte und Wege Jesu* (Gütersloh: Gerd Mohn, 1924); A. Alt, 'Die Stätten des Wirkens Jesu in Galiläa territorialgeschichtlich betrachtet,' *Kleine Schriften zur Geschichte des Volkes Israels,* 3 vols. (Munich: C. H. Beck, 1953–64), vol. 2, 436–55.

archaeology together with Jesus conjures up images of pious pilgrims rather than serious academic research.

This is not the place to discuss the reasons for these biases in contemporary scholarship or to trace the independent growth of various disciplines that could and should have contributed to a shared enterprise. It is encouraging to note signs of change in this regard from both sides of the divide. For some time archaeologists such as Eric Meyers and James Strange have been insisting on the importance of their findings for the study of early Christianity.[4] Some New Testament scholars are becoming more conscious of the need for dialogue with their 'dirt' colleagues. Thus, during the annual meeting of the Society of Biblical Literature (Chicago, 1994) the sections dealing with Archaeology of the New Testament World and the Historical Jesus had several joint-meetings to which scholars from both sides contributed, marking an important turning point in the dialogue, even if no firm conclusions were reached.[5] The large attendance at all the sessions indicates a growing awareness that the time is ripe for a fruitful dialogue between literary, historical and archaeological approaches to the understanding of the rise and identity of early Christianity.

What has changed and how do we define the 'new' in both areas? Several developments are worth mentioning. To begin, Biblical Archaeology itself has changed considerably in its objectives and method, influenced by developments within the field generally.[6] These have to do not just with the greater scientific sophistication, e.g., of pottery analysis, underwater exploration and radar testing, but also owe a good deal to the dialogue with the social sciences. As an independent discipline, archaeology is no longer text-driven, as in its earliest phase. It has been developing its own methodology, which usually includes a published report following area mapping and the detailed stratigraphic analysis of sites. However, an increasing number of studies are concerned with regional and inter-regional comparisons, based on detailed surveying and surface sherd-collecting from all existing settlements within regions or sub-regions.[7] In this context

---

[4] E. Meyers and J. Strange, *Archaeology, the Rabbis and Early Christianity* (London and Nashville: SCM and John Knox Press, 1981).

[5] Cf. the various articles by J. D. Crossan, R. Horsley, J. Reed, J. Strange in *SBLASP 1994*, ed. D. Lull (Atlanta: Scholars Press, 1994)

[6] E. Scott, ed., *Theoretical Roman Archaeology: First Conference Proceedings*, Worldwide Archaeology Series (Aldershot: Avebury, 1993).

[7] S. Dar, *Landscape and Pattern: An Archaeological Survey of Samaria 800 B.C.E.– 636 C.E.* (Oxford: BAR International Series 308 i, 1986); id., *Settlements and Cult Sites on Mount Hermon, Israel: Iturean Culture in the Hellenistic and Roman Periods* (Oxford: BAR International Series 589, 1993); D. Urman, *The Golan. A Profile of a Region during the Roman and Byzantine Periods* (Oxford: BAR International Series 269, 1985); C. Dauphin, *La Palestine Byzantine du IVe au VII Siécle. Peuplement et Population*, 3

increased attention is being given to lesser-known and smaller sites as well as to the larger urban centres. Thus, life in the countryside is gradually being brought into focus as consideration is given to settlements and landscape patterns, the proximity to water and other natural resources, roads, the size of fields and the nature of agricultural cultivation, field towers, wine and olive presses, industrial installations and the like[8] In order to interpret the mass of data emerging from such surveys, inevitably there is an increasing attention to social models that help to map out more comprehensively life as it was lived in pre-industrial societies. In this broader approach archaeology is a natural dialogue partner with ethnography, cultural anthropology and other relevant branches of the social sciences in its efforts to contribute to a more rounded picture of life at various strata of the social spectrum.[9] It has also meant that archaeology has to correct its positivistic image and self-consciously engage in a hermeneutic enterprise that not only underlines the provisional nature of its findings but also becomes aware of the modern biases which have often determined its findings. In this regard the feminist critique has recently drawn attention to the invisibility of women in many of the current archaeological accounts, thereby challenging modern stereotypes about distinctions that have been drawn between public and private space along gender lines.[10]

At the same time the study of the social world of early Christianity has become increasingly important for many New Testament scholars, especially, but not exclusively from North America. Studies by Malherbe (1977), Kee (1980), Meeks (1983) in particular, were trail-blazers following a pioneering article of Smith (1976).[11] Until recently Theissen (1983)

---

vols. (Oxford: BAR International Series 726, 1998); G. Barker and J. Lloyd, eds., *Roman Landscapes: Archaeological Surveys in the Mediterranean Region,* Archaeological Monographs of the British School at Rome 2 (London: British School at Rome, 1991).

[8] S. Applebaum, 'The Settlement Pattern of Western Samaria from Hellenistic and Byzantine Periods,' in Dar, *Landscape and Pattern;* D. Fiensy, *The Social History of Palestine in the Herodian Period* (Lewiston, NY: The Edwin Mellen Press, 1991); I. Roll, 'The Roman Road System in Judea,' in *The Jerusalem Cathedra,* ed. L. Levine, vol. 3, 136–81; M. Nun, *Ancient Anchorages and Harbours around the Sea of Galilee* (Kibbutz Ein Gev: Kinneret Sailing, 1988).

[9] E. Meyers and C. Meyers, 'Expanding the Frontiers of Biblical Archaeology,' *Eretz Israel. 20. The Yigael Yadin Volume* (Jerusalem: The Israel Exploration Society, 1989) 140*-47*.

[10] M. Sawicki, 'Archaeology as Space Technology: Digging for Gender and Class in the Holy Land,' *Method and Theory in the Study of Religion* [Berlin: de Gruyter] (1995) 319–48.

[11] J. Z. Smith, 'The Social Description of Early Christianity,' *RelSRev* 1 (1975) 19–25; A. Malherbe, *Social Aspects of Early Christianity* (Baton Rouge: Louisiana State University Press, 1977); H. Clark Kee, *Christian Origins in Sociological Perspective*

has ploughed a lonely furrow among continental European scholars.[12] The Context group, spearheaded by Neyrey (1991), Malina and Rohrbaugh (1992), Elliott (1993) and Esler (1995), have been consistent in their application of social theory to explain various aspects of early Christianity.[13]

Biblical Archaeology and New Testament studies, at least that branch that is most concerned with the social world, have, therefore, a common and natural meeting place in the social description of the movement and the circumstances – social, political, economic and religious – that gave rise to this distinctive configuration within the context of Second Temple Judaism. Yet, despite the growing recognition of this on both sides, there is still no consistent method for the wedding of archaeological findings and literary descriptions. Clearly, the old approach whereby certain pieces of archaeological evidence are introduced to show that the biblical narratives are trustworthy will not do. Apart from the fact that this approach subordinates archaeology as an independent discipline to the literary evidence, it also smacks of a positivistic outlook that views archaeology as provider of discrete, incontrovertible hard data, that can then be exploited at will by the interpreter of the texts. If archaeology should not be made subservient to the needs of literary historians, neither should it be too dismissive of what have been described as sectarian writings,[14] giving the impression that archaeologists alone are scientific and objective in their approach, whereas the interpreters of religious texts such as the gospels, may easily fall into the trap of adopting uncritically the partial and therefore biased accounts of the texts with which they deal. An approach that was concerned only with interpreting the remains of material culture is equally open to mistaking the parts for the whole, given the chance nature of many of the most important finds and depending on whether or not the deposition of objects in their present context was accidental or intended. It could equally ignore the fact that those aspects of ancient people's lives which gave rise to the sectarian documents may have left very incomplete or indeed no trace at all in the archaeological record.

(London: SCM, 1980); W. Meeks, *The First Urban Christians* (New Haven and London: Yale University Press, 1984).

[12] G. Theißen, *Studien zur Soziologie des Urchristentums* (Tübingen: J. C. B. Mohr, 1983).

[13] J. Neyrey, ed., *The Social World of Luke-Acts: Models for Interpretation* (Peabody: Hendrickson, 1991); B. Malina and R. Rohrbaugh, *A Social-Scientific Commentary on the Synoptic Gospels* (Minneapolis: Fortress Press, 1992); J. Elliott, *What is Social-Scientific Criticism?* (Minneapolis: Fortress Press, 1993); P. Esler, ed., *Modeling Early Christianity: Social Scientific Studies of the New Testament in its Context* (London and New York: Routledge, 1995).

[14] R. Vale, 'Literary Sources in Archaeological Descriptions. The Case of Galilee, Galilees and Galileans,' *JSJ* 18 (1987) 210–28.

Each discipline should give its own version of the situation from its perspective, avoiding any easy conflation of these divergent accounts. Rather, they should be juxtaposed and critically evaluated in a two-way dialogue between text and spade. Each account challenges the other in various ways, pointing to gaps, possible distortions and emphases that are not likely to have verisimilitude or, alternatively, are capable of illuminating more fully the situation being reconstructed. In such an 'inter-textual' exercise it is important to recognise the methods, shortcomings and assumptions of each discipline, thereby bringing a hermeneutic of suspicion into play. Only after this critical comparison has taken place is it possible to achieve more adequate answers to some pressing questions to do with the historical Jesus and his movement, and the real contribution of archaeology to the debate can be properly evaluated. In the remainder of this paper I want to engage such an exercise in the hope of developing a more adequate method and of testing its possibilities around specific questions.

The Geography of Jesus' Ministry

Crossing boundaries, be they social, political or religious, is usually also making a statement, especially if the boundaries are crossed freely. Because of the territorial nature of the Jewish religion which viewed *Eretz Israel* as Yahweh's gift, there was a particular need to pay attention to the precise boundaries of the land, as defined by the religious establishment, irrespective of whether or not these coincided with the political realities of the day. There is later evidence, both literary and inscriptional, to suggest that the rabbis were exercised about the matter, particularly in the north.[15] This may have reflected their own concerns after emigrating to Galilee in the wake of the Bar Cochba defeat in the second century. However, the incident reported by Josephus concerning the desire of the Jewish inhabitants of Caesarea Philippi to purchase oil produced within the land (*Life* 74) shows that at least some northern Jews were troubled with the issue of purity already in the first century. Thus the movements of Jesus into the non-Jewish areas of Tyre, the Dekapolis and Caesarea Philippi (Mk 5,1–19; 7,24.31; 8,27) present an intriguing interpretative problem in regard to his ministry and its primary focus. All three regions, though lying well outside political Galilee of the Roman period, nevertheless fall well within the borders of what might be described as 'greater Israel' in accordance with Jewish hopes of restoration as these found expression in various strands of Second Temple literature, dating back to the sixth century BCE

---

[15] J. Sussman, 'The Inscription in the Synagogue in Rehob,' in *Ancient Synagogues Revealed*, ed. L. Levine (Jerusalem: The Israel Exploration Society, 1981) 146–53.

(Ez 47,15–20). Should all these travels be viewed as part of a single strategy, as Mark seems to suggest, or could different issues have been at stake in each case?

Various interpreters view the historical significance of these notices within the Markan narrative differently. Thus F. Lang argues for the historical plausibility of the journey of 7,31, while acknowledging that it now functions within a section of the gospel (7,24–8,9) which seeks to anchor the gentile mission to the actual ministry of Jesus, a position espoused by others also.[16] In a similar vein, T. Schmeller has studied thoroughly all these notices from an historical and socio-cultural perspective and concludes that while redactionally they do indeed function as a legitimating of the post-Easter mission, historically they contain a core dealing with the activity of Jesus among Jewish communities within the territories of the Greek cities. After Easter, however, others, non-Jews who also felt alienated in the shadow of the cities and who obtained a new identity in Jesus, were interested in seeing themselves as having been addressed by him also.[17] The story of the Syrophoenician woman has attracted the attention of Theissen from the perspective of the local colouring of the narrative. He concludes that because it presupposes an original narrator and audience who are well acquainted with the concrete social and cultural conditions of the region between Tyre and Galilee, it is not so easy to trace the story's origins exclusively to the issue of the legitimacy of the gentile mission.[18] He does not, however, speculate as to whether the incident belongs to the actual ministry of Jesus.

It would seem then that we are faced with two options for interpreting these geographic notices if in fact they should be seen as referring to the career of Jesus. Either he was engaged in a mission to his co-religionists, and possibly also to other natives, non-Jews who were equally oppressed by urban elites, or he was already concerned with crossing the Jew/Gentile divide, thus opening up the possibility of a gentile mission before either Paul or the Hellenists. As has been pointed out, one crosses boundaries for various reasons – to emigrate, to trade, or to visit. Accordingly, it is important for historians and archaeologists to operate with various models in order to test all the possibilities. Both Schmeller and Theissen are quite

---

[16] F. Lang, '"Über Sidon mitten ins Gebiet der Dekapolis": Geographie und Theologie in Markus 7,31,' *ZDPV* 94 (178) 145–60; W. Marxsen, *Der Evangelist Markus. Studien zur Redaktionsgeschichte des Evangeliums,* FRLANT 67 (Göttingen: Vandenhoeck & Ruprecht, 1959) 43–46.

[17] T. Schmeller, 'Jesus im Umland Galiläas: zu den Markinischen Berichten vom Aufenthalt Jesu in den Gebieten von Tyros, Caesarea Philippi und der Dekapolis,' *BZ* 38 (1994) 44–66.

[18] G. Theissen, *The Gospels in Context. Social and Political History in the Synoptic Tradition* (Edinburgh: T. & T. Clark, 1992) 61–80.

sensitive to the complexity of the literary and archaeological evidence, but the question still needs to be asked whether this necessarily allows for a single interpretation of all the journeys or whether different conditions might not have prevailed in different territories and at different periods. Thus, if Mark's gospel is to be dated close to the Jewish War of 66–70 and located somewhere within the region of Syria/Palestine, as an increasing number of interpreters seem to agree, then one would have to ask whether or not the tensions between Jew and Greek in the north which Josephus describes (*JW* 2,457–65; cf. *Life* 113), might have had a bearing on the ethnocentric references both in the Syrophoenician story and in the earlier one dealing with the Gadarene demoniac.[19] Can an independent canvassing of the archaeological evidence help, while being true to the methods of the discipline?

With regard to immigration, archaeology can provide some important perspectives. In 1976 the Meiron excavation project headed by Eric Meyers, James Strange and Denis Groh conducted a survey of 19 sites in all, in upper and lower Galilee and just two in the Golan, all at locations where the remains of ancient synagogues were known. They concluded that a cultural continuum existed between upper Galilee and the Golan on the basis of obvious similarities of architectural styles for synagogues, the absence of representational art and the predominance of Hebrew/Aramaic inscriptions as well as common pottery types. This pattern was not in their opinion maintained in lower Galilee where different influences could be detected.[20] While some of their conclusions have had to be modified in the light of subsequent findings, the cultural relationship between upper Galilee and the Golan has been reinforced by a more detailed surveys in the Golan.[21] According to these findings the number of settlements in the Golan increased from 75 in the Hellenistic to 182 in the Roman period. There are variations in different sub-regions and Urman does not distinguish between the early, middle and late Roman periods. Nevertheless, when all the factors are taken into account, especially the strong Jewish presence there of later times, the steady increase points strongly in the direction of internal migration from the early Roman period onwards, probably already following the Hasmonean annexation of the north. The region in question

---

[19] S. Freyne, 'The Geography, Politics and Economics of Galilee and the Quest for the Historical Jesus,' in *Studying the Historical Jesus: Evaluations of the Current State of Research*, ed. B. Chilton and C. Evans (Leiden: Brill, 1994) 75–124, especially 82–84.

[20] E. Meyers, J. Strange, D. Groh, 'The Meiron Excavation Project: Archaeological Survey in Galilee and Golan, 1976,' *BASOR* 230, 1–24; E. Meyers, 'Galilean Regionalism as a Factor in Historical Reconstruction,' *BASOR* 221 (1976) 93–101; and id., 'Galilean Regionalism: A Reappraisal,' in *Approaches to Ancient Judaism*, ed. W. Scott Green, vol. 5 (Missoula: Scholars Press, 1978) 115–31.

[21] Urman, *The Golan. A Profile of a Region during the Roman and Byzantine Periods.*

within the Golan could easily be covered by the rather curious Markan phrase 'in the midst of the Dekapolis', once it is recalled that according to Pliny, Damascus to the north east was one of the ten cities of this region, even though the others are clustered much further to the south.[22] In that event Jesus' journey would have been to a thoroughly Jewish territory, a fact that Josephus also seems to take for granted more than once by saying in one place that Judas the Galilean, the founder of the Fourth Philosophy, was a native of Gamala in the Golan (*JA* 18,4), and by describing his own appointment as governor by the revolutionary council in 66 CE to the two Galilees and Gamala (*JW* 2,566–68).

The situation with regard to the territory of Tyre and Sidon and Caesarea Philippi is rather different, at least from an archaeological profile. No remains of a Jewish presence such as synagogues or *mikwaoth*, have been found above a line that runs from Sasa through Baram to Qatzyon.[23] In the west, similarly, a clear demarcation can be drawn between places yielding evidence of Jewish culture in the material remains and those that do not,[24] and this would presumably correspond with ancient territorial boundaries. This does not mean, of course, that no Jews lived outside those lines. The later rabbinical concerns suggest that such was not the case, and there are indications from Josephus, as we have seen, that Jews lived in both Caesarea Philippi and Tyre. It must, however, signify a very different ethos, even for Jews living in country places, than that which would have obtained for their counterparts in the Golan. Were Jesus to have visited these latter, one could thus conceive the purpose and function of the visit in rather different terms to a visit to Jewish communities in the Golan.

This raises the second reason for boundary crossing, namely, trading purposes. Links between Tyre and Galilee in this regard go back to the time of Solomon, and were also emphasised by Ezekiel in the sixth century BCE (1 Kgs 5,11; 17,7–16; Ez 27,17). Because of its location on a island with a very narrow strip of land between it and the mountainous, mainland promontory, Tyre, despite its wealth from seafaring, was, nevertheless, dependent on its hinterland for its basic sustenance (Acts 12,20). As a recognised port it would also have functioned as a collecting and export centre for any surplus goods such as grain and oil. It comes as no surprise, therefore, to find that Tyrian coins predominate at the Jewish sites in upper

---

[22] Lang, '"Über Sidon mitten ins Gebiet der Dekapolis",' 147–52.

[23] Z. Ilan, 'Galilee. A Survey of Synagogues,' *Excavations and Surveys in Israel* 5 (1986/87) 35–37.

[24] M. Aviam, 'Galilee: The Hellenistic to Byzantine Periods,' *NEAEHL* 2, (1993) 452–58, especially 454.

Galilee excavated by the Meiron Expedition.[25] What is more surprising is that the same holds for lower Galilee also,[26] though we must await the publication of the numismatic evidence from the various digs currently in progress, especially at Sepphoris, before coming to any definitive conclusions for this region.

A number of reasons can be suggested for this situation. In all probability Tyre, because of its traditional status, was allowed by Rome to mint a far greater number of coins than was permissible at local mints such as Sepphoris and Tiberias, or even Akko/Ptolemais. This might mean, as Horsley claims,[27] that too much should not be read into the frequency of these coins in Galilee in terms of trading links with Tyre. It is true that, unlike pottery remains which we shall presently discuss, coin finds can only tell us about their place of origin and final deposition, but nothing about their intermediate use for trading or other purposes. However, Horsley's critique of Meyers and Hanson is too dismissive of the literary evidence supporting such links. Nor does it do justice to the fact that in all the hordes of coins found in the North (Magdala, Gischala and especially Isfija, Carmel) city coins from Tyre predominate. This latter hoard of some 5000 Tyrian tetradrachmas and didrachmas contained coins dated to the few years before Nero put an end to their production, replacing them instead with provincial coins of a lower silver content and weight. Most of the coins struck in antiquity were required for the payment of a resident Roman army. Since there was none such in Palestine in the first century, the existence of such a large hoard suggests major trading links with Tyre, unless one were to posit their collection for religious purposes alone. Yet then, the money must have been obtained through some transaction. Because of their stable value, compared with other currencies, the Tyrian didrachma continued to be 'the coin of the sanctuary' according to rabbinical ruling (*m. Bek.* 8,7; *t. Ketub.* 13,3) and they remained in circulation for well over a hundred years after their last striking. Thus, in addition to the secular economy, the temple economy meant that there was a demand for Tyrian money in Palestine throughout the first century.[28] This was all the more surprising in view of the pagan religious symbolism of the coins associated with the city, and can only be attributed to the buying power

---

[25] R. Hanson, *Tyrian Influences in Upper Galilee* (Cambridge, MA: ASOR Publications, 1980); J. Raynor and Y. Meshorer, *The Coins of Ancient Meiron* (Winona Lake: Eisenbrauns, 1988).

[26] D. Barag, 'Tyrian Currency in Galilee,' *INJ* 6/7 (1982/83) 7–13.

[27] R. Horsley, 'The Historical Jesus and Archaeology of the Galilee: Questions from Historical Jesus Research to Archaeologists,' in *SBLASP 1994*, ed. D. Lull (Atlanta: Scholars Press, 1994) 91–135, especially 105 f.

[28] A. Ben David, *Jerusalem und Tyros. Ein Beitrag zur Palästinensischen Münz- und Wirtschaftsgeschichte* (Basel: Kyklos Verlag, 1961.)

and consistency of the money. This underlines the continued importance of the city for both the religious and everyday economy of the hinterland.

If the case for trading links between Tyre and Galilee can still be generally maintained, it does not yet explain why a Galilean teacher/prophet might want to visit the region of the city, especially in view of Jesus' critique of wealth and possessions. One could argue, as does Schmeller,[29] that Jews living in the countryside of these city territories were just as likely to be exploited as were their non-Jewish peasant neighbours, given the way in which the economy in all ancient agrarian societies was controlled politically. Schmeller bases his conclusion on the fact that within Galilee itself, Jesus' ministry seems to have been conducted in the villages of lower Galilee for the most part, a sub-region where, according to the Meiron survey (1978), the influences of Hellenistic culture were being felt. He interprets this to mean that the traditional way of life was coming under threat from the effects of urbanisation in the region. This will be discussed in detail in the next section. Here it is of importance in its suggesting a possible socio-economic reason for Jesus' visit to the region of Tyre as well as to the villages of Caesarea Philippi. The force of the suggestion stems from the fact that it plausibly links the ministry of Jesus in these places with that in Galilee itself. On the other hand the visit to the Dekapolis region could not be so easily explained on the same basis, provided our suggestion of the Jewish ethos of such a visit has any merit.

At this juncture recent discussion of the pottery trade opens up interesting possibilities for understanding such forays beyond the Jordan. The focus has been on the ceramic industry at two Galilean villages, both of whom were known from Rabbinical literature for the quality of their pottery – Kefar Hanania, located between upper and lower Galilee and Shikhin, near Sepphoris. Detailed neutron activation analysis (NAA) of the provenience and distribution of the Kefar Hanania household ware by David Adan-Bayewitz points to a network of trading links between this Galilean village, not just with other centres within Galilee itself, notably Sepphoris, but with both Jewish and non-Jewish settlements in the Golan also.[30] In competition with local ware there, Kefar Hanania is estimated to have provided between 10–20% of the total needs. The distribution pattern shows that the closer any given location was to the production centre the greater the total percentage of wares from that centre was. Nevertheless, products from Kefar Hanania were also found at Akko/Ptolemais and Banias/Caesarea, but significantly not south of the Nazareth ridge nor in the

---

[29] Schmeller, 'Jesus in Umland Galiläas,' 49f.

[30] D. Adan-Bayewitz, *Common Pottery in Roman Galilee. A Study of Local Trade* (Ramat-Gan: Bar-Ilan University Press, 1993) especially 224–50; D. Adan-Bayewitz and I. Perlman, 'The Local Trade of Sepphoris in the Roman Period,' *IEJ* 40 (1990) 153–72.

urban centres of Scythopolis and Samaria, thus confirming local separatism based on religious animosities (cf. Lk 9,53; Jn 4,9). Though the identification of Shikhin is still under debate, the opinion of recent studies is that it is to be identified with Asochis mentioned by Josephus, and located a few kilometres north of Sepphoris. A definite identification would enable a study of the sherds and their distribution pattern similar to that conducted for Kefar Hanania. It seems to have specialised in stone jars, which were important in the maintenance of purity, and supplied not just Sepphoris, but other centres also, possibly even Cana (Jn 2,6).[31]

In view of the fact that the wares from both centres are singled out for special mention in the Rabbinic literature, one could argue with some justification that the appearance of Kefar Hanania ware at centres outside Galilee, even non-Jewish ones, is best explained by halachic concerns of some of the inhabitants of these places, by analogy with the Jews of Caesarea Philippi who, according to Josephus, were prepared to pay extra in order to obtain oil from the land because of similar concerns (*Life* 74 f.; cf. *JW* 2,591 f.) This is not the conclusion that Adan-Bayewitz draws from his study, however. The absence of the competing Golan ware at any of the Galilean sites calls for some explanation, especially if one is to talk about trading networks and Galilean culture being open to outside influences, as others drawing on his conclusions have done. In this regard it is important to avoid modern ideas about both manufacture and market, given the nature and scale of the operations which were very much rooted in local needs, and were small-scale and family-based in terms of production and distribution.[32]

It is clear from this discussion that archaeology cannot settle the question of either the fact or the function of Jesus' visits to the surrounding territories. What it can do is to help in better understanding the day-to-day contacts that did exist in that region, and provides us with a number of alternatives for judging both the verisimilitude and possible intention of any such visits against that background. In the end one's understanding of any given episode and its likely impact will depend on the assumptions one brings to the discussion of what Jesus' overall intentions might have been. Schmeller's suggestion that a ministry to Jews living in these outlying areas because of the pressures they were experiencing in economic rather than cultural terms, is attractive in that it does point to a deliberate pattern

---

[31] Cf. J. Strange, D. Groh, T. Longstaff, 'Excavations at Sepphoris: The Location and Identification of Shikhin,' Part I, *IEJ* 44 (1994) 216–27, and Part II, *IEJ* 45 (1995) 171–87.

[32] F. Vitto, 'A Look into the Workshop of a late Roman Galilean Potter,' *Bulletin of the Anglo-Israel Archaeological Society* 5 (1983/84) 19–22; R. McMullen, 'Market Days in the Roman Empire,' *Phoenix* 24 (1970) 333–41.

which, we shall presently see, appears to be consistent with Jesus' strategy in Galilee also, namely that of avoiding the urban centres. There must surely be something significant in Mark's careful portrayal of his visiting the land of the Gadarenes, the borders of Tyre and the villages of Caesarea Philippi, but not the actual urban centres. But what are the reasons for such a strategy? All one can say definitively is that on the basis of our present knowledge of Jewish settlement patterns in the area in the first century, such journeys and contacts would not be inconsistent for someone who was not only concerned with the socio-economic oppression of co-religionists and the consequent erosion of kinship values, but who also believed himself to have a ministry to call all Israel to a new vision of its own destiny. Indeed, both concerns would have been mutually reinforcing.

Jesus and the Herodian Culture of Galilee

Apart from Luke's account, the virtual absence of Herod Antipas and his court from the story of Jesus is remarkable, particularly in view of the close association with the Baptist, whom Herod perceived to be a political threat (*JA* 18,116–19). The silence becomes even more striking when one considers that during the life-time of Jesus Antipas had refurbished Sepphoris and had founded Tiberias, probably in the year 19 CE, thereby seeking to emulate the building feats of his father, Herod the Great, in the south, on a more modest scale to be sure. Both foundations were undoubtedly intended to honour his imperial patron, possibly in the hope of eventually becoming king of the Jews, instead of mere tetrarch.

The silence of the gospels concerning these urban centres of lower Galilee should have raised questions for historical Jesus researchers. Yet, with one or two exceptions this does not seem to have occurred. Already in 1926 Shirley Jackson Case discussed the issue of Jesus and Sepphoris, attempting to explain some of Jesus' attitudes – his pacifism and his openness to strangers – on the basis of his having grown up close to Sepphoris and possibly having worked there as a τέκτων. As yet no serious archaeological work had been done at the site, but more recently, Richard Batey has attempted to revive Case's approach, drawing on his experience as part of the University of South Florida Sepphoris Project under the direction of James Strange. He attributes, among other things, Jesus' friendship with tax collectors to his experience of the pro-Roman, anti-Zealot stance of the people of Sepphoris in the first century.[33]

---

[33] R. Batey, 'Is not this the Carpenter?' *NTS* 30 (1984) 249–58; id., 'Jesus and the Theatre,' *NTS* 30 (1984) 563–74; id., *Jesus and the Forgotten City. New Light on Sepphoris and the Urban World of Jesus* (Grand Rapids: Baker Books, 1991).

While Case and Batey attempt to explain certain aspects of Jesus' ministry, including some of the attributed sayings, to his contact with the urban environment of Sepphoris, Albrecht Alt adopted the opposite position. He argued for Nazareth's isolation from the capital on the basis of rather dubious geophysical grounds. According to him 'a wall of separation' existed between the two places, with Nazareth oriented more to the great plain in the south, and Sepphoris inclined towards the plain of Akko.[34]

These attempts to discuss the issue of Jesus and Sepphoris must be deemed unsatisfactory, because the question is being addressed from a far too narrow focus, giving rise to highly speculative arguments from silence that are ultimately unconvincing. Recent developments in socio-archaeology, already mentioned, are concerned with discerning the pattern of relationships between town and country and offer a more realistic possibility for addressing the question in a meaningful way.[35] The contribution of James Strange is particularly noteworthy, insofar as he deals directly with the matter for Sepphoris and its environs. He speaks of an urban overlay which in his view indicates close bonds between the city and the countryside, the city being dependent on its hinterland for such natural resources as its water supply, while at the same time providing an outlet for goods produced by the peasants, whether agricultural produce (grain, oil and wine) or pottery and stone jars from Kefar Hanania and Shikhin, as previously discussed.[36] The discovery in Sepphoris of large underground silos, presumably for storage, and also a lead weight referring in Greek to the *agoranomoi* or market inspectors, point to the city as having both a market and an administrative role in lower Galilee.[37] Josephus is also aware of this dual role, on the one hand chiding Sepphoris for not resisting the Romans even though it was well supplied by surrounding villages, and on the other mentioning the jealousy of Justus of Tiberias because under Nero his native place had to cede to it both banking and the archives (*Life* 38,346).

In arguing for a symbiotic relationship between Sepphoris and its hinterland, Strange is challenging the dominant view, associated with Moses Finley, that ancient cities were parasitic on the countryside[38] Against this view, others have argued that from the Hellenistic age onwards, cities en-

---

[34] Alt, 'Die Stätten des Wirkens Jesu,' *Kleine Schriften* 2, 444 f.

[35] J. Rich and A. Wallace-Hadrill, eds., *City and Country in the Ancient World* (London and New York: Routledge, 1991).

[36] J. Strange, 'Some Implications of Archaeology for New Testament Studies,' in *What has Archaeology to do with Faith?* ed. J. H. Charlesworth (Valley Forge: Trinity Press International, 1992) 23–59.

[37] E. M. Meyers, E. Netzer and C. L. Meyers, 'Sepphoris: Ornament of All Galilee,' *BA* 49 (1986) 4–19; E. Meyers, E. Netzer, C. Meyers, *Sepphoris* (Winona Lake: Eisenbrauns, 1992).

[38] M. Finley, *The Ancient Economy,* 2nd ed. (London: Chatto and Windus, 1977).

gaged in production and increased marketing, and so were able to pay the peasants for their produce, thus enabling these to pay their taxes in money rather than in kind.[39] There appears to be grounds for modifying somewhat Finley's views, as can be easily documented from both literary and archaeological sources, but without blurring the undoubted distinctions between city and country in antiquity.[40] Urbanisation and 'urban overlay' could easily become terms for a one-way process that does not do justice to the complex relationship that undoubtedly existed. It may well be the case that strictly on the basis of the data drawn from the material remains, this is in fact the picture that suggests itself to field archaeologists in view of the formal continuities between urban and smaller settlements. They must recognise, however, that when it comes to interpreting those same data within a more general theory of social relations in antiquity, they require theoretical models appropriate to the task they set themselves.[41]

Strange assumes that the encounter with Hellenism had prepared the Galileans for Antipas' aggressive Romanisation, thus enabling the locals to make a powerful symbolic statement in stone of how they viewed the world, grafting together the native and the imported without any real confrontation between them. This can be seen from the material remains of Jewish Sepphoris where the process has, in his view, reached down to the very lowest levels of city life, and extended itself to the surrounding region as well. Even the words of Jesus reflect the process, echoing as many urban images and types as rural ones.[42]

This view of the matter assumes that the 'urban overlay' which Strange detects in the material culture of lower Galilee was seen in the same light by all the inhabitants of the region. One must ask whether all might have benefited equally from the contacts. Was the symbolic statement celebrating the power of Rome which Sepphoris and Tiberias were intended to make, perceived in the same way at all levels of the social spectrum even

---

[39] K. Hopkins, 'Economic Growth and Towns in Classical Antiquity,' in *Towns in Societies: Essays in Economic History and Historical Sociology*, ed. P. Abrams and E. Wrigley (Cambridge: Cambridge University Press, 1980) 35–77; A. Wallace-Hadrill, 'Elites and Trade in the Roman Town,' in Rich and Wallace-Hadrill, *City and Country*, 241–72.

[40] C. R. Whittaker, 'The Consumer City Revisited: the *Vicus* and the City,' *JRA* 3 (1991) 110–18.

[41] Cf. 'Herodian Economics in Galilee. Searching for a Suitable Model,' above pp. 86 ff. for a fuller discussion of this issue.

[42] Strange, 'Six Campaigns at Sepphoris: The University of South Florida Excavations 1983–1989,' in *The Galilee in Late Antiquity*, ed. L. Levine, 339–56; 'Some Implications of Archaeology for New Testament Studies,' in *What has Archaeology to do with Faith?* ed. J. H. Charlesworth (Valley Forge: Trinity Press International, 1992) 23–59. Cf. 'Town and Country Once More. The Case of Roman Galilee,' above pp. 59 ff.

among the urban inhabitants? Given that no individual or sub-group ever fully internalises a culture in all its aspects, can one confidently assume that the Galilean peasants, even those tied to Sepphoris by economic or other reasons were equally impressed by all aspects of the dominant culture represented by the city? To be sure, Sepphoris differed in this regard from such centres as Beth Shean/Scythopolis and Akko/Ptolemais, where even from the early Hellenistic age both literary and archaeological evidence point to aggressive Hellenisation. Yet, despite the more modest signs of Romanisation that the Herodian centres represented, it is difficult to explain Galilee's participation in the revolt of 66 CE, if they had been as successful in creating a single symbolic world, as Strange's analysis would seem to suggest. There are many ways of resisting imperialist ideology, even when the external trappings of colonial power, including language, have to be adopted for commercial or administrative reasons.

My query to those who espouse the urbanisation hypothesis, therefore, is not about the urban overlay that may be detected in the material culture, but rather about the ways in which people felt free to resist, dissent, select or develop counter-cultural models to the prevailing ones. It is doubtful if archaeology can assist us directly in answering this question. As Strange recognises, apart from the Jerusalem temple, the synagogue is the most typically Jewish building where a different cultural experience could be fostered. Closely allied to this are the *mikwaoth* or ritual baths where the separation that the purity laws embodied was ritually expressed on a regular basis. The pre–70 archaeological evidence for both structures is sparse, though existing at Gamala (both synagogue and *mikweh*), Khirbet Shema and Sepphoris (*mikwaoth*) and Magdala (presumed synagogue), Iotapata (reported *mikweh*). This scarcity of evidence so far for the instrumentalities of the Jewish way of life from the pre–70 period is all the more surprising in view of the fact that the gospels, and to a lesser extent Josephus, seem to assume the presence of synagogues throughout the region (Mk 1,39; Mt 4,23; Lk 4,15; *Life* 277), causing some to challenge its Jewish character, in favour of either a Hellenised or an Israelite alternative. On the other hand, Zvi Ma'oz has proposed the novel theory that since the building of synagogues was a political act in Roman Palestine as elsewhere, they were allowed from the time of Herod onwards only at the larger urban centres and the district capitals, but not in the villages. It was only in the third century and afterwards, when Jewish resistance as a political threat had been broken that synagogue building occurred on the grand scale, even in remote areas. Even then, however, it was not without political significance that a Greco-Roman urban architectural type was defiantly transferred and adapted to lesser Jewish settlements. Prior to that,

Jewish communities in more remote settlements gathered in less formal contexts such as court-yards or private dwellings, or even in the open air.[43] This situation inevitably recalls the strategy of Jesus, as least as it is represented in the gospels. His ministry avoided the urban centres, not just in the surrounding territories, as we have seen, but even in the heartland of Galilee itself. He concentrated instead on the villages where the worst aspects of the pressure downwards from the top of the social pyramid were most keenly felt. In terms of the kingdom of God which he proclaimed, it was the πτωχοί that he declared blessed. These are not the poor simply, but rather they are those who have lost their status or had it removed from them through loss of property, and are, therefore, destitute.[44] At the same time he castigated the rich and called on them to share their goods with the needy, thereby radically challenging the social norms of honour, power and patronage as these operated at centres such as Sepphoris. Elsewhere, I have attempted to show that Jesus' critique of secular kingship, in one instance in the context of declaring the imminent downfall of Beezebul's kingdom, is best understood as a covert critique of Herodian kingship rather than a generalised set of remarks.[45] But what was the inspiration for this movement of protest and what was the shared understanding of prophet and addressees? Those who see the region as a whole as highly urbanised and Hellenised assume a total openness of the inhabitants to the religio-philosophical ideas emanating from the cities, particularly Cynicism, the popular counter-cultural philosophy of Greco-Roman society.[46] The support for this position is sought in the archaeological record as propounded by Overman and Edwards,[47] both of whom follow Strange's position broadly speaking. This provides Crossan with the perfect setting for his a priori and unlikely construct of a peasant Jewish Cynic. Yet perhaps archaeology has something more to say on this topic, namely the provenance and religious affiliations of Galileans. It is to this crucial issue in historical Jesus research that we must now finally turn.

---

[43] Z. Ma'oz, 'The Synagogue in the Second Temple Period. Architectural and Social Interpretation,' *Eretz Israel* 23, *The A. Biran Volume* (Jerusalem: The Israel Exploration Society, 1992) 331–44 [Hebrew].

[44] Malina and Rohrbaugh, *A Social-Scientific Commentary on the Synoptics,* 48 f.

[45] 'Jesus and the Urban Culture of Galilee,' below pp. 183 ff.

[46] B. Mack, *A Myth of Innocence: Mark and Christian Origins* (Philadelphia: Fortress Press, 1988); J. D. Crossan, *The Historical Jesus. The Life of a Mediterranean Jewish Peasant* (Edinburgh: T. & T. Clark, 1991); L. Vaage, *Galilean Upstarts. Jesus' First Followers according to Q* (Minneapolis: Fortress Press, 1992).

[47] A. Overman, 'Who were the First Urban Christians?' and D. Edwards, 'First-Century Rural-Urban Relations in Lower Galilee: Exploring the Archaeological Evidence,' in *SBLASP 1988*, ed. D. Lull (Atlanta: Scholars Press, 1988) 160–68 and 169–82.

A Jewish Galilee?

The issue of the religious and cultural affiliations of the Galilean population in the first century is central to historical Jesus research because of its
theological, as well as its historical implications. H. D. Betz has shown
that those who currently espouse a Cynic Jesus are, unwittingly or otherwise, successors of those who in the last century sought to revive Cynicism as a world philosophy, particularly under the patronage of Friedrich
Nietzsche. As a forerunner to his *Weltphilosophie*, he too considered a Jesus who had left behind the narrow confines of Judaism and had not yet
been christianised.[48] In a similar vein the notion of a cosmopolitan Galilee,
open to and receptive of all the cultural influences of the Greco-Roman
society, also has nineteenth-century forerunners from the History of Religions School[49] in the work of Schürer, Bauer and Bertram. The result, if not
the intention, was to detach Jesus from his Jewish roots, a conclusion that
reached its explicit formulation in the 1941 declaration of Grundmann that
Jesus 'kein Jude war.' This anti-Jewish bias in much of nineteenth-century
scholarship, already blatantly expressed in Renan's contrasting depictions
of the Galilean and Judean landscapes and the different religious orienta-
tions in terms of gospel and law emanating from each, has been exposed in
recent times.[50] It would be a false ecumenism in a post-Holocaust era to
attempt to gloss over the tensions between the nascent Jesus movement
and its Jewish matrix. At the same time it is equally incumbent on scholars
to consider all the implications of their scholarly reconstructions and to
examine as dispassionately as possible all the available evidence.

Archaeology can assist by giving its own independent account of the
data that would point to the ethnic mix within the population of first-
century Galilee. While general adaptation to the environment of a particular place is common to all people, irrespective of their ethno-religious affiliations, certain features of lifestyles may be discernible in such material
remains as public buildings, baths, coins etc. that can point strongly in one

---

[48] H. D. Betz, 'Jesus and the Cynics: Survey and Analysis of a Hypothesis,' *JR* 74
(1994) 453–75.

[49] E. Schürer, *The History of the Jewish People in the Age of Jesus Christ,* 3 vols., re-
vised by G. Vermes, F. Miller, and M. Black (Edinburgh: T. & T. Clark, 1973–84) [first
German edition: 1886]; W. Bauer, 'Jesus der Galiläer,'(1924), in *Aufsätze und Kleine
Schriften,* ed. G. Strecker (Tübingen: J. C. B. Mohr, 1967) 91–108; W. Bertram, 'Der
Hellenismus in der Urheimat des Evangeliums,' *Archiv für Religionswissenschaft* 32
(1935) 265–81; J. Colin, 'La Galilée de l'Évangile et les villes paiennes de la Palestine,'
Antiquité Classique 34 (1965) 183–92; W. Grundmann, *Jesus der Galiläer und das Ju-
dentum* (Leipzig: Georg Wigand, 1941).

[50] C. Klein, *Anti-Judaism in Christian Theology* (London: SPCK, 1978).

direction or another. In the case of first-century Galilee three different proposals can be detected in recent and contemporary discussions – the Galileans were the remnants of an old Israelite population (Alt); there was an enforced Judaisation by the Hasmoneans of the Iturean people who had infiltrated most of Galilee (Schürer); or a colonisation from the south following the Hasmonean conquest of the north in the late second and early first century BCE. While none of these suggestions necessarily exclude one or both of the others, it would seem legitimate to draw wider inferences according to which background was likely to have been the more dominant among the first-century population of Galilee. A process of inculturation over a few generations can begin to blur any distinctions that large-scale population disruptions may have initially given rise to. Yet, group traits are also shaped by tradition and memory, especially if imposed colonisation has brought about the disruptions in the first instance. With these caveats in mind, the question to be addressed has to do with how archaeology might assist in determining the religious loyalties in the first century of those whom our literary sources call 'Galileans' .

The findings of Zvi Gal's survey of Iron Age III sites (i.e. 7th–6th century BCE) challenge Alt's contention, argued from the literary sources for the most part, that the Israelite population in the Galilee was relatively undisturbed throughout centuries, thus providing the framework for the incorporation of the region into the ἔθνος τῶν Ἰουδαίων by the Hasmoneans in the second century BCE. Alt believed that Galilee had fared better in the first Assyrian onslaught of 732 BCE than Samaria did in 721, when the native population was replaced by people of non-Israelite stock (2 Kgs 15,29; 17,6.24). However, the absence from 83 surveyed sites in lower Galilee of four different pottery types, dated to that particular period on the basis of stratified digs at Hazor and Samaria, has convinced Gal that there was a major depopulation of the area in the century after the fall of Samaria.[51] Only additional stratified digs will decide whether this population gap was the result of the Assyrian aggression or was due to the migration of the country people to larger settlements. In any event, the theory that the rural population of Galilee remained untouched by the Assyrian invasion would seem to be challenged by such findings.

What can archaeology say about the Iturean hypothesis? Josephus reports (*JA* 13,318 f.) on the enforced Judaisation by Judah Aristobulus I in 105 BCE of the Itureans, a semi-nomadic Arab people who became sedentarised in the Hellenistic period and who are associated particularly with

---

[51] A. Alt, 'Die Assyrische Provinz Megiddo und ihr späteres Schicksal,' and 'Die Umgestaltung Galiläas durch die Hasmonäer,' in *Kleine Schriften*, vol. 2, 374–84 and 407–23; Z. Gal, *Lower Galilee during the Iron Age*, ASORDS 8 (Winona Lake: Eisenbrauns, 1992).

the Hermon and the region north of Damascus, where the centre of their kingdom of Chalcis lay.[52] The claim is that with the break-up of the Seleucid empire during the second century BCE, the Itureans infiltrated Upper Galilee. According to Schürer and those who have followed him uncritically, this includes 'almost all of Galilee' which, it is suggested, was hitherto sparsely populated.[53] Recent archaeological evidence, however, poses a number of difficulties for this scenario. Firstly, upper Galilee was not so sparsely populated in the early Hellenistic period, as the results of the Archaeological Survey already alluded to make clear.[54] Nor is the character of the settlements similar to those confidently identified as Iturean in the Golan such as, e.g., Kh. Zemel, for the upper Galilean settlements reflect a sedentarised and agricultural rather than a semi-nomadic, pastoral milieu, so obvious in the Golan remains, at least for the initial phase of sedentarisation there in the Persian and early Hellenistic periods.[55] The majority of these Iturean sites are in the east (i.e. upper Golan), but there are signs of expansion to the south-west in the direction of Galilee.[56] According to Aviam many settlements in upper Galilee were abandoned in the Hellenistic period, only to have been replaced by others which he regards as Jewish, probably from the period of the expansion in the second century BCE, based on the preponderance of Hasmonean coins at bedrock. There may well have been Iturean settlements also, since sherds have been found in upper Galilee which, in terms of clay composition (pinkish brown with coarse grits) and style (from large storage jars, poorly finished), are not dissimilar to so-called 'Iturean ware' from Hermon/Golan.[57]

The current political situation has prevented further surveying of the Western Hermon region (modern southern Lebanon), which might reveal a greater Iturean presence than can be postulated at present. Irrespective of what might be the final judgement on that issue, the notion of Iturean conversions accounting for most of the Jews of the Galilee comes from an uncritical reading of Josephus. He is reporting Strabo's citation of Timagenes, which is taken to parallel a similar description (*JA* 13,257f.) of the treatment of the Idumeans in the south by the Hasmoneans. It is noteworthy, however, that unlike Idumeans such as Herod, no Galilean is ever described as a half-Jew in the rabbinic literature, despite the suspicion of

---

[52] W. Schottroff, 'Die Ituräer,' *ZDPV* 98 (1982) 125–47; Schürer, *History of the Jewish People,* vol. 1, appendix I, 561–73.

[53] *History of the Jewish People,* vol. II, 7–10.

[54] Aviam, 'Galilee: the Hellenistic to Byzantine Periods,' above note 24.

[55] M. Hartel, 'Kh. Zemel, 1985/6,' *IEJ* 37 (1987) 270–72.

[56] M. Hartel, *Northern Golan Heights. The Archaeological Survey as Source for Local History* (Qatzrin: Israel Department of Antiquities and Museums, 1989) [Hebrew].

[57] Urman, *The Golan,* 162–64; Hartel, *Northern Golan Heights,* 124–26.

Galileans as *'ammei ha-'aretz* by the standards of the sages.[58] Thus, neither literary nor archaeological evidence supports the hypothesis, but indicates rather that if there were Itureans in upper Galilee in the early Hellenistic period, they left with the advance of the Hasmonean armies of conquest, an option which they were given according to Josephus (*JA* 13,318 f.).

It was only in the Persian and Early Hellenistic periods that signs of new settlements began to appear in this area once more. Preliminary results from the Archaeological Survey of Israel for upper Galilee show an upward curve from 93 sites in the Hellenistic period to 138 for the Roman and 162 for the Byzantine periods respectively (Aviam). As already noted, this trend corresponds to the results of Urman's survey of the Golan carried out for the Association for the Archaeological Survey of Israel and the Israel Antiquities Authority (1985). It is best explained in terms of the incorporation of the whole Galilee/Golan region into the Jewish state and the need for new settlements and military outposts on both sides of the Jordan. The further increase of settlements in the Roman and Byzantine periods is directly attributable to internal Jewish migration for the most part, both in the wake of the second revolt and as a result of the increased Christian presence in the south from the fourth century CE onwards.

The task of identifying sites as Jewish or not is a difficult one, since, as already noted, such instrumentalities of Jewish life as synagogues and *mikwaoth* are scarce for the pre–70 period. The presumption, nevertheless, is that sites which can be clearly identified as Jewish on the basis of the synagogue remains, with their distinctively Jewish iconography, inscriptions, and liturgical architecture, especially in Upper Galilee/Golan from the middle Roman to the early Arab period, in all probability were not all new foundations. Rather, in some instances at least, they were based on existing Jewish settlements from the earlier period. Stratified digs have been able to confirm this assumption at such sites as Meiron, Khirbet Shema, and Gush ha-Lab in upper Galilee. Architectural remains of synagogues from lower Galilee are less well preserved, with a few notable exceptions (Chorazin, Capernaum, Hammath Tiberias). Nonetheless, Ilan's survey of some seventy sites shows almost as many remains for lower as for upper Galilee. This evidence would seem to support the third possibility suggested, Hasmonean colonisation from the south, as the most likely hypothesis for explaining the dominant Jewish element in first-century Galilee presumed by the literary sources. It is the preponderance of Hasmonean coins at bedrock in several of these sites that has convinced Aviam that these were in fact Jewish sites, especially in view of the propaganda nature of those early Jewish coins. Such an hypothesis would

---

[58] A. Oppenheimer, *The 'Am ha-'aretz. A Study in the Social History of the Jewish People in the Hellenistic-Roman Period* (Leiden: Brill, 1977) 200–218.

best explain the continued resistance to Herod the Great in Galilee because of his ousting of the Galilean nobles which Josephus reports, and it would also account for the ongoing Jerusalem-Galilee relations which both Josephus and the gospels assume.[59] The absence of any human or animal representations on the coins of Herod Antipas, the first to be struck in Galilee itself, would appear to support such a general conclusion, particularly when compared with those of his brother Philip in the neighbouring kingdom. The coin of the First Revolt from Gamala with the inscription, 'For the Redemption of Jerusalem, the Holy', together with the *mikwaoth* already mentioned, point to some concern with purity and holiness as represented by the Jerusalem temple in the archaeological remains there also.

This does not mean that non-Jews or Jews of another provenance, possibly even those of old Israelite stock, did not also make up part of the population mix. Josephus tells of the distinctively Jewish way of life that the Babylonian Jews whom Herod the Great had planted in Gaulanitis and Trachonitis were able to maintain (*JA* 17,23–31). There is also evidence that Dan continued as a cult-centre in the Hellenistic age on the basis of the bilingual (Aramaic and Greek) dedicatory inscription 'to the God who is in Dan.'[60] Only a narrow view of observant Jewish practice and its inability to live in mixed communities requires an ethnically-cleansed Galilee. What emerges from the map of known Jewish settlements, especially where synagogue remains have been claimed, is a concentration of sites in certain areas of both Galilees. In those districts there are few remains of a non-Jewish presence, whereas outside those sub-regions the evidence is unmistakable. The situation is most obvious in upper Galilee where a Roman temple from the second century CE at Qedesh points to a thriving pagan (Phoenician) culture.[61] Farther north the bilingual inscription from Dan, as well as the grotto of Pan at Banias dating from Seleucid times at least show that the region south of Hermon was thoroughly Hellenised from an early period.[62] Herod the Great dedicated a temple to Augustus at Caesarea Philippi (*JW* 1,404–6; *JA* 15,360). As mentioned previously, no

---

[59] Cf. 'Galilee-Jerusalem Relations,' above pp. 73 ff.

[60] A. Biran, 'To the God who is in Dan,' in *Temples and High Places in Biblical Times*, ed. A. Biran (Jerusalem: HUC-JIR, 1981) 142–51.

[61] M. Fischer, A. Ovadiah, and I. Roll, 'The Roman Temple at Kedesh, Upper Galilee: a Preliminary Study,' *Tel Aviv* 11 (1984) 142–72; and id., 'The Epigraphic Finds from the Roman Temple at Kedesh in the Upper Galilee,' *Tel Aviv* 13 (1986) 60–66.

[62] V. Tzaferis, 'Cults and Deities Worshipped at Caesarea-Philippi (Banias),' in *Priests Prophets and Scribes. Essays on the Formation and Heritage of Second Temple Judaism in Honour of Joseph Blenkinsopp*, ed. E. Ulrich et al., JSOT Supplements 149 (Sheffield: Sheffield Academic Press, 1992) 190–203; id., 'The "God who is in Dan" and the Cult of Pan at Banias in the Hellenistic and Roman Periods,' *Eretz Israel* 23, *A. Biran Volume* (Jerusalem: The Israel Exploration Society, 1992) 128*-35*.

material remains of Jewish presence have been found above a line that runs just north of Sasa, Baram and Qatzyon, all of which show unmistakable signs of having been Jewish communities. To the west/south-west, no synagogal remains have been found west of the line Peqi'in to Rama in Upper Galilee. A similar situation obtains in Lower Galilee west of the line running from Rama through I'billin to Tiv'on.[63] In the south no clear evidence of Jewish communities have been found south of the Nazareth ridge. Outside these lines one is moving in the orbit of the Greek cities, especially Beth Shean/Scythopolis and Akko/Ptolemais, while to the north Tyre was the dominant urban influence, even on Jewish Galilee.[64]

As well as the absence of synagogues or other material signs of Jewish presence in these areas, dedicatory inscriptions to pagan gods have been found only on the fringes of Galilee, such as the third-century CE inscription addressed in Greek to the Syrian gods, Hadad and Atargatis from the region of Akko/Ptolemais, or the one addressed to the Heliopolitan Zeus on Mount Carmel.[65] On the other hand, the only remains of pagan worship from Jewish Galilee (apart from some votive objects from Sepphoris) is the Syro-Egyptian shrine at Har Mispe Yamim in the Meiron massif, a site which was abandoned already in the second century BCE.[66] The Jewish and non-Jewish areas were not hermetically sealed from one another, however. The evidence points only to the predominant ethnic identities being localised. The literary evidence that there were Jews living in the city territories of Palestine and that some non-Jews were also to be found in Jewish areas, is not negated. In both cases they constituted minorities that were more or less influential on their immediate environment at different periods.

This distinction between Jewish and non-Jewish elements in Galilee is strikingly confirmed by Christian remains. Early archaeological work concentrated on the important Christian sites associated with the life of Jesus, such as Nazareth, Mt Tabor, Capernaum and Tabhga. In these areas Jews and Christians lived side by side from the Middle Roman period (i.e. second century CE onwards) until the Persian conquest in 614 CE.[67] A similar pattern emerges for the Golan also, whereas in Western Galilee on the

---

[63] Above, notes 23 and 24.

[64] *Cf. S. Freyne, 'Galileans, Phoenicians and Itureans: A Study of Regional Contrasts in the Hellenistic Age,' in *Hellenism in the Land of Israel*, ed. J. J. Collins and G. E. Sterling (Notre Dame: University of Notre Dame Press, 2000).

[65] M. Avi-Yonah, 'Mt Carmel and the God of Baalbek,' *IEJ* 2 (1951) 118–24; and id., 'Syrian Gods at Ptolemais-Acco,' *IEJ* 9 (1959) 1–12.

[66] R. Frankel, 'Har Mispe Yamim, 1988/9,' *Excavations and Surveys in Israel* 9 (1989/90) 100–102; R. Frankel and R. Ventura, 'The Mispe Yamim Bronzes,' *BASOR* 311 (1998) 39–55.

[67] Cf. B. Bagatti, *Antichi Villaggi Christiani di Galilea* (Jerusalem: Franciscan Publications, 1971); 'Christianity in Sepphoris and Galilee, below pp. 299 ff.

other hand there are many Christian settlements, identified by the number of crosses as well as dedicatory inscriptions on remains of tombs and churches.[68] Some of the inscriptions are in Syriac and others are in Greek, suggesting that some of the local Semitic, non-Jewish population may have converted to Christianity. This concentration of a Christian presence in Western Galilee seems to corroborate the fact that in that area at least, bordering on the territories of the Phoenician cities, the non-Jewish element continued to predominate from pre-Christian to Christian times.

Conclusion

This examination of archaeology's contribution to our understanding of the population patterns of Galilee in the first century CE appears to challenge the picture of a predominantly non-Jewish region, or at least one that was thoroughly open to all and every cultural influence coming from the larger Greco-Roman society. The kind of cultural ambience that is required to support the Cynic hypothesis, at least in the rural areas, would appear to be missing. The conclusion does not of itself disprove the hypothesis, but simply points to the fact that the population of Galilee, upper and lower, in the first century CE contained a sufficient number of people whose cultural and religious roots were linked with the south, thereby identifying with Jerusalem and its temple. This suggestion corresponds to what the literary sources in their very different ways also portray. The extent to which Jesus was inspired by such links cannot be determined from archaeology. Only detailed comparison of the ethos of his sayings, critically examined, with both their Jewish and non-Jewish parallels, can decide how far his world-view was shaped by the Jewish religious experience or by that of popular Greco-Roman philosophy. What this study has hopefully shown is that those who seek to support their picture of Cynic influences on Jesus and his audience cannot do so unambiguously on the basis of the archaeological evidence. It has also sought to demonstrate that by allowing archaeology its own voice, it can act as a challenge and a corrective to our texts, ancient and modern, while acknowledging the provisional nature of its own conclusions. Only an ongoing critical dialogue in which both disciplines operate on an equal footing will ensure that the mistakes of the past will not be repeated and that the new archaeology and the new quest for Jesus can be mutually enriching for each other.

---

[68] C. Dauphin, 'Jewish and Christian Communities in the Roman and Byzantine Gaulanitis. A Study of Evidence from Archaeological Surveys,' *PEQ* 114 (1982) 129–42; Aviam, 'Galilee: the Hellenistic to Byzantine Periods,' *NEAEHL,* 456–58.

9. Jesus and the Urban Culture of Galilee

The past 20 years have witnessed an unprecedented interest in Galilee in antiquity for several reasons, not all of which have to do with the fact that Jesus was from Nazareth in Galilee. A number of academic disciplines which previously had operated quite independently of each other have of late begun to show a convergence of interests that makes it possible to achieve a more comprehensive picture of Galilean life. Foremost among these is the archaeological work performed by a number of different teams who are interested in situating the results of their work at individual sites within the framework of the wider social and cultural context of the region as a whole, an area that should not be confined to political Galilee as known to Josephus (*JW* 3,35). More detailed analysis of the pottery has also achieved a much clearer impression of trading patterns on both an intra- and inter- regional basis. Social scientific models, especially those that deal with pre-industrial cities, are increasingly employed as an aid to a better understanding of the scattered pieces of evidence that are available, by situating these within a coherent theoretical framework for ancient societies. Textual studies too have contributed to the discussion. The impact of his Galilean sojourn on the writings of Josephus has been clearly exposed, and redactional studies of both the gospels (especially Mark and *Q*) and the rabbinical corpus have sought to relate the various strata of these writings to specific historical moments and social contexts of Galilee.

All of these developments have understandably played a role in the most recent wave of interest in the historical Jesus. However, the marriage of Galilean studies and historical Jesus research is fraught with its own difficulties which have not always been successfully negotiated. Some latter-day Schweitzer will, no doubt, critically evaluate the current crop of Jesus books, even if none of them can match Ernest Renan's romantic idealisation of Galilee. The danger is the way in which the Galilean social world can so easily be manipulated to suit the particular Jesus figure that is being presented. The problem is exacerbated by the fact that the gospels, the very documents that provide us with access to Jesus, are also quite important literary evidence for reconstructing the larger picture. When it comes to dealing with Galilee it is difficult, even for critical scholars, not to put Jesus at the centre and paint the picture of the region accordingly.

The explosion of specialised information on so many different fronts, even when dealing with a limited area such as Galilee, as well as the demand for methodological awareness in several disciplines, make it increasingly difficult for any one scholar to keep all aspects in focus. As one trained to deal with literary texts it has been my experience that the ongoing dialogue with archaeology, especially socio-archaeology, can be both fruitful and challenging. I am not thereby suggesting that archaeology provides the 'hard' facts which prove the gospels were right (or wrong). Rather, the dialogue between text and spade is highly complex, each with its own methodological constraints. It needs also to be recognised that, if it is true that 'our texts are tellings rather than showings', it is equally true that archaeology is a showing that requires a telling, that is an interpretation, to which texts have a very real contribution to make. Insofar as is possible each should be allowed to tell its different story before any attempt is made to generate a single converging account.

These methodological observations are prompted by a reading of two of the most imposing of the recent crop of books on Jesus, those of J. D. Crossan and J. Meier.[1] The description 'Mediterranean' and 'marginal' as applied to Jesus in the titles of the two works seemed promising from a Galilean perspective, yet in this regard at least both disappointed in different ways. We shall have to await further volumes of Meier's projected study before it becomes clear what particular importance he gives to the Galilean setting of the ministry. He acknowledges it more than once in this first volume, but without any real engagement with the recent archaeological evidence. Crossan's methodology is a deliberate attempt to keep literary, historical and social scientific procedures in critical dialogue, without giving precedence to any of them. Regardless of what one might think about the possibilities of such a hermeneutical stance, there is lacking here an engagement with the specific *Galilean* contours of Jesus' career, in contrast to the more generalised category of Mediterranean. This results from the archaeological evidence not being allowed to play any part in the historical reconstruction in part two of his work which surveys the social and political world of first-century Palestine. 'Mediterranean' enters the picture not primarily as an historical but as an anthropological category. It can then be used to make plausible the appearance in Galilee of those most pervasive of Mediterranean counter-culturalists, the Cynics.

In effect Crossan has repeated, in a highly nuanced and sophisticated manner to be sure, the History of Religions approach to Galilee, namely, that the epithet, 'Galilee of the gentiles' (Is 8,23; 1 Macc 5,15) should be regarded as an accurate cultural and ethnographic description of the region

---

[1] J. D. Crossan, *The Historical Jesus. The Life of a Mediterranean Jewish Peasant* (Edinburgh: T. & T. Clark, 1991); J. Meier, *A Marginal Jew. Rethinking the Historical Jesus*, vol. I (New York: Doubleday, 1991).

in the first century.[2] Bauer, for example, writing in a manner that scarcely disguises the then prevalent views on Pharisaic Judaism, states: 'Der Galiläer Jesus vertrat das Judentum in einer dem allgemein Menschlichen zugewandeten oder, wenn man so will, in einer synkretistisch erweichten Form.' Such claims provided the scholarly (sic!) basis for W. Grundmann's claim that because 'Galilaea heidnisch war', 'Jesus kein Jude war.'[3] To be fair to Crossan, he is at pains to retain a Jewish element to the picture. His Jesus is a Mediterranean Jewish peasant, but when one analyses the data base on which this picture of Jesus is constructed, very little of the distinctively Jewish concerns of the Jesus tradition as a whole is considered to be relevant.

It is indeed useful to see Galilee, or any other region for that matter, within the larger context – cultural, social and economic. The categories of honour/shame e.g., which Crossan regards as pivotal Mediterranean values, are applicable to Galilean life also, and have been used with excellent results by a number of scholars in clarifying the Jesus tradition. But within such a general perspective more immediate geographical, historical and socio-cultural factors which apply to particular regions also need to be articulated in order to present a balanced picture that has the best chance of approximating the real lives of people in that region in a given period. This must surely be the goal of all historical research, however much we need interpretative models that are more general in nature in order to make sense of the data. It is for this reason that I choose to start with the actual gospel narratives rather than with any reconstructed data base either of deeds or words, since the narratives, in their different ways to be sure, all anchor the ministry of Jesus within a coherent social world in Galilee. It is to an actual Galilee as 'the world behind the text' that these accounts point, and at the risk of being unfashionable, I want to look at those narratives about Jesus, particularly as they apply to Galilee and re-present the ethos there.[4] My aim is to test the ways in which these narratives situate the ministry of Jesus in that context with a view to judging how their tellings do or do not approximate to that world as we today can reconstruct it,

---

[2] W. Bauer, 'Jesus der Galiläer,' in *Aufsätze und Kleine Schriften* (Tübingen: J. C. B. Mohr, 1967) 91–108; W. Bertram, 'Der Hellenismus in der Urheimat des Evangeliums,' *Archiv für Religionswissenschaft* 32 (1935) 265–81; W. Grundmann, *Jesus der Galiläer und das Judentum* (Leipzig: Georg Wigand, 1941).

[3] Bauer, 'Jesus der Galiläer,' 104; Grundmann, *Jesus der Galiläer,* 166–75.

[4] This is the approach adopteded in my study, *Galilee, Jesus and the Gospels. Literary Approaches and Historical Investigations* (Dublin: Gill & Macmillan, and Philadelphia: Fortress Press, 1988). Cf. G. Theissen, *The Gospels in Context. Social and Political History in the Synoptic Tradition* (Edinburgh: T. & T. Clark, 1992), who has very effectively applied the notion of 'local colouring' (*Lokalkoloritforschung*) to the Synoptic Tradition at various stages of its development from small units to complete gospels.

and to judge how the actual Jesus might have related to it on the basis of a
critical use of the traditions about him that have been received.

Galilean Regional Geography and Jesus

By taking the gospel narratives as the starting point one is immediately
confronted with the geography of Jesus' ministry, especially the Galilean
geography. Much has been made of the symbolic intentions of the different evangelists in terms of their geographic references, especially in the
wake of Lohmeyer's study of Mark and Conzelmann's treatment of Luke.[5]
Such symbolism need not, however, obliterate all actual reference, especially in a context in which the land and its different regions had always
had definite religious associations from the Israelite experience and history
(cf. e.g., Is 8,23). Yet when one compares the gospel geography with the
accounts of Palestine that pagan writers such as Strabo, Pliny and Tacitus
provide us with, not to speak of Josephus and the Rabbinical writings,
there is a stark contrast. Despite various inaccuracies and confusions that
are easily attributable to the absence of maps or any other technical helps,
there is a far greater sense of place in the pagan writers and a keener
awareness of the natural resources. Josephus also has a very clear sense of
boundaries, distances between various places and the length of time required for journeys between different destinations, as well as the topography of certain key sights – all matters we would expect someone who had
been active in the field as a military and political commander to be well-
informed about. In the Rabbinical writings, on the other hand, geographical interests are directly related to halachic ordinances to do with the observance of tithing laws and the settling of disputed cases with regard to
the place of provenance of various products. That these discussions were
not purely academic emerges from Josephus' account about John of Gischala's exploitation of his co-religionists' desire to obtain native oil (*Life*
74), as well as from the mosaic floor in the synagogue at Rehov in the
Beth Shean valley, a section of which reproduces a text also found in several rabbinical writings, which describes the borders of *Eretz Israel*. It may
well be no accident that the list of places is most detailed for the borders
between Tyre and Galilee. The concern apparently was to define precisely
the area within which tithes and other offerings would have to be set aside.
For this purpose the rabbis sought to temper strict observance with leni-

---

[5] E. Lohmeyer, *Galiläa und Jerusalem,* FRLANT 34 (Göttingen: Vandenhoeck & Ruprecht, 1936); H. Conzelmann, *The Theology of St. Luke* (London: Faber and Faber,
1960).

ency in their description, especially in view of the economic hardships of the third century CE.[6]

By comparison, the gospels show relatively little interest in these matters, even though there is a general awareness of such aspects as the regional divisions of the land (Galilee, Samaria and Judea), the surrounding territories and cities as well as other features of the physical geography, such as the lake and the activities associated with it. While there is no concentrated attention on these details within the narratives, the apparent distance, even vagueness, should not lull us into dismissing the geographical notices of the gospels as mere window-dressing, devoid of any intention of actual reference, however imprecise. Rather they summon us to discern more fully the intentions of these notices against their immediate historical background. For example, does the fact that Jesus is depicted as moving freely from Galilee to its environs, though never entering any of the cities, but only the 'the territory of the Gerasenes', 'the borders of Tyre' or 'the villages of Caesarea Philippi' (Mk 5,1; 7,24; 8,27), reflect the situation in Mark's own day in relation to Christian communities in the region? Or does it tell us anything about Jesus' attitudes as these were remembered as significant? And how might one go about answering such a question in historical terms? More intriguing still is the question why there is no mention of either Sepphoris or Tiberias, the former refurbished and the latter founded during Jesus' life-time. Both played a very significant role in the commercial and administrative life of Galilee, as Josephus makes abundantly clear.

The excursions of Jesus to outside territories in Mark (7,31) are generally believed to fit into the evangelist's gentile and missionary perspective.[7] There are, however, certain problems with that position from a purely historical perspective. On the assumption that Mark was written during or immediately after the Jewish war, easy movement between Galilee and the surrounding non-Jewish territories would be rather difficult. Episodes like the insistence of the inhabitants of Tarichaeae that the refugee noblemen from Trachonitis should be circumcised (*Life* 113) show just how fraught relations were in that period. This is not surprising in the aftermath of the Jew/Gentile hostilities that had broken out in the territories of the Greek cities of Palestine immediately prior to the revolt (*JW* 2,457–65). In such a climate would Mark have presented a Jesus figure who seemed so indifferent to such tensions? Perhaps so. One can think of sev-

---

[6] J. Sussman. 'The Inscription in the Synagogue at Rehob,' in *Ancient Synagogues Revealed*, ed. L. Levine (Jerusalem: The Israel Exploration Society, 1981) 146–53.

[7] F. Lang, "'Über Sidon mitten ins Gebiet der Dekapolis." Geographie und Theologie in Markus 7,31,' *ZDPV* 94 (1978) 145–60; T. Schmeller, 'Jesus im Umland Galiläas,' *BZ* 38 (1994) 44–66.

eral reasons why such a presentation might have been significant at that juncture, especially if his gospel was directed to Christian communities in the Galilee or southern Syria, as has been suggested. On the other hand such a cavalier attitude to religious and social boundaries could only have been extremely provocative to Jews in the region, and made Christian communities there more vulnerable to attacks from Jewish neighbours.

What if we were to think of such inter-regional movements some thirty years earlier, informed by the evidence from the archaeological data? How well do they fit the situation then? Palestine, like other regions of the Mediterranean world seems to have enjoyed the relative peace of Tiberius' reign. In Galilee Antipas had political quarrels with the Nabateans only. The Phoenician city territories, the territory of Herod Philip and the Dekapolis would all have been accessible to Jewish traders and craftsmen, and the Herodian cities of lower Galilee were certainly no less likely to be unfriendly to gentiles then than later. The archaeological data mentioned earlier are highly relevant here, in that recent neutron activation analysis of common household pottery in the Roman period shows that there was a thriving export industry of Kefar Hanania wares to the surrounding cities, especially in the Golan, at both Jewish and non-Jewish sites, but also to Ptolemais and Caesarea Philippi. In other words, the trade was both inter-regional and inter-ethnic, in all probability.[8] Significantly, however, no wares emanating in Galilee are found in sites south of the Nazareth ridge, e.g., at Beth Shean or Samaria, or farther south in Judea, equally supporting the notices of Lk 9,52; Jn 4,10, that Jews and Samaritans do not have any intercourse. The preponderance of Tyrian coinage not only at most of the upper Galilean sites, but also at those in lower Galilee (including a number of hordes) supports the existence of such trade across religious and cultural boundaries in the north.[9]

In other words, both the political realities and the material remains make the kind of free movement between Jews and gentiles in the north more plausible for the period of Jesus than for that of the proposed dating of Mark. The material remains show that such movement was a fact of everyday life, and was interrupted only by concern for halachic observances at periods of heightened tension. When the political and religious climate was right, Jews had long since learned how to live their traditional way of life among gentiles and to deal with them commercially on a daily basis. The hostility that operated between Jew and non-Jew in the Helle-

---

[8] D. Adan-Bayewitz, *Common Pottery in Roman Galilee. A Study of Local Trade* (Ramat-Gan: Bar-Ilan University Press, 1993).

[9] R. Hanson, *Tyrian Influence in Upper Galilee* (Cambridge, MA: ASOR Publications, 1980); J. Raynor and Y. Meshorer, *The Coins of Ancient Meiron* (Winona Lake: Eisenbrauns, 1988).

nistic city territories prior to the Great Revolt was, therefore, exceptional. The differences with the Samaritans ran deeper, presumably because of the shared religious heritage that was disputed, thereby precluding any possibility of normal everyday relations.

These observations are not intended as an uncritical vindication of the gospel narratives with regard to the historical Jesus in the Galilean setting, nor should they be read as providing further evidence for Bauer's and more recent claims for a syncretised ethos in Galilee. Such generalised accounts ignore the fact that despite the everyday contacts which the material culture can illustrate, real differences on religious and ethnic grounds could and did surface when Jewish self-identity in the region was under threat. Gerd Theissen's analysis of the story of the Syrophoenician woman has shown that despite its being made to serve Mark's gentile purposes now, he does not remove the Jewish bias of the pre-Markan account when viewed from the perspective of its local colouring.[10] This suggests a much stronger ethnocentric focus to Jesus' ministry than some of the recent accounts want to claim. We would also have to ask whether his other excursions to so-called 'gentile territory' did not have a similar purpose: Jesus' interest in visiting such places was not to 'go to the gentiles', but rather to 'the lost sheep of the house of Israel', particularly in view of the fact, again on the basis of the material evidence, that it is possible to speak of a 'cultural continuum' between upper Galilee and the Golan, the precise district that would have to be traversed in order to get to the region of the Dekapolis from the borders of Tyre.[11] Nor should it be overlooked that the restoration of Israel included the gentiles in messianic blessings also, according to varied strands of Second Temple literature (Is 2,2–4; 45,2; Zeph 3,9; Zech 8,20–22; Tob 13,11; Sir 36,11–17; Sib Or 3,616). Thus a concern for the restoration of Israel, inspired by the prophetic tradition would not have been xenophobic as far as Jesus was concerned. Mark's careful presentation of his visiting the territories and villages of the surrounding cities, but not the cities themselves, would fit easily into such a pattern. Yet Mark also intimates that Jesus, despite his healing powers, was not welcomed by the people of Gerasa, who on hearing of his successful exorcism of the legion of demons asked him to depart their territory (Mk 5,17). In other words, the Markan narrative does not totally dilute the Jew/Gentile divisions in cultural as well as religious terms in its handling of Jesus' movements, as Theissen notes, even when we might assume that it was in its own theological interests to do so.

---

[10] Theissen, *The Gospels in Context,* 61–81.

[11] E. Meyers, 'Galilean Regionalism as a Factor in Historical Reconstruction,' *BASOR* 221 (1976) 93–101; and id., 'Galilean Regionalism: A Reappraisal,' in *Approaches to Ancient Judaism,* ed. W. Scott Green vol. 5 (Missoula: Scholars Press, 1978) 115–31.

Such a conclusion makes the complete silence concerning Sepphoris and Tiberias all the more baffling. If the reasons for the omission is the lack of success that Jesus had in such centres then we might have expected a series of woes against them similar to those expressed against Chorazin, Bethsaida and Capernaum. On the other hand if Jesus was prepared to visit gentile territories to address Jews living there, why exclude these cities from the ambit of his ministry, since they both were thoroughly Jewish in character in the first century, despite a minority gentile presence? Reading the gospels with the more complete picture of Galilee, both geographical and historical, as the subtext, the silence appears not just as an omission, but as quite deliberate. It seems impossible for anyone to have conducted the kind of ministry attributed to Jesus in lower Galilee without having encountered in some way these two Herodian cities and their spheres of influence. Perhaps a consideration of the political and economic roles of these centres will help to explain the enigma that our geographic considerations have thrown up with regard to the intention of Jesus' ministry.

The Role of Sepphoris and Tiberias

Our discussion of the geographic realities of Jesus' ministry as these are reflected in the gospel narratives raises the question of the Herodian cities of lower Galilee in a particularly acute manner. The usual ways of raising the issue of Jesus and Sepphoris are too simplistic, focusing as they do on the personal impact that growing up beside such a centre, or even possibly plying one's trade there as a τέκτων, might have had on him. To pose the question in this way is to run the risk of psychologising Jesus after the manner of the nineteenth-century liberals.[12] What should not be forgotten is that both centres were new foundations. As such they symbolised and embodied rapid social change in Galilee as a whole under Antipas. Such a claim might appear to be unwarranted in view of the rather phlegmatic character that comes across in the gospel portraits, especially Luke's, and because Josephus does not give the same detailed account of his reign as he does of Herod the Great. Antipas had hoped to succeed his father, and unsuccessful, he was even more likely to have thrown himself into the task of proving himself to the Romans, never relinquishing the hope of kingship to the very end. Indeed the name αὐτοκράτωρ as applied to Sepphoris and the calling of Tiberias after the Emperor shows how much he kept

---

[12] R. Batey, *Jesus and the Forgotten City. New Light on Sepphoris and the Urban World of Jesus* (Grand Rapids: Baker Books, 1991), assumes without adequate testing that proximity to an urban centre means sharing the dominant values and ethos of the place.

Roman imperial patronage in his sights. Rome allowed him a personal income of 200 talents. To collect this he had need of a well disciplined, loyal and efficient administrative bureaucracy – tax collectors, notaries, judges, military personnel, store and market managers – in short, a whole range of retainers, who could insure that he and his court would reap the full benefits of a relatively fertile region within an agrarian economy. Antipas' reign, therefore, marked the rapid development of the Galilean economy along lines that were directly opposed to the Jewish patrimonial ideal, as this had been enshrined in the Pentateuch, upheld by the prophets and re-enacted by reformers such as Nehemiah (Neh 5,1–11).

The archaeological evidence has a particular contribution to make towards a discussion of the import of these developments on Galilean life generally. While surveys have shown a cultural continuum between upper Galilee and the Golan in terms of linguistic habits and architectural styles, lower Galilee presents a somewhat different profile in that Greek inscriptions occur more frequently here than Aramaic or Hebrew ones, giving rise to the general assumption that lower Galilee is more 'open' to the prevailing wider atmosphere, largely, but not entirely attributable to the presence of the two Herodian centres.[13] However, when compared with such nearby urban centres as Beth Shean/Scythopolis or Caesarea Philippi e.g., the material remains suggest a profile for the city in the first century that is very different. No statues, temples or other public signs of pagan cult (apart from a few domestic figurines) have so far come to light. The numbers of *mikwaoth* especially in the residential area near the acropolis where presumably the more affluent residents dwelt, strongly suggest an observant Jewish ethos, despite the presence of the theatre, one of the trappings of Greek culture, possibly from the first century already. The rightly acclaimed Dionysiac and Nile mosaics point in a different direction. However, these are to be dated to a much later period when, as Diocaesarea, the city's character had changed considerably, while still not precluding an affluent and influential Jewish presence there as we know from rabbinical sources. Thus, archaeology has not provided the kind of clear evidence that would be considered necessary to support the case that Sepphoris was a centre of dissemination of Greek influences in lower Galilee, to the detriment of Jewish religious affiliations.

In fact the ceramic evidence examined by D. Adan-Bayewitz, already referred to, would appear to preclude such a possibility. Following NAA analysis of the Sepphoris pottery remains, it is his conclusion that Kefar Hanania, known from the Mishnah as being situated on the dividing line between upper and lower Galilee as a pottery-making centre, had produced

---

[13] A. Overman, 'Recent Advances in the Archaeology of the Galilee in the Roman Period,' *Currents in Research. Biblical Studies* 1 (1993) 35–58.

all the household wares for Sepphoris (and indeed all Galilee). In addition stone storage jars for the city were produced at another village, Shikhin, which has been identified with a site close to Sepphoris.[14] These findings suggest a pattern of co-operation between the city and the villages in the hinterland that would appear to rule out any idea of tension between them, however we are to interpret the literary evidence. Sepphoris, on the basis of this evidence could not be seen as a typical 'consumer' city parasitically related to its hinterland, since it provided a market outlet for the village wares, and may have acted as a collection centre for grain and other produce from the fertile Bet Netofa valley, something that the many underground storage chambers at the site strongly suggests. In addition the evidence of local villages specialising in different kinds of pottery production dispels the notion of the Galileans as boorish peasants, a representation that one sometimes encounters in various authors, ancient and modern.

Nevertheless, this evidence must not be allowed to tilt the picture so far in the opposite direction that all distinctions between city and hinterland are entirely obliterated. At this point a more general model of urban-rural relations can help in sorting out and interpreting the data, rather than simply juxtaposing discrete pieces of evidence either from archaeology or literary sources and making generalised claims from these. There is general agreement today among historians of antiquity, that ancient, as distinct from medieval cities were symbiotically related to their immediate countryside, a shift in perspective which has been brought about by archaeological surveys at many different locations throughout the Mediterranean world, and which is, of course implied in the term πόλις.[15] Yet this does not answer the question of whether the relationship was balanced or not. Certainly, insofar as urban centres had administrative and military roles they were perceived as mediators of distant power and control on a region, and were often not experienced as benevolent by the non-elite regionals. It was Roman policy generally to encourage concentration of resources at certain centres, leading to the evolution of local elites who would vie with each other in expending their resources at the urban centre, only to be eventually assimilated with the Roman provincial ruling class. Thus the peasantry were deprived of an independent local leadership, who might be more sensitive to their needs.

The Herodians can be thought to fit this category rather well for first-century Galilee. The building projects at Sepphoris and Tiberias presumably created a certain demand for local labour, yet if the system of *angaria*,

---

[14] D. Adan-Bayewitz and I. Perlman, 'The Local Trade of Sepphoris in the Roman Period,' *IEJ* 40 (1990) 153–72.

[15] J. Rich and A. Wallace-Hadrill, eds., *City and Country in the Ancient World* (London and New York: Routledge, 1991).

or forced labour was employed, as seems to have happened in the founding of Tiberias (*JA* 18,37), then these projects did little to improve the lot of the peasants. As Martin Goodman has persuasively argued, the problem of debt was one of the factors that lead to the Jewish revolt, and it was the direct result of the elites drawing off the resources of the countryside, but without any productive reinvestment.[16] Thus the political rebellion against Rome quickly degenerated into a social revolution, in which impoverished Jews from the countryside turned on their own aristocracy, replacing the reigning high priest with one elected on egalitarian lines. While these developments were associated in particular with Jerusalem and Judea, nevertheless the attacks of the Galilean peasants on both Sepphoris and Tiberias (*Life* 66, 376) should be seen as expressions of the same feelings. In these actions we are surely seeing symptoms of a peasantry frustrated with centres which were not prepared to offer the kind of solidarity between town and country that might have been expected but which was not in fact forthcoming. Thus the archaeological evidence which suggests close ties between Sepphoris, in particular, and its hinterland, in no way precludes resentment of the elites which comprised the bulk of the influential population in both centres.

What then was the character of such places? The appellation πόλις as applied to them needs to be carefully evaluated, since undoubtedly they were not 'free and autonomous' as this was understood within the Roman administrative system and as it applied to such places as Beth Shean/ Scythopolis or the Phoenician cities of the coast, who were empowered to mint their own coins as well as Roman imperial ones from the first century CE. Rather, under Antipas, as distinct from later times, they were both eparchies or administrative centres within the framework of a client kingdom. Thus they shared a common ethos as administrative centres whose population for the most part was from the retainer class, without excluding wealthy landowners as a native aristocracy as well. Josephus paints a picture of the mixed character of the population of Tiberias at its foundation – people from every quarter and background being brought together either by force or with blandishments of gifts of land in return for loyalty to Antipas (*JA* 18,36–38), thus presumably violating Jewish law not merely in terms of building the city on a burial ground, but also in forcibly appropriating the land of others. This picture was maintained subsequently as we see in the account of the citizenry when Josephus himself arrived in the region in 66 CE – a combination of Herodian landowning residents with

---

[16] M. Goodman, 'The First Jewish Revolt: Social Conflict and the Problem of Debt,' *JJS* 33 (1982) 417–27. See further his *The Ruling Class of Judaea. The Origins of the Jewish Revolt against Rome, A.D. 66–70* (Cambridge: Cambridge University Press, 1987), especially 51–108.

estates across the lake, various officials at the Herodian court such as Justus of Tiberias, a man well-educated in the Greek ways, and the service classes – 'sailors and destitutes' as the aristocratic Jerusalemite describes them (*Life* 32–38). The fact that in 66 CE Tiberias has the trappings of a Greek city with its βουλή and ἄρχων should not disguise the fact that it had a subordinate position within the Herodian administrative framework from the outset. Even that role had been diminished when Nero transferred it to the territory of Agrippa II in 54/55, thus ceding primacy in banking, market and other administrative functions to its rival Sepphoris, something that Justus bemoans. It was only in 66 that Sepphoris struck its first coins and Tiberias had to wait until 100 CE, i.e. after the end of the Herodian dynasty, before it enjoyed the same privilege by favour of Trajan.[17]

Since land was the primary resource in antiquity in general and in Galilee in particular, the issue of Herodian land policy is crucial to the point here, namely, an intensification of agrarian values in Antipas' Galilee as demonstrated by the emergence of the two centres. The question is whether there was an appreciable move away from small family-run holdings, in which reciprocity was still the basic mode of exchange, towards a situation of land used as a revenue-generating resource. Previously, I have maintained that on the literary evidence (Josephus, the gospels, the Jewish writings and the Zenon papyri), landownership patterns in Galilee were mixed – large estates such as Beth Anath and small, family-run holdings that were part of the Jewish ideal as we have seen (1 Macc 14,10; cf. Neh 5,1–11).[18] Undoubtedly, pressure had come on these latter since the Hellenistic age, as increased taxation and narrow margins in terms of yields left the small landowner increasingly vulnerable. Once a person was caught in the situation of having to borrow money for whatever reason, thus mortgaging their holding, it was extremely difficult for them to recover.[19]

The *Similitudes of Enoch*, which most commentators date to the Herodian period, reflect this situation with their repeated condemnation of 'the kings, the governors, the high officials and the landlords' (*1 Enoch*

---

[17] Y. Meshorer, *The City Coins of Eretz Israel and the Dekapolis in the Roman Period* (Jerusalem: The Israel Museum, 1985) 33 and 36.

[18] S. Freyne, *Galilee from Alexander the Great to Hadrian. A Study of Second Temple Judaism* (reprint, Edinburgh: T. & T. Clark, 1998) 156–70. Cf. further 'Herodian Economics. Searching for a Suitable Model,' above pp. 86 ff.

[19] B. Isaac, 'The Babatha Archive. A Review Article,' *IEJ* 42 (1992) 62–75, especially 72, notes that in the village of Engedi there were both crown property and privately owned farms side by side. Document 11 from the cache relates how a centurion stationed in the town had made a loan of sixty denarii of Tyrian silver to a local Jewish resident, who pledged his courtyard should he be unable to repay the loan. Documents 19 and 20 indicate that the loan was in fact repaid, suggesting somebody engaged in commercial activity rather than subsistence farming.

38,4; 46,3–5; 48,8; 53,5; 62), whereas the holy and just ones will 'possess the earth', thus echoing the beatitude of Jesus (Mt 5,5). Clearly, whatever about the ideal the reality was that pressures on peasant ownership had increased considerably. The bequests of land that went with the foundation of Tiberias were at somebody's expense, yet when it and Tarichaeae were transferred to the kingdom of Agrippa II by Nero, significantly these places are not said to have a χώρα but rather they are given σὺν ταῖς τοπαρχίαις, that is, they were toparchic capitals rather than cities in any strict sense (*JW* 2,252; cf. *JA* 20,159). Equally Josephus assumes that Sepphoris had villages associated with it which could have provided it with sufficient resources to resist Rome, had it so wished (*Life* 65, 346). In neither case can there be any question of a city territory in the strict sense, and hence these references must point to a situation of wealthy citizens owning land in the countryside around, but residing in the city itself, as in the case of Crispus, the prefect under Agrippa I, who resided in Tiberias and was part of the elite of the city, but who was absent at his estates across the Jordan when Josephus arrived in Galilee in 66 CE (*Life* 33 f.). Recently David Fiensy has produced the most up-to-date study on the topic of landownership in Herodian times in which he challenges my views about the persistence of the small landowning class, on the basis that the evidence does not allow us to decide between ownership of land and leasing. Yet later in the same work he acknowledges that the small landowners bore the brunt of the tax burden, which was considerable as we have seen.[20] To some extent the issue is academic in this context as on either reading of the evidence the tension between two very different systems was real and growing all the time.

The intensification of the market that is represented in the emergence of Sepphoris and Tiberias as administrative centres within an agrarian economy brought about considerable changes in the lives of Galilean peasants. In such a climate it is the small landowner that is most vulnerable since there is no protection built into the system against the failure of a bad harvest, illness or some other catastrophe. By contrast leaseholders may be fortunate enough to be protected by a benign landlord in a culture where magnanimity could be seen as worthy of honour within a patron-client relationship. Archaeological evidence suggests that the single holdings were not large – an average of 6 to 9 acres has been estimated – and hence there was little possibility of increased output through more intense labour or specialised production. In all probability many engaged in mixed farming in an effort to meet the family's basic dietary requirements – vines, olives and grain. The demands of the tribute, other taxes and the religious dues

---

[20] D. Fiensy, *The Social History of Palestine in the Herodian Period* (Lewiston, NY: The Edwin Mellen Press, 1991) 55–57 and 92 f.

had first to be met and in the case of grain crops the following year's seed requirements had to be set aside. This meant scarcity for domestic use with low nutrition resulting in a high incidence of illness and infant mortality.[21] In such conditions the reciprocal system of exchange with its in-built concerns for all members of the extended household or clan is more favourable to the poor than is the market economy which functions in favour of the ruling elite and their administrative retainers. The tensions between these two types of economic system and the increasing dominance of the latter in Herodian Galilee generated the social situation that many gospel parables depict – day labourers, debt, resentment of absentee landlords, wealthy estate owners with little concern for tenants' needs, exploitative stewards of estates, family feuds over inheritance etc. In these vignettes we can catch glimpses of both systems in operation and the clash of values that are inherent, a topic we shall presently address.

The picture here emerging suggests considerable tensions between Sepphoris and Tiberias on the one hand, and the Galilean rural hinterland on the other. Essentially, they represented two very different value systems which could not easily co-exist, for the success of the one was dependent on the exploitation of the other. The situation was complicated by the fact that the new Herodian elite represented by the two centres in question continued to maintain allegiance to a Jewish way of life, while being imbued with the values of the Roman agrarian economy. A shared religious belief system with its stress on temple offerings based on ownership of land was difficult to maintain in such an atmosphere of social inequality. Only in distant Jerusalem, and then occasionally, was it possible to bridge the gap between symbolic universe and social experience. Is this the religio-social vacuum within the region that Jesus sought to fill with his message of the coming kingdom of God and the implications of such a proclamation for the social life of those who heard his word? As already suggested, there are several possible explanations for the absence of any mention of Sepphoris and Tiberias in the gospels – a strategic avoidance in view of the fate of his mentor the Baptist; a failed visit that went unrecorded unlike similar ones to Capernaum, Chorazin and Bethsaida; or a principled avoidance as an act of solidarity with the victims in order to generate a prophetic critique of their oppressors. It is this latter suggestion that will be pursued in the final section of this essay.

---

[21] G. Hamel, *Poverty and Charity in Roman Palestine. The First Three Centuries C.E.* (Berkeley: University of California Press, 1990) 94–140; D. Oakman, *Jesus and the Economic Questions of his Day* (Lewiston NY: The Edwin Mellen Press, 1986) 57–72.

Jesus in Galilee

Crossan and others with different nuances view the ministry of Jesus in Galilee in the light of Cynic ideals for coping with life's problems that, it is claimed, were widely diffused in the early empire. This claim is based on a number of different assumptions: 1) the similarity of Jesus' life-style and that of his followers with the Cynic counter-cultural attitudes towards home, family and possessions; 2) the proximity of Galilee to the Dekapolis where it is believed Cynic ideas had widespread currency in view of the fact that Meleager of Gadara is known for his espousal of these ideas at Tyre in the second century BCE already;[22] 3) as urban centres in lower Galilee, Sepphoris and Tiberias would have mediated these ideas to the country people who visited for market or for other reasons. Thus Crossan believes that the most natural understanding of Jesus' talk about the kingdom of God among his peasant audience was not that of apocalyptic but rather the Cynic belief that the wise person is king. Burton Mack, another influential proponent of the Cynic Jesus, believes that Jesus did for Jewish belief at a popular level what Philo had attained on a more intellectual plane, namely to open it to a broader understanding of life that was synonymous with the Hellenistic world-view.[23] In addition, there are the views of F. G. Downing, based on an intimate knowledge of the Cynic sources. According to his latest statement of the case the presence of Cynic elements in such a wide variety of early Christian writings, ranging from *Q* and Mark through Paul to James, is more readily explained if these ideas emanated with Jesus himself, rather than that his ideas were later subjected to a process of 'Cynicisation'. Thus, despite his acknowledgement of 'the Jewish palette' in the earliest strata of the Jesus tradition and the presence of 'older, native Jewish influences on Jesus', Downing also claims that a pervasive Cynic influence on Galilee at a popular level provides the most appropriate communicational context for Jesus' sayings, including those to do with the kingdom of God.[24]

It is beyond the scope of this paper to deal with these arguments in detail.[25] The most significant aspect for the case being argued here is the as-

---

[22] M. Hengel. *Judentum und Hellenismus. Studien zu ihrer Begegnung unter besonderer Berücksichtigung Palästinas bis zur Mitte des 2.Jh.s v. Chr.* 2nd ed. WUNT 10 (Tübingen: J. C. B. Mohr, 1973) 152–61.

[23] Crossan, *The Historical Jesus*, 72–88 and 265–302; B. Mack, *A Myth of Innocence. Mark and Christian Origins* (Philadelphia: Fortress Press, 1988) 72–74.

[24] F. G. Downing, *Cynics and Christian Origins* (Edinburgh: T. & T. Clark, 1992) 146–48.

[25] Cf. H. D. Betz, 'Jesus and the Cynics: Survey and Analysis of a Hypothesis,' *JR* 74 (1994) 453–75; cf. 'Galilean Questions to Crossan's Mediterranean Jesus,' below pp. 208 ff.

sumption that close proximity to an urban culture meant assimilation of the ideas prevalent among the urban elites by the peasants. All the archaeological evidence from both upper and lower Galilee shows clear signs of a distinctive Jewish presence in certain areas of both sub-regions, many of the sites dating to the early Roman period (i.e. first century CE), if not earlier.[26] They had been able to maintain a religious and cultural identity, even when a case can be made for Greek being the *lingua franca*, at least in lower Galilee, especially along the lake shore. Are we to suppose that these people abandoned their inherited beliefs and values for those emanating from outside and mediated by centres that were treated with suspicion, if not hostility? I remain unconvinced by such a scenario, preferring to see Jesus espousing a prophetic critique of the dominant prevailing ethos, based on covenantal ideals for a restored Israel, within an apocalyptic framework that made it possible to imagine and propose a radically different life-style and values. Such an understanding of the kingdom of God was much more likely to be familiar to Jewish peasants from synagogal prayers and scriptural readings than those touted by Cynic teachers in urban contexts, even if we were to suppose that these latter found expression in the urban centres of Galilee also.

Most treatments of Jesus' ministry begin by discussing the opposition which it generated among Jewish religious circles over issues of Torah observance. In a Galilean context, however, that may be the wrong starting point, especially in the light of E. P. Sanders' discussion within the context of what he describes as 'common' Jewish practice among the ordinary people who would have regarded themselves as Jewish throughout the Galilean villages.[27] In suggesting that his most immediate target was the rapidly developing Herodian economy of Galilee, one should avoid turning him into a social revolutionary, devoid of any religious intentions with regard to the renewal of Israel. In order to keep both aspects in proper focus it is important to recall the collusion between Herodian rule and an increasingly venal Jerusalem aristocracy, among whom were the upper echelons of the priesthood itself (*JA* 20,181.206 f.). It was in their interest to maintain the fiction of the theocratic ideal of the temple-state, while themselves being thoroughly imbued with the values of the elite rich of the Greco-Roman world, as can be seen graphically from the discovery of luxury items in the Jewish quarter in Jerusalem. With this backdrop in view we shall approach the Jesus tradition in search of a critique of both Herodian political power and the values of the market economy which were shared by provincial Herodian and Jerusalem aristocracy alike.

---

[26] M. Aviam, 'Galilee: the Hellenistic to Byzantine Periods,' in *NEAEHL* 2, 452–58.

[27] E. P. Sanders, *Judaism: Practice and Belief, 63 B.C.E.–66 C.E.* (London: SCM Press, 1992).

Jesus and Herodian kingship

Three items from the sayings tradition suggest themselves for consideration in terms of a possible critique of the values of Herodian kingship: a) the saying which contrasts the standards of human rulers with those which should operate in the community of Jesus (Mk 10,42–45 and parallels; b) the reference to divided kingdoms and houses in the Beelzebul controversy (Mk 3,24; *Q*Mt 12,25 = *Q*Lk 11,17); c) the disparaging reference to those who dwell in royal palaces in the encomium on the Baptist (*Q*Mt 11,9; *Q*Lk 7,25 = *Gos. Thom.* 78). While various redactional aspects of all three items can be readily recognised, there is still a very good case to be made for hearing in these sayings echoes at least of Jesus' voice, which warrants our considering their impact in terms of the situation in Antipas' Galilee, irrespective of their use in later gospel settings.

a) A dispute among the disciples over places of honour in the kingdom is the immediate context for Jesus' contrast between his standards and those of the world with regard to leadership. Luke has transferred the saying to the context of the last supper (Lk 22,25), where it forms part of a more general farewell discourse about attitudes in the community, thus reflecting later discussions about authority. He has also softened the implied criticism of secular kingship by acknowledging that kings can also be benefactors (εὐεργέται). The context of early Christian leadership may also be operative in Mk's setting already, but in contrast to Lk both he and Mt employ rare compound verbs by use of the preposition κάτα together with κυριεύειν and ἐξουσιάζειν, suggesting a repressive, downward force or total dominion. Finally, whereas Mt and Lk speak directly of βασιλεῖς, kings of the gentiles, Mk is decidedly more ironic, speaking of 'those who supposedly rule over gentiles' (οἱ δοκοῦντες ἄρχειν, cf. Gal. 2,6.9). There is nothing in the allusion that would automatically refer it to Herodian kingship, and it could, arguably, be seen as a piece of generalised comment. Indeed the reference to ἔθνη/gentiles, might appear positively to exclude such an implied reference. At Acts 4,26, however, the Ps. text which refers to 'the kings of the earth' is applied both to Herod Antipas and to Pilate, the representative of Roman rule. From a pious Jewish perspective the Herodians could, it would seem, be regarded as analogous to gentile rulers, despite their continued interest in, and in some instances, observance of their subjects' religious practices.

What if we were to read the reference to earthly kings as directly inspired by conditions in Antipas' Galilee? Could it agree with Theissen's category of 'local colouring' for that period, even though he himself considers the present saying only in the context of the immediate post–70 situation, when Christian disciples as well as Jews in the region had to come to terms with the might of Rome?[28] As is well known, though Antipas aspired to kingship, he never actually obtained it, losing out in the end to his nephew, Agrippa I. He sought to play a role in international affairs, as his father had done, by arranging for a treaty between the Roman legate of Syria, Vitellius, and the Persian king, Artapanus (*JA* 18,101–5). Josephus, as distinct from the gospel writers (especially Luke), has little doubt about his ruthless character in lording over his subjects. His account of the peremptory justice for John the Baptist, as well as those compelled to inhabit Tiberias, is set in immediate contrast with the attitude of Antipas' brother Philip, who conducted sittings of his court at various places in order to facilitate his subjects (*JA* 18,106–8.116–19). Here is someone who regards himself more highly than his status as ethnarch within Roman imperial administration warranted, and behaved accordingly. Against such a background perhaps the critique in Mk's remark about kingship, especially with the implied put-down of the verb δοκέω, should not be understood as a generalisation. It could, justifiably, be heard as a direct swipe at Antipas and to have originated within the circumstances of his rule, as we know them from other sources.

b) In both the *Q* and Markan versions Jesus counters the charge of being in league with Beelzebul by the image of a kingdom (βασιλεία) or house (οἰκία) divided against itself not being able to stand (Mk 3,24–25), or being left desolate (*Q*Mt 12,25; *Q*Lk 11,17). The *Q* version as represented by both Mt and Lk agree with the more generalised form of the saying – every kingdom/πᾶσα βασιλεία – suggesting again ordinary wisdom based on everyday experience. Mk's use of the singular, but with a conditional 'if' (ἐὰν) of itself would scarcely warrant seeing here a more direct reference to the immediate circumstances. However, in both versions, the overall context of the passage is the contrast between the kingdoms of Satan and that of God. The classic apocalyptic framework sees earthly kingdoms, especially repressive ones, as representative of the present evil age which will be replaced by the kingdom of 'the saints of the most high', as in the Danielic version of the mythic pattern (Dn 11,23). Thus, it would be natural for hearers to identify the image with the most immediate source of repression, either Herodian or Roman. While the context of Vespasian's ascent to imperial power in 69 CE, the year of the three emperors, is suggestive as far as Mk's readership is concerned, *Q*'s dating is earlier, even if we were to assign this passage with Kloppenborg to *Q*2, as part of the later judgement/apocalyptic strand of that document.[29]

---

[28] *The Gospels in Context*, 286.

[29] J. Kloppenborg, *The Formation of Q. Trajectories in Ancient Wisdom Collections* (Philadelphia: Fortress Press, 1987) 121–27.

Again, therefore, we are justified in seeking a *Sitz im Leben Jesu* in terms of Herodian politics. The internecine struggle between the sons of Herod the Great over the terms of his will, leading eventually to Augustus' decision not to appoint any of them as king, immediately come to mind. Neither was the kingship restored on the deposition of Archelaus in 6 CE, nor subsequently in 37 CE on the death of Philip. Apart from the brief reign of Agrippa I (41–44, CE), Herod's kingdom was never reconstituted, falling foul of the Roman principle '*divide et impera.*' While some of these events are later than the career of Jesus, the dispute over Herod's will has left its traces in the Jesus-traditions in the Lukan reference to the 'king who went into a far country to obtain kingship and then return' but whose subjects 'did not want him to rule over them' (Lk 19,11–15). This shows how the memory of that time and its uncertainty continued to be fresh. Antipas too had his ambitions, as we have seen. If kingship was denied to him he seems to have received the dynastic title 'Herod' on the deposition of Archelaus, thereby maintaining the semblance of a single house.[30] Yet the difficulties generated by his marriage to Herodias, his brother's wife, shows just how tenuous such unity really was. Again, our conclusion can only be tentative. Yet it must be admitted that if this saying was uttered by Jesus, his audience would have had little enough difficulty in hearing here a prophecy of the demise of Herodian rule, especially in view of all the circumstances surrounding Herod the Great's succession.

c) The third possible reference to the Herodian presence in the sayings of Jesus occurs in the *Q* passage dealing with John the Baptist (*Q*Mt 11,9; *Q*Lk 7,25). Recent discussion of this encomium tends to see it having a composite tradition-history, though there is fairly general agreement that some elements do go back to Jesus, including the double section of immediate concern in this context, which has a parallel saying in the *Gos. Thom.* 78,1–3.[31] The form of the section is that of three questions, the first two expecting the answer 'no', followed by one which calls for a 'Yes, indeed, John was a prophet!.' The negative contrast of the first two questions insists that John is neither a reed shaken by the wind nor someone dressed in fine garments; and to this latter statement is added 'those who wear luxurious clothes (those who are gorgeously apparelled and live in luxury, Lk) are in the houses of kings' ('royal palaces', Lk). If Gerd Theissen's identification of 'the reed shaken by the wind' is to be accepted as a veiled reference to Antipas on the basis of the emblem on his coins, then the men-

---

[30] H. Hoehner, *Herod Antipas*, SNTSMS 17 (Cambridge: Cambridge University Press, 1972) 105–9.

[31] Kloppenborg, *The Formation of Q*, 108–10; D. Catchpole, *The Search for Q* (Edinburgh: T. & T. Clark, 1993) 43–45; R. Funk and R. Hoover, *The Search for the Authentic Words of Jesus. The Five Gospels* (New York: Macmillan/Polebridge, 1993) 178–82.

tion of 'houses of kings' or 'royal palaces' would inevitably also refer to the Herodian court.[32] While the Matthean and Lukan wordings vary slightly, they both agree in the more general plural reference. This brings the comparison into line with the two previous passages discussed, but in this case as well it does not thereby preclude a specific allusion to an actual situation, from the point of view of both speaker and hearer. The plurals οἴκοις / βασιλείοις are quite natural with reference to a Herodian royal residence, as is clear from Josephus also (*Life* 66).

Confirmation of this implied criticism of the luxurious life-style of the court, at least as viewed from the world of the peasant (cf. *Gos. Thom.* 78 'Why have you come out to the countryside?'), may be seen in the account of Antipas' birthday, when John was beheaded in a wanton act (Mk 6,14–29). Josephus also reports that on the occasion of Augustus' deliberations over Herod's will a Jewish delegation appeared before him complaining about the bribery and corruption of those sent to collect the tribute, and bemoaning the corruption of their wives and daughters in drunken orgies (*JA* 17,304–9; *JW* 1,511). The mention of those sent out to collect the tribute in association with such conduct is all the more intriguing in view of the frequent allusions to Jesus' table-fellowship with tax collectors that occur in the tradition, more especially in the immediate context in *Q* of the passage being discussed here (Mt 11,16–19; Lk 7,31–35). The parable of the children in the market place, refusing to rejoice or mourn, is applied by the *Q* redactor to the different stances of John and Jesus. John's is an ascetic life-style, whereas Jesus' celebratory attitude earns for him the sobriquets of 'glutton and wine-drinker' and 'the friend of tax collectors and sinners.' Thus, Jesus' behaviour and association with tax collectors gains for him the same criticism as that levelled against the Herodian officials in Josephus, a criticism which is even more pointed still if, as has been recently claimed, 'sinners' should be identified with women whose presence at public meals gave them a doubtful reputation.[33] Jesus rejects the charge, having aligned himself with John against 'this generation', whose stance, like that of the children in the parable, is regarded as petty and childish.[34] Yet the implications of his actions and associations were double-edged. On the one hand he ran the risk of being rejected by the pious circles who

---

[32] Theissen, *The Gospels in Context,* 26–29. Cf., however the criticism of F. W. Burnett and G. A. Philips, 'Palm Re(a)ding and the Big Bang: Origins and Development of the Jesus Traditions,' *RelSRev* 18 (1992) 296–99.

[33] F. Herrenbrück, 'Wer waren die Zöllner?' *ZNW* 72 (1981) 178–84; K. Corley, *Private Women. Public Meals. Social Conflict in the Synoptic Tradition* (Peabody: Hendrickson, 1993) 103–8. Cf. further 'Jesus the Wine-Drinker, A Friend of Women,' below pp. 271 ff.

[34] W. Cotter, 'The Parable of the Children in the Market Place, Q(Lk) 7, 31–35,' *NovT* 29 (1987) 289–304.

deplored the life-style of the court, while at the same time he was engaging in a subtle act of subverting the Herodian officials, probably of lower rank in the villages, by summoning them to listen to his and John's prophetic word to Israel.

This attempt to read the three sayings against the sharpened focus of the Herodian court, especially that of Antipas, may not be wholly conclusive. Nevertheless, enough has emerged from the exercise to suggest that Jesus was remembered among other things for his outspoken criticism of the standards of royal power and privilege as these were exercised in that world. The very use of such comparisons with their implied negative comment can only be described as daring, even provocative. There is here no idealisation of kingship in terms of the philosopher-king of the Cynic-Stoic worldview. Rather the inspiration for the sayings is much more that associated with the apocalyptic understanding as this had received expression in various Jewish writings of the Second Temple period and which viewed the foreign rulers as belonging to the present evil age which was soon to be replaced by God's just rule on behalf of the oppressed. The situation of rapid change postulated for the period of the ministry of Jesus as this was outlined in the second part of this paper might be considered sufficiently traumatic to have elicited a prophetic response such as was found in the words and deeds of Jesus, not least in his critique of the prevailing value-system of the ruling elite.

Jesus and the Values of the Market Economy

The argument in the second section of this paper was that coincidental with the arrival of the adult Jesus in Galilee from the Jordan, there were obvious signs present of the intensification of a very different value-system to that which was enshrined in the Jewish theocratic ideal of all Israel sharing in the fruits of the land. This ideal still continued to appeal to many, especially the Galilean Jewish peasants, despite the erosion of the vision and its basic values among its ruling, priestly elite, as distinct from the ordinary priests. Josephus, who himself came from that background makes no attempt to hide this stark reality (*JA* 20,181.206 f.). As mentioned earlier it could well be that there were already in Galilee those who were critical of the Jerusalem cult-centre and its priesthood. However, if that were the case they certainly do not appear as an organised network within the region in the way that the Essenes or, later at the time of the first revolt, the Zealots had functioned in Judea. It is only in the Jesus movement that we find such a critique. If the argument to this point is at all sustainable, the task now is to show that it was with an essentially Jewish understanding of history and from a decidedly Jewish hope of restoration and renewal that Jesus and his movement mounted their critique of

both value-systems, Herodian and theocratic alike. I do not believe that
what began as a set of insights for coping with life, which is what Cynicism of a popular kind essentially was, could have been transformed into
an apocalyptically inspired renewal movement with a radical social agenda
in such a short space of time and with only the memory of a discredited
teacher of aphorisms to inspire it.[35] At least I find that scenario historically
less plausible and logically less probable than the one which I am proposing. Here I can only sketch the briefest outline of the case to be argued.

The social setting I am now proposing as the most immediate and significant for the earthly Jesus' ministry of deed and word, namely, the need
to resist the changing values and attitudes represented by the rise of Sepphoris and Tiberias, requires something other than a strategy for coping
with life, though of course in many instances in the ancient as well as in
the modern world, that is all that is possible. There are traces of a popular
wisdom akin to that of Proverbs and Sirach to be found in the earliest stratum of the Jesus tradition also. If material as well as cultural factors are to
be used in our attempt to explain, as distinct from merely describe, the Jesus movement and its emergence in this particular place (Galilee, not
Judea or Idumea) and at this particular time (the reign of Antipas rather
than 66 CE, e.g.), then we must attempt to show how its strategy and approach fit into the totality of life in that society at that particular time. We
must illuminate how precisely it was aimed at alleviating the perceived
condition of alienation that was threatening as a result of the new developments under Antipas. Which of the following alternatives was likely to
be better news for Galilean peasants threatened with loss of land and the
kinship values associated with it, without any redress: to hear that if they
honoured what was best they would be like kings, and would have the
freedom 'to dare to be different', or to be reassured that the advent of
God's reign which was occurring now in their midst (ἐντὸς ὑμῶν of Lk
17,21) would mean the reversal of all the dominant values which were currently destroying their lives at every level? The former merely accepts the
status quo and hopes to alleviate its most baneful effects. The latter calls
for envisaging the world differently. It is the dramatic suddenness of the
changes which were occurring in their midst that in my opinion called
forth the latter rather than the former understanding as the more adequate
way of addressing the situation.

According to T. Carney, rapid economic change can occur when not
only are markets and money available, but also a change of values is present which supports exploitation of resources for profit rather than simply

---

[35] I am unconvinced by Crossan's attempt to see such a Cynically-inspired movement
as capable of generating an organised counter-cultural challenge to existing social structures (*The Historical Jesus*, 128).

for providing subsistence.[36] This calls for very different attitudes towards nature, other people within the kinship network and the purpose and goal of life itself. Jesus' attitude towards possessions, money and the family, when read against the backdrop of the situation we have suggested merit the description which Theissen has proposed in another context, namely, 'a values revolution,'[37] thereby attempting to counter the new dominant value system on which the Herodian economic policy rested.

The very founding of Tiberias and the allotment of land to the inhabitants must have meant some displacement. Similarly, the pressure on the private landowner meant the break-up or diminution of the small holdings, leading to intra-family feuding about property and inheritance rights that are echoed in the parables of Jesus. For those who were exposed to these harsh realities and who had the will to resist, there remained only a downward spiral of options – from landowning to leasing, to day-labouring, to slavery or banditry. All of these possibilities remained within the existing structures and not even banditry which was the most violent response to the unequal situation had any alternative to put in its place, but was simply reactive. By contrast, Jesus' vision of shared goods and rejection of the normal securities, including money (*Q*Mt 6,19–21.24; *Q*Lk 12,33–34; 16,13; *Gos. Thom.* 47,1–2; 76,3), which, apart from land, was the most important commodity in the market economy, though utopian in its intention, did provide an alternative vision. This vision viewed the world of human relations, based on status maintenance, in a very critical light and allowed instead for oppressors and oppressed to relate as equals. In proposing such an ideal Jesus was not seeking to revert to a *status quo ante* for Israel as stated in the Pentateuch, but was operating within a genuinely prophetic framework of adapting the tradition to the demands of a new situation, and doing so in the name of God's final prophetic word to Israel.

A similarly radical stance can be discerned in his dealing with the crisis that the family faced within the new situation. Again, Carney has remarked that the family unit bonded by factors other than economic ones is singularly ill-equipped for the market-economy which calls for specialised skills and the maximisation of resources. Under such pressures kinship values can easily be eroded. Josephus, relying as he was on his status as a Jerusalem priest to win the support of the Galilean country people, repeatedly appeals to kinship values in order to appease their hostility towards the Jewish retainer class in Sepphoris and Tiberias, with, it must be said, only limited success (*Life* 55, 100, 171). Jesus, by contrast, challenges the abso-

---

[36] T. F. Carney, *The Shape of the Past. Models in Antiquity* (Lawrence, KS: Coronado Press, 1975) 139–52.

[37] G. Theißen, 'Die Jesusbewegung als charismatische Werterevolution,' *NTS* 35 (1989) 343–60.

lute nature of kinship values which can of course legitimate situations of great inequality, proposing instead an ideal of community based on love, forgiveness and shared reciprocity (*QLk* 6,27–35; *QMt* 5,38–44). In these sayings one can detect a subtle, yet firm critique of the prevailing patriarchal family structure, which was one of the cornerstones, not just of the Herodian, but also of the theocratic systems that were competing with each other in Galilee as elsewhere in Palestine (*QLk* 9,57–61; *QMt* 8,20–22; Mk 1,16–20; 10,29–31). Family imagery and values were applied to the new social configuration that was emerging around Jesus and in his name. This occurs despite his refusal to endorse certain aspects of the existing family reality, recognising instead that adherence to his way would be disruptive of those set patterns, with their economic and social rootedness (Mk 3,33–35; *QMt* 10,37; *QLk* 14,26; *Gos. Thom.* 55,1; 101,1–3).

Not everybody in Jesus' putative audiences or who had benefited from his charismatic healing ministry was ready for such a message. The threat to landownership was real and the signs of rapid change were now very tangible in terms of the new foundations. Yet as long as a tenuous link could be maintained with the old, many were uncertain about the new, at least such a radically new vision. The Galilean peasantry who in 66 CE were still prepared to bring their tithes to Josephus and his colleagues and to support as leader one of Jerusalem priestly stock rather than any native leader, shows how powerfully the old symbol system of temple and land still functioned. An idealisation of the destitute and a declaration that in the new economy theirs was the kingdom of heaven were only likely to resonate with those who were in reality destitute. On the other hand many of the sayings attributed to Jesus were not addressed to these but to people who did in fact own land or had other possessions. The relative failure of the Jesus movement as an inner-Galilean Jewish renewal movement must be judged not only in terms of the absence of clear archaeological or literary evidence for a Christian presence there in the first century, but also by the extent to which the Herodian and the theocratic system, each vying with the other for control of the resources, were still in place in 66 CE.

Conclusion

In this paper I have attempted to perform a critical reading of certain aspects of the Jesus tradition against the backdrop of the larger picture of Galilean social life as this can be reconstructed from both archaeological and literary sources, without, I hope, engaging in a too easy conflation of the two pictures. The attempt to keep both in focus, or better, the exercise of bringing both into focus by critically juxtaposing them, seems to be the best methodology for understanding how the Jesus tradition could have directly addressed certain pressing issues within that original setting, even when these traditions may have been used subsequently in other settings, both historical and geographical.

The question is particularly complex in view of the fact that recent studies of the sayings tradition, generally designated *Q* have attempted to highlight the geographical and social location of the so-called *Q* community, and Galilee has featured prominently in those discussions also.[38] The fact that greater precision has been introduced into the study of *Q* as a literary document in its own right means that, unlike the nineteenth century, no easy bridge can be built from *Q* to Jesus.[39] Kloppenborg's study on the formation of *Q* has been particularly influential with its separation of an earlier sapiential layer from a later apocalyptic/judgement one, which can then be related to two different stages of the *Q* community's history of mission and rejection in Galilee throughout the second half of the first century CE.[40] Kloppenborg himself stresses that this literary analysis of *Q* does not prejudge the issue of whether or not elements from the apocalyptic stratum originate with Jesus. Others who have found his analysis congenial to their own positions have used it to that effect, thereby postulating a sapiential (i.e. popular Cynic) rather than apocalyptic understanding of the kingdom as the primary inspiration of Jesus' own strategy.[41]

This study has argued that if a co-relation between social situation and an apocalyptically inspired response is to be postulated, then the period of Jesus' ministry in Galilee in the reign of Antipas can be plausibly construed in such a way as to provoke that kind of response. In fact that precise period with its rapidly changing ethos exemplified in the two Herodian foundations in lower Galilee is perhaps more suited to such a response than any other time in the first century, at least until the immediate outbreak of hostilities with Rome in 66 CE. Then, however, as Theissen and others have convincingly argued, it is in Mark rather than *Q* that we can sense the rumblings of those particular events in the background as far as Galilee is concerned.

---

[38] Theissen, *The Gospels in Context,* 203 f.; J. Kloppenborg, 'The Sayings Gospel Q: Recent Opinion on the People behind the Document,' *Currents in Research. Biblical Studies* 1 (1993) 9–34.

[39] Cf. D. Kosch, 'Q und Jesus,' *BZ* 36 (1992) 31–58.

[40] J. Kloppenborg, 'Literary Convention, Self-Evidence and the Social History of the Q People,' *Semeia* 55 (1991) 77–102.

[41] Thus e.g., B. Mack, *The Lost Gospel. The Book of Q and Christian Origins* (San Francisco: HarperCollins, 1993).

10. Galilean Questions to Crossan's Mediterranean Jesus

In this paper I would like to engage in an exercise of inter-textual reading of a kind. I read John Dominic Crossan's book, *The Historical Jesus. The Life of a Mediterranean Jewish Peasant* with great enjoyment and not a little profit, as I hope will emerge from this discussion.[1] However, it would be naive to suggest that I was a disinterested reader. At every step of the way I found myself interacting in the light of my own preoccupation with many of the themes and issues that he has dealt with in such a lucid and challenging way. This paper is then a report on the light that has been generated for this critical reader by rubbing Crossan's book against my own perspective on Jesus and his ministry, to borrow Harold Bloom's image for the reading process I have been engaged in. Though disagreeing with him in many fundamental respects I have been forced to revise and sharpen my own construal of Jesus by critically interacting with his persuasively argued positions. In the book's preface the author asks those colleagues who disagree with his moves to replace them with better ones. I am not sure that my moves are better, nor would I be certain by what criteria I could come to such a judgment. My moves are certainly different for reasons that I hope will become explicit as my argument develops.

The Question of Sources

I have followed the work of the Jesus seminar with interest and was, therefore, familiar with the meticulous concern for bedrock tradition that has marked the discussions of its members, published in *Forum* (vols. 1–10, 1985–94). Crossan has clearly been one of the main fashioners of the rigorous methodology that has been developed and the results are now put to the test in the present study.[2] While the logic of this approach might appear to be impeccable in dealing with individual items of the Jesus tradition, I do have serious reservations about its advisability when it comes to build-

---

[1] J. D. Crossan, *The Historical Jesus. The Life of a Mediterranean Jewish Peasant* (Edinburgh: T. & T. Clark, 1991).

[2] See J. D. Crossan, *Four Other Gospels: Shadows on the Contours of the Canon* (Minneapolis: Winston Press, 1985); and 'Materials and Methods in Historical Jesus Research,' *Forum* 4/4 (1988) 3–24.

ing an edifice from the scattered bits and pieces that eventually get the black, or even the grey vote. Only those items that have a double attestation from the earliest stratum will be used, we are told, in the reconstruction, and overall this very stringent criterion is adhered to. Nevertheless, how realistic is this fastidious concern with bedrock and whence this desire for unimpeachable criteria? The elaborate stratification of all the early Jesus traditions, canonical and non-canonical alike is of course a matter that could be debated as regards details. I could not help but note in passing that all the stratum one material is either extra-canonical or not very helpful in the quest for Jesus (the Pauline material). Mark finds himself relegated to stratum two, and even then supplanted by *Secret Mark*. At least the nineteenth-century questers were kinder in their judgement of him, perhaps too naively as it transpired. At all events the difficulties with claiming that only the earliest documents can serve as genuine sources in historical reconstruction have been exposed for a long time now. No amount of refinement of criteria can overcome the epistemological problems inherent in such an approach.

Rather than entering into debate on matters of detail I would prefer to query the very model that is being used – stratification – that is drawn from archaeology and shows a predilection for so-called hard facts. In dealing with a living and oral tradition I suspect that it is an unhelpful, and in the end potentially distorting model in identifying literary sources for historical writing. Reminiscences, quotations of pithy sayings, reporting of incidents and the like, all occur in lived and living contexts. Nothing is frozen in time, awaiting the arrival of the modern historical critic with his or her trowel to release it from the later 'fill' that has obscured it from view for centuries. In his concern to arrive at bedrock Crossan freely admits that he may well be ignoring important pieces of evidence from other strata, just because they do not meet his rigid criteria. Surely that is being methodologically correct to the point of distorting the picture from the outset by limiting the field of vision. Indeed if one were to follow Crossan's methodology to its logical conclusion, that is, use only material from stratum one, it would be difficult to locate Jesus anywhere in particular, certainly not in Galilee. In the end I found myself wondering whether the 'atopicality' which is so important a feature of Crossan's Jesus (pp. 345–48) was the result of the minimalist position adopted from the outset with regard to the appropriate sources, or whether the image of such a figure already determined a predilection only for a certain kind of evidence.

My own approach to the issue of the sources for the historical Jesus begins in quite a different place. While I am well aware that the canonical gospels represent choices, often ideological ones of the second century, it is they and not the other gospels that have shaped Christian self-understanding down the centuries. The Synoptic portrait does after all pre-date the search for sources by two millennia, contrary to what some of proponents of the extra-canonical Jesus seem to think. Even within the ca-nonical gospels one has to decide between the Synoptics and John in terms of the main location and chronology of Jesus' ministry, not to speak of other aspects of the narratives, in determining one's starting point. This does not mean that other, extra-canonical portraits should not be consid-ered, even when they appear to conflict with the canonical accounts in a fundamental way. S. Patterson is surely correct in objecting to using *Gos. Thom.* only when its traditions can be shown to corroborate the traditional accounts. However, there are a number of critical questions to be ad-dressed before one can go to the other extreme and postulate a minimalist common core of sayings that were subsequently developed by *Gos. Thom.* and the Synoptics along different trajectories, and claim that in that core 'we can catch a glimpse of that common beginning, extremely important for understanding who Jesus was.'[3]

There seems to be an assumption among some of those who seek to limit themselves to such an early stratum, be it best represented in *Gos. Thom.* or *Q* (stratum one), shared also by Crossan, that the existence of such a putative wisdom portrait of Jesus means that it was the only portrait available to the tradents of that particular set of traditions. As E. P. Sand-ers remarks in a similar context, there may have been genre constraints that allowed only certain aspects to be included in a particular document. Even more fallacious would be the assumption that these people were op-posed to that about which they do not speak.[4] It is possible to imagine a situation in which collections of wisdom sayings, accounts of his mighty deeds and a primitive passion story might have been utilised in different contexts by the same people, and at an early stage in the tradition (cf. 1 Cor 11,23–25; 15,3–6). If one is attempting to escape 'the tyranny of the Synoptic portrait of Jesus', as one member of the Jesus seminar puts it, then one must be careful not to become slave to another tyranny, the con-straint of the earliest stratum, on the principle of one group, one portrait.[5]

---

[3] S. J. Patterson, 'The Gospel of Thomas and the Historical Jesus: Retrospectus and Prospectus,' in *SBLASP 1990*, ed. D. Lull (Atlanta: Scholars Press, 1990) 614–36, espe-cially 622.

[4] E. P. Sanders, *Jewish Law from Jesus to the Mishnah* (London: SCM Press, 1990) 322–25.

[5] C. W. Hedrick, 'Introduction: The Tyranny of the Synoptic Jesus,' *Semeia* 44 (1988) 1–8; B. L. Mack, 'All the Extra Jesuses: Christian Origins in the Light of Extra-Canonical Gospels,' *Semeia* 49 (1990) 169–76. J. S. Kloppenborg, 'Literary Convention, Self-Evidence and the Social History of the Q People,' *Semeia* 55 (1991) 77–102, espe-cially 79–81, is aware of the problem of moving from text to social entity, but still be-lieves that the document was canonical for the group and hence mirrors its social world.

I am declaring a preference for the canonical gospels as my starting point, not because I necessarily believe that they contain more reliable historical information about Jesus, nor because I subscribe to canonical criticism as that phrase is usually employed, but rather because in the first instance they point to an historical trajectory that interests me in the light of their subsequent reception and continued authority in shaping Christian identity today. I make no apologies for declaring my interest, as I want to suggest that this theological concern need not in principle be any more distorting of my historical judgments than are the claims to objectivity of those who show different interest in the issue of the historical Jesus. It will of course remain to be debated on both historical and hermeneutical grounds whether or not those portraits have so distorted the intention of Jesus as to call for their rejection in favour of the other accounts which by an accident or conspiracy of history got lost until our own time.

In my book, *Galilee, Jesus and the Gospels* (1988) I took as my starting point for enquiry the very specific setting of Galilee as a way of exploring the traditions about Jesus, since it plays a determining, though differing role in shaping the plots of all four canonical gospels. In view of the methodological difficulties associated with the search for the earliest stratum and in an attempt to see how literary and historical concerns might co-operate in gospel studies I decided to experiment with the notion of narrative realism as applied to the final redactions of the evangelists. In choosing to experiment in this way I realized that I was leaving myself open to the charge of confusing the realism of narrative fiction with historical fact. My criticism of the experiment now would be that I did not carry through with sufficient rigour my initial insight of allowing the individual writers' differences in their descriptions of the Galilean social world to emerge, before attempting to show that each, in their different ways and despite their other immediate concerns, had paid their debt to the past of the real Jesus in the real Galilee through the various traces of that past that were available to them, or as they imagined how it was with Jesus in that setting. Paul Ricoeur has helped me considerably in seeing the overlap between narrative fiction and history-writing and how a consideration of this overlap might assist in freeing us from the objectivist fallacy with its unending and fruitless search for the earliest source, without thereby abandoning a critical historical perspective. Because both enterprises are mimetic, that is re-presenting the world of human affairs through emplotment, they both involve an active imagination. In the case of history-writing the events, characters and situation to be emplotted are only present insofar as individual historians can imaginatively bring about the presence of the past though the traces of past events available to them, so that the past is present 'like it was.' In other words all history-writing en-

gages in the metaphorical mode through the perception of likeness between the present account and the real past, which has gone forever and
can only be imagined. Thus history-writing has in common with fictional
narrative the fact that they both are the product of the active imagination
working on the past, the one to render it *like* it was, the other to present it
as if it was.[6] For those of us caught up in the paradigm of the real as
equivalent to sense presence, there is little comfort in the notion that all
history-writing is interpretation so that the past is only mediately accessible to us despite our most rigorous efforts to produce objective sources.

I am not of course suggesting that the gospels are purely fictional narratives, nor am I advocating a return to a naive conflation of the various accounts, as though all we have learned through form and redaction criticism
can now be abandoned, as one North American reviewer of my book
seems to think, accusing me of all things of an uncritical approach, 'characteristic of British scholarship!' When we today with our historical consciousness and asking our historical questions approach these texts we
must of course critically evaluate how they rendered their debt to the past
of Jesus and his world that they were configuring and refiguring, to use
Ricoeur's terminology. What traces of that past were available to them?
How did they imagine the real Galilee without our first-hand knowledge
through maps, photographs and artefacts from the past? That their intentions were historical there can be little doubt since they have left them in-
delibly printed in their works – Luke most explicitly, but all by implication
in their adoption of the narrative mode. In accomplishing their task they
had, we know, their sources, and it is good that we today can identify these
with a reasonable amount of certainty. Equally, however, they had their
imagination and their convictions, which caused them to wonder about the
past in the light of the present and the future. In putting their questions to
the past they created the past, but not in a way that violated that metaphorical likeness which is essential to all rendering of the past in the narrative mode, whether fictional or historical.[7] At least that is the hypothesis
that we today are called on to test as historically conscious readers of these
works. We render our debt to their past by taking seriously their intentions
which they have left for us to decipher in and through those texts.

It will be obvious that by taking seriously as my starting point the narrative mode of the gospels, rather than any putative earliest stratum, my

---

[6] See in particular P. Ricoeur, *Time and Narrative,* 3 vols., (Chicago: University of
Chicago Press, 1984–88) vol. 3, 104–240.

[7] Here I am indebted to the reflections of B. F. Meyer, building on Bernard Loner-
gan's theory of human cognition, in 'The Challenge of Text and Reader to the Historical-
Critical Method,' in *The Bible and its Readers, Concilium,* ed. W. Beuken, S. Freyne and
A. Weiler (London: SCM, 1991) 3–12.

approach, and thus also, my end result are likely to be different from Crossan's. One must deal with Galilee directly and not easily abandon it for a
Mediterranean atopicality which Crossan's Jesus finds more congenial.
This will also mean a considerable difference of emphasis in two important respects. Because my focus throughout is on Jesus in Galilee, I will
not be happy with merely painting a background from Josephus of Palestinian life and then construct a Jesus image that is never made to engage
seriously with that world, presumably because such engagement is not to
be found in the 'earliest stratum.' If the impact of Jesus' socio-religious
vision and movement is to be properly elucidated and evaluated, the values
inherent in the embattled brokerage and the brokerless kingdom will need
to be brought into direct and critical confrontation with each other. Secondly, in view of the use of archaeological imagery in dealing with the literary evidence, a greater debt might have been rendered to the accounts of
Galilean social life that is now emerging from the application of the methods of the 'new archaeology' to Galilee. Not that these stones will speak
with one voice! Yet in many instances they present us with aspects of
Galilean social life that are just as challenging to the gospel portraits as are
the extra-canonical gospels. The critical co-relation of both the literary and
archaeological remains is then in my opinion an essential prerequisite for
anybody interested in locating the real Jesus in the real Galilee.

Where is the Fox? Antipas and Jesus

'Foxes have holes and the birds of the air have nests' (Mt 8,20), as Jesus
remarked, not directly referring to Antipas, I take it, despite Theissen's
imaginative uncovering of the reed of Tiberias.[8] Nevertheless Antipas was
a fact of life in the Galilee of Jesus, and his almost complete absence from
Crossan's book is strange, but predictable in light of the discussion in the
previous section. The omission is all the more significant in view of the
fact that the reign of Antipas in Galilee had a direct bearing on the situation of the local peasants to whom the message of Jesus was addressed.

What difference did Antipas make? In previous discussions I have espoused the view that the reign of Antipas provided a buffer for Galilee
from the excesses of Roman provincial rule and that conditions under him
should not be confused with those obtaining in Judea after the deposition
of Archelaus nor with those in Galilee itself on the eve of the first revolt.
We should pay Matthew the compliment of taking his aside seriously
(2,23) by exploring the contrasting social worlds in the two regions. In this

---

[8] G. Theissen, *The Gospels in Context*, (Edinburgh: T. & T. Clark, 1992), 'The Shaken
Reed and the Foundation Coins of Tiberias,' 26–42.

regard Crossan's ignoring of the archaeological evidence shows up particularly since so much of the data points to regional differences and their importance in terms of trade and commerce, language, social conditions generally, religious affiliations etc. It is not that now suddenly we discover that Galilee was not Jewish at all, à la Grundmann and others, and as some recent studies have implied.[9] It is a matter of sensitively estimating the way in which Jewish faith was lived and expressed in terms of everyday life in a region that was both part of *Eretz Israel* and yet cut off from its cultic-centre and so forced to develop its own brand of Jewishness in response to the social factors operating there at different periods.

It so happens that the career and ministry of Jesus coincided with the emergence for the first time of a local Galilean ruler, somebody who had been frustrated in his ambition to succeed his father as king and who yet operated with a relative degree of independence as ethnarch. The fact that there was no protest in Rome calling for his deposition may or may not be significant. The aniconic coins of Antipas show a sensitivity to Jewish religious concerns, unlike his palace which was destroyed in 66, ostensibly because of the human representations (*Life* 66). We should not go to the opposite extreme and paint an idyllic picture. Josephus contrasts him unfavourably with his brother Philip in terms of the administration of justice in their respective territories (*JA* 18,106–8). The pre-emptive strike against John the Baptist shows that Antipas could be ruthless. It also raises sharply the question of how Jesus avoided a similar fate at his hands. If the scenario suggested by the adoption of Ted Robert Gurr's model of a peasantry suffering from decremental deprivation is to apply (Crossan, pp 218–22), then close attention will need to be paid to the shifting social world of Antipas' reign, especially as this was symbolized in the emergence of Sepphoris and Tiberias as administrative centres in Lower Galilee.

The usual way of posing the question of Jesus and Sepphoris are in my view far too simplistic, focusing as they do on the psychological or personal impact that growing up beside such a centre or even possibly plying his trade there as a τέκτων, might have had on him.[10] To pose the question

---

[9] W. Grundmann, *Jesus der Galiläer und das Judentum* (Leipzig: Georg Wigand, 1941). Cf. 'Archaeology and the Historical Jesus,' above pp. 160 ff.

[10] R. Batey, *Jesus and the Forgotten City. New Light on Sepphoris and the Urban World of Jesus* (Grand Rapids: Baker, 1991), although attractively presenting some of the recent archaeological evidence for Sepphoris, assumes but does not prove that close association with a place means sharing its ethos and values. Equally, A. Overman, 'Who Were the First Urban Christians?' in *SBLASP*, ed. D. Lull (Atlanta: Scholars Press, 1988) 160–68 and D. Edwards, 'First-Century Urban/Rural Relations in Lower Galilee,' ibid., 169–82, and id., 'The Socio-Economic and Cultural Ethos of the Lower Galilee in the First Century: Implications for the Nascent Jesus Movement,' in *The Galilee in Late Antiquity*, ed. L. Levine (New York and Jerusalem: The Jewish Theological Seminary of

in this way is to fall into the nineteenth-century liberal trap of psychologising Jesus. What is forgotten is that both centres symbolized and embodied rapid social change in Galilee as a whole under Antipas.[11] Such a claim might appear to be unwarranted in view of the rather phlegmatic character that comes across in the gospel portraits, especially Luke's, and because Josephus does not give the same detailed account of his reign as he does of his father's. Antipas had hoped to succeed his father, and foiled in that hope he was all the more likely to have thrown himself into the task of proving himself to the Romans, never relinquishing the hope of kingship to the very end. Indeed the name *autokratoris* as applied to Sepphoris and the calling of Tiberias after the Emperor shows how much he kept Roman imperial patronage in his sights. Rome allowed him a personal income of 200 talents. To collect this he needed a well disciplined, loyal and efficient administrative bureaucracy – tax collectors, notaries, judges, military personnel, store and market managers – in short, a whole range of retainers, who could insure that he and his court would reap the full benefits of a relatively fertile region within an agrarian economy. Antipas' reign, therefore, marked the rapid development of the Galilean economy along lines that were directly opposed to the Jewish patrimonial ideal, as this had been enshrined in the Pentateuch, upheld by the prophets and re-enacted by reformers such as Nehemiah (Neh 5,1–11).

Sepphoris and Tiberias shared a common ethos as administrative centres whose population was that of the retainer class for the most part, without excluding wealthy landowners as a native elite aristocracy also. Josephus paints a picture of the mixed character of the population of Tiberias at its foundation – people from every quarter and background being brought together either by force or with blandishments of gifts of land in return for loyalty to Antipas (*JA* 18,36–38). He was thus presumably violating Jewish law not merely in terms of building the city on a burial ground, but also in forcibly appropriating the land of others. This picture was maintained subsequently as we see in the account of the citizenry when Josephus himself arrived in the region in 66 CE, comprising as it did a combination of Herodian landowning residents with estates across the lake, various officials at the Herodian court such as Justus of Tiberias, a man well-educated in the Greek ways, and the service classes – 'sailors

---

America, 1992) 53–73, although using the evidence (especially the gospels) more critically, are both in danger of operating with the same assumptions. The classic expression is that of Shirley Jackson Case, 'Jesus and Sepphoris,' *JBL 45* (1926) 14–22.

[11] Cf. 'Herodian Economics in Galilee: Searching for a Suitable Model,' above, pp. 86 ff. See also J. L. Reed, 'Population Numbers, Urbanization, and Economics: Galilean Archaeology and the Historical Jesus,' in *SBLASP*, ed. Eugene H. Lovering, Jr. (Atlanta: Scholars Press, 1994) 203–19.

and destitutes' as the aristocratic Jerusalemite describes them (*Life* 32–38). The fact that in 66 Tiberias has the trappings of a Greek *polis* with its βουλή should not disguise the fact that it had a subordinate position within the Herodian administrative framework from the outset. Its role had been diminished when Nero transferred Tiberias to the territory of Agrippa II in 54/55, thus ceding primacy in banking, market and other administrative functions to its rival Sepphoris, something that Justus bemoans. It would be a mistake to think of either place being on a par with other cities in the environs where the epithet 'free and autonomous' meant much more in terms of developing their own ethos and lifestyle. It was only in 66 that Sepphoris struck its first coins and Tiberias had to wait until 100 CE, i.e., after the end of the Herodian dynasty, before it enjoyed the same privilege by favour of Trajan.[12]

Mediterranean and Cynic or Galilean Jewish and Apocalyptic?

Mediterranean has replaced Hellenistic or Greco-Roman among those who adopt a social-scientific approach in N.T. studies, largely due to the influence of Bruce Malina and the Context Group.[13] I do not wish to deny the advantages of employing categories that will aid us in better understanding the social codes and values that were operative in cultures other than our own. However, as an instrument in historical investigation it could become a very blunt tool indeed, if it were to mean that all historical, cultural, and social differences were to be obliterated. The issue surely is to find out the extent to which generalized categories can apply in particular contexts, or whether they must be modified or abandoned entirely in the light of contrary evidence. In terms of Crossan's Jesus the question is whether Mediterranean is more important than Jewish in the sub-title, and even more specifically whether Galilean Jewish does not introduce another dimension of particularity that will have to be considered also. Administrative Galilee did not reach the Mediterranean, and indeed a culture that could describe the largest inland water complex as sea rather than lake suggests that its orientation was not directly towards the west.[14] The history of Judaism, especially in the land of Israel in the Second Temple period was one of

---

[12] Y. Meshorer, *City Coins of Eretz Israel and the Dekapolis in the Roman Period* (Jerusalem: The Israel Museum, 1985) 33, 36.

[13] B. Malina, *The Social World of Jesus and the Gospels* (London and New York: Routledge, 1996); J. Neyrey, ed., *The Social World of Luke-Acts: Models for Interpretation* (Peabody: Hendrickson, 1991); K. C. Hanson and D. Oakman, *Palestine in the Time of Jesus. Social Structures and Social Conflicts* (Minneapolis: Fortress Press, 1998).

[14] G. Theißen, '"Meer" und "See" in den Evangelien: Ein Beitrag zur Lokalkoloritforschung,' *Studien zum Neuen Testament und seiner Umwelt* 10 (1985) 5–25.

resisting any easy assimilation to the universal values that were then in circulation. Fergus Miller has drawn our attention to the ways in which the Semitic cultures of the east, including the Jews, adopted and adapted Hellenistic influences. It was by no means a one-way process, nor did the older local indigenous people become absorbed in a pan-Hellenic culture that shared a common ethos and value system to the point of wiping out all difference.[15] There are far too many examples, both ancient and modern, some heroic, some tragic, of resistance by the Little Tradition to the Great Tradition. Certainly, if we are going to use the category Mediterranean for Jewish peasantry it will need to be refined and defined carefully. Anyone who has read Josephus' *Life* must be aware of just how distinctive Jews in the Galilee regarded themselves, even as they were participating in aspects of the larger world in their own midst, such as trade and commerce. The fact that archaeological data, especially coins, point to strong trading links between Tyre and Upper Galilee[16] no more means that a cultural continuum existed between this city and the Galilean rural hinterland in terms of core values, than that today Arab traders who look for U.S. dollars are thoroughly imbued with all aspects of American culture.

Crossan accepts the view of Overman and others that Lower Galilee was urbanized, and the acceptance of that position proves to be an important step in the development of his argument.[17] Undoubtedly, Lower Galilee, especially around the lake does present a more mixed cultural aspect than does Upper Galilee/Golan, as has been shown by various archaeological surveys.[18] This difference is no doubt attributable to the trading and other links that were possible in the Valley region as a result of the ease of communications between the various city territories and across the lake. These provided a natural outlet for any surplus production as well as markets for the pottery and fish industries which we know were developed in Lower Galilee.[19] Not all cities present the same aspect, however. Relations

---

[15] F. Millar, 'Empire, Community and Culture in the Roman Near East: Greeks, Syrians, Jews and Arabs,' *JJS* 38 (1987) 143–64; U. Rappaport, 'The Hellenization of the Hasmoneans,' in *Jewish Assimilation, Acculturation and Accommodation: Past Traditions, Current Issues, Future Prospects*, ed. Menahem Mor (Lanham: University Press of America, 1991) 1–13; Louis Feldman, 'How Much Greek in Jewish Palestine?' *Hebrew Union College Annual* 57 (1986) 82–111.

[16] J. Raynor and Y. Meshorer, *The Coins of Ancient Meiron* (Winona Lake: Eisenbrauns, 1988). See above 'Archaeology and the Historical Jesus,' pp. 160 ff.

[17] Overman, 'Who were the First Urban Christians?' 160–68.

[18] E. M. Meyers, J. F. Strange and D. Groh, 'The Meiron Excavation Project: Archaeological Survey in Galilee and Golan, 1976,' *BASOR* 230 (1978) 1–24; D. Urman, *The Golan. A Profile of a Region during the Roman and Byzantine Period* (Oxford: BAR International Series 269, 1985).

[19] D. Adan-Bayewitz, *Common Pottery in Roman Galilee. A Study of Local Trade* (Ramat-Gan: Bar-Ilan University Press, 1993); D. Adan-Bayewitz and I. Perlman, 'The

can vary considerably with the surrounding territories, and one must make a very clear distinction between the ethos in the autonomous cities such as Scythopolis, Caesarea Philippi, Tyre and Ptolemais, and the Herodian administrative centres of Sepphoris and Tiberias. As regards the former, relations were never far from strained, and could easily erupt between the non-Jewish inhabitants and their Jewish neighbours (*JW* 2,457–65). Their avowedly pagan ethos which can be documented from inscriptions as well as the literary sources marks them off as an essentially hostile environment for Jews. Sepphoris and Tiberias were different, however, and even though there probably were some non-Jewish elements in their population from the start, neither shared the pagan ethos of the cities in the circle, certainly not in the early part of the first century CE. Antipas was careful not to offend the Jews in terms of his coins, and he had no desire to propagate actively pagan culture in the Jewish part of his realm any more than did his father. Despite the essentially Jewish ethos of these cities, it is my conviction that the hostility shown to them by the Galileans according to Josephus' *Life* was not just due to the circumstances leading up to the revolt but was inherent in the very nature of the relationships of these centres with their rural environs. In sociological terms they were heterogenetic rather than orthogenetic, despite their Jewishness, and their overall impact on Galilean peasant life must be judged accordingly.[20]

Could these and other lesser centres have been the bearers of a popular Cynicism – that pervasive and quintessentially Mediterranean philosophy for coping with the inequalities of life within an agrarian society, as Crossan argues? This is what Crossan's book strongly implies and it has been argued or assumed by a number of recent studies. In my view this is extremely unlikely, especially for the rural peasants, yet the case deserves a full hearing. I agree with F. G. Downing that Mack assumes too readily that Galilee was just the right kind of environment for the transmission of popular Cynic ideas, without considering the alternative.[21] Downing himself mounts an impressive case for a broad social basis for Cynic ideas, every place from the law courts to the street corners. His analysis of *Q* shows persuasively that there is a strong Cynic influence both in form and content – with a few important exceptions to be discussed presently. The core of his argument is that Cynic influence is so pervasive in early Chris-

---

Local Trade of Sepphoris in the Roman Period,' *IEJ* 40 (1990) 153–72; M. Nun, *Ancient Anchorages and Harbours around the Sea of Galilee* (Kibbutz Ein Gev: Kinnereth Sailing, 1988).

[20] Cf. 'Urban-Rural Relations in First-Century Galilee,' above, pp. 45 ff.

[21] F. G. Downing, *Cynics and Christian Origins* (Edinburgh: T & T Clark, 1992) 146 n. 7, referring to Burton L. Mack, *A Myth of Innocence: Mark and Christian Origins* (Philadelphia: Fortress Press, 1988), especially 72–74 and 148.

tian writings (Mark, Special Matthew, James, 1 Thess as well as *Q*) that the most plausible explanation is that this influence emanated from Jesus himself rather than that a Jewish Jesus was later 'Cynicized' by different groups in various social settings. The social milieu of Galilee is still sufficiently open for debate to allow for a Cynic presence there at a popular level, to the extent that it was natural and possible to present 'characteristically and distinctively "Cynic-friendly" ideas, attitudes and practices' and that these were 'readily communicable' in that setting.

Downing's position is well argued and nuanced. He is aware that there are counter arguments, but in his view they lack both the scope (i.e. the capacity to explain the broadest possible number of salient facts) and the force (the capacity to convince over against the other possible alternatives) of his own position. However, despite his conviction of a pervasive Cynic presence in Galilee at a popular level that provides an appropriate communicational context for Jesus' sayings, Downing avoids any sweeping generalizations. He accepts the tensions between town and country that might block any easy spread of what could be seen as urban ideas among country folk; he repeatedly refers to 'the Jewish palette', 'older native Jewish influences' on Jesus, the teaching material 'unmistakably drawing its colour from Jewish sources', etc. Thus Downing is conscious of the distinctively Jewish dimension of the Jesus tradition also. The question then is whether both strands – the Jewish and the Cynic – go back to Jesus and if so how that particular amalgam is best expressed in the light of all the circumstances. In terms of Crossan's subtitle, will Jesus be seen as more Jewish than Mediterranean? One way of answering that question is to say that the Jewish element comes from Jesus and then the Cynic element in *Q* will have to be explained in terms of the move to the urban environment of Galilee and its surrounds by the tradents of those traditions. The effect of such a solution would be of course to drive a wedge between *Q* and Jesus thereby challenging the assumption that earliest is best in terms of historical reconstruction.

In my opinion it is unrealistic to assume that close proximity to an urban culture means that the population as a whole was likely to be imbued with the attitudes and values, alleged or real, of those centres. One would have to ask to what ends certain strata of the population adopted those attitudes and values and why they might have abandoned older ones. Those older values were, I have argued, grounded in the Jewish, theocratic ideal that was built on the realities of land, temple and Torah. As a result of the archaeological evidence I am now dubious about my earlier views, following Alt, that an old Israelite presence was maintained in Galilee over the centuries.[22] However, the Pentateuchal traditions did function to legitimate the inclusion of the northern regions within *Eretz Israel* once the possibility of a Jewish national state emerged under the Hasmoneans. Archaeology is helping to identify those sites in the Galilee/Golan where new Jewish foundations occurred in the late Hellenistic period. The presence of *mikwaoth*, the nature of the art work and the absence of any signs of pagan worship in Galilean Jewish sites of the first century (as distinct from the evidence from the surrounding city territories where several pagan inscriptions have been found) all point to the essentially conservative nature in terms of religious observance of the Jewish settlements in Galilee (Upper and Lower) even when the archaeological evidence points at the same time to trading links with those non-Jewish centres, as already noted.[23] It is difficult not to see in this attachment to the Jewish way of life a legitimation for the peasants in terms of access to the resource of the land. Despite a critique of the Jerusalem priesthood and its cult-centre with a Galilean flavour (*1 Enoch* 14,18–22; 15,3 f.), when all was said and done that cult-centre supported a symbolic universe which could on the whole rely on Galilean peasants' loyalty to the very end (*Life* 63, 348 f.).

It was in Jerusalem's interest to foster those links. The visits of scribes to Galilee (Mk 3,22; 7,1) fit into a larger pattern of such visits by influential Jerusalemites like Johanan ben Zakkai or the delegation sent to unseat Josephus in 66 CE. Synagogue remains from the pre–70 period are meagre for the whole country, but that does not mean that as an institution it did not function in Galilee as both a place of prayer and of instruction. If Downing can point to second-century characterisations of Christians as Cynics as an argument for a trajectory going back to Jesus, then one is equally entitled to argue from the migration of Jews to the north in the wake of the Bar Cochba revolt to a Jewish trajectory going back well beyond Jesus. They would scarcely have moved to an alien or a hostile culture in the light of their experiences in Judea. Indeed the tensions between the Rabbinic teachers and the synagogue leaders that are echoed in later Jewish writings suggests that the synagogue had had an independent life of its own in the region before the advent of the sages and was determined to maintain such a role for the ordinary people. This provides the context for Bruce Chilton's Targumic studies in which he finds echoes of what later came to be the Palestinian Targum in the sayings of Jesus in terms of lan-

---

[22] S. Freyne, *Galilee, Jesus and the Gospels. Literary Approaches and Historical Investigations* (Dublin and Philadelphia: Gill & Macmillan and Fortress Press, 1988) 167–75, especially 169 f.

[23] E. M. Meyers, 'Galilean Regionalism as a Factor in Historical Reconstruction,' *BASOR* 221 (1976) 93–101; E. M. Meyers, E. Netzer and C. L. Meyers, 'Sepphoris: Ornament of all Galilee,' *BA* 49 (1986) 4–19.

guage, content and style.[24] Clearly then the Cynics had their competitors in the Jewish villages of Galilee!

Downing concedes that one important element in the *Q* material that finds no parallel in the Cynic tradition is the notion of an eschatological judgment (Lk 3,17; 6,20–23; 10,12–15; 17,23–27), a theme that is pervasive in Jewish apocalyptic writing as is well known. One might have expected that an apocalyptic rather than a sapiential understanding of Jesus' kingdom language would therefore have suggested itself to Crossan. Following Mack and others, however, and in line with the Cynic hypothesis generally, he opts for a decidedly this-world understanding as the one that would suggest itself most naturally to the peasants, 'a kingdom of the nobodies and the destitute, a kingdom performed rather than just proclaimed,' as he describes it (p. 292). Leaving aside the issue of the social situation of the peasants that this statement presupposes, one would have to query its probability in the light of the arguments just presented for a vibrant and conservative Jewish practice in Galilee, especially when an unlikely hybrid, Jewish Cynicism, has to be constructed in order to support such a claim. It is of course based on the analysis of *Q* that has now become almost standard, namely a sapiential stratum followed later by an apocalyptic one, a concern for the present rather than with any future, other-worldly kingdom. It would seem then that this is a conclusion that is forced on Crossan through his rigorous adherence to the stratification of the Jesus tradition, even though he has difficulty in finding the right label for the particular mix as far as Jesus is concerned: 'Call it, if you will, Jewish and rural Cynicism rather than Greco-Roman Cynicism' (p. 340). Unfortunately, there are no examples of this rural Cynicism that can be drawn on, but there is a tradition of proverbial wisdom from the Ancient Near East that is much older than Cynicism which had all to do with trying to understand and cope with the vagaries of life, often those to do with life in the country. Centuries earlier the Jewish religious tradition had shown itself sufficiently flexible to be able to incorporate this tradition into its own theocratic framework, and the rabbinic writings indicate that it was not incompatible with their world-view either. Perhaps such a precedent might have suggested a more adequate framework for interpreting the presence of the sapiential elements in both Jesus and *Q*, while doing far greater justice to the Jewishness of both Jesus and Galilee. On the analogy of the international character of proverbial wisdom this would not at all preclude the inclusion of Cynic aphorisms to do with life's struggles, but within a comprehensively Jewish theocratic framework.

---

[24] See, e.g., B. Chilton, *A Galilean Rabbi and his Bible. Jesus' Use of the Interpreted Scripture of his Time* (Wilmington: Glazier, 1984).

Part of the problem has to do with the understanding of apocalyptic as being totally other-worldly and future-oriented, and therefore lacking an ethical impulse for the present. Yet as Chilton, Malina and others have recently emphasized from quite different perspectives, the distinction between present and future as this has become a received orthodoxy in N.T. scholarship, especially German, is a creation of our logical thinking rather than a genuine reflection of Jewish thought processes. Chilton in particular emphasizes the eschatological nature of the notion of the kingdom of God in the Targumim, as referring to God's definitive, yet present intervention on behalf of his people now.[25] Confirmation of this understanding comes from the very setting in which the Targumim functioned, namely the synagogue service, where the prayer, the *18 Benedictions*, celebrated God's triumph over Israel's enemies as a reality that could be experienced now in and through cultic performance.[26] Surely this setting is as close as we can reasonably hope to come to an appreciation of how common people, even peasants, might have had their anticipation of and appetite for the arrival of God's kingdom prepared and whetted. Even when one moves from this setting where an eschatological understanding of God's rule in the present could be affirmed and experienced, to a more thorough-going apocalyptic symbolization of the event, the collection of Jewish apocalypses which now constitute *1 Enoch* show how the circles in which this material was developed and transmitted could integrate this-world wisdom, Hellenistic cosmic speculation and varied expressions of the divine combat myth into a single narrative. Far from being some Utopian fantasy of the future, this synthesis was directly addressed to coping with the challenges that Hellenism as an economic and cultural force was posing even from within Judaism itself.[27] Philo of Alexandria and the Book of Wisdom are the Jewish

---

[25] B. Chilton, 'Kingdom Come, Kingdom Sung: Voices in the Gospels,' *Forum* 3/2 (1987) 51–75.

[26] See the important study of Th. Lehnhardt, 'Der Gott der Welt ist unser König: Zur Vorstellung von der Königsherrschaft Gottes im Shema und seinen Benediktionen,' in *Königsherrschaft Gottes und himmlischer Kult im Judentum, Urchristentum und in der hellenistischer Welt*, ed. M. Hengel and A. M. Schwemer (Tübingen: J. C. B. Mohr, 1991) 285–307, who shows that the central declaration of the synogogue liturgy, Dt 6,4, was interpreted in terms of God's kingship which was first experienced at the Red Sea (Ex 15,18). This connection provided the context for the association of the kingship of God and the acceptance of the requirements of the Torah in the rabbinic literature. Thus an eschatological and an everyday understanding of kingdom were quite feasible within a thoroughly Jewish context.

[27] M. Hengel, *The "Hellenization" of Judaea in the First Century after Christ* (London: SCM, 1989) 45–52, with copious bibliographical references to the Hellenistic influences in Jewish apocalyptic literature in the notes; see also M. Barker, *The Older Testament: The Survival of Themes from the Ancient Royal Cult in Sectarian Judaism and Early Christianity* (London: SPCK, 1987) 83–103. Both texts show that ethical wisdom and apocalyptic kingship motifs were not incompatible.

witnesses that Mack and Crossan can adduce for their sapiential (i.e. Cynic-Stoic) understanding of the kingdom as applying to the individual who has achieved inner self-control through wisdom.[28] Yet even if one were to allow for such an intellectual understanding in certain circles in Galilee, in Philo's view the individual's participation in the world process is ultimately dependent on the creative and sustaining power of God, whereby he alone is king of the cosmopolis, and on whom all human kingship depends.[29] In other words, behind the Philonic philosophical expression of the individual wise person as king stands a thoroughly Jewish theocratic conception that cannot disguise its true parentage.

Conclusion: Jesus in a Jewish Galilee[30]

My critical reading of Crossan's book has helped me to sharpen the focus on how a Galilean setting and a more grounded Jewish Jesus would lead to a different construal to that which a Mediterranean perspective offers. It is my opinion that a less rigid approach to the question of sources and a greater attention to the real social world of Galilee has a better chance of doing justice to the real Jesus, however inaccessible that figure may still remain.

The accounts of Palestine that pagan writers such as Strabo, Pliny and Tacitus give us, not to speak of Josephus and the Rabbinic writings, provide an interesting contrast to the gospels. Despite various inaccuracies and confusions that are easily attributable to the absence of maps or any other technical helps, there is a far greater sense of place in the pagan writers and a keener interest in describing the natural resources.[31] Josephus has a very clear sense of boundaries, distances between various places and the length of time required for journeys between different destinations, as

---

[28] B. L. Mack, 'The Kingdom Sayings in Mark,' *Forum* 3/1 (1987) 3–47, especially 11–21; Crossan, *Historical Jesus,* 282–92.

[29] See N. Umemoto, 'Die Königsherrschaft Gottes bei Philon,' in *Königsherrschaft Gottes,* 207–56; and J. G. Williams, 'Neither Here nor There: Between Wisdom and Apocalyptic in Jesus' Kingdom Sayings,' *Forum* 5/2 (1989) 7–30. The latter directly addresses Mack's proposal in a manner with which I would concur, by suggesting that genres such as wisdom and apocalyptic were not pure types mutually excluding each other.

[30] The final section of this chapter is an abridged version of the original, since several of the topics touched on in that presentation have been developed in other essays, cross-references to which in this volume are given in the notes.

[31] M. Stern, *Greek and Latin Authors on Jews and Judaism,* 3 vols. (Jerusalem: Israel Academy of the Sciences and the Humanities, 1974–84), vol. I, 305 and vol. II, 21.

well as the topography of certain key sites – all matters we would expect somebody who had been active in the field as a military and political commander to be well informed about. In the Rabbinic writings, on the other hand, geographical interests are directly related to halachic ordinances to do with the observance of tithing laws and the settling of disputed cases in terms of the place of provenance of various products. That these discussions were not purely academic emerges from such notices as that of Josephus concerning John of Gischala' exploitation of his coreligionists' desire to obtain native oil (*Life* 74) as well as the mosaic floor in the synagogue at Rehov in the Beth Shean valley, which has a most detailed description of the borders of Israel in the north, especially that between Tyre and Galilee.[32]

Despite the unfavourable comparison in terms of the Gospels' lack of interest in such details, we are not entitled to categorise their geographic references as purely symbolic. In particular, the visits of Jesus to the outlying regions – the borders of Tyre and Sidon, the territory of the Gerasenes, the middle of the Dekapolis and the villages of Caesarea Philippi – all call for careful analysis in the light of both the historical and political realities of the first century CE, especially the shift from client kings to direct provincial rule after the death of Agrippa I in 44 CE. What might such crossing of boundaries signify in socio-religious terms in the light of increasingly hostile relationships between Jews and gentiles in the region immediately prior to the first revolt (cf. *Life* 113; *JW* 2,457–65) and how did these circumstances differ from those thirty years earlier?[33]

Though Antipas may not intrude directly into the story of Jesus as this is related in the gospels, the changing socio-economic realities in Galilee following directly on the emergence of the two Herodian cities of Sepphoris and Tiberias certainly leave their imprint on the narratives. Jesus' revolutionary message about the blessedness of the poor, coupled with the frequent references to absentee landowners, day-labourers, debts etc. all seem to correspond rather well with what we might have anticipated from the new, emerging set of relationships, even within the village culture, to which in the main Jesus' ministry was addressed. The *Similitudes of Enoch*, which most commentators date to the Herodian period, reflect this situation also with their repeated condemnation of 'the kings, the governors, the high officials and the landlords' (*1 Enoch* 38,4; 46,3–5; 48,8; 53,5; 62), whereas the holy and just ones will 'possess the earth.' Does this explain the silence with regard to Sepphoris and Tiberias in the gospels' accounts? Certainly the drain on resources, natural and human, in-

---

[32] J. Sussman, 'The Inscription in the Synagogue at Rehob,' in *Ancient Synagogues Revealed*, ed. L. Levine (Jerusalem: The Israel Exploration Society, 1981) 146–53.

[33] Cf. 'Archaeology and the Historical Jesus,' above pp. 160 ff.

volved in Antipas' building projects provides the most immediate context for the period of Jesus' young adulthood in Galilee. It is difficult to see how they could not have made an impact on the consciousness of any would-be reformer, prophet or charismatic within a Jewish framework of reference.[34]

In the light of this picture we can readily understand the hatred that the Galilean peasants displayed for both foundations in 66 CE. Crossan's analysis has helped considerably in sorting out what happened then and the mediating role that Josephus played in Galilee.[35] In Judea/Jerusalem the Zealot takeover turned what was at first a political rebellion under the control of the aristocracy into a social revolution that turned the lower classes, clergy and laity alike, against the ruling priestly aristocracy. A similar situation existed in Galilee also, except that the aristocracy was for the most part Herodian rather than priestly, and beneath them the upper echelons of the retainer class were equally hated. In this situation the Jerusalemite, Josephus, was able to mediate between the rival factions, acting as a broker between them until Vespasian put an end to both the rebellion and the possibility of the social revolution alike. But that was in 66 CE and many things had changed in Palestine since the twenties, when the intensification of the social changes associated with the development of an agrarian market economy came to Galilee also, disrupting older patterns of relationships and the values associated with these, as we have seen. Such changes were clearly and unambiguously embodied in the two foundations which from the start must have been experienced as heterogenetic by the peasant population, in a way that Jerusalem was not, despite its frequent exploitation of peasant loyalties to its cult-centre.[36]

I argued earlier that in addressing peasants in Galilee kingdom language and imagery was much more likely to have been received in Jewish eschatological terms than in the purely Cynic mode that Crossan and others have claimed, irrespective of how one seeks to introduce a Jewish colouring to what was in essence a decidedly un-Jewish world-view. The levels of practice and attachment to the Jewish theocratic ideal were too vigorous and too developed for such a watered down version to have had any wide-scale currency, least of all among the peasants. The social setting I am now proposing as the most immediate and significant for the earthly Jesus' ministry (as distinct from that of *Q* or *Thomas*), namely, the need to resist the changing values and attitudes represented by the rise of Sepphoris and Tiberias, requires, it seems to me, something other than a strategy for cop-

---

[34] Cf. 'Jesus and the Urban Culture of Galilee,' and 'Herodian Economics in Galilee. Searching for a Suitable Model,' above pp. 183 ff. and 86 ff. respectively.

[35] Crossan, *The Historical Jesus*, 193–96.

[36] Cf. 'Urban-Rural Relations in First-Century Galilee,' above pp. 45 ff.

ing with life, though of course in many instances in the ancient as well as in the modern world, that is all that is possible. If material as well as cultural and religious factors are to be employed in our attempt to explain, not just describe, the Jesus movement and its emergence in this particular place (Galilee, not Judea or Idumea) and at this particular time (the reign of Antipas rather than 66 CE), then we must attempt to show how its strategy and approach fit into the totality of life in that society and how precisely it was aimed at alleviating the perceived condition of alienation that was threatening as a result of the new developments under Antipas. Which of the following alternatives was likely to be better news for Galilean peasants threatened with loss of land and the kinship values associated with it, without any redress: to hear that if they honoured what was best they would be like kings, and would have the freedom 'to dare to be different,'[37] or to be reassured that the advent of God's reign which was occurring now in their midst (ἐντὸς ὑμῶν, Lk 17,21) would mean the reversal of all the dominant values which were currently destroying their lives at every level? The former merely accepts the status quo and hopes to alleviate its most baneful effects. The latter calls for envisaging the world differently. It is the dramatic suddenness of the changes which were occurring in their midst that in my opinion called forth the latter rather than the former understanding as the more adequate way of addressing the situation.

How did Jesus propose to confront this situation in the light of his kingdom language and praxis? Crossan's 'open commensality' is a good place to start. There can be no doubting the radical social dimensions of such a programme. However, its real point is lost, or at least considerably weakened unless it is located in a social world in which its political implications are seen in all their immediacy. To espouse table-fellowship with tax collectors and sinners (which probably should be taken to mean women[38]) is not just to incur the condemnation of those whose programme is based on temple purity, but rather throws down the gauntlet to the very institutions on which the current repressive regime was based in terms of both its patriarchal value-system and retainer class structure. As a result of his meals with such 'undesirables' Jesus was accused of being a wine-bibber and a glutton, a friend of tax collectors and sinners (Lk 7,33; Mt 11,19). Such an accusation takes on its full vilificatory force only when it is heard against the critique by orthodox Jewish circles of the Herodian court. Ac-

---

[37] This is Burton Mack's approximation of what kingdom language in the Cynic mode would have meant on the lips of Jesus, 'The Kingdom Sayings in Mark,' 17.

[38] K. Corley, *Private Women. Public Meals. Social Conflict in the Synoptic Tradition* (Peabody: Hendrickson, 1993) 103–8; cf., 'Jesus the Wine-Drinker, A Friend of Women,' below pp. 271 ff.

cording to Josephus one of the complaints of the Jewish delegation in Rome seeking an end to Herodian kingship had to do with the bribery and corruption of those sent to collect the tribute and the corruption of their wives and daughters in drunken orgies (*JA* 17,304–9; *JW* 1,511). Such an ethos is at least evoked by the legendary story of Antipas' birthday also with its local Galilean colouring (Mk 6,21 f.).

A similarly radical stance can be discerned in his dealing with the crisis that the family faced within the new situation. Thomas Carney has remarked that the family unit bonded by factors other than economic ones is singularly ill-equipped for the market-economy which calls for specialized skills and the maximization of resources.[39] Under such pressures kinship values can easily be eroded. Josephus, relying as he was on his status as a Jerusalem priest to win the support of the Galilean country people, repeatedly appeals to ὁμοφυλία, that is, kinship, in order to appease their hostility towards the Jewish retainer class in Sepphoris and Tiberias, with, it must be said, only limited success. Jesus, by contrast, challenges the absolute nature of kinship values which can of course legitimate highly repressive situations in all cultures, proposing instead an ideal of community based on love, forgiveness and shared reciprocity. Once again one can detect a subtle, yet firm critique of the prevailing patriarchal family structure, which was one of the cornerstones, not just of the Herodian, but also of the theocratic systems that were competing with each other in Palestine generally, and specifically in the Galilee of Jesus. Family imagery and values are appropriated to the new social configurations that were emerging around Jesus and in his name, even as he refuses to endorse certain aspects of the existing family reality, recognizing instead that adherence to his way would be disruptive of those set patterns, with their economic and social rootedness in the past.

My starting point in the gospel narratives does not require the existence of *Q*, at least in the refined form in which modern North American scholarship has been able to identify this putative document and the group for whom it functioned as a foundation myth. Yet I do have to acknowledge that the sayings tradition came to the evangelists by some channels and circulated independently in others also – Q, *Thomas*, the *Apocryphon* of James, oral tradition, etc. Since John Kloppenborg's analysis of a two-layered *Q* is the currently accepted one among most scholars, I am happy to see how his profile might co-relate with my proposals in the light of the social situation that I have postulated for Jesus. Kloppenborg does not seek to identify his earliest sapiential stratum with Jesus in the way that Harnack's *Q* was construed. It represents a studied production within a

---

[39] T. F. Carney, *The Shape of the Past: Models and Antiquity* (Lawrence, KS: Coronado, 1975) 149–51.

known sapiential genre. Thus, he claims, we can see in Q a stage in which the Jesus tradition was already shaped by various factors, social as well as theological (the words of Sophia incarnate) within a circle of *petit bourgeois* class. These are to be identified with the village administrators rather than the rural peasants. The social disruption caused by the transfer of political jurisdiction in Galilee under Nero in the fifties would have represented difficulties for this class and their social standing and it is these circumstances that can be discerned in their shaping and transmission of the Jesus material which they had inherited. In this account the apocalyptic element in Q comes at the stage in which this group who originally did not require social boundaries, now felt the need to do so because of pressure from their rejection by the local Pharisees.[40] Though Kloppenborg does not suggest this, the circumstances immediately prior to the revolt and the anti-Jewish feelings in the surrounding city territories might have been the catalyst for this second step in the Q-people's social formation.

The situation envisaged in this scenario represents a rather different stage in the social transformation of Galilee to that which in our account Jesus encountered in the twenties. We have maintained that Jesus' message was addressed both to landowning peasants (the majority of the population of lower Galilee) and the lower levels of the retainer class. We have claimed that his message was eschatological in tone ('after whom there would be no other', as B. Meyer puts it) and apocalyptic in inspiration, involving a total renewal of the social order based on a reversal of the existing value-system. In contrast, the situation envisaged by Kloppenborg is not quite so drastic – the need to cope with changing fortunes within a particular class. In my opinion a radically transformative statement about what was called for would have been required if Jesus had any hope of receiving a hearing across the class divisions and the different social pressures that each was under. If, as reconstructed by Kloppenborg, Q can indicate that some of the lower retainer classes were attracted to Jesus' social programme as presented in this collection including its Cynic sounding elements, thereby causing dissensions in their own ranks (the Pharisees), Josephus' *Life* would seem to suggest strongly that many of the landowning peasants were not so impressed, despite their hostility towards the Herodian centres. No doubt the call to abandon all, trusting the gracious providence of God in radical, Jubilee-style hope, proved a stumbling block for those who already experienced that care sufficiently to be able to hold on to their own plot of *Eretz Israel*.

The Jesus tradition had retained a memory of his refusal to take on the role of popular kingship in Galilee, when the ordinary people expected as

---

[40] J. Kloppenborg, 'Literary Convention, Self-Evidence and the Social History of the Q People,' *Semeia* 55 (1991) 77–102.

much from him in view of his words and ministry (Jn 6,14 f. and possibly Mk 6,45). Perhaps it was this refusal and the rejection of the violent means that it would have involved that caused the disillusionment of the country people with Jesus. On the death of Herod one Judas son of Hezechias, aspiring to kingship (βασιλεία) had invaded the royal arsenal at Sepphoris, and in 66 CE a religious Zealot, Jesus son of Sapphias, had lead the attack on the royal palace in Tiberias, joined by some Galileans (*JA* 17,271 f.; *Life* 66 f., 134 f.). Josephus had a difficult role to play in maintaining the loyalties of the country Galileans and at the same time restraining them from acts of violence against both Herodian centres. Someone who had established his authority among them as prophet, healer, and teacher and who in the name of God's kingdom had proposed a radically different lifestyle and values might have been expected to engage in a similar action. His refusal to do so explains at once his avoidance of these places and the failure of the country peasants to heed his proposal. Since his message was grounded in his own experience as a religious charismatic it was to another urban centre that he directed his gaze, Jerusalem, the cult centre that continued to have such a hold on the village people of Galilee, despite its sharing the oppressive economic value-system represented by the Herodian centres in their midst.[41]

I do not expect that my account will win over many Cynics or doubting Thomases! At least I have been able to identify my differences with Crossan which have to do with recognizing the distinctive ethos of Galilee and the social transformation that was occurring there during the reign of Antipas. It was this situation which provided the best context for explaining both the emergence of the Jesus movement then and the particular form of social critique that it embodied. It appears to me to have scope, but that is a relative term, depending on what pieces of evidence are regarded as essential. Has it force? That is for others to decide obviously. For me it has the force of taking the Galilean indicators of our narratives seriously, by attempting to follow the historical trajectories that they suggest. One should not minimize the difficulties inherent in such a construction in view of the many gaps in our knowledge of that society. The dangers of creating a social world to fit our own perceptions of the main character are all too obvious. Nevertheless, the use of archaeological as well as literary evidence can help to ground our best guesses! The value of such an exercise is that it also grounds the career and ministry of Jesus in a particular historical and social context, and contemporary liberation theologians have shown us how theologically important that insight is.

---

[41] Cf. 'Messiah and Galilee,' below pp. 230 ff.

11. Messiah and Galilee

'Surely the Messiah does not come from Galilee? Does not Scripture say that he is of the seed of David, and the Messiah comes from Bethlehem, the village where David is from' (Jn 7,41 f.).

'With the footprints of the Messiah: presumption increases and dearth increases . . . and Galilee will be laid waste and the Gablan (Golan) will be desolate, and the men of the frontiers will go around from town to town and none shall take pity on them' (*m. Sota* 9,14).

These two citations, one from a Christian source and the other from a Jewish one, might suggest that the topic I propose to address is somewhat redundant. On the one hand the messiah cannot be from Galilee, and on the other, his coming spells disaster for the region, as well as for other neighbouring ones. When each citation is examined in its immediate literary and historical context, however, it provides a window on the debates between Jews and Christians and among Jews themselves as to the identity and function of the messiah in the wake both of the destruction of the Second Temple in 70 CE and the failure of the messianic war of Bar Cochba in 132–35 CE.

So what was the relation between messianic expectation and Galilee? For Christians the question is more easily answered, since Galilee will forever be tied to the career of Jesus of Nazareth, which their foundational sources have interpreted messianically, despite the criticism of such claims which the Johannine citation given at the outset reflects. For Jews on the other hand, Galilee has no such resonances in terms of messianic hopes. Indeed the forced movement of the rabbinic schools to the region in the second century CE brought nothing but bitter memories of messiahs and messianic struggles. This move marked a phase of Jewish theological development in which the messiah concept remained 'systemically inert', according to Jacob Neusner. It was only much later, in the fourth and fifth centuries CE that the redactors of the Palestinian Talmud felt free to reintroduce this figure, now transformed, however, into their own image and likeness.[1]

---

[1] J. Neusner, *Messiah in Context. Israel's History and Destiny in Formative Judaism* (Philadelphia: Fortress Press, 1984).

In this essay I propose to go behind such developments and examine the ways in which, in the centuries prior to the destruction, the messiah concept functioned within the multi-dimensional reality labelled today as Second Temple Judaism. Next the aim will be to explore the ways these various images might have impacted in a regional context, namely Galilee, away from the ruling elites and scribal schools who were responsible for their formulation. Finally, I shall turn to Jesus of Nazareth, the only Galilean to whom our sources, however polemically, ascribe the role of messiah. My hope is that by bringing into active dialogue these two very different and apparently irreconcilable realities – Messiah and Galilee – new light may be shed on both. How does the expected future figure relate to the outlying geographical region, which in the eyes of some at the centre had an insignificant role to play in their vision of the future destiny? I trust that such a thought experiment may also suitably honour the memory of Sigmund Mowinckel, who though sharing the notions of his time about a 'half-heathen Galilee', was also conscious of the ways in which regional diversity might give rise to different images of the messiah.[2]

The Messiah in Recent Discussion: Some aspects

Like many other aspects of Second Temple studies the issue of the messiah has received a considerable impetus from the latest publication of the remaining Dead Sea Scrolls. Not that messianic expectation among the Essenes should be exaggerated. As John Collins notes, the messiahs did not play a causal role in the origins of the sect, and as far as its hopes are concerned they were 'merely players in a larger scenario.'[3] It is also now part of the emerging consensus that the idea of a developed unitary doctrine of the messiah, as earlier scholars such as George Foot Moore and Emil Schürer and even Sigmund Mowinckel supposed, is anachronistic and may well have been driven by Christian theological interests.[4] In a similar vein there is widespread recognition that discussion of the messiah should not

---

[2] S. Mowinckel, *He that Cometh* (Oxford: B. Blackwell, 1956), especially 291 and 450. This paper was originally delivered as the annual Mowinckel lecture of the University of Oslo in October 1998. I am deeply grateful to all the members of the Faculty for their invitation, but particularly to Professor David Hellholm and his family.

[3] J. J. Collins, *Apocalypticism in the Dead Sea Scrolls* (London and New York: Routledge, 1997) 90.

[4] J. J. Collins, *The Scepter and the Star. The Messiahs of the Dead Sea Scrolls and Other Ancient Literature* (New York: Doubleday, 1995) 3 f.; cf. also the pertinent discussion of W. Scott Green, 'Messiah in Judaism: Rethinking the Question,' in *Judaisms and their Messiahs at the turn of the Christian Era*, ed. J. Neusner, W. S. Green and E. Frerichs (New York: Cambridge University Press, 1987) 1–13.

be restricted to a mere word study of *mashiah/christos* where these appear in the sources, but that other end-time figures of redemption should also be included in discussion. As Mowinckel insisted 'an eschatology without a messiah is conceivable, but not a messiah without a future hope.'[5] Thus, not all Jewish eschatological statements should be labelled messianic, but only those which envisage an end-time figure, usually, but not always identified with the Davidic king, since other figures such as ideal priest, prophet and other-worldly being also appear in the role of Israel's saviour, however that role may be further specified in political and/or religious terms.[6]

Another aspect that recent studies stress is the fact that the messiah in the sense of the later understanding of an end-time liberator figure, does not occur in pre-exilic Israel. While the term *mashiah* (Hebrew: משיה) does occur, it can be applied to kings, priests or prophets, but without the eschatological significance that it later came to carry. Certain texts which in their original, pre-exilic reference spoke of hope in Yahweh's promises came to be identified as having a surplus of meaning for the future, when Israel's self-understanding was being sorely tested. These texts have been described by various scholars as being pre- or proto-messianic, in that they supply the seedbed from which different utopian pictures of the future could grow and develop. These pictures functioned, not to legitimate the existing king, but as a critique in the light of the experiences which kingship had brought to Israel, by projecting a counter-picture of how different the future king would be.[7] Texts such as Gn 49,9–10; Nm 24,17; Pss 2 and 110; Is chs. 6, 9 and 11, were previously explained in terms of royal messianism arising from Nathan's prophecy to David (2 Sam 7,13–16) which promised that Yahweh would 'establish the throne of his kingdom forever', and would never 'take his steadfast love' from his descendant. Now, however, they are seen as the pre-texts for the messianic ideas of such later compositions as the *Psalms of Solomon*, the *Similitudes of Enoch*, *4 Ezra*, as well as various messianic texts from Qumran, especially 4Q 246, the

---

[5] *He that Cometh*, 8.

[6] G. S. Oegma, *The Anointed and his People. Messianic Expectation from the Maccabees to Bar Kochba*, JSP Supplement Series 27 (Sheffield: Sheffield Academic Press, 1998), has a useful discussion about efforts to introduce some precision into this debate (20–27). His own definition, 'A Messiah is a priestly, royal or otherwise characterised figure, who will play a liberating role at the end time' (26), is similar to that of Collins, *Scepter and Star*, 11–14, except that the latter makes the Jewish dimension explicit.

[7] E. Zenger, 'Jesus von Nazareth und die messianische Hoffnungen des alttestamentlichen Israel,' in *Studien zum Messiasbild im Alten Testament*, ed. U. Struppe (Stuttgart: Verlag Katholisches Bibelwerk, 1974) 23–66, especially 36–38; W. Beuken, 'Did Israel need the Messiah?' in *Messianism through History, Concilium*, ed. W. Beuken, S. Freyne and A. Weiler (London: SCM Press, 1993) 3–13.

'Son of God' text, in that allusions to the earlier biblical passages can read-ily be established, especially, it must be said, Nm 24, Is 11 and Ps 2.

This acknowledgement that messianic speculation is primarily a herme-neutical exercise of re-actualising earlier texts naturally raises the question of the precise contexts which have given rise to this enterprise and the par-ticular horizons of understanding of those engaged in it. What emerges is a much more fluid and variegated picture of the messiah and the expectation associated with his coming. Particularly striking is the fact that after a brief burst of activity in the Persian period reflected in the prophet Zechariah, the messiah(s) disappears from view until the Seleucid period after c. 200 BCE. Thereafter, speculation continued until c. 150 CE, when, as we have seen, it again disappeared, at least in official Jewish sources. However, such Christian writings as Justin's *Dialogue with Trypho* and Origen's *Contra Celsum* show that the debates between Christians and Jews about the messiah did not cease, at least in some circles, despite the changed Christological climate among Greek-speaking Christians, influenced by Gnosticism and other currents of thought.[8] Indeed Neusner believes that the re-introduction of the Messiah figure in the Palestinian Talmud in the fourth and fifth centuries was due in part at least to the triumphalist Chris-tological developments associated with the reign of Constantine as re-flected in Eusebius of Caesarea and others.[9]

For the aim of this paper the Hasmonean and Herodian periods are parti-cularly relevant. Under the Hasmoneans the Jewish territory was expanded to include Galilee and the emergence of an independent Jewish king for the first time since the Babylonian exile in the sixth century (*JA* 13,301). The kings of Judah, Hezekiah and Josiah are reported to have extended their reforms to the north also (2 Kgs 23,15.19 f.; 2 Chr 34,6 f.) but the extent and permanence of their success is disputed. One might therefore speculate that the arrival of a Jewish king, Aristobulus I (104 BCE), followed after one year by his brother Alexander Jannaeus, would have been invested with messianic meaning, especially in Galilee, since it expressed the rise of an independent Jewish nationalism. In contrast, Herod the Great was pro-claimed king of the Jews at the behest of the Roman senate, and had a very difficult time extending his authority to Galilee (*JA* 14,395.413–17.421–30.433.452–3). Herod's successors were never to achieve the same profile,

---

[8] M. Simon, *Verus Israel. A Study of the Relations between Christians and Jews in the Roman Empire* (Oxford: Oxford University Press, 1986) 156–78; N. de Lange, *Origen and the Jews. Studies in Jewish-Christian Relations in third-century Palestine* (Cam-bridge: Cambridge University Press, 1976) 98–102; W. Horbury *Jews and Christians in Contact and Controversy* (Edinburgh: T. & T. Clark, 1998.)

[9] J. Neusner, *Judaism and Christianity in the Age of Constantine* (Chicago: University of Chicago Press, 1987) 59–80.

with the brief exception of the reign of Agrippa I, 41–44 CE. We must look at the general discussion on how these developments gave rise to messianic speculations among religious Jews, before attempting an estimate of their likely impact in a specifically Galilean setting.

The Hasmonean Period

There is no evidence that any of the first Maccabean leaders saw themselves in terms of the expectations associated with a Davidic royal messiah. Certainly neither the Maccabean propagandist author of 1 Macc nor the epitomist who produced 2 Macc from Jason's longer history regarded them in that light.[10] The apocalyptic response of the *hasidim* to the crisis engendered by Antiochus' reform, which is to be found in Daniel (chs. 7–12) and *1 Enoch* (chs 85–90, the animal apocalypse) envisages various otherworldly figures of redemption, but not a royal messiah figure.[11] True, the deeds of Judas, Jonathan and Simon are presented in heroic form in 1 Macc, echoing earlier biblical narratives, but the author seems to diminish the idea of God's direct action in history, as represented e.g., in the Book of Judges, thus showing himself thoroughly imbued with the Hellenistic *Zeitgeist*.[12] The titles that are eventually ascribed to Simon by the people are those of *archiereus*, *strategos* and *ethnarches*, 'until a trustworthy prophet should arise' (1 Macc 13,42; 14,41.47).

John Hyrcanus, the founder of the Hasmonean dynasty, is, on the other hand, attributed by Josephus with the gift of prophecy as a result of his special divine intimacy in the exercise of his roles of priest and leader (*JA* 13,300). However, the exact import of the attribution is not clear, since in the actual account his prophesying is restricted to foretelling of future events to do with his reign, and he is not, directly at least, identified with the prophet who was to come of 1 Macc 14,41. One might therefore justifiably suspect some Josephan self-interest at work here, since he too claims a priestly and prophetic role, especially in his period as governor of Galilee (*Life* 63, 80; *JW* 3,351–55). Hyrcanus' destruction of Shechem and Gerizim (*JA* 13,255) is justified by the author of Jubilees by omitting in

---

[10] J. A. Goldstein, 'How the Authors of 1 and 2 Maccabees Treated the Messianic Promises,' in *Judaisms and their Messiahs*, 69–96.

[11] Cf. G. W. Nickelsburg, 'Salvation without and with a Messiah: Developing Beliefs in Writings Ascribed to Enoch,' in *Judaisms and their Messiah*, 49–68, especially 55 f., and J. J. Collins, 'Messianism in the Maccabean Period,' in *Judaisms and their Messiahs at the turn of the Christian Era*, ed. J. Neusner, W. S. Green and E. Frerichs (New York: Cambridge University Press, 1987) 97–110, especially 101–3; Oegma, *The Anointed and his People*, 67–69.

[12] U. Rappaport, 'A Note on the Use of the Bible in 1 Maccabees,' in *Biblical Perspectives: Early Use and Interpretation of the Bible in Light of the Dead Sea Scrolls*, ed. M. Stone and E. Chazon (Leiden: Brill, 1998) 175–79.

the treatment of the Genesis account of the rape of Dinah, both Jacob's reprimand for the incident and the fact that the Shechemites had undergone circumcision, as the original account in Genesis reports (Gn 34; Jub 30).[13] Yet the author does include Levi together with Judah for special blessing in the very next chapter (Jub 31,14.18). Even though Collins believes that this passage need not be interpreted eschatologically, it does indicate that there was dissatisfaction with the fact that the Hasmoneans had arrogated to themselves the priestly as well as the political leadership. Josephus reports two such incidents of discontent (*JA* 13,291.372–74).[14] While the tradition-history of the *Testaments of the Twelve Patriarchs* is highly complex, it seems certain that the messianic interpretation of Levi together with Judah can be dated to the redaction of the work during the Hasmonean period (*T. Levi* 8,11–17; 18,2–4; *T. Judah* 21,2–4).[15] Likewise, this bifurcation of the messianic role in terms of priest and king is to be found in all the major rule and law-books of the Qumran sect (1QS; 1QSa; 1QM; CD). This is surely indicative of the fact that although the origin of the notion is to be dated to Zechariah's 'sons of oil' of the Persian period (Zech 4,14), it provided an appropriate model for expressing deep-felt dissatisfaction with the Hasmoneans on the part of the Essenes, something that is a recognised feature of the sect.[16]

Control of the high priesthood was clearly of prime importance and it was only with Aristobulus I, followed immediately by his brother Alexander Jannaeus, that the title 'king' was also adopted. This move does not seem to have been an issue, initially at least. The fact that the Hasmoneans did not lay any claims to Davidic succession may have played a role in this regard, but the whole experiment clearly intensified the longing for the long-awaited Davidide, as emerges in the *Psalms of Solomon*. This collection of psalms from pious (possibly Pharisaic) circles is dated in its present form to the period after Pompey's entry into Jerusalem in 63 BCE and the

---

[13] D. Mendels, *The Land of Israel as a Political Concept in Hasmonean Literature* (Tübingen: J. C. B. Mohr, 1987) 70–73; Collins, *Scepter and Star*, 84–86; R. Meyer, *Der Prophet aus Galiläa* (reprint, Darmstadt: G. Olms, 1970) 60–70.

[14] Collins, *Scepter and Star*, 84–86.

[15] A. Hultgard, 'The Ideal Priest, the Davidic Messiah and the Saviour Priest in the *Testaments of the Twelve Patriarchs*,' in *Ideal Figures in Ancient Judaism*, ed. G. Nickelsburg and J. J. Collins (Chico, Ca: Scholars Press, 1980) 93–110. For a discussion of the relationship between Aramaic *T. Levi* and the *Testaments*, cf. Collins, *Scepter and Star*, 86–95, and Oegma, *The Anointed and his People*, 73–81. Cf. also G. Brooke, '4Q Testament of Levi (?) and the Messianic Servant High Priest,' in *From Jesus to John. Essays on Jesus and New Testament Christology in Honour of Marinus de Jonge,'* ed. M. De Boer, JSNT Supplement Series 84 (Sheffield: Sheffield Academic Press, 1993) 83–100.

[16] Collins, *Scepter and Star*, 76 f. and 95.

subsequent profanation of the temple, events which are reflected in a number of different psalms: 2,1–2. 26. 29–31; 8,15–20; 17,14. While the Roman general is certainly not seen as a liberator figure, unlike the Persian king, Cyrus, who was called 'Yahweh's anointed' (Is 45,1), the wrath of the psalmist, especially in *Pss. Sol.* 17 is firmly directed at the Hasmoneans. After recalling the election and promise to David, the psalmist addresses 'those to whom you did not make the promise who took away by force and despoiled the throne of David.' This does not necessarily imply that the Hasmoneans laid claim to the Davidic throne, but that from the author's point of view the only legitimate kingship in Israel should be based on the promise to David. The reign of these impostors which was brought to an end by 'a man alien to our race', namely Pompey, was marked by injustice, greed, fornication, and profanation of the temple. By contrast, the ideal king, the Son of David, whom God is asked to raise up, will purge Jerusalem of gentiles and sinners, and gather them as a holy people, 'dividing them according to their tribes upon the land' (17,28), judging justly and destroying the unlawful nations 'by the word of his mouth', a phrase that echoes LXX Is 11,4. Interwoven with this image of the messiah as wisdom teacher, which is further developed in *Pss. Sol.* 18 (vv. 5–7), are other images of a more war-like kind such as 'smashing the arrogance of sinners like a potter's jar' and 'shattering their substance with an iron rod' (vv. 23–24). At the same time there is the statement that the future king 'will not put his trust in horse and rider and bow, nor gather confidence from a multitude for the day of battle' (*Pss. Sol.* 17,37), statements that seem to reflect a critique of the Hasmonean adoption of Hellenistic military strategies, including foreign mercenaries.[17] Trust in God rather than arms, and the practice of piety rather than war seems to be the keynote, even when violent imagery is seen as appropriate for the cleansing of Jerusalem of gentiles and the gathering of the tribes, themes that are important in a Galilean context as we shall see.

In earlier Israelite history the Deuteronomic code of the king (Dt 16,18–18,22) offers a critique of the previous experience of kingship by seeing it

---

[17] Collins, *Scepter and Star,* 53–56, stresses the war-like traits of this royal figure in the Psalms, whereas others, notably, J. Klausner *The Messianic Idea in Israel from its Beginning to the Completion of the Mishnah* (London: Allen and Unwin, 1956) 317–24 stress the spiritual dimension. Mowinckel, *He that Cometh,* 306–21, favours the more spiritual understanding of his mission, while also recognising the militantly nationalistic dimensions. Oegma, *The Anointed and his People,* 103–8, following J. Schüpphaus, *Die Psalmen Solomos* (Leiden: Brill, 1977), favours the notion of a development within the collection from earlier to later psalms, especially between *Pss. Sol.* 17 and *Pss. Sol.* 18, reflecting changes in the political situation during the reign of Alexandra Salome. On the Hasmonean military achievements see I. Shatzman, *The Armies of the Hasmoneans and Herod from Hellenistic to Roman Frameworks* (Tübingen: J. C. B. Mohr, 1991).

as one office among several in Israel (17,14–20), namely those of judge (16,18) and priest (18,1–8). All three are subordinated to the free, charismatic role of the prophet (18,9–22). This realignment constituted a diminution of kingly power and a critique of militarism by the king as idolatrous.[18] While such a utopian structure never actually functioned subsequently, the Deuteronomic 'rule of the king' provided the basis for a similar critique of the Hasmonean kings in the *Temple Scroll* from Qumran (11QT 57,1–59,11).[19] Contrary to what might have been expected, this passage does not envisage the king as an eschatological figure. Indeed there is the possibility that his posterity would be cut off for ever and several of the prescriptions can be plausibly read in the light of the career of Alexander Jannaeus. The king is to be subordinate to the authority of the High Priest, a hierarchy which is in line with other passages in the scrolls, notably, 1QSa 2 (the Messianic Rule), 4Q 285 (the so-called 'dying messiah' text) and 4QpIsa. as well as CD 14,18–19.[20] There would seem to be little doubt but that such a division of leadership which the community endorses so emphatically as the eschatological ideal has its immediate roots in the Hasmonean experience.

We might summarise this first stage of the examination of recent discussion about the messiah in the following points:

1) The messiah idea in Judaism is primarily a linguistic construct, based on the midrashic development of some key O.T. passages as applied to the political and social situation of the later Hellenistic period.

2) Consequently, there is a fluidity about the notion, depending on the historical context and the circles within which the idea is being developed.

3) The relevant themes which emerge from this first phase are: the restoration of Israel; the control of the priesthood, the administration of justice, the treatment of the gentiles and the character of the messiah as peaceable or as militaristic.

The Roman Period

Whereas the Hasmoneans had carved out a niche for themselves as the Seleucid empire collapsed, the rise of the Herodians was subject to Roman imperial ambitions after the civil strife of the previous decades. Herod the Great was appointed 'king of the Jews' by the Roman senate in 40 BCE, in effect a client king. It took him three years to oust the last of the Hasmone-

---

[18] Zenger, 'Jesus von Nazareth und die messianische Hoffnungen des alttestamentlichen Israel,' 38–41.

[19] M. Hengel, J. Charlesworth and D. Mendels, 'The Polemical Character of "On Kingship" in the Temple Scroll: An Attempt at Dating 11Q Temple,' *JJS* 37 (1986) 28–38.

[20] Collins, *Scepter and Star*, 74–77 and 109–11.

ans, Antigonus, and he seems to have had particular difficulties in Galilee, as previously mentioned. This may have been due to the fact that Galilee was strongly pro-Hasmonean and memories of Herod's earlier rule there as governor of the province were less than enthusiastic.[21] If the idea of filling the role of the messianic king had ever occurred to Herod, he was politically too astute to voice it, since it would have run directly counter to the ideology of empire that was emanating from court circles in Rome, namely that the age of Augustus meant a new beginning of good news for the whole *oikumene*, as expressed in such writings as Virgil's *Fourth Eclogue* and Horace's *Carmen Saeculare*. While Herod's rebuilding of the Jerusalem temple on the grand scale might conceivably have been interpreted messianically, it seems far more likely that he intended it to bolster his image at home and abroad as a benevolent Hellenistic-style monarch.[22] His biographer, Nicholas, followed by Josephus, sought to give him the image of a pious and devoted Jew on occasions such as the announcement of the rebuilding programme: 'to make full return to God for the gift of this kingdom' (*JA* 15,387). Yet his overall policy of Hellenisation, coupled with his disregard for Jewish customs and institutions, meant that he could never be seen as anything other than a self-serving tyrant, as emerges from the delegation that went to Rome on behalf of the people, 'seeking the dissolution of the kingdom' (*JA* 17,304).[23]

Herod may have had no delusions of messianic status, but his reign was likely to have fostered a desire for the ideal king among pious circles on the basis of the experience of the Hasmonean period. Certainly many of the recently published texts from Qumran that can, with some confidence, be dated to the Roman period indicate a messiah figure that is both royal and war-like. There is less evidence of the speculation about two messiahs which occurs in texts datable to the Hasmonean period. Herod had in fact re-instituted the high priesthood as a separate office, albeit with his own appointees. These later texts include *pesherim* or biblical interpretations of Habakkuk (1QpHab) and Psalm 37 (4Q 171), the apocalyptic War Scroll (1QM), a Commentary on Genesis (4Q 252) and a Midrash on Eschatology (4QFlor or 4Q 174). Perhaps the most important text of all is the so-called 'Son of God Aramaic text' (4Q 246), dated by J. T. Milik on palaeographic grounds to the last third of the first century BCE, i.e., the Herodian period,

---

[21] S. Freyne, *Galilee from Alexander the Great to Hadrian. A Study of Second Temple Judaism* (reprint, Edinburgh: T. & T. Clark, 1998) 63–71.

[22] D. Mendels, *The Rise and Fall of Jewish Nationalism* (New York: Doubleday, 1992) 285–87.

[23] P. Richardson, *Herod, King of the Jews and Friend of the Romans* (Columbia: University of South Carolina Press, 1996), is a valiant and interesting attempt to revise this standard picture of Herod's relation to Jewish religion, but is not in my opinion wholly convincing on this issue.

though of course it may originally have referred to an earlier period. This text which has some affinities with the annunciation story in Luke is variously interpreted. Much depends on whether or not the figure introduced in the opening line as 'Son of God he shall be called and they shall name him Son of the Most High' (cf. Lk 1,32.35), is to be seen as a positive or negative character.[24] After the introduction of this figure the fragment goes on to describe a picture of universal chaos: 'people shall trample on people and city on city,' before the people of God arises. Then peace shall reign, the sword shall cease and all cities shall pay him (Son of God) or it (people of God) homage. The great God alone will make war on behalf of the people or the Son and cast down the nations before it or (him).

I agree in general with Collins that this text is best interpreted messianically, following a general pattern found originally in Dn 7 which recurs in The *Similitudes of Enoch* and *4 Ezra*, where the Son of Man figure is interpreted individually and identified as 'anointed' (*1 Enoch* 48,10; 52,4; 4 Ez 12,33; 13,37).[25] However, the Danielic echoes which are quite strong in this fragment, though the Son of Man is not mentioned, means that the representative meaning need not be ruled out also.[26] The notion of the messiah as a representative figure who includes the messianic people is not at all foreign to many of these texts, especially in an apocalyptic framework, influenced by Dn 7,23, and was known also in early Christianity (cf. Mt 19,28; 1 Cor 6,2; Ap 3,21; 20,4). Whatever may have been the original background to this text, a setting in the Herodian period when Roman propaganda about the *pax Augusta* was being spread abroad seems singularly appropriate for a *relecture*. In true counter-cultural fashion, as befitted the circles who preserved such texts (or, as in the case of the early Christians, who produced their own messianic narratives), the establishing and maintenance of peace could only be achieved by the great God and his representative(s). It was not achieved from men like the Roman emperor, Gaius Caligula, who sought 'to be considered and called a god' (*JW* 2,184).

The Essenes belonged to what Richard Horsley calls the elite, scribal classes, who drew their inspiration about the future messiah from reworking ancient texts and the promises they offered in new situations. He has also argued for a model of popular kingship which operated among the illiterate peasants, and was based on stories of deeds of daring by David,

---

[24] Cf. Oegma, *The Anointed and his People*, 123 lists five quite different proposals as to the identity of the figure.

[25] Cf. *The Scepter and Star*, 154–72 for a full discussion.

[26] Cf. G. Theißen, 'Gruppenmessianismus. Überlegungen zum Ursprung der Kirche in Jüngerkreis Jesu,' in *Jahrbuch für Biblische Theologie* 7 (1992) 101–23; M. Hengel, *The Son of God* (London: SCM Press, 1976) 44 on the collective use of the term.

Saul and others.[27] Such figures took on a revolutionary character and could always command strong popular support, as distinct from the royal ideology which, he claims, was highly unpopular with the masses. He regards the exploitation of the Herodian period as providing the socio-economic conditions for the resurgence of such popular messianism in the various uprisings which occurred on the death of Herod the Great. Josephus reports three in particular in some detail: those of Judas, son of Hezechias in Galilee, Simon in Perea and Athronges in Judea (*JA* 17,269–85; *JW* 2,55–79). Horsley describes all three as messianic uprisings, but this must be open to question in view of the actual descriptions, even allowing for Josephus' biases against such popular movements in general.

It is indeed possible that someone who 'desired royal honour' (Judas), 'donned the diadem' (Simon), or 'dared to aspire to kingship' and who 'enjoyed the title king for a long time' (Athronges), might seek to support their claims by deliberately presenting themselves in the guise of end-time messianic figures, especially if they were prompted by feelings of alienation arising from the nature and style of Herodian kingship. Were that the case, it would represent highly significant information for the subject of this paper, since it would document regional (including Galilean) interest in, and use of the messianic ideal in certain social settings. Closer inspection of Josephus' narratives casts doubt on Horsley's interpretation, at least in the case of Judas, son of Hezechias. While all three uprisings are presented under the common heading of 'aspiring to sovereignty' (*JW* 2,55), or as examples of 'tumults that filled Judea' (*JA* 17,269), the fact is that the account of the Galilean revolt is much less embellished than those in Perea and Judea. Both Simon, whose revolt is also known to Tacitus (Hist. V,9), and Athronges are described as being endowed with great physical strength, thus deliberately, it would seem, putting them in the *gibbûr* or strongman tradition of the biblical narratives like Gideon and David, prior to his election as king (Judg 6,12; 8,22; 1 Sam 16,18). By contrast there is no such heroic colouring of Judas, whose violence against his local opponents is all that is mentioned. In addition, both Simon and Athronges are said to have actually been acknowledged as kings, the former having put on the diadem (Ps 89,19), whereas Judas merely aspired to kingly honour, but is never said to have actually achieved this. In the case of Simon, who had been a slave of Herod, there was also a strong popular expectation from which he drew his support, whereas Athronges, a shepherd like David, actually set up a council, sharing power with his brothers as his regents in various districts. Missing from both the *JW* and *JA* accounts of

---

[27] R. A. Horsley, 'Popular Messianic Movements,' *CBQ* 46 (1984) 473–78; R. A. Horsley and J. S. Hanson, *Bandits, Prophets, and Messiahs. Popular Movements at the Time of Jesus* (Minneapolis: Winston Press, 1985) 88–134.

Judas are any such details, other than his capture of arms and other booty in the raid on Sepphoris, which he then distributed among his followers. It may well be, therefore, that Josephus in his desire to portray disturbances in all three Jewish regions of Herod's kingdom on his death, availed himself of various reports and included them under a common umbrella, even though in fact they had quite different motivation and backgrounds.[28]

Horsley identifies three further examples of his type, two at the outbreak of the first revolt, namely, Menahen, the leader of the *sicarii* and Simon bar Giora, and the leader of the second revolt, Simeon bar Koziba. All three would seem to fall into the messianic category more convincingly than those just discussed. In the case of Simeon bar Koziba, there is the literary evidence in which Rabbi Akiba is reputed to have applied to him the Balaam oracle which spoke of 'a star going forth from Jacob' (Nm 24,17), and proclaimed him 'King Messiah', so that his name subsequently became transformed to Bar Cochba, 'the Son of a Star' (*y. Ta'an.* 68d; *b. Sanh.* 93b).[29] Archaeological evidence from the Judean desert in terms of both coins and documents confirm this picture, but he appears to have styled himself *nasi'* rather than king, in accordance with Ez 37,42ff., where the end-time ruler of Israel of Davidic line is described similarly. As regards the various leaders of the first revolt, the messianic-style character of their claims seems fairly well established, despite the fact that Martin Hengel's construction of the Zealot party as a messianic movement, dating from the founding of the Fourth Philosophy by Judas the Galilean in 6 CE, is now queried.[30] Thus, even Josephus, who is at pains to distance the Jewish people as a whole from the revolt, blaming instead the small band of militant hot-heads who had initiated the uprising, has coloured his account of both leaders in a highly religious manner.[31] Menahen, after storming Masada and arming his group of followers, is depicted as 'approaching the

---

[28] Cf. Freyne, *Galilee from Alexander the Great to Hadrian,* 213–16, for an alternative proposal regarding the background to Judas' revolt, but this proposal has been dismissed rather summarily by Horsley, *Galilee. History, Politics, People,* 60 and 268–71, even though he strikes a note of caution here about his idea of popular kingship, not found elsewhere in his writing on the topic, as e.g., in *Bandits, Prophets and Messiahs,* 114f. Cf. further, Theißen, 'Gruppenmessianismus,' 105f., who also notes the different treatment of Judas from that of Simon and Athronges by Josephus.

[29] P. Schäfer, *Der Bar Kokhba-Aufstand* (Tübingen: J. C. B. Mohr, 1981), especially 51–77; M. Hengel, 'Die Bar-Kokhbamünzen als politisch-religiöse Zeugnisse,' in *Judaica et Hellenistica. Kleine Schriften,* vol. 1 (Tübingen: J. C. B. Mohr, 1998) 344–50.

[30] M. Hengel, *The Zealots. Investigations into the Jewish Freedom Movement in the Period from Herod I until 70 A.D.* (Edinburgh: T. & T. Clark, 1989), especially his response to his critics in the Foreword, XI-XVII, 'Zealots and Sicarii.'

[31] D. Rhoads, *Israel in Revolution. 6–74 C.E. A Political History Based on the Writings of Josephus* (Philadelphia: Fortress Press, 1976) 11–122 and 140–48; Hengel, *The Zealots,* 296–308.

temple in state to pay his devotions, arrayed in royal robes and attended by his suite of armed fanatics' (*JW* 2,242–48). Simon bar Giora on the other hand 'proclaimed liberty for slaves and rewards for the free', a description which has some echoes of Is 61,1, a passage which is interpreted messianically both in Qumran (4Q 521) and in Luke's gospel as applied to the ministry of Jesus (Lk 4,18). Josephus also refers to the effect an ambiguous oracle from the Scriptures, claiming that 'one from their country would rule the world', had on the populace at large in the immediate pre-revolt period (*JW* 6,312; cf. Tacitus *Hist.* V, 13). The two apocalyptic works, *4 Ezra* and *2 Baruch*, are to be dated to the post-revolt period, and are often said to have transformed the royal, warrior messiah, whose kingdom is preliminary and provisional into an other-worldly figure, but this did not necessarily mean the abandoning of the messiah's role in the political realm and the eventual overthrow of Rome.[32] In such a climate, therefore, it is quite understandable that the figure of a royal and militant messiah would have appealed to those who felt the time to strike against Roman rule had come. The fact that internecine strife led these various pretenders to betray the expectations of justice and peace associated with that figure and to fail in their objective to overthrow Rome's domination of Palestine, does not take from the perception that a warrior messiah figure had special appeal for the Jews, not merely in Palestine but also in the Diaspora, throughout the first and early second centuries CE.[33]

It is unclear to me therefore, how useful Horsley's rigid distinction between elite and popular notions of the messiah is, in the task of sorting out the tangled skein of messianic speculation to be found in the writings of the time, including the N.T. In the case of Bar Cochba for example, while he undoubtedly had popular support, he was allegedly acknowledged as messiah by no less a person than Rabbi Akiba. Josephus too belonged to the scribal elites, yet he did not remove all traits of messianic colouring from his accounts of some of Horsley's popular kings, as we have seen, despite his distaste for such characters. Undoubtedly, royal figures of a militant kind seem to have had the most widespread popularity, and the support for these varied with different strata of the population, since the aristocracy was reluctant to become involved in messianic wars against Rome. Indeed almost all the messianic texts that have come to us are from

---

[32] Cf. J. J. Collins, *The Apocalyptic Imagination. An Introduction to the Jewish Matrix of Christianity* (New York: Crossroad, 1984) 166f. on the introduction of the eagle, the symbol of Rome into the animal vision of Dn 7 (*4 Ezra* 13); Oegma, *The Anointed and his People*, 224–26; M. Stone, 'The Question of the messiah in Fourth Ezra,' in *Judaisms and their Messiahs*, 209–24.

[33] M. Hengel, 'Messianische Hoffnung und politischer "Radikalismus" in der jüdisch-hellenistischen Diaspora. Zur Frage der Voraussetzungen des jüdischen Aufstandes unter Trajan, 115–117 n. Chr.,' in *Judaica et Hellenistica. Kleine Schriften*, vol. 1, 314–43.

groups who may indeed be described as scribal elites, like the Pharisees and Essenes, but who, it should not be forgotten, were rivals, if not dissidents in terms the Hasmonean and Herodian ruling classes. Other messiah types in addition to those of king and priest, especially that of the teacher/prophet occur, but they appear to be less popular, and there was also a tendency for them to become absorbed into the picture of the ideal king (*Pss. Sol.* 17,32.36.43).[34] However, the Essene material shows how the teacher figure in particular resisted such an absorption, no doubt because it was important to the community and its own history, however the figure of 'the teacher of righteousness of the end of days' is related to the historical teacher (CD 6,7–11; 4QFlor(174).[35] Thus, insofar as Horsley's category of a scribal elite applies, it was the teacher-messiah rather than the royal-messiah that was more likely to have been attractive to them.

The various sign and oracular prophets that Josephus also documents were likewise a response to the social anomie of the period and appear to have had some popular appeal. The form of this response was the expectation of God's imminent intervention on behalf of his people, similar to the founding acts of the desert wandering, the crossing of the Jordan and collapse of the walls of Jericho, except that now it was the collapse of Jerusalem's walls that was expected (*JW* 2,259; *JA* 20,97–98; *JA* 20,169–71).[36] These two different strands, the one based on the expectation of a militant messiah, the other more passive, relying on God's protective care for Israel, stand in some tension with each other, though clearly the former is dependent on the latter, since all messiahs of whatever hue are God's anointed. The views of Judas the Galilean, founder of the Fourth Philosophy, appear to show no interest in a royal messianic figure relying instead on a radical theocracy, which acknowledges 'God alone as king.' Among all the rebellious leaders mentioned by Josephus, he is the only one to have been described as a *sophistes* (*JW* 2,118; cf. *JA* 18,9,23). His form of rebellion, the withholding of taxes, represented a different strategy to that of the messianic pretenders. Thus each strand could give rise to quite different practical responses to the prevailing situation. To some extent they can be seen to come together and be transformed in the process in the *Similitudes of Enoch* (*1 Enoch* 37–41), now commonly dated to the first century CE. Here the figure of a latter-day judge is heavily dependent on that of the

---

[34] Thus M. de Jonge, *Jesus the Servant Messiah* (New Haven: Yale University Press, 1991) 72. However, the possibility that Son of David could have included prophet and exorcist, and therefore, was used by Jesus as a self-designation during his own life, has been challenged by H. J. de Jonge, 'The Historical Jesus' View of Himself and his Mission,' and W. Meeks, 'Asking Back to Jesus' Identity,' in *From Jesus to John*, 26 f. and 46–48. See also Collins, *Scepter and Star*, 116.

[35] Collins, *Scepter and Star*, 111–14.

[36] Horsley and Hanson, *Bandits, Prophets, Messiahs*, 135–89.

Son of Man in Daniel, yet he can also be designated 'the chosen one', 'the righteous one' and 'the anointed one' or messiah (*1 Enoch* 48,10; 52,4).[37] Thus, the messiah figure is transformed from an earthly, militant, royal figure into an other-worldly judge, whose saving act for Israel is the vindication of the righteous and the condemnation of its enemies.[38]

When one compares Jewish messianic expectation of the Roman period with that of the previous, Hasmonean one, it is clear that the Roman presence has had a major impact on both the frequency and the colouring of the messiah image. The dominance of the royal messianic figure with his war-like traits must surely be attributed to the desire in various circles to be rid of the Roman yoke, and this in turn played a major role in the two revolts against Rome in the homeland, as well as that in Egypt, Cyrenaica and Cyprus under Trajan. As well as the militaristic interpretation, however, there were other strands discernible, notably that of the teacher/prophet, who in some circles took precedence over the royal son of David figure, without being absorbed by it. On the other hand the radical theocracy of apocalyptic literature seems also to have been operative, as we have seen. Even when these two strands were brought together in the combination of the messiah with the other-worldly Son of Man figure expected in apocalyptic literature, this development was by no means apolitical, but left the resolution of Israel's difficulties to God's intervention, when the wicked would be finally judged and the righteous vindicated. The synoptic gospels, with their combination of an earthly, non-militant messiah figure and the expectation of an apocalyptic redeemer/judge, provide an interesting mutation within this overall scenario in a climate of intense speculation about the issues that messianic hopes addressed. As already noted, the very notion of a messianic, saviour figure disappears in the early rabbinic writing (the *Mishnah*) after the failure of the Bar Cochba revolt, but it should be remembered that this represented only one circle of opinion within the Jewish community. The dating of the Targums is indeed a difficult issue, but even if the portrayal of the messiah in these works is to be dated to the pre-Bar Cochba period, the mere fact of the continued presence and vitality of the war-like messiah in the later transmission of such writings as the Targums to Gn 49 and Dt 33 (the blessings of Jacob and Moses to the tribal leaders) or Is 53 (the suffering servant), is surely an indication that that particular expression of messianic hope had not been totally lost sight of.[39]

---

[37] J. Van der Kam, 'Righteous One, Messiah, Chosen One and Son of Man,' in *The Messiah. Developments in Earliest Judaism and Christianity*, ed. J. H. Charlesworth (Minneapolis: Fortress Press, 1992) 167–91.

[38] Oegma, *The Anointed and his People*, 140–46.

[39] For a recent discussion of the many aspects of this intriguing phase of Jewish history cf. Oegma, *The Anointed and his People*, 235–86. On the Targums in question cf. R.

The revolt under Gallus, which incidentally took place in the environs of Sepphoris in Galilee in 351/52 CE and which has left some traces in pagan, Christian and Jewish writings, may reasonably be seen as a sign that Jewish nationalistic hopes, and with them the expectation of a militant messiah figure, were never totally abandoned. They had only required an environment such as that created by the increased Christian presence in the Holy Land under Constantine to spark them off again.[40]

Galilee and Jewish Messianic Hopes

While Galilee has received considerable attention in recent studies of Early Judaism and Christianity, mainly because of the connection with the quest for the historical Jesus, it is sometimes overlooked that it was only one of several regions of first-century Palestine with their own distinctive ethos. This aspect of the situation was graphically illustrated by the revolts that occurred on the death of Herod the Great, with uprisings in three different regions, Galilee, Perea and Judea, each with a native strong man laying claim to the title king. Apart from Judas, the son of Hezechias, the messianic character of whose rebellion is at best dubious, Jesus of Nazareth is the only Galilean to whom the title messiah has been ascribed in the literature of the period. As a result, any discussion of Jesus and Galilee runs the risk of searching for a suitable fit between the recorded ministry of Jesus and the presumed Galilean social world of his time. There are several dangers in this approach. In the first place it suggests that social world was a static and uniform reality and fails to acknowledge that there was considerable diversity within the region as a whole, differences that might be described as geographical (e.g., upper and lower Galilee and the valley), historical (Hasmonean and Roman periods), ethnographical (e.g., Israelite, Judean and gentile) and socio-cultural (urban and rural tensions). Another difficulty in allowing the quest for the historical Jesus set the agenda for understanding the social world of Galilee is the fact that the quest for the latter then becomes laden with the same difficulties that have bedevilled the former for over 200 years. Thus in the current 'third wave' of historical Jesus studies the case has been made, with varying degrees of plausibility, it must be said, for a thoroughly Hellenised, even gentile Galilee, a Galilee

---

Syren, *The Blessings in the Targums. A Study on the Targumic Interpretation of t.Genesis 49 and Deuteronomy 33* (Abo: Abo Akademi, 1986), especially 101–23; B. D. Chilton, *The Isaiah Targum,* The Aramaic Bible, vol. 11 (Edinburgh: T. & T. Clark, 1987) 28 f. and 103–5.

[40] B. Geller Nathanson, 'Jews, Christians and the Gallus Revolt in Fourth Century Palestine,' *BA* 49 (1986) 26–36.

that was a hot-bed of Jewish revolutionaries (i.e., Zealots) and a Jewish Galilee that was Torah-observant, each corresponding to the picture of Jesus that was being presented.[41]

We shall return to the messianic career of Jesus in Galilee in the third section of this paper, but for now it seems important to reframe the question to be addressed in the light of the discussions about the messiah outlined above. These have demonstrated that messianic speculation in all circles of Jewish life combined mythopoeic imagination, exegetical expertise in reworking older texts and socio-political realism. All three were operating in a dynamic tension and gave rise to new images of the messiah and his role. With this broader perspective on the factors at work in messianic thinking during the Second Temple period, we can now ask some different and interesting questions which may throw further light on both Galilean social life and the various images of the messiah that had evolved. Did special conditions operate in Galilee that might have given rise to images of the messiah that were different from those which were formulated among the Jewish religious elites, and inevitably, therefore, had a Jerusalem bias? If so, were there any native Galilean figures, narratives or symbols that could have been drawn upon in developing these distinctive images of the messiah and messianic blessings? Who would have been likely to have developed such images – native Galilean or outsider – and for what circles of Galilean life? While obviously difficult to answer in any definitive way, questions such as these, when addressed from the perspective of our knowledge, both of messianic speculation within various branches of Judaism and the Galilean social world, should offer new perspective on both issues.

In this context, however, Galilee really stands for Galileans, since it is people who engage in messianic speculation and are carried forward by the hopes which such an activity engenders, no matter how much weight is placed on landscape and political boundaries in developing regional attitudes. Who really were the Galileans in Hellenistic and Roman times, and how might their cultural and religious affiliations best be described? Several different opinions have been put forward, and it is important to describe each briefly in order to have the most complete picture of all the various possibilities in addressing our questions.

---

[41] See for example, W. Bauer, 'Jesus der Galiläer,' in *Aufsätze und Kleine Schriften*, ed. G. Strecker (Tübingen: J. C. B. Mohr, 1967) 91–108; B. Mack, *A Myth of Innocence: Mark and Christian Origins* (Philadelphia: Fortress Press, 1988) 53–78; E. Bammel, 'The Revolution theory from Reimarus to Brandon,' in *Jesus and the Politics of His Day*, ed. E. Bammel and C. F. D. Moule (Cambridge: Cambridge University Press, 1984) 11–68; G. Vermes, *Jesus the Jew. An Historian's Reading of the Gospels* (London: Collins, 1973) 43–57.

1) Γαλιλαία ἀλλοφύλων/Galilee of the Gentiles is deemed to have been an accurate designation of the Galileans up to the Maccabean times (1 Macc 5,15). Thereafter, so the theory goes, the Hellenistic cities of 'the circle' continued to play a very active role in ensuring an overall Hellenistic ethos for Galilee. This can take the extreme form of a continued 'pagan' Galilee in terms of its cultural affiliations, so that 'Jesus kein Jude war' (Grundmann), or the more moderate version of a thoroughly Hellenised Jewish Galilee, which spawned that curious hybrid of contemporary scholarship, namely, a Jewish Cynic Jesus, who would be quite at home there.[42]

2) At the opposite end of the spectrum is the view that the Galileans should be characterised as Israelites, because, unlike Samaria in 721 BCE, the inhabitants of the northern region were largely undisturbed when the first wave of Assyrian deportations occurred in 732 BCE after the campaign of Tiglath-Pileser. Albrecht Alt argued that this Israelite background to the Galilean population meant that when the opportunity arose for Galilee to be integrated into the Jerusalem temple community, the ἔθνος τῶν Ἰουδαίων, in the wake of the Maccabean successes, they willingly availed of it.[43] On the other hand, Richard Horsley, while also espousing the Israelite background of the Galileans with their own local traditions maintained over centuries, sees the relationship with the Judeans as more confrontational, these latter imposing their laws on the unwilling Galileans. Thus, the Hasmonean expansion was a disruptive event as far as Galilee was concerned and the relationship of Galilee with the south continued to be fraught, even after the Bar Cochba revolt, when the rabbinical schools were established in Galilee.[44]

3) Another variation on the Galileans' relationship with Jerusalem is to take Josephus' account of the enforced Judaisation of the Itureans by Aristobulus I at face value (*JA* 13,319; *JW* 1,76).[45] This can easily lead to the assumption that Galileans as 'new converts' were somehow less authentically Jewish in the Roman period, and thus easily fell prey to Hellenistic influences like their Samaritan counterparts.

---

[42] E. Schürer, *The History of the Jewish People in the Age of Jesus Christ*, revised by G. Vermes, F. Millar, and M. Black, 3 vols. (Edinburgh, T. & T. Clark, 1973–84), vol 1, 142; Bauer, 'Jesus der Galiläer,' *Aufsätze und Kleine Schriften*, 91–108; W. Grundmann, *Jesus der Galiläer und das Judentum* (Leipzig: Georg Wigand, 1941); J. D. Crossan, *The Historical Jesus. The Life of a Mediterranean Jewish Peasant* (Edinburgh: T. & T. Clark, 1991).

[43] A. Alt, 'Galiläische Problemen: Die Umgestaltung Galiläas durch die Hasmonäer,' *Kleine Schriften zur Geschichte Israels*, 3 vols. (Munich: C. H. Beck, 1953–64), vol. 2, 407–23.

[44] R. A. Horsley, *Galilee. History, Politics, People* (Valley Forge: Trinity Press International, 1995).

[45] Schürer, *History of the Jewish People*, vol. 2, 7–10.

4) Finally, there is the view that the population of Galilee was indeed Judean, in that in the Hellenistic period many new settlements appear which have clear Hasmonean associations.[46] The presumption is that these were settled by Hasmonean sympathisers, as the northern territory gradually came to be included within the borders of *Eretz Israel* in the period from John Hyrcanus to Alexander Jannaeus. Their cultural and religious affiliations, therefore, were Jerusalem oriented. The question becomes one of assessing how far these settlements should be designated 'fortresses' because of the allegedly hostile attitude of the native Galilean 'Israelites' towards the new arrivals, as Horsley maintains, or whether they should be considered natural extensions of claims to the old tribal territories which had been sparsely populated for several centuries.[47]

I cannot obviously deal here with all the issues raised by these varying and partially, at least, competing claims. Though previously I was persuaded by Alt's arguments for the continuity of the population from earlier times, in a number of different recent publications I have adopted the fourth position, since I believe that the archaeological evidence strongly supports it.[48] This includes the most recent data from both Sepphoris and Iotapata, crucial sites in lower Galilee in terms of our understanding of the nature of the Hasmonean expansion to the north.[49] Of course it would be naive to believe that the population of Galilee was not to some extent mixed; what is at issue is the dominant cultural and religious affiliation of those inhabitants of the region whom we meet in our sources and who are often, but not always described as Galileans. In our discussion of messianic resonances in Galilee we shall keep the various options in mind, as clearly different backgrounds would be likely to give rise to quite diverse understandings and emphases of the expected figure's role within the same region.

We have seen already that the differences between the Hasmonean and Herodian periods manifested themselves in the issues that emerged in each in the context of messianic speculation, relating to different political and

---

[46] E. Meyers, J. Strange and D. Groh, 'The Meiron Excavation Project: Archaeological Survey in Galilee and Golan, 1976,' *BASOR* 230 (1978) 1–24; M. Aviam, 'Galilee: the Hellenistic to Byzantine Periods,' in *NEAEHL*, ed. E. Stern, 4 vols. (Jerusalem: The Israel Exploration Society, 1993), vol. 2, 452–58; Z. Gal, *Lower Galilee during the Iron Age*, ASORDS 8 (Winona Lake: Eisenbrauns, 1992).

[47] Horsley, *Galilee. History, Politics, People*, 42–45.

[48] S. Freyne, *Galilee from Alexander the Great to Hadrian*, 23–26; *Galilee, Jesus and the Gospels* (Dublin: Gill & Macmillan, 1988) 170 f.; 'Archaeology and the Historical Jesus,' above pp. 160 ff.

[49] E. Meyers, E. Netzer, C. Meyers, *Sepphoris* (Winona Lake: Eisenbrauns, 1992); D. Adan-Bayewitz and M. Aviam, 'Iotapata, Josephus, and the Siege of 67: Preliminary Report on the 1992–94 Seasons,' *JRA* 10 (1997) 131–65.

social experiences. Presumably what was true on the macro-level would be equally true in the micro-world of Galilean regionalism. In fact both periods impacted quite differently on Galilee, in terms both of its place within the larger Jewish world and the role that outside political control played there. As already mentioned, Galilee was included in the greater Israel during the Maccabean/Hasmonean period, with the emergence of an independent and united state, that for the first time since the days of David and Solomon included the northern region. There are various opinions as to the effects of this extension of the borders of *Eretz Israel* on the natives of the region and the changes in the population that it brought about. Yet irrespective of one's answers to those questions, it certainly must have raised such issues as to how the gentiles were to be dealt with, both 'those round about' and those living in the midst of the land, a recurring theme in the messianic speculation of the time, as we have seen. By contrast, the Herodians were not independent rulers, but client kings of Rome. Their policies were, therefore, determined by the demands of Roman propaganda, and the building projects of Herod the Great (Temple of Augustus at Banias) and Antipas (Sepphoris and Tiberias) were above all architectural statements of Roman power and Roman domination in Galilee. They were also a serious drain on the resources of the populace, as forced labour, expropriation of property and increased taxation placed a heavy burden on the peasants, creating resentment of the new class of retainers in their midst dwelling in the cities.[50] The degree of Galilee's participation in the two revolts becomes a measure of how far these pressures were felt in the region and the likely demand for an alternative style of rule.

In both periods the relationship of Galilee to Jerusalem as a religious centre was of crucial significance, but for different reasons. In order to consolidate their control of Galilee, it was important politically for the Hasmoneans to extend the sphere of influence of the temple, as a symbolic centre of unity for the whole nation. In doing this, applying the language of the anthropologist Clifford Geertz, they would be 'creating long-lasting motivations and feelings of loyalty' among the population as a whole, irrespective of their regional and social differences.[51] In the Roman period, the emergence of such centres of civil rule as Caesarea Maritima, which was to become the permanent seat of the Roman administration, and to a lesser extent, Jericho, Masada and Herodion as royal residences, meant that Jerusalem, its temple and priesthood, were no longer important as a political

---

[50] Cf. 'Herodian Economics in Galilee: Searching for a Suitable Model,' above pp. 86 ff.

[51] C. Geertz, 'Religion as a Cultural System,' in *Anthropological Approaches to the Study of Religion,* ed. M. Banton, ASA Monograph series 3, (London, 1966) 3 f.

centre, but were relegated to a more isolated religious role.[52] This was in line with Roman policy generally in regard to national shrines, and they therefore monitored carefully any attempt to restore the political centrality of Jerusalem by militant groups, ultimately turning it into a pagan city, Aelia Capitolina, after 135 CE. Its role in various depictions of the future was, therefore, a matter of some importance to the Roman authorities also.

Against this background we can now begin to address the questions already formulated, not in the hope of giving comprehensive and definitive answers, but of sketching out certain lines of approach which would appear to offer fruitful avenues for further exploration.

1) In dealing with the contrast between the impact of the Hasmonean and Herodian periods on Galilee we have already hinted at the main themes which could have provoked there a distinctive approach and colouring to the expectation of the messiah, or at least made certain formulations more attractive than others for Galileans. The inclusion of the region into the Hasmonean state was the result of military campaigns by John Hyrcanus, Aristobulus and Alexander Jannaeus. Insofar as these developments were viewed by Galileans as a form of 'home-coming' to the one cultic community, these figures might conceivably have taken on the status of liberators, and their adoption of the title 'king' as well as their militarism in dealing with the gentiles would have been both natural and appropriate. However, as we saw in the first part of this paper, there is little evidence that in adopting the title king, the later Hasmoneans thought of themselves as Davidides. It was their arrogation of the role of the high priesthood that seems to have provoked more of a reaction from religious circles as expressed in the idea of the two messiahs. Besides, to employ foreign mercenaries, as the Hasmoneans had done, was certainly not part of a Jewish war-like messiah's profile: one of his tasks was to rid Israel and Jerusalem of its gentile enemies and relocate the tribes in their place as a purified people 'so that neither sojourner nor alien shall dwell with them anymore' (*Pss. Sol.* 17,28). Indeed, for northern Israelites the destruction of Shechem by John Hyrcanus could scarcely have been judged as one of the blessings of the messiah's arrival. As noted already the pro-Hasmonean author of Jubilees felt the need to justify this action by re-writing the original story in such a way that the Shechemites were uncircumcised and could therefore, be slaughtered without any feelings of guilt (Gn 34,19.24).[53] In a Galilean context such court propaganda was also relevant to the treatment of the Itureans, who were given the option of being circumcised or of leaving the country (*JA* 13,319). In a similar vein Jubilees' treatment of the relations between Jacob and Esau, representing Jews and

---

[52] D. Mendels, *The Rise and Fall of Jewish Nationalism*, 277–320.

[53] Mendels, *The Land of Israel as a Political Concept*, 72–76.

Arabs, so that the brothers are eventually reconciled, had significance not just for the Idumeans in the south, but for the Itureans also. Insofar as both Idumeans and Itureans were prepared to adopt the ways of the Jews, they were no longer considered aliens in the land, but could be seen as full participants in the cultic community.

For Judeans who had been settled in Galilee as part of the re-appropriation of the national territory, the links with Jerusalem were highly important, both symbolically and politically. This situation would appear to have been addressed in surviving fragments from the court historian, Eupolemus' work, *On the Kings of Judea*, usually dated to 158/157 BCE. In rewriting the biblical narrative, this writer clearly had the situation of his own day in view, particularly the centrality and sanctity of the temple, possibly as a response to its profanation by Antiochus.[54] The building of Solomon's temple with the aid of the king of Tyre (1 Kgs 5; 2 Chr 2) is retold in the second fragment to emphasise Solomon's superior status to the kings of Egypt and Tyre, and the size of his kingdom is extended to include Moab and Ammon as well as Galilee, Gilead and Samaria. These different regions are expected to send the necessary provisions from the land – wine and wheat – with Judea supplying the oil and Arabia (Nabatea) the meat, in order to feed the Tyrian workmen whom Souron, king of Tyre, had sent in response to Solomon's letter. Later in the same fragment, this politico-geographical arrangement is described in religio-cultural terms of the twelve tribes, each tribe taking charge of supplies for one month. Galilee, then, is an integral part of an enlarged, ideal Israel, the centre of which is the Jerusalem temple, which all areas of the land are expected to support. In this way those living in the provinces are connected intimately with the centre and can share in its sanctity, while ensuring its economic as well as its religious status.

These aspects of Hasmonean politics, reflected on religiously in the court literature, are treated in terms of a rewriting of past history to mirror the present situation. The combination of the notion of an extended territory coinciding with that of former Israel, and the centrality of the Jerusalem temple, reflect both the Deuteronomic ideal of the land and the vision of the restored temple at the centre of the twelve tribe territories as described by Ezekiel (47,13–48,29).[55] They can, therefore, be ascribed to

---

[54] Schürer, *History of the Jewish People*, vol. 3.i, 513–17; Ben Zion Wacholder, *Eupolemus. A Study of Judeo-Greek Literature* (Cincinnati: Hebrew Union College, 1974) 155–69.

[55] The *Temple Scroll* develops this link further with the names of the twelve tribes inscribed on the gates leading into the courtyard of the Israelite males who pay the half shekel offering, in the eschatological temple (11QT 39, 11–13). However there is no mention of any messianic figure in this restoration of the temple which God himself will build (col. 29).

Jewish eschatology in a general way, but what is missing is the idealisation of any one person in bringing about that situation, even though the possibility offered itself in terms of the Hasmonean kings. This may be due to the fact that as a court historian, Eupolemus was more interested in addressing a Hellenistic than a Jewish audience. Therefore, while developments with regard to Galilee in the Hasmonean period fitted well into the eschatological hopes for restoration of the Jewish community, they do not appear to have generated a messianism that was specifically addressed to the Galilean situation, at least insofar as we can judge from the extant literature, selective and court-centred though it may be. Not even in terms of Horsley's popular messianism can we detect traces of Galilean unrest with the Hasmonean expansion, as might have been expected among native Israelites. Perhaps this is a further indication that the majority of the population consisted of new arrivals from the south whose allegiance was firmly with the Hasmonean rulers.

Was the new urgency which the Roman/Herodian period brought to messianic speculation generally felt in Galilee also? As previously mentioned, Herod the Great had difficulty in establishing his rule in the area after being appointed king by the Roman senate in 40 BCE. The nature of this opposition is unclear in Josephus' account. While I have attempted to understand it in the context of continued Hasmonean support in the region, Richard Horsley has argued for a two-tiered opposition, one 'a feeble, short-lived effort by the garrisons of the ousted Hasmonean claimant, Antigonus', and the other, more persistent, popular unrest, associated in particular with the brigand chief, Hezechias, whom Herod had murdered earlier when he was governor of the region (*JW* 1,204; *JA* 14,159). This unrest resurfaced again on Herod's death with the attempt of Hezechias' son, Judas, to claim kingly honour in 4 BCE.[56] Irrespective of which is the more accurate view of the social and political background to the continued unrest, the messianic status of both Hezechias and Judas is, as we saw earlier, highly dubious.

Dissatisfaction with the existing kingship, Hasmonean and Herodian alike, had created the conditions in which the notion of the ideal, future king could be appealed to, as in the *Psalms of Solomon*. However, apart from Jesus of Nazareth, no other specifically messianic movement is recorded for Galilee, and as we shall see in the final section of the paper, it is disputed whether or not messianic claims were a feature of Jesus' own ministry or were attributed to him later by his followers. Attempts have been made to project the views of Judas the Galilean, the founder of the Fourth Philosophy, who espoused freedom and refusal to accept anyone as

---

[56] Freyne, *Galilee from Alexander the Great to Hadrian*, 211–16; Horsley, *Galilee. History, Politics, People*, 60 f.

master except God (*JA* 18,23–25; *JW* 2,118) on to Galileans generally. This gives rise to the view that Galilee was the home of revolutionary messianism, since the Fourth Philosophy has been identified with the Zealots, and Judas' family appear later in the first century as revolutionary figures opposed to Rome. Under the procurator Tiberius Alexander (c. 48 CE), his sons James and Simon were crucified, and Menahen, the leader of the Sicarii, was either his son or grandson (*JW* 2,433). Consequently, according to Hengel and others, he was the founder of a dynasty that was implacably opposed to Roman rule in first-century Palestine and that appealed to the messianic ideal.[57] It was in Judea, however, not Galilee, that Judas himself and Menahen subsequently, were active. While the latter may indeed fall into the category of royal messianic claimant, Judas' own programme did not explicitly involve violence. He espoused total reliance on God alone rather than expecting a messianic liberator figure, as previously discussed. It is noteworthy that no clearly recognisable messianic figure appeared in Galilee during the first revolt. Local leaders such as John of Gischala, and Jesus of Tiberias, were revolutionary in the sense of wishing to be free of Roman rule, but there is no suggestion that either had any messianic pretensions, and this is equally true of Josephus, sent by the revolutionary council in Jerusalem to organise the province. The Galilean phase of the campaign was at best sporadic, with Gamala and Iotapata alone offering the kind of resistance associated with the messianically motivated groups in Jerusalem. Nor did Galilee participate very actively, if at all, in the second revolt insofar as can be discerned from the accounts. Thus, no matter how much the war-like character and courage of the Galileans is emphasised by Josephus (*JW* 3,40), the truth is that no war-like messiahs appear among them, even though, as we shall see, the ministry of Jesus might have raised the possibility of such, at least for some of the population.

2) The second set of questions posed above referred to texts or events from Israel's past which had to do specifically with Galilee and which thus could have been reworked in order to engender a distinctive messianic hope there. Alternatively, one may ask: were there native characters who might have had special resonances for the Galileans in formulating their hopes for the future? Dealing first with texts to do with Israel's past, the Assyrian conquest in the eighth century BCE was probably the most traumatic to affect Galilee, since it struck at the heart of the promises to the land to which all Israel had felt itself heir. It is noteworthy, however, that future restoration was always envisaged in terms of the return of the twelve tribes, but the kings of Israel have no part to play in it. In Isaiah's oracle of salvation for the north (Is 8,23), which Alt has convincingly argued must have been uttered close to the first Assyrian attack of 732 BCE,

---

[57] Hengel, *The Zealots*, 79–94; Rhoads, *Israel in Revolution*, 94–150.

the land of Zebulun and the land of Naphtali, two of the five northernmost tribes, are explicitly mentioned as having been brought low.[58] We know from Assyrian records that they had organised the conquered territory into three separate provinces, Dor, Megiddo and Gilead, and it is to these three areas that promises are now given that they 'will be made glorious': the way of the sea (Dor), the land beyond the Jordan (Gilead) and Galilee of the Gentiles (Megiddo).[59] It is important to note that in its present context within the Book of Isaiah, this oracle is now linked with the Davidic promise of Is 9,1–6. Darkness and gloom will give way to light and rejoicing; slavery and war will be replaced by justice and peace with the birth of the child whose names include 'Wonderful Counsellor', 'Mighty God' and 'Prince of Peace.' Set in the context of a restoration eschatology – 'you have multiplied the nation' (9,3) – the north is also included in the blessings associated with the ideal Davidic king of the future.

The Targumic reworking of the text reflects a moment of messianic caution, emphasising in particular the theme of judgement for Israel: 'As in former time the people of the land of Zebulun and the people of the land of Naphtali have gone into exile, and a strong king will exile what remains of them, because they did not remember the prodigy of the sea, the wonders of the Jordan, the war of the Gentile fortresses. The people, the house of Israel who walked in Egypt as in darkness have come out to a great light.' The emphasis is on obedience to the law, following the example of the child who is born: 'He will be called before the Wonderful Counsellor, the Mighty God: the Messiah in whose days peace will increase upon us.' Thus the specific fate of Zebulun and Naphtali under the Assyrians is largely bypassed to stress universal judgement for all Israel, and the restoration of light is applied to the exodus from Egypt of the house of Israel in the past, not to future restoration. Even the newborn child's role is diminished. No longer is he given the names Wonderful Counsellor, Mighty God or Prince of Peace, but rather he is brought before this lofty character to be named the Messiah. Because of his obedience to Torah, peace will remain in the kingdom of David.[60] The continued importance of this text is further evidenced in its use by the Jewish Christian sect, the Nazoreans. According to Jerome, they applied the reference to the land of Zebulun and Naphtali to Jesus' ministry of 'removing the heavy weight of Jewish traditions

---

[58] See the discussion of A. Alt, 'Jesaja 8,23–9,6. Befreiungsnacht und Krönungstag,' *Kleine Schriften*, vol. 2, 206–25. W. Werner, *Eschatologische Texte in Jesaja 1–39: Messias, Heiliger Rest, Völker* (Munich: Echter Verlag, 1982) 20–46 also sees Is 9, 1–6 as a later reworking of the Nathan prophecy and quite separate from 8, 23.

[59] Freyne, *Galilee from Alexander the Great to Hadrian*, 24 f.

[60] Chilton, *The Isaiah Targum*, 20–22.

from their necks,' and the mention of 'the borders of the gentiles' and 'the way of the universal sea' to Paul's preaching to the nations.[61]

The blessings to the tribal leaders by Jacob (Gn 49) and by Moses (Dt 33), ascribing various characteristics to the different tribes within the twelve-fold league, also have important resonances for Galilee in the later period. They acknowledge the territories ascribed to each, an aspect that is more fully elaborated in Ez 47, where the geographical location of the different tribes is indicated. This form of the parting speech was expanded in the Second Temple period into various testamentary books, the longest of which is the *Testament of the Twelve Patriarchs*, whose composition history was originally Jewish, despite later Christian redactions.[62] In contrast to Gn and Ez, both of which extol Judah in particular, but in line with Dt, the figure of Levi is singled out for a special blessing in which royal messianic traits are conferred on him, but as a new, eschatological priest (*T. Levi* 18). Furthermore, he is given a heavenly vision on Sirion (which is another name for Mt Hermon, Dt 3,9), near to which he was shepherding his flock at Abel Main (*T. Levi* 2,9), in order to validate his special election (*T. Levi* 3). This location and vision seem to draw on a similar vision situated in the same location, which Enoch received 'by the waters of Dan' (*1 Enoch* 13,7), in which he is brought to the heavenly temple and charged with a mission to pass judgement on 'the watchers of heaven' who have forsaken their station and mingled with women and polluted themselves (*1 Enoch* 15,3–4).[63] Levi also receives a charge to execute vengeance on one who has committed a sexual irregularity, namely, the Shechemites who had raped Dinah (*T. Levi* 5,3–7).

Thus Galilee can provide an alternative location for divine revelation. In a place that would have been deemed pagan from a Jerusalem perspective, judgement was passed on the Jerusalem priesthood. It was also suggested that its patriarch, Levi, had received his commissioning there. In view of the genre of the literature, it is difficult to say whether or not these accounts reflect a separate Galilean tradition, pointing to visionary experience in the area, a further example of which would be the revelation to Pe-

---

[61] Cf. Freyne, *Galilee from Alexander the Great to Hadrian*, 353 f.

[62] Above note 15. Cf. also Collins, *The Apocalyptic Imagination,* 106–13.

[63] That Dan continued as a sacred site in the Hellenistic period at least, is shown by the bi-lingual inscription discovered there by A. Biran, 'To the God who is in Dan,' in *Temples and High Places in Biblical Times,* ed. A. Biran (Jerusalem: HUC-JIR, 1981) 142–51. More recently there is also the 'House of David' inscription from the same location, suggesting that the king of Judah had assisted the northern king in a battle against the Syrian king. This presupposes continuing links between north and south that one might not suspect from reading the Deuteronomic history: A. Biran and J. Naveh, 'An Aramaic Stele Fragment from Tel Dan,' *IEJ* 43 (1993) 81–98, and 'The Tel Dan Inscription: A New Fragment,' *IEJ* 45 (1995) 1–18.

ter on the way to Caesarea Philippi (Mt 16,16), as George Nickelsburg
claims.[64] Even if one is hesitant to agree with this aspect of his reconstruction, what Nickelsburg's analysis of the texts indicates clearly is that Galilee could be seen to play a vital role in the restoration that was associated
with the patriarchs in the messianic age, even to the extent of providing an
alternative to Jerusalem. Judah also has a messianic role based on various
eschatological texts from the Scriptures (*T. Judah* 24), and this
commissioning is followed by a list of all twelve tribes, which will
constitute 'one people' when the patriarchs come back to life (*T. Judah*
25). While none of the northern tribes receives any special treatment, they
still form an integral part of the complex picture, based both on the ideal of
pre-monarchic Israel and that of the priestly and royal messiahs from the
monarchic period at the centre of Israel's cultic and political life. Thus,
Galileans, insofar as they might identify with Israelite ancestry, could
continue to feel included in the hopes for the future, indeed to form an
essential part of that hope, while at the same time stressing the need for
maintaining their ties with the Jerusalem centre (cf. e.g., *T. Napthali* 8).

A third example of biblical figures particularly relevant for Galilee from
the past are the prophets Elijah and Elisha who operated within the orbit of
the northern kingdom. The former's victory over the priest of Baal, signifi-
canttly, is also located on a mountain, Carmel, on the borders of lower
Galilee. It is also a place that, like Dan, continued to have special religious
significance in the first century CE (Tacitus, *Hist.* II,78,3). In a scene
reminiscent of the making of the Mosaic covenant (Ex 24) and its renewal
under Joshua (Jos 24), Elijah gathers all the people around an altar made of
twelve stones representing the twelve tribes, 'the sons of Jacob to whom
the word of the Lord came, saying "Israel shall be your name"' (1 Kgs
18,30–32). This particular scene is part of an artfully constructed narrative
in which Elijah stage-manages Yahweh's victory over the prophets of
Baal. The Israelite king Ahab is a mere bystander in this scene, a witness
to Yahweh's victory and the people's choice. The issue now becomes one
of whether or not he and his wife, Jezabel, will continue with their policy
of foreign associations, so that Yahweh and his laws are abandoned in Israel. In all probability this whole collection of stories functioned independently, legitimating the revolution whereby the house of Omri was replaced with Yahweh's approval by Jehu, prior to its incorporation into the
Deuteronomic history. Richard Horsley sees this cycle as playing an important role in the memory of his Galilean Israelites, projecting 'an ideal
that could become a rallying symbol for more active resistance to oppressive rule.' Thus, while the cycle may have been shared with Jerusalem in-

---

[64] G. W. Nickelsburg, 'Enoch, Levi and Peter: Recipients of Revelation in Upper
Galilee,' *JBL* 100 (1981) 575–600.

sofar as it was adapted for use in the Deuteronomic History, it would have evoked very different responses in the north because of 'eight centuries of separate development in the two regions.'[65]

There is, however, little direct evidence that this was the way in which the Elijah cycle functioned subsequently, even though many aspects of his story recur in later Jewish writings, including the New Testament. The fact is that even in its Deuteronomic re-telling the stories lose nothing of their originality in terms of the independence of the prophet. Thus, the Jerusalem scribal elite may not have been as hostile to such a character as Horsley's hypothesis suggests. It was Elijah's translation into heaven and his expected return that captured later Jewish imagination, not his role as social agitator. The returning Elijah becomes identified with the promised messenger, who would precede the final coming of God himself, in order to restore social harmony in a domestic setting, thereby averting God's anger (Mal 3,1.21 f.). Subsequently, his role as restorer is embellished in various ways, and it is in this setting that his miraculous deeds are recalled and expected (Mk 15,33–36).[66] In a particularly interesting development for the argument of this paper, Ben Sirach extends the prophet's role from the family (as in Malachi) to the notion of 'restoring the tribes of Jacob' (Sir 48,10), a theme that picks up the role of the servant of Yahweh as described in Is 49,6. The expectation of Elijah's return is well represented in the gospels also, as both John the Baptist and Jesus are identified with him (Jn 1,21; Mk 6,15; 8,28). Indeed the Markan Jesus ascribes a cosmic role to him: 'Elijah indeed is coming to restore all things' (Mk 9,12). While there is a strong tendency to identify John the Baptist with the returning Elijah (Mt 11,14), this identification does not fit particularly well, either with the roles of the returning Elijah or those of the Baptist.[67] In fact several of the miracles of Jesus have Elijah-like traits, especially in Luke. It is in Luke also, with his strong social concerns, that Elijah's contacts with the widow of Sidon, Zarephath and the Syrian ruler, Naaman are deliberately recalled (Lk 4,23–25), despite his opposition to the religious syncretism, even in the pre-Dt cycle of stories. We shall return to these aspects of the Elijah career later in discussing Jesus as messiah. It is important, however, to note here that there were several aspects of the prophet's career, both as it is reported in the cycle of stories preserved in the historical cycle

---

[65] Horsley, *Galilee. History, Politics, People,* 25 and 50. Cf. further the interesting discussion by several scholars in *Elijah and Elisha in Socioliterary Perspective,* ed. Robert B. Coote (Atlanta: Scholars Press, 1992).

[66] Meyer, *Der Prophet aus Galiläa,* 31–37; J. L. Martyn, *The Gospel of John in Christian History* (New York: Paulist Press, 1978), 'We have found Elijah,' 9–54, especially 12 f. and 22–26.

[67] Martyn, *The Gospel of John,* 19 f.

and as it was developed in later Jewish tradition, which might be expected to resonate in a particular way in Galilee, not least his projected role as end-time restorer of all Israel.

3) The third question previously posed, namely who either from Galilee itself or from outside might have formulated a specifically Galilean portrayal of the messiah, and for what circles, has to some extent been answered in the discussion of the previous two issues. While it has not been possible to discover a distinctively Galilean image of the messiah, it seemed plausible to speculate that certain aspects of general messianic speculation were particularly appropriate to Galilee, e.g., the war-like figure who would destroy the nations round about, or the restorer figure who would reconstitute Israel to its original condition, symbolised by the twelve tribe league. We can say, therefore, that the expression Galilean messianic hopes were in the hands of outsiders, namely, Horsley's scribal and ruling elites, and the extent to which they might have been formulated with a view to inner Galilean concerns must be open to question.

We are poorly informed as to how far Jerusalem and Judean scribal elites might have extended their influence to Galilee prior to 135 CE. True, Mark informs us of the arrival of Jerusalem scribes within the region on hearing of Jesus' ministry (Mk 3,21; 7,1). John has a similar delegation to inquire about John the Baptist's identity, in this case priests and Levites sent by the Pharisees, the champions of orthodoxy in the Fourth Gospel (Jn 1,19.24). These delegations recall the particular make-up of the one sent by the council in Jerusalem to remove Josephus, their own appointee as governor, prior to the first revolt: the party consisted of two laypeople (δημοτικοί) who were also Pharisees and two priests, one of whom was also a Pharisee and the other, Simon, was from the high-priests (*Life* 197f.). One cannot but note the strong Pharisaic presence, presumably because of their likely influence with the Galileans, but also because of their friendship with local Galilean leaders such as John of Gischala, one of Josephus' implacable enemies in the province.[68] There is also the account of Johanan ben Zakkai spending 20 years at Arav in Galilee and having to deal with only three halachic cases in all that time, but this probably relates to later rabbinic experiences there rather than to the time of the historical Johanan.[69] Only a few native Galilean teachers are referred to in the literary sources. One such was the Eleazar who came from Galilee and was said to have been 'extremely strict when it came to ancestral laws' and who advised Izates king of Adiabene that he should be circumcised (*JA*

---

[68] Cf. 'Galilee-Jerusalem relations according to Josephus' *Life*,' above pp. 73 ff.

[69] J. Neusner, 'The History of a Biography. Johanan ben Zakkai in the Canonical Literature of Formative Judaism,' in *Formative Judaism V. Religious, Historical and Literary Studies*, Brown Judaic Studies 91 (Chico: Scholars Press, 1985) 79–86.

20,43). Others such as Judas the Galilean, the founder of the Fourth Philosophy, or later, Yose the Galilean, an important figure among the Jamnia rabbis, are indicative of a trend of gravitating to the south rather than being active within their native region. Yet, it seems reasonable to suggest that some form of Jewish schooling must have been instituted in the region from the time of the Hasmoneans onward. In all probability this would have been associated with local synagogues, even though the architectural as distinct from the literary evidence for such a development is singularly lacking before the second century at the earliest.[70]

One difficulty with Horsley's notion of separate local traditions existing for centuries is that it presumes some form of communal life that would support and give expression to these experiences, thus ensuring their continuance. We know virtually nothing about the village institutions of the sort that he suggests, however, other than that of the synagogue, first established to meet the needs of Jewish communities in the Diaspora.[71] In this regard the prayer service and scripture reading that are later documented for synagogue worship must have played a vital role in establishing and maintaining separate Jewish identity, in Galilee also. The fact that the *Shemoneh Ezre*, or *18 Benedictions*, included the themes of the coming of the messiah and the restoration of Israel, surely meant that this was one location where the gap between the scribal and the popular expectations must have been bridged.[72] In addition, the targumic elaboration of the scriptural readings would have played a similar role. While the question of dating these traditions is notoriously difficult, the war-like messiah figures prominently in the later targumic compilations, as has been already noted, even though he is largely ignored (or rabbinised) in the other contemporary literary corpus emanating from the rabbinic circles.[73] This contrast suggests that the war-like figure continued to be attractive in popular circles, something that may be inferred from some later synagogue floor mosaics also.[74]

---

[70] L. Levine, ed., *The Synagogue in Late Antiquity* (Philadelphia: ASOR Publications, 1987), especially Levine, 'The Second Temple Synagogue: the Formative Years,' 17.

[71] Cf. his discussion in *Galilee. History, Politics, People*, 222–38.

[72] Th. Lehnhardt, 'Der Gott der Welt ist unser König,' in *Königsherrschaft Gottes und himmlischer Kult im Judentum, Urchristentum und in der hellenistischer Welt*, ed. M. Hengel and A. M. Schwemer (Tübingen: J. C. B. Mohr, 1991) 285–307. I. Elborgen, *Die Jüdische Gottesdienst in seiner geschichtlichen Entwicklung* (reprint, Hildesheim: G. Olms, 1967) 27–41.

[73] Cf. B. Chilton, *A Galilean Rabbi and his Bible. Jesus' Use of the Interpreted Scripture of his Time* (Wilmington: Glazier, 1984); for a discussion of the issue of targumic dating and their use in interpreting the Jesus tradition. Cf. also Syren, *The Blessings in the Targums*, above note 39.

[74] S. Muczbik, A. Ovadiah and C. Gomez de Silva, 'The Meroth Mosaics Reconsidered,' in *JJS* 47 (1996) 286–93.

Messianic speculation in its varied forms was provoked in the main by dissatisfaction with aspects of the existing situation, as we saw in the opening section of this paper. Since it operated through the re-working of scriptural texts in new contexts, it demanded some training in scribal techniques, giving rise to the kind of social elitism one can observe in Ben Sirach, for example (Sir 38,24–39,11), who himself walks a thin line between the roles of social prophet and establishment scribe. A similar attitude underlies the dispute in the Fourth Gospel, which was alluded to at the outset: 'This people who do not know the law is accursed. . . . Surely you (Nicodemus) are not also from Galilee. Search and see that no prophet is to arise from Galilee' (Jn 7,49.52). The later rabbinic disparagement of the Galilean *'am ha-'aretz* is merely a continuation of that attitude.

Jesus of Nazareth, a Galilean Messiah?

On the basis of the discussion up to this point the understanding of Jesus of Nazareth as a messianic figure was an innovation as far as Galilee was concerned, since he is the only Galilean whose career has unambiguously been interpreted messianically in the sources. Apart from the inherent interest in such a claim for Christians, a consideration of its historical basis can function as a testing of the working hypothesis of this paper, namely, that messianic speculation of the Second Temple period always mirrored in some way the particular social and historical conditions that gave rise to it. In this regard it is interesting to note in passing that among the spate of books that constitute the so-called 'third wave' of historical Jesus research, his messianic status is scarcely an issue any longer. It would seem that a virtual consensus has been reached with regard to the topic, namely, that messiahship did not belong to the self-understanding of Jesus but was the product of the later Christian community's myth-making activity based on his memory. Yet the recent publication of the Qumran messianic fragments has at least re-opened the issue, in that the nearest parallels to some of those texts are found in the Gospels themselves.[75] We shall, therefore, begin by surveying briefly the way in which those various gospel portraits link the messianic career of Jesus to Galilee, before re-examining the historical question in the light of the discussion in the second portion of this paper.

---

[75] Collins, *The Scepter and the Star*, 204–09; Oegma, *The Anointed and his People*, 147–68.

The Gospels and the Messiah Jesus

The contrasting roles of Galilee and Jerusalem in Mark's gospel have been variously understood.[76] All, however, are agreed that Galilee is presented in a positive light. It is there, in upper Galilee, that Jesus is proclaimed messiah by Peter, as spokesperson for the specially chosen core group of the Twelve. That recognition of Jesus' identity was based on a ministry of healing and nature miracles, which, though largely located in Galilee, could involve an outreach to the territories of Tyre and Sidon and the Dekapolis also. While the evangelist clearly supports the claim to Jesus' messianic status, he displays a certain reserve, as the journey to Jerusalem commences. Peter is ordered to remain silent and Jesus alludes to himself, not as the Christ, but as the Son of Man who will suffer at the hands of the religious authorities in Jerusalem. He is in fact a hidden messiah, even in Galilee: 'He was going through Galilee and he did not want anyone to know it' (9,30). Even the entry to Jerusalem is muted, though a blind man addresses him as son of David. However, his action of overthrowing the tables of the money changers provokes the denouement of arrest, trial and crucifixion as 'Messiah, son of the Blessed' and as 'King of the Jews' (Mk 14,61; 15,18.26.32). Yet before this he has made a farewell address to his disciples, both warning them of the dangers of false prophets and false messiahs and reassuring them of his return as the glorious son of Man to gather his elect 'from the four winds' (Mk 13,22.26). The story ends with an injunction to Peter and the disciples from an angelic being that they should return to Galilee, 'there to see him' as he had foretold (Mk 14,28; 16,7).

In contrast to Mark's hidden messiah, Matthew openly proclaims Jesus' messianic status as Son of David from his infancy. The author is at pains to show that Galilean associations do not disqualify Jesus; he was born in Bethlehem, David's city, and only came to live in Galilee to escape the evil king, Herod.[77] The beginning of Jesus' ministry in Galilee is authenticated by a citation of the Isaian oracle of salvation for the north already discussed (Is 8,23; Mt 4,13–16). This ministry of teaching as well as healing, described as 'the works of the messiah' (Mt 11,1), is directed to 'the lost sheep of the house of Israel' both by Jesus himself and by the Twelve (15,24; 10,5–6), leading to a fuller messianic acclamation by Peter than in Mark of Jesus as 'Christ, the son of the living God' (Mt 16,15–17). This takes place in upper Galilee, and is attributed by Jesus as a revelatory experience for Peter, reminiscent of Enoch and Levi. He then embarks on a

---

[76] E. Struthers Malbon, 'Galilee and Jerusalem: History and Literature in Markan Interpretation,' *CBQ* 44 (1982) 242–55.

[77] K. Stendahl, 'Quis et Unde? An Analysis of Matthew 1–2,' reprinted in *The Interpretation of Matthew*, ed. G. Stanton (London: SPCK, 1983) 56–66.

much more explicitly messianic journey to Jerusalem, where his rejection leads to a stinging judgement on the holy city, after its destruction has been cryptically alluded to in allegory (Mt 22,6). Matthew also closes on a Galilean note as the Twelve reassemble 'on a high mountain in Galilee', there to receive the commission to bring Jesus' teaching 'to all the nations', thus transcending the 'Israel only' perspective of the earlier part of the work (Mt 28,16–20).

Luke also establishes the messianic career of Jesus from his infancy, presenting the birth of the child within the context both of Jewish restoration hopes and Roman imperial ideology with its claims of universal peace. The public career receives a formal inauguration in the synagogue at Nazareth, when Jesus applies to himself the Isaian text which speaks of God's anointing of his chosen one in order to proclaim good news to the poor, liberation to captives and the 'acceptable year of the Lord' (Lk 4,18 f.). This prophetic commission inaugurates a journey that begins in Galilee, passes through Samaria and ends in Jerusalem, where he is arraigned with the charge of subverting the people, refusing to pay taxes to Caesar and proclaiming himself Christ the king (Lk 23,3). Unlike the other two synoptists, there is no return to Galilee for the disciples, however. Having been reconstituted formally in their symbolic role as the Twelve, they must await the gift of the spirit in Jerusalem before beginning there a journey of witness that would eventually lead to Rome, 'the end of the earth' (Acts 1,6). Thus, the twofold mission of restorer of Israel and light to the nations of Is 49,6, which Ben Sirach had applied to the returning Elijah, now provides the frame of reference for Luke's presentation of the messianic career of Jesus and his followers, a movement which, Luke hints, was a serious challenge to Rome's claim to rule the world.

Finally, there is the Fourth Gospel, where the messianic status of Jesus and its Galilean associations, appear to have been bypassed in favour of more lofty theological ideas, inspired by the glorious Son of Man figure. Yet, on closer inspection, the issue of the messiah – his origins, destiny and functions – is nowhere more hotly debated than in this work (Jn 7,25–44; 10,24–25; 12,34–35). It is the judgement of the Pharisees – a stereotypical term for the leaders of the obdurate Jews in this gospel – that Jesus cannot fulfil the messianic role, since he is from Galilee. Yet with typical Johannine irony, the certainty of the Jewish leaders is in stark contrast to the Galilean disciples assertion at the outset: 'we have found the messiah' (Jn 1,41). This recognition is set within the larger framework of John the Baptist's rejection of the designations 'Christ', 'Elijah' or 'the prophet' and the disciples acknowledgement of Jesus as 'the Christ', 'the one whom Moses in the law and also the prophets wrote', and 'the Son of God, the King of Israel', thus giving a cross-section of the variations of messianic speculation that could occur. Affirmative as these designations are, they are merely the forerunners of a more comprehensive understanding that is promised to the disciples in terms of the heavenly Son of Man, as the locus of the divine presence among humans (Jn 1,19–51).[78] This progression of understanding on the part of the original disciples is generally interpreted today in terms of different stages in the Johannine community's faith-journey. Yet the fact that the earlier, 'Galilean' understanding is retained seems highly significant in light of the Pharisees' dismissal of the possibility of such claims later, operating within the narrow confines of a Davidic messiahship in the strict sense. While Judea and the Jerusalem temple feasts purposely provide John with the main theatre for Jesus' messianic utterances and the ensuing debates, the Galilean dimension is not lost sight of.[79] The region is not just the scene of his two Cana miracles, but it also serves as a haven of refuge when he is under pressure from the Jerusalem authorities, since 'the Galileans received him' (Jn 4,45). Yet from the author's perspective these Galilean sojourns are not without their dangers. The people in the environs of the sea of Tiberias who experienced the feeding miracle declared him 'to be the prophet who was to come into the world', and Jesus 'fled to the mountain alone', fearing that they would 'take him by force and make him king' (6,14f.). It is only later in the trial before Pilate that both titles, 'prophet' and 'king' can be applied to Jesus, but in suitably Johannine terms as the revealer who has come into the world. Significantly, the political connotations of both are retained, only to be rejected as inappropriate for an understanding of Jesus' true messianic status, as enunciated by the fourth evangelist.

This rapid survey of the links between Jesus' messianic status as this was proclaimed in Early Christianity and his Galilean ministry presents a variegated picture.[80] Yet that variety itself is a witness to the difficulties and challenges presented in proclaiming Jesus the Galilean as the messiah of Israel among the competing claims of first-century Judaism, in the wake of Herod the Great's reign. If Jesus is to be understood as messiah Mark wants to ensure that this does not involve him or his followers in the Jewish war of 66–70. This would explain the reserve regarding the recognition of Jesus in Galilee once his messianic status has been claimed. John' gospel would appear to reinforce the point, that however Jesus' messiahship is to be understood, it is not in nationalistic terms, and hence he must avoid

---

[78] J. Ashton, *Understanding the Fourth Gospel* (London and New York: Oxford University Press, 1991) 238–91.

[79] See J. Bassler, 'The Galileans: A Neglected Factor in Johannine Research,' *CBQ* 43 (1981) 243–57.

[80] For further detail and discussion cf. Freyne, *Galilee, Jesus and the Gospels*, especially 219–72.

his would-be king-makers. At the same time the memory of messianic claims for Jesus that were less exalted than his own theological understanding is important for the author of the Fourth Gospel, claims that he could be identified with Elijah or the coming prophet as well as in royal terms.[81] One might conjecture whether the threefold designation of Christ, Elijah and the prophet which John the Baptist rejects for himself at the outset, and which therefore point to Jesus, might not be intended to cover the geographic spread of the gospel itself – Galilee (Elijah), the prophet of whom Moses wrote (Samaria) and messiah, king of Israel (Judea) – thereby implying the inclusive nature of Jesus' messianic status for all areas of traditional Israelite territorial claims. Such claims were still important for the Johannine community in its bitter struggles with the synagogue. By including in their gospels the *Q* material which itself does not seem to have had any messianic, as distinct from eschatological, claims, both Luke and Matthew were able to stress other aspects of Jewish messianic expectation: that of teacher (Matthew) and prophet of justice for the poor (Luke). In their views, being from Galilee did not in any way negate such claims. Matthew is particularly aware of the issue, but turns it to good effect, alluding to Galilee's role in the divine plan as against that of a discredited Jerusalem in the post–70 period. This is in line with the criticism voiced by the authors of *1 Enoch* and *Testament of Levi*. For Luke the twofold role of restorer of Israel and bringer of salvation to the nations, suited well the schema of the mission which he sought to project in the post-Pauline era. As the gospel arrived at Rome, 'the end of the earth', the messiah Jesus is the bringer of peace, justice and salvation for the world in ways other than those inspired by imperial propaganda. The nationalistic messiah has been transformed into a political messiah who offers an alternative to Rome and its claim to rule the world.

Jesus' Galilean ministry and its messianic claims

The line of argument I have been pursuing suggests that, like other branches of Judaism, early Christianity developed its various messianic images in response to the needs and circumstances of the new movement. One aspect that is shared by all these portraits is the avoidance of any suggestion of a war-like stance, a feature that was strongly represented in the other strands examined. In this regard the gospel portrayals resemble most closely that of the *Similitudes of Enoch* in that there also the linking of the messiah with such other images as the Son of Man had lead to a de-politicisation of his role and a greater emphasis on his eschatological judg-

---

[81] Martyn, 'We have found Elijah,' 16–29.

ing functions. The concern with the messiah's role in the restoration of Israel, likewise symbolised by the twelve-tribe confederation, is not so central to the evangelists' concerns as might have been anticipated. Though the role of the Twelve is clearly remembered, especially in the Synoptics, less so in John, its symbolic function in terms of national aspirations is transformed, losing its territorial and tribal aspects, and instead being made to serve other ecclesial interests to do with the Christian community's claims to be the true Israel.[82] On the other hand the theme of the messiah as champion of the poor and oppressed is strongly featured in the Jesus tradition, based on the prophetic critique of wealth in Q and developed further by both Matthew and Luke. Finally, there are the links of the messiah with Jerusalem, the capital and symbolic centre of David's kingdom and therefore, central to any image of restoration built on his memory. This aspect is also well represented in all the portrayals of Jesus as messiah, but the focus is on the religious rather than the political role of Jerusalem. Thus the incident in the temple is pivotal in the three synoptic portrayals, whereas the festivals of Passover, Tabernacles and Dedication provide the backdrop to Jesus' Jerusalem ministry in John.

We may now push our investigation back one step further and ask how far these themes might fit in with the career of Jesus, as this can be plotted in its broad lines within the Galilee of Antipas' day. This seems to be a better way of posing the question of the messianic status of Jesus than an approach which begins with his own putative messianic consciousness. Our approach is less specific but it leaves the issue of Jesus as messiah in the public arena, and therefore, in principle at least capable of being discovered. Our question then is, how well do the concerns of Jesus' public ministry fall within the parameters of possible messianic expectation in Galilee, so that both he himself and others who encountered him might have felt prompted to claim messianic status for him and his activity?

Clearly the absence of the militancy one associates with Jewish nationalist aspirations of the first century would have disqualified Jesus in the eyes of many, including many Galileans. While other strands of Jewish thinking also sought to distance themselves from this understanding they seem to have been in the minority. Both Mark and John stress that, contrary to his intentions, Jesus' career was likely to have been misunderstood in terms of nationalist hopes, and both are at pains to distance him from this. This concern of the evangelists raises the issue of whether or not we are dealing here with later problems of the Christian community, caused by the first revolt, rather than with the actual career of Jesus. Whatever aspirations of kingship Judas son of Hezechias espoused on the death of Herod

---

[82] See S. Freyne, *The Twelve: Disciples and Apostles. An Introduction to the Theology of the First Three Gospels* (London: Sheed and Ward, 1968).

the Great, these had been snuffed out pretty ruthlessly by the Romans. It is significant that Judas the Galilean, the founder of the Fourth Philosophy, propagated the notion of God alone as king rather than any earthly ruler who might be described as his 'anointed', just ten years later on the deposition of Archelaus in Judea in 6 CE. While Antipas, as ruler of Galilee, aspired to the title 'king', he did not dare to arrogate it to himself; his building projects, though intended to honour the imperial house, were not on the grand scale of his father's buildings, nor were they so self-promoting. In addition, Antipas' military difficulties were with the Nabateans in Perea rather than in Galilee. For all these reasons it seems legitimate to conclude that the conditions in Galilee under Antipas were not such as to generate an intense longing for the ideal Jewish king as a replacement for a situation deemed to be intolerable, such as the *Psalms of Solomon* reflected at the end of the Hasmonean dynasty. Of course it might be countered with Brandon and others that the militant dimension of Jesus' career has been largely suppressed by the later evangelists and that he was in fact a militantly nationalistic messiah. However, as already discussed, the Zealot hypothesis was based on a misrepresentation of Galilean social conditions as well as a misreading of Josephus' apologetic handling of the pre-revolt period.[83] The view that Jesus is best understood as a militant nationalist is, therefore, largely discredited today, and much less probable than one which sees him as highlighting other aspects of the prevailing messianic repertoire, especially those of teacher and prophet. While there was, as we have seen, a tendency for the son of David title to include these aspects, the notion of the prophet like Moses, sometimes at least coalescing with the returning Elijah, had retained a separate identity.[84]

It is noteworthy that in both Mark and John the figure of the prophet appears side by side with that of the messiah. Mark warns against false prophets as well as false messiahs and John suggests that because Jesus had been perceived as the prophet he might have been forcibly made king, thereby implying a close link between the two roles. If Antipas' career had not created the conditions to spark an intense desire for the arrival of the ideal king, it certainly did give rise to circumstances in which a prophetic voice of criticism was called for. Elsewhere, I have argued in detail that the refurbishing of Sepphoris and the foundation of Tiberias during his reign were a serious intrusion into Galilean social life as they introduced elements of a politically controlled economy into a situation of free land-

---

[83] S. G. F. Brandon, *Jesus and the Zealots* (Manchester: The University Press, 1967); M. Hengel, *War Jesus Revolutionär?* (Stuttgart: Calwer Verlag, 1970).

[84] Cf. Martyn, *Gospel of John,* 26 f. for a discussion of the possibility of such a coalescence in Jn 1,21 f. and Jn 6,14.

owning peasants.[85] Land, a primary resource in all pre-industrial societies, was at a premium and in short supply. Labour, often enforced, was required for the building projects as well as to service the needs of the ruling, Herodian elites who dwelt in these cities. Primary resources such as water were channelled into the new foundations, as can still be so dramatically seen today at Sepphoris. Debt, penury and homelessness were the inevitable results of such changes. These are the conditions that best explain the particular thrust of Jesus' teaching ministry – the blessings for the poor and the woes on the rich, the call for total trust in God's provident care, the injunction to share with the needy and the refusal to endorse retaliation, even of a limited kind when it had been provoked. In all this we are hearing the voice of a prophet with a passion for justice, rather than the voice of a would-be king, such as Judas, son of Hezechias, whose militant campaign as described by Josephus was previously discussed.

Thus, the role of Elijah as miracle worker on behalf of the marginalised in the environs of Galilee seems quite apposite also in terms of the understanding of Jesus' ministry. As already discussed, the 'fit' between Elijah and John is not that obvious in terms of their respective careers. The linking of the two may well be secondary in the tradition, the pre-cursor role of Elijah with respect to the messiah, known in the later Jewish tradition, being applied to John, once Jesus' messianic status was assured. This would leave the way open for an identification of Jesus and Elijah at a very early stage, certainly in *Q*, and possibly even during Jesus' own lifetime. This case has been argued by Martyn with respect to the source underlying Jn 1,19–50[86] and it may now be further supported in the light of the so-called Messianic Apocalypse from Qumran (4Q 521). The similarities between this text and the responses of Jesus to the disciples of John the Baptist in *Q* (Mt 11,2–6; Lk 7,18–35) have been noted on the basis of their common citation of Is 61,1. In both, however, there is mention of raising of the dead, which is not referred to in the Isaian passage, but it is one of the remembered aspects of Elijah's miracle-working career (Sir 48,4; *m. Sota* 9,15). It is this fact, together with the discovery of another fragment of the same Qumran text which refers to Mal 3,23 (Elijah's creating family harmony), which has convinced Collins that the 4Q 521 text, which opens with a reference to 'his messiah', in fact refers to Elijah.[87] In that case, not merely have we certain similarities in terms of the miracle tradition between Elijah and Jesus, but also their prophetic ministry of preaching good news to the poor, and they both thereby earn the epithet messiah!

---

[85] Cf. 'Herodian Economics in Galilee. Searching for a Suitable Model,' and 'Jesus and the Urban Culture of Galilee,' above pp. 86 ff. and 183 ff. respectively.

[86] Martyn, *The Gospel of John*, 29–42.

[87] Collins, *Scepter and Star*, 117–23.

Elijah's contest with the prophets of Baal had, we saw, connections with the twelve tribe tradition of all Israel gathering before Yahweh (1 Kgs 18,30–32), and this same theme is also suggested in the Jesus' tradition with the symbolic role of the Twelve.[88] In contrast to the *War Scroll* in particular where the twelve tribal leaders are engaged in the final holy war, the primary role of the Twelve in the Jesus tradition has both a present and future dimension that are intimately connected. As missionaries they share in Jesus' ministry to Israel and they will act as future judges of the tribes as part of the end-time scenario in which the ministry as a whole is cast.[89] As already discussed, this was an important aspect of much of Jewish restoration eschatology, which came to be associated with the role of Elijah or the ideal king of *Psalms of Solomon*. The restoration ideal encapsulated in this symbol was a reversal to the pre-monarchic state of Israel, and therefore, one that was not immediately associated with the messiah role and its Davidic, royal associations. Nevertheless, these two strands from Israel's past, the pre-monarchic tribal league and the monarchic centrality of Jerusalem, as David's city, had become intertwined in Ezekiel, Eupolemus and the Temple Scroll long before the Roman period. Sometimes, as in the *War Scroll* and *Psalms of Solomon*, it involved a war-like messiah who would destroy the *Kittim* or the nations, and could, therefore, have a strongly xenophobic colouring, foreign to the aims of Jesus insofar as we can discern them. The tribal territories in Ezekiel were linked to the notion of a vastly expanded Israel stretching from the borders of Hamath and Damascus to the Wadi of Egypt and from the borders of Hauran to the great sea (Ez 47,13–23). The Targumic versions of the blessings of Jacob envisage Zebulun incorporating Sidon in its territory.

Jesus' Galilean ministry, especially as depicted by Mark involved journeys to these surrounding territories, and while stories such as those of the Syrophoenician woman and the Gadarene demoniac do retain the Jew/gentile distinction, it is clear that these journeys were not motivated by an aggressive campaign of Judaisation, such as had allegedly occurred with the Itureans under the Hasmoneans. Indeed the absence of any mention of circumcision as the hallmark of separate Jewish identity in the recorded sayings of Jesus is highly noteworthy. What then was the purpose of these journeys which took him to the territories of Tyre and Sidon, Caesarea Philippi and the Dekapolis, but not to the cities themselves? Had they to do with gathering 'the lost sheep of the house of Israel', a perspective that is important for Matthew in particular (10,6; 15,24), but which should not, therefore, automatically be denied to Jesus also? Such a minis-

---

[88] John P. Meier, 'The Circle of the Twelve: Did it Exist during Jesus' Public Ministry?' *JBL* 116 (1997) 601–12.

[89] W. Horbury, 'The Twelve and the Phularchs,' *NTS* 32 (1986) 503–27.

try to Jewish villages situated outside the borders of political Galilee, but within those of an ideal Israel, would cohere well with a non-aggressive restoration model. This is true especially because these villages were within the orbit of city-states, and their inhabitants were likely to have come under the same economic hardships as those which the Galilean peasants had experienced under Antipas.[90] Such an actualisation of the messianic hope was more realistic than that later attributed to the messiah in the post–70 apocalypse, *4 Ezra*, which envisages the future liberator figure miraculously bringing home the ten and a half exiled tribes who, it was believed, had lived the Jewish way of life separately for centuries (4 Ez 13,12–13.39–47).

Finally, there is Jesus' relationship with Jerusalem. While this is much more accentuated in the Fourth Gospel than in the Synoptics, these also see the goal of Jesus' ministry in relation to the holy city, and establish the links with Jerusalem and its religious establishment in different ways. The early lament for the city, reported in *Q*, is spoken from the perspective of the country prophet, whose fate is nevertheless tied up with that of the city itself (Mt 23,36–38; Lk 13,34–35). Espousal of the restoration model based on the twelve tribes did not exclude concern for Jerusalem, as we have seen. There are many examples in the tradition, from Jeremiah to Jesus son of Ananias, of country prophets challenging the religious centre and calling for a more authentic realisation of its own symbolic role, something that the messiah would achieve in an unparalleled manner.[91] The story of Jesus, son of Ananias, is a particularly suggestive comparison to Jesus of Galilee, particularly as he is reported in Jn 7–8. The son of Ananias is also deemed 'a rude peasant', who for seven years immediately prior to the first revolt, especially on the occasion of the festivals, continued to issue his woes on Jerusalem, the people and the temple, until he was eventually killed by a stone hurled at him (*JW* 6,300–9). Jesus of Nazareth had a Galilean rural background and, as we have seen, Mt Hermon and its region had in the past provided an alternative location for God's heavenly sanctuary, by way of criticism of the Jerusalem temple and its priesthood. There was, therefore, some precedent upon which a Galilean prophet such as Jesus could have drawn, even if his critique of the temple, in line with his own passion for justice, seems to have had more to do with its economic exploitation than with its clergy's failures to observe the purity regulations as this expressed in *1 Enoch* and *Testament of Levi*.

---

[90] T. Schmeller, 'Jesus im Umland Galiläas: zu den Markinischen Berichten vom Aufenthalt Jesu in den Gebieten von Tyros, Caesarea Philippi und der Dekapolis,' *BZ* 38 (1994) 44–66.

[91] G. Theißen, 'Die Tempelweissagung Jesu. Prophetie im Spannungsfeld zwischen Tempel und Land,' *Theologische Zeitschrift* 32 (1976) 144–58.

Conclusion

It is not easy to decide whether or not these emphases in the recorded career of Jesus of Galilee amount to a full-scale messianic claim either by him or by his followers during his lifetime. They certainly seem adequate to cast him in the role of end-time prophet, whose concerns with justice for the oppressed strikes a deep messianic chord, even as his eschewing of a militant nationalism does not fit easily with popular hopes and aspirations, in Galilee as elsewhere. At the very least his career has opened up some intriguing windows, or should one say, peep holes, on the fascinating, if sometimes confusing world of Jewish messianic speculation in the late Hellenistic and early Roman periods. Once the issue of the messiah is approached in a flexible and contextually sensitive manner, the claim that Jesus may have been deemed to have fulfilled that role for his contemporaries need not be as divisive for Jews and Christians as is often claimed. Later Christian theological and philosophical speculation gave an ontological status to what in the sources was thinking of a mythopoeic nature which lacked the systematic precision later attributed to it. One can concur with the assessment of George MacCrae, namely that, 'to the extent that the title *Christos* became progressively more central to early Christian proclamation, to that extent it departed further from the Jewish understanding of the messiah.'[92] For that very reason the importance of retrieving the range of symbolic potential that the figure of the messiah could have in its original setting has important implications for both Jews and Christians today. After centuries of animosity in which claim and counter-claim have provoked bitter disputes, both religions might do well to seek to rediscover their common roots in a shared world of hope for God's future.

---

[92] G. MacCrae, 'Messiah and Gospel,' in *Judaisms and their Messiahs*, 169–86, especially 174.

12. Jesus the Wine-Drinker: A Friend of Women

It is noteworthy, though perhaps predictable, that the role of women in the Jesus movement has received relatively little attention in recent writing, despite the remarkable resurgence of historical Jesus studies in the past decade or so. With the notable exception of Elizabeth Schüssler Fiorenza, feminist scholars have concentrated on literary rather than historical investigations in dealing with the androcentrism of the New Testament writings.[1] The omission is all the more regrettable since many of these studies, including my own, have focused on the social world of Jesus, who appears to have ignored or deliberately set aside the stereotypical social role of women in that world. This article is, therefore, an attempt to redress the imbalance in my own explorations of that social world. Taking a cue from one particular hint in the gospels, namely the charge that Jesus was a wine-drinker, hitherto unexplored to the best of my knowledge, I seek to open up a larger vista on the issue of women members of the original Jesus movement.

Each of the Synoptic Gospels indicates that women formed part of the permanent retinue of Jesus in Galilee, though Luke is the most explicit (Mk 15,40–41; Mt 27,55–56; Lk 8,1–3; 23,55). While the Fourth Gospel does not focus on a Galilean ministry except in passing, the intimate relationship between Jesus and Mary Magdalene is a feature of the presentation (Jn 11,2; 20,1–2,11–18). Even more interesting than these reports is the saying of Jesus from the triple tradition which profiles his movement as one in which those who do the will of his Father take on a fictive kin relationship with him as mothers, brothers *and sisters* (Mk 3,31–35; Mt 12,46–50; cf. Lk 8,19–21). The addition of sisters, strangely omitted by Luke, is all the more noteworthy in view of the fact that the response of Jesus is prompted by a report that his mother and brothers (but no mention of sisters) are outside seeking him. That women as well as men feature in the orbit of Jesus' activity is clear from other instances in the gospels: the woman with the issue of blood, the Syrophoenician woman, the woman who anointed him for burial; the daughter of Jairus, the Samaritan woman, the poor widow all come to mind. Perhaps even more significant, because of its social implications, is Jesus' own comment on the purpose of his ministry: 'Do not think that I have come to bring peace upon the earth. I

---

[1] E. Schüssler Fiorenza, *Jesus. Miriam's Child, Sophia's Prophet. Critical Issues in Feminist Christology* (New York: Crossroad, 1995).

have not come to bring peace but a sword. For I have come to set a man against his father and daughter against her mother and daughter-in-law against her mother-in-law' (Mt 10,34–36; Lk 12,49–53). Affiliation to the Jesus movement meant, therefore, a radical re-ordering of the most basic relationships within a kinship society.

How are we to evaluate this evidence historically and culturally? While redactional and later community concerns have been identified by various commentators of these episodes and sayings, and allowing for the fact that the androcentrism of the texts silences the presence of women, the evidence available clearly supports the idea that from the very beginning the Jesus movement included women as well as men as permanent members. More significant, therefore, is our evaluation of this evidence in terms of its socio-religious implications. The Jesus movement was undoubtedly disruptive in social terms because its value system violated prevailing norms with regard to property and other areas of life, such as use of violence against one's enemy, the honour/shame codes of Mediterranean society and ritual purity concerns as these are known to us from Jewish sources.[2] Yet what was the social impact of the inclusion of women as permanent members of an itinerant movement of renewal? This is a highly significant, if difficult, question to answer, and yet it is one that the sources raise, especially the *Q* saying alluded to above: Mt 10,34–36/Lk 12,49–53. Once we begin to read the gospel traditions, not as generalized statements of universal significance, but as implying localized settings to which they are specifically directed, they resonate in an altogether new way.

The attempt to understand Jesus' attitude towards women within the setting of first-century Galilean society calls for caution, however, in the light of some recent efforts to portray him as a Cynic-style philosopher in that setting. In order to provide the proper social milieu for such a portrayal, some scholars have in my view grossly distorted the picture of Galilean society, making it a crossroads of Greco-Roman culture, without any distinctions being drawn between urban and rural contexts, not to speak of the demands which Jewish religious life and practice imposed, even for urban dwellers in Galilee.[3] The questions therefore are: What conceivable circumstances might give rise to a movement that was equally attractive to men and women, and how plausibly can such circumstances be postulated for a Galilean Jewish setting of the first century?

---

[2] G. Theißen, 'Die Jesusbewegung als charismatische Werterevolution,' *NTS* 35 (1989) 343–60.

[3] Cf. 'Galilean Questions to Crossan's Mediterranean Jesus,' above pp. 208 ff.

A Wine-drinker and the Associations

One avenue of enquiry that has particular resonances for Galilee, as we shall see, is the charge by Jesus' opponents that he was a glutton and a wine-drinker (Mt 11,19; Lk 7,33). While in the context this might readily be dismissed as a rhetorically motivated label of disparagement,[4] it does bear further investigation because of its realistic local colouring and possible associations with the cult of the wine god, as we shall argue. At least it raises the question as to how outsiders might have perceived the religious reformer's and his followers' practices in that setting. A Dionysiac background has been discussed in regard to the wine-making miracle of Cana, but it has not won wide acceptance outside the History of Religions School of interpretation.[5] To the best of my knowledge, however, no attempt has been made to discuss the historical Jesus himself against that background, yet the evidence that such a culture obtained in Galilee is more compelling than that which is often suggested in support of the presence of Cynics there.

The significance of such an association, were it to be established, would be its potential to explain the attraction of the Jesus movement to women in particular. It is generally accepted that certain mystery cults held a special appeal for women within Greco-Roman society of the first century. This can be documented for the cults of Isis and Osiris from Egypt, the Magna Mater (Cybele) cult from Phrygia and the Dionysus cult from Greece. The fact that women were central to the mythological framework of the first two of these cults might explain their particular attraction. Yet in the case of the Dionysus cult the hero is the god himself, who, having escaped Zeus' thunderbolt which struck down his mother while he was still in the womb, was eventually raised by the nymph, Nysa, and travelled the earth bringing his gifts to people, especially the gift of wine.[6] According to Euripides' play, the *Bacchae,* the worship of this god consisted in orgiastic celebrations conducted at night by women initiates, who, tempo-

---

[4] The term οἰνοπότης is a rare word in secular Greek, a *hapax* in the NT in the Q passage under discussion and is not found in the LXX. Polybius (*Histories* XX, 8,2) describes Antiochus the Great as a 'wine-drinker and rejoicing in drunkenness' by way of explaining his infatuation with a young virgin from Chalcis, whom he desired to marry. Dionysiac associations are at best implicit, but not improbable in view of the Seleucid espousal of the wine-god. At all events the connection between wine-drinking and improper sexual behaviour is clearly intended in the passage from Polybius.

[5] M. Smith, 'On the Wine God in Palestine,' *Salo M. Baron Jubilee Volume* (Jerusalem: Israel Academy of the Sciences and the Humanities, 1975) *815–*829.

[6] R. Shepard Kraemer, *Her Share of the Blessings. Women's Religions among Pagans, Jews, and Christians in the Greco-Roman World* (New York and Oxford: Oxford University Press, 1992).

rarily abandoning their homes and maternal duties, engaged in dancing and merry-making in a state of frenzy which had been induced by drinking a mixture of wine, honey and milk, and who were clothed in ritual dress. Instead of feeding their infants they disgorged their flowing breasts by feeding wild animals, who were subsequently torn apart and the raw flesh eaten. It is by no means certain that these rites as described in the play reflected actual practice in fifth-century Athens. Nevertheless, subsequent accounts by writers such as Demosthenes, Diodorus Siculus (c. 40 BCE) and much later, Plutarch and Strabo, as well as epigraphic evidence, would seem to corroborate the general picture. The spread of the worship of Dionysus in Hellenistic and Roman times and the general suspicion towards it from official Roman circles meant a moderation of some of the excesses as described in the *Bacchae,* but also the significant change that men as well as women could become initiates.[7]

At first sight it would appear that there is little resemblance between groups of Dionysiac initiates just described and the Jesus movement, at least as it appears in the gospels. In particular the induced ecstasy which seems to have been an essential part of the Bacchic rites is entirely absent. It is in the Pauline churches that ecstatic experiences occur within early Christianity. The most significant contrast, perhaps, is the fact that for the Dionysiac initiates the celebrations were a temporary release from their daily chores and responsibilities, whereas in the Jesus movement the call was for total abandonment of home and family on a permanent basis. However, before concluding that this particular analogue has little heuristic value for understanding our topic of Jesus and women, we should examine the likely forms which associations with Dionysus would have taken in differing social situations in Galilee, and whether or not anything might be learned about Jesus' women followers from such an investigation.

Dionysus in a Galilean Jewish Setting

It appears that the wine-god was familiar throughout the Ancient Near Eastern world as a vegetation deity associated with the harvesting of the grape. It was in this guise that Dionysus first appeared in Greece also, long before the more restricted rites of Dionysiac devotees became current.[8] The Syria-Palestine region was also familiar with such a deity, who was connected with fertility in humans and beasts. Wine, the gift of this god,

---

[7] Kraemer, *Her Share of the Blessings*, 36–45.

[8] H. Seesemann, Article οἶνος, in *Theological Dictionary of the New Testament*, ed. G. Kittel, VIII vols. (Grand Rapids: W. Eerdmans, 1968), vol. V, 162–66.

had special importance in cultic settings, where imbibing was thought to lead to a close fellowship with the divine world, a view that is echoed in the Hebrew Scriptures also: 'wine that cheers gods and mortals' (Judg 9,13; Ps 104,15). In Hebrew lore Noah, the postdiluvian patriarch, was the first to cultivate the vine (Gn 9,20), and thereafter a plentiful wine-harvest was seen as a gift from God (Gn 27,28.37) and associated with messianic blessings to come (Gn 49,10–12; Joel 2,23–24; cf. Mk 2,22 and par.). At the same time prophetic critique of wine-drinking is reflected in the example of the Rechabites who obeyed the command of their ancestor not to drink wine, among other ascetic practices (Jer 35), as well as in the condemnation of Baal worship with which it was associated (Hos 2,10–13). Both these examples have significance for our discussion. The contrast between Jesus and John with regard to wine-drinking echoes the abstinence of the Rechabites (cf. Lk 1,15), whereas the behaviour of Hosea's wife is described in terms not dissimilar to those of the Bacchae with mention of merrymaking, the use of incense and festive clothing at the various festivals of Baal, which, according to the prophet, would lead to the destruction of the vine and revenge of the wild animals as a punishment from Yahweh.

Despite the prophetic critique, the use of wine in a Jewish religious context continued, especially at Passover, and there is some evidence that it also continued to be used in temple sacrifice (*JW* 5,565; cf. Ex 29,28–31). Furthermore, several of the symbols associated with Dionysus were also used in Jewish settings. Thus, the coins of one of the Hasmoneans, Antigonus Mattathias who opposed Herod the Great in the name of Jewish religious claims, bore the ivy wreath and the grape cluster. Likewise, the coins of both the first and second revolts against Rome bear such emblems as the wine-cup, a pitcher, grape-leaf and grape, iconography that was undoubtedly inspired by the messianic associations of the vine and its fruit in the prophetic texts already referred to. More significant still was the great vine with hanging grape clusters, 'a marvel of size and artistry', which, according to Josephus, adorned the entrance to Herod's restored temple (*JA* 15,395; *JW* 5,224).[9] Tacitus relates that this decoration was understood by some to mean that it was Dionysus who was worshipped in the Jerusalem temple (*Hist.* V,5).

Thus the Jews were certainly no strangers to the joys and mystery of wine and its religious resonances were shared with the wider Mediterranean and Near Eastern cultures. This was so widespread that it was natural to associate Yahweh and Dionysus, as Tacitus reports. Plutarch also has similar information, intimating that the Jewish feast of Tabernacles was a feast in honour of Dionysus (*Quaestiones Conviviales* 6,1 f.). The irony of

---

[9] Smith, 'On the Wine God in Palestine,' 820–24.

that particular association is that in all probability the Feast of Tabernacles had been an old nature festival associated with the grape harvest, which had later been given a Yahwistic colouring related to the wandering in the wilderness. The fact that it was one of the festivals which the Deuteronomic reform sought to centralise in Jerusalem alone (Dt 16,13–17) is surely an indication that the older associations continued to function throughout the countryside, as indeed we might expect with a festival that had an essentially local significance in a rural rather than an urban setting. Indeed there is evidence from Rome that already in the second century BCE Jews were expelled from the city because they were deemed to worship the god Sabazios, who already in antiquity was identified with Dionysus, due to the similarity of the rites practised in his honour. It has been claimed that it was Roman Jews themselves who made the identification of Yahweh and Sabazios, leading to their expulsion, because of Roman unease with eastern cults in general. Such an identification may have been facilitated by the Hebrew epithet *Sabaoth*/Hosts which became attached to Yahweh earlier. This would represent an extreme form of the *interpretatio Graeca* of the Jewish god, something that had occurred earlier in the same century in Jerusalem itself where the introduction of the worship of Ζεὺς ὕψιστος had been inspired by Jews who had opted for an extreme form of Hellenism (1 Macc 1,11; 2 Macc 6,4). Yet among Jews who had maintained a strong sense of religious identity, various haggadic anecdotes and iconographic representations suggest that even observant circles of a later period were not averse to adapting and adopting Dionysiac motifs that had a very wide currency throughout the eastern Mediterranean from the beginning of the Hellenistic age.[10]

Against this more general background how can one describe Galilean connections with Dionysus? The Seleucids had been ardent promoters of the god, culminating in the attempt to impose his formal worship together with that of Zeus on the Jews in the Hellenistic reform of 167 BCE. While the reform failed due to the success of the Maccabean resistance movement, the coins of Scythopolis/Beth Shean continued to bear the name Nysa, the nurse who had cared for the infant god according to the myth. This indicates that once the city had been restored after the Roman intervention in Palestinian politics in 67 BCE, its earlier connection with the god continued. There is also numismatic as well as literary evidence for the cult of Dionysus in the Phoenician cities of Tyre and Sidon, the former

---

[10] M. Hengel, 'The Interpretation of the Wine Miracle at Cana: John 2:1–11,' in *The Glory of Christ in the New Testament. Studies in Christology in Memory of G. B. Caird*, ed. L. D. Hurst and N. T. Wright (Oxford: Clarendon Press, 1987) 83–112, especially 108–11.

having important commercial links with upper Galilee in particular.[11] Thus the likelihood must be that even rural Galilee was not immune to festivals associated with the gift of wine, under whatever guise these might have been celebrated.

The discovery in 1988 at Sepphoris in lower Galilee of a beautifully executed Dionysiac mosaic dating from the third century CE raises the question as to whether or not actual worship of the god may have taken place there at an earlier date also.[12] This particular mosaic, adorning the floor of a *triclinium* in a large villa, situated close to the theatre, consists of some seventeen panels with Greek labels on each. These deal with a drinking contest between Dionysus and Hercules, who incidentally appeared on the coins of Tyre, identified with the older Phoenician god Melqart. It contains various scenes depicting mythological themes from the god's life, but also more realistic ones in which real life people (men and women) are portrayed carrying gifts in procession. These panels are surrounded by 'an elaborate frame of intertwining acanthus leaves', forming a number of medallions. The central medallion on one side contains the bust of a beautiful woman, who has been aptly described by the archaeologists who discovered the mosaic as 'the Mona Lisa of Galilee.' Presumably this exquisitely executed head is a portrait of the matron of the house, who may well have been a Dionysiac devotee herself and who arranged for the mosaic to be placed in this banqueting hall of the villa.

Two possibilities present themselves in terms of Jesus' Galilean audiences as devotees of the wine god, according to this evidence, fragmentary though it may be. They might have been members of the elite urban upper class, pagan or Jewish in name at least, who engaged in the full-blown worship of Dionysus. Or, alternatively and more likely, they would have been peasants for whom the distinction between Yahweh and the wine god may have been somewhat blurred, especially at wine-making festivals, provided they were not in the practice of going to Jerusalem for the feast of Succoth/Tabernacles (cf. Jn 7,1–9). It is in the larger Herodian centres such as Sepphoris and Tiberias that one might reasonably expect to find Dionysiac associations, attractive to wealthy women such as the Sepphoris matron depicted on the mosaic. The links between Dionysus and the theatre go back to the very dawn of Greek drama, and there had been a theatre in Sepphoris from the first century, possibly even from the time of its refurbishment by Herod Antipas during the life-time of Jesus. There is no comparable archaeological evidence for first-century Tiberias, but we do

---

[11] G. Foerster and Y. Tsafrir, 'Nysa-Scythopolis – A New Inscription and the Titles of the City on the Coins,' *INJ* 9 (1986/87) 53–60.

[12] E. Meyers, E. Netzer, C. Meyers, 'Artistry in Stone: The Mosaics of Ancient Sepphoris,' *BA* 50 (1987) 223–31; *Sepphoris* (Winona Lake: Eisenbrauns, 1992) 38–59.

hear of Antipas' palace there which, because it had animal representations, was destroyed by 'the destitute class', aided by some country Galileans, prior to the first revolt (*Life* 65–66). Given his easy association with people from every background and ethnic origin, as well as those of both genders, there is no reason to rule out *a priori* Jesus' contact with devotees of Dionysus also. Though even then the crucial question would remain: What possible attraction could the Jesus movement as known to us have for such devotees? However, the silence of the gospels about any visit by him to either of the two Herodian urban centres would seem to make such contact less likely, provided his avoidance was a principled one, as I have argued elsewhere.[13] This, of course, does not exclude affluent women being part of his retinue, as Luke informs us (Lk 8,1–3). However, there is a strong suspicion that Luke is here interested in painting a picture of the new movement's social make-up suitable for his own time.[14] The most that can be stated now is that a charge of being a wine-drinker because some of his permanent followers were or had been members of a Dionysiac circle, is possible, though less probable, given the social location of the Jesus movement within first-century Galilean society, insofar as this can currently be reconstructed.

The alternative suggestion, namely, that many of Jesus' Galilean peasant followers might be identified as dedicated to a particular understanding of Yahweh under the guise of the wine god, also has its difficulties, however. It raises questions about the nature of Galilean Jewish attachment to the 'Yahweh alone' claims emanating from Jerusalem, and how likely the peasants would have been to resist any easy assimilation. In the light of the evidence from pre-revolt Galilee it seems clear that a majority of the country people retained undivided allegiance to the Jerusalem temple, despite the influences of the urban centres, both the older ones such as Tyre, Sidon and Scythopolis, or the newer Herodian foundations of Sepphoris and Tiberias.[15] Yet the fact is that wine was one of the principal products of Galilee according to all the literary sources, and archaeological evidence indicates winemaking activity at various sites.[16] The plain of Gennesar has been particularly praised for its lush vegetation, including the vine, by Josephus (*JW* 3,519), and this territory seems to have figured promi-

---

[13] Cf. 'Jesus and the Urban Culture of Galilee,' above, pp. 183 ff.

[14] M. Rose D'Angelo, 'Women in Luke-Acts: A Redactional View,' *JBL* 109 (1990) 529–36.

[15] Cf. 'Urban-Rural Relations in First Century Galilee: Some Suggestions from the Literary Sources,' above, pp. 45 ff.

[16] S. Krauss, *Talmudische Archaeologie*, 3 vols. (reprint, Hildesheim: G. Olms, 1966), vol.2, 227–43; R. Frankel, *The History of the Processing of Wine and Oil in Galilee in the Period of the Bible, the Mishna and the Talmud* ([Hebrew] Ph.D. Diss., Tel Aviv University, 1984).

nently in the earliest activities of the Jesus movement also (Mt 11,19–24). Magdala, the home of Mary, who is repeatedly named as one of the women in the retinue of Jesus (Mt 27,56.61; 28,1.9; Jn 20,11–18), was not far away along the lakefront also. Even though the town had received the Greek name Tarichaeae, associated with the fish-salting industry there, it did not have the same ethos as Tiberias, as became evident later in the first century when it differed from the newer, more cosmopolitan centre nearby in adopting a more nationalistic stance towards the revolt. If association with women such as Mary was the reason for Jesus being described a 'wine-drinker', therefore, it was far more likely to have been in a Jewish, rather than a pagan, Dionysiac context. Sharing in the revelry during the wine harvest rather than engaging in self-induced ecstatic experiences was the much more probable setting for earning such a designation.

Re-examining the Charge

The use of the Dionysus analogy to explain the charge that Jesus was a wine-drinker and friend of women has not proved particularly illuminating thus far. The evidence of a suitable background that might make the charge realistic rather than a piece of vituperative rhetoric, has at best been inconclusive, even if Jewish peasant circles might conceivably have blurred distinctions between certain aspects of their Yahweh worship and a more generalized version of the wine god as a vegetation deity. A closer examination of the charge in its context may help to decide its implications, if any, for our topic of Jesus and women.

The charge occurs in a *Q* passage and has been variously analysed in terms of its tradition and redaction. The complete unit consists of three elements: 1) an initial parabolic comparison – the children in the market-place; 2) an application of this to the contrast between Jesus and John, and 3) a concluding proverbial reflection on wisdom's vindication. Recent proposals suggest that these three units reflect three stages of the redaction of *Q*, relating to the experiences of the so-called *Q* community as it progressed from witnessing, to rejection by 'this generation', to vindication of its claims.[17] Such detailed reconstructions must always remain problematic in view of the putative nature of the source they begin with. Yet, they do raise the question as to whether the various elements may have pre-

---

[17] J. Kloppenborg, *The Formation of Q. Trajectories in Ancient Wisdom Collections* (Philadelphia: Fortress Press, 1987) 111; D. Smith, 'The Historical Jesus at Table,' in *SBLASP*, ed. D. Lull (Atlanta: Scholars Press, 1989) 466–86, especially 477–80; W. J. Cotter, 'The Parable of the Children in the Market-Place, Q(Lk) 7:31–35: An Examination of the Parable's Image and Significance,' *NovT 29* (1987) 289–304.

existed, possibly emanating from the historical Jesus, or whether they are purely a later construct of the community faced with rejection by the vast majority of their fellow Jews.

One way out of this impasse which is adequate for our present purposes is to read the whole passage *as presently constructed* as a commentary on the career of Jesus, but for that reason no less important in terms of its historical implications for understanding that ministry in its setting. The opening question, 'to what shall we liken this generation?' should be read as applying to the whole situation described in the parabolic contrast, namely, the unreasonableness of this generation with regard to God's emissaries. Thus understood, one does not have to find correspondences between individual items in the parable and in the application, a problem that has beset many interpretations. Just as petulant children cannot be easily satisfied, so 'this generation' was unhappy with the contrasting styles of John and Jesus. Wisdom's children, by contrast, acknowledge wisdom's gifts and accept them gladly.

When the passage is read in this way, there is in fact an a,b–a',b' pattern. Jesus' life-style (a') matches the piping and dancing in the marketplace (a), whereas John's ascetic conduct (b') is represented by the wailing and dirging (b). Thus, the activities of merry-making and mourning represent the two extremes of a joyful (messianic) existence and an ascetic (penitential) one. Neither is acceptable to 'this generation', that is, those who are not open to the surprise of a totally alternative understanding of God's dealing with Israel, opting instead for the safety of the status quo. What is significant about the contrast of the two lifestyles for the purposes of this discussion is the choice of imagery. Piping and dancing are universal human activities of merry-making, but there may well be a definite local colouring also with religious significance. A clay plaque from a bronze-age cultic location at Dan represents a male dancing figure with a lute in his hand, which the archaeologist, A. Biran has named 'The dancer from Dan.'[18] Piping is associated with the god Pan, who from the Hellenistic age was celebrated at the nearby grove of Banias at the foot of Mt Hermon. Coins of Banias represent him playing the pipes, sometimes with a goat beside him, a symbol also associated with Dionysus. Pan was also depicted as the escort of Dionysus, as on an altar with an inscription dedicated to Dionysus, 'founder' of the city, from Scythopolis and dating from the year 11/12 CE.[19]

---

[18] A. Biran, 'The Dancer from Dan, the Empty Tomb and the Altar Room,' *IEJ* 36 (1986) 168–87.

[19] V. Tzaferis, 'The "God who is in Dan" and the Cult of Pan at Banias in the Hellenistic and Roman Periods,' *Eretz Israel*, vol. 23, *A. Biran Volume* (Jerusalem: The Israel Exploration Society, 1992) 128*-35*; Foerster and Tsafrir, 'Nysa-Scythopolis,' 53, n. 2.

Thus, there was a very long tradition of both these gods in the neighbourhood of Galilee and the pagan resonances of piping and dancing would surely not have been lost on Jesus' Galilean opponents. They could, therefore, categorise him as a devotee of these locally venerated deities, presumably because of his general infringement of Jewish identity markers as these were defined by more orthodox circles. His and his followers' joyful attitude, grounded in messianic claims, was capable of being misrepresented and thereby discredited, and there was ready to hand a set of associations which could easily have been evoked to pillory his conduct as betrayal and un-Jewish.

That vilification is the prime intention of the charge may be deduced, not merely from the term 'wine-drinker' and its nuance of pagan religious worship, but also from the other terms used, 'glutton' and 'friend of tax collectors and sinners.' The association of these terms evokes the setting of meals, often, connected with lewd conduct including women. Thus, according to Kathleen Corley, Matthew's linking of tax collectors with prostitutes (Mt 21,31), instead of the usual 'tax collectors and sinners' is a natural one. In Hellenistic literature the term ἁμαρτωλός / sinner referred to various kinds of moral failure, but especially those involving sexual promiscuity. Equally, 'tax collector' may not just have the usual connotations of cheating or collaboration with the enemy, but also with prostitution, being closely related to brothel-keeping in the literature.[20] While all these various associations were no doubt grounded in the everyday social life of the Mediterranean world in which the presence of women at public meals was still regarded as improper, the terms inevitably passed over into use as part of vituperative rhetoric, that highly developed art-form in the ancient, no less than the modern world, in order to discredit one's opponent. In a culture where honour was so highly prized any such character assassination was intended to shame the opponent publicly, thereby depriving them of their right to status and the influence that went with it.

Our brief examination of the charge that Jesus was a wine-drinker in its original *Q* setting has, therefore, all the signs of an attempt to discredit him and his movement by religious opponents unhappy with his apparent lack of regard for the mores of Galilean Jewish society. This does not mean that we should discount entirely the particular terms in which this vituperation is couched. Vernon Robbins in particular has drawn our attention to the fact that all rhetorical devices are social codes which can give us insight into the values and ethos of particular societies.[21] Thus our pas-

---

[20] K. Corley, *Private Women. Public Meals. Social Conflict in the Synoptic Tradition* (Peabody: Hendrickson, 1993) 89–93.

[21] V. Robbins, 'Socio-Rhetorical Criticism: Mary, Elizabeth and the Magnificat as a Test Case,' in *The New Literary Criticism and the New Testament*, ed. E. Struthers Mal-

sage tells us something of how women in public were perceived in that culture, participating fully in the values that were prevalent in Greco-Roman society generally. Such women were cast in the roles of whore, temptress, dangerous and open to foreign and lewd practices under the guise of religion. When such images are compared with those of orthodox Jewish women as described in the, admittedly later, rabbinic writings the contrast is marked. There, too, women are dangerous, not as objects of sexual temptation but as a potential source of impurity. It is for this reason that they had to be excluded from any direct contact with the sacred. As Jacob Neusner has shown, control of women in terms of board and bed is the generative principle of the Mishnah's division, *Nashim*.[22] Aspects of the social role of women are of no interest to the framers of the Mishnah, other than in removing any grey areas in the law concerning the circumscribing of women and their protection, as potential sources of impurity. While it is not possible to ascribe these detailed rules to first-century Galilee with any great assurance, recent archaeological evidence (e.g., ritual baths, stone jars and absence of pig bones) from Sepphoris, Iotapata and elsewhere suggest that issues of purity were important in some Galilean Jewish circles of the period.[23] The significance of such a public statement of concern for purity in certain households has particular implications for the daughters of the house in terms of their marriage prospects, as Marianne Sawicki notes.[24] It is to such groups, probably of a priestly caste, that we should attribute the efforts to vilify the Jesus movement, as being not just unobservant in regard to purity but as being un-Jewish in its basic affiliation.

Taking Vilification Seriously

Those who chose to vilify Jesus and his movement in the terms mentioned in the *Q* passage we have been discussing were only too happy to characterize them in ways that were quite familiar to Greco-Roman audiences,

---

bon and E. V. McKnight, JSNT Supplements 109 (Sheffield: Sheffield Academic Press, 1994) 164–209.

[22] J. Neusner, *Method and Meaning in Ancient Judaism,* Brown Judaic Series, 10 (Missoula: Scholars Press, 1979) 79–100.

[23] D. Adan-Bayewitz and M. Aviam, 'Iotapata, Josephus and the Siege of 67: Preliminary Report on the 1992–94 seasons,' *JRA* 10 (1997) 131–65, especially 163–64; E. Netzer and Z Weiss, *Zippori* (Jerusalem: The Israel Exploration Society, 1994) 20–24.

[24] M. Sawicki, 'Spatial Management of Gender and Labor in Greco-Roman Galilee,' in *Archaeology and the Galilee. Texts and Contexts in the Greco-Roman and Byzantine Periods,* ed. D. Edwards and C. T. McCollough (Atlanta: Scholars Press, 1997) 7–28, especially 15 f. and nn. 29 and 67.

and the added suggestion of possible complicity in pagan worship merely strengthened the case for rejection. By the same token this observation also supports the claim that women were members of Jesus' permanent retinue. One cannot agree with Morton Smith's principle that outsiders invariably give a more accurate account of things than insiders, yet at the same time their views, even when hostile, cannot be discounted entirely.[25] Distortion and misrepresentation of the truth, rather than pure fiction, is the normal stock-in-trade of vilification. Thus, while we cannot take the charge against Jesus at face value, we should ask why in fact he is characterized in this precise way. While Jesus and his followers almost certainly should not be viewed as forming a Dionysiac group, clearly there were sufficient similarities at a superficial level to make such a comparison possible, even plausible for some of the uncommitted of Galilee. In that event it is worth asking whether the social reasons which made Dionysiac associations attractive to women in the Mediterranean world might not have applied in the case of the Jesus movement also.

Ross Kraemer has drawn on the group/grid theories of Mary Douglas, combined with I. M. Lewis' notion of 'oblique aggression strategy', to explain the attraction of Dionysiac rites for women.[26] While the group/grid theory with its strong/weak co-relates is by now familiar in biblical studies, Lewis' idea is based on the observation of Polynesian women who were able 'to redress the imbalance of power between themselves and men without directly challenging the status quo.' Kraemer suggests that, in a similar fashion, through the rejection of socially ascribed roles of mother and nurse and the adoption instead of traditional male roles of warrior and hunter, women Dionysiacs effected a temporary role reversal. The fact that this was achieved 'under inspiration' of the god meant that they were inculpable, engaging in a form of ritual release at the behest of the deity. In the classical period and as evidenced in the *Bacchae* women displayed strong group relations but weak grid identity. However, as the character of the Greek city evolved in the Hellenistic period, the role of women in society also changed. The new cosmopolitanism resulted in both weakened group and grid in the form of traditional roles, but consequently a greater freedom and variety even for women at the lower end of the social spectrum. At the same time this would also explain why men were now becoming members of Dionysiac associations because of their need for a strong group connections.

Such models from the social sciences are of necessity, highly generalised. Nevertheless, they can function heuristically by suggesting the most

---

[25] M. Smith, *Jesus the Magician* (New York: Harper and Row, 1978) 1–7.
[26] Kraemer, *Her Share of the Blessing*, 46–9; 'Ecstasy and Possession: The Attraction of Women to the Cult of Dionysus,' *HTR* 72 (1979) 56–80.

appropriate questions to be posed to the data to hand. Greater attention to the changing social context of Galilee in the Herodian period is called for in order to understand not just the fact but also the particular shape of the Jesus movement. Elsewhere I have attempted to highlight this situation in terms of the building of two urban centres – Sepphoris and Tiberias – during the life-time of Jesus.[27] Since the pre-industrial city was heavily dependent on its hinterland the emergence of the two centres inevitably put pressure on the traditional way of life in the village culture of lower Galilee. Landownership patterns were affected and the shift from a subsistence to a market economy changed both the means of production and the market exchange system. An integral part of such changes is the 'values revolution' that makes the transition from one system to the other possible. Kinship concerns are replaced by those which have to do with maximizing profits, giving rise to a more stratified society. It was the urban elites and their retainers who stood to benefit most from these changes, while the peasant class come under increasing pressure. The slide from ownership to day labouring to homelessness could be rapid. Brigandage or alternative movements, such as the Jesus movement, became real options for those who found themselves on the margins of the new social reality.

The lives of women were inevitably affected by these changes. Within the structure of a peasant village economy women's presence and labour are essential to the maintenance of the status quo. Many of the tasks necessary for subsistence, for example animal tending, fruit gathering, vine treading, etc. are shared by men and women, in addition to the more traditional female activities such as textile production, baking and child nurturing. The tension between group and grid is minimized when everyday existence dominates the ethos so that the public/private dualism is not as marked as in more advanced economies. It was this way of life that was being eroded by the changes occurring in Galilee. Land was confiscated in order to provide allotments for those who were compelled to inhabit the new foundation, Tiberias. Debt is a constant feature in the tradition of the Synoptic Gospels and this led to brigandage. The male population was further depleted by the political disturbances on the death of Herod the Great, especially in the region of Sepphoris which was sacked by the Roman general Varus in 4 BCE. Many women were either prematurely widowed or deprived of the opportunity to marry, such an essential feature of women's status in the ancient world, including the Jewish one. The rigid patriarchal structures which controlled marriage were certainly not conducive to women's autonomy, but the alternatives of penury or menial services, including prostitution at the larger centres, were deemed to be shameful.

---

[27] Cf. 'Herodian Economics in Galilee. Searching for a Suitable Model,' above pp. 86 ff.

Thus, class as well as gender were operative factors in women's full participation in the Jesus movement. The involvement of upper-class women in Greco-Roman religious practices, especially from the early empire, has been well documented.[28] A similar case has recently been argued for upper-class Jewish and non-Jewish women's attraction to Pharisaism, and various reasons, social and psychological, have been suggested for this.[29] In a similar vein Luke can speak of the Herodian women caring for Jesus "from their own resources" (Lk 8,3). As we have suggested, this may reflect a later situation in which women of means acted as patronesses of such movements. That there were such women of means, either widowed or divorced, can be documented from the Babatha archive in the province of Arabia, for the early second century. Her *ketubba*, or marriage dowry in the event of divorce or death of her husband, was worth 100 Tyrians, that is 400 denarii, recalling that a silver denarius was the average daily wage.[30] Yet Babatha was deemed a 'noble' (or free) woman. The situation I am suggesting for the earliest Jesus movement is its attraction for women of a lower social class, those who had been marginalized by the changing circumstances in that world. It was presumably the particular view-point and life-style that would have attracted them to that movement rather than those of the Pharisaic associations, which may not have appealed to these village women, since Josephus tells us that the Pharisaic movement was generally attractive to the townspeople.

It would appear, therefore, that we can posit social conditions in Galilee that might have been conducive to women as well as men joining the permanent retinue of Jesus. The social circumstances we are positing are different to those which would have obtained in the case of Dionysiac gatherings with their temporary release from family chores. Rather than providing such a temporary escape, the Jesus movement supplied a real social need by offering an alternative, based on a radically different world-view. Faced with the rapidly changing circumstances of their lives, some women of Galilee found that the Jesus movement was offering a viable and attractive alternative. The apparent lack of concern around purity issues must

---

[28] J. Bremmer, 'Why did Early Christianity attract Upper-Class Women?,' in *Fructus Centesimus. Mélanges offerts à Gerard J. M. Barrtelink*, ed. A. A. R. Bastiaensen, A. Hilhorst and C. H. Kneepkens (Steenbrugis: In Abbatia S. Petri, 1989) 37–47; id., 'Pauper or Patroness. The Widow in the Early Christian Church,' in *Between Poverty and Pyre. Moments in the History of Widowhood*, ed. J. Bremmer and L. van den Bosch (London and New York: Routledge, 1995) 31–57.

[29] T. Ilan, 'The Attraction of Aristocratic Women to Pharisaism,' *HTR* 88 (1995) 1–34.

[30] Y. Yadin, J. C. Greenfield, A. Yardeni, 'Babatha's *Ketubba*,' *IEJ* 44 (1994) 75–101; M. A. Friedmann, 'Babatha's *Ketubba* : Some Preliminary Observations,' *IEJ* 46 (1996) 55–76.

have been a factor of some importance, but it was not the only reason for the appeal.[31] The message of blessing for the poor and setting captives free undoubtedly resonated with the experiences of repression that such women encountered in their daily lives. The promise of reversal of fortunes that the apocalyptic world-view held out was far more attractive than any alternative. Pilgrimage to Jerusalem offered a thoroughly legitimated escape from familial chores, if such were required. Only the permanent following of Jesus could provide the incentive to remake the world in ways that were different to anything that either Rome or Jerusalem might have to offer.

Conclusion

The search for an adequate social location for permanent women followers of Jesus on the basis of our initial hunch did not at first prove particularly fruitful. However, the implied unfavourable comparison in the description of Jesus as a wine-drinker opened up another avenue for investigation. A social-scientific perspective that is sensitive not only to gender but also to class can disclose the hidden lives of women in a particular context, even when hard facts are scarce. Approaches to various aspects of women's life in antiquity that can combine such insights with the evidence provided by the new archaeology will surely help considerably in clarifying what was at stake for women in making choices such as joining the Jesus movement and the kind of vilification that they were likely to encounter even from within their own families. Thus, the very silence of our androcentric sources provides a challenge to the historical imagination to re-image critically the world of women in antiquity in ways that may be suggestive for the present and the future also.

---

[31] R. Horsley, *Galilee. History, Politics, People* (Valley Forge: Trinity Press International, 1995) 197–8.

13. Locality and Doctrine: Mark and John Revisited

The symbolic meaning of place is common to all cultures and finds expression in many different literary creations. Previous generations of New Testament scholars have explored this aspect of early Christian self-expression also, as the title of this essay, recalling R. H. Lightfoot's *Locality and Doctrine in The Gospels* (London, 1938), acknowledges. However, it was not just this title, but also a remark of Lightfoot's elsewhere that has prompted the topic I wish to explore in this essay: 'Every theological idea that one finds rough-hewn in the gospel of Mark is finely honed in the gospel of John.'[1] I have found this to be a most stimulating suggestion for studying these two gospels over the years, since they do, in my view, share more than the common number of traditions that previous studies have proposed. Questions nevertheless remain, such as how we can best explore this phenomenon and where should we begin? Lightfoot speaks of shared theological ideas, but that remark may be somewhat premature. Recent gospel studies with a literary bent stress that we should not separate form and content too readily, a temptation to which those with formal theological and philosophical rather than literary training are all too prone to yield.

Much of the close and detailed analysis of source criticism in regard to John and the Synoptics can find a new context through an inter-textual approach to the gospels. Intertextuality as applied to the gospels, however, is not simply a matter of comparing and contrasting similarities and differences, since such an exercise does not adequately explore the common discourse of the different works, with a view to uncovering their shared possibilities for meaning.[2] This shared meaning can be examined and expressed, irrespective of our decisions about possible relationships of interdependence in the production of the texts in question.

For some practitioners of the historical-critical method such an approach is far too subjective and lacking in proper criteria. It should be stressed, however, that the continued fascination of our classic texts (but to some degree of all texts) is their ability to provoke different generations of readers to appropriate their meanings in ever-changing circumstances.

---

[1] 'Consideration of Three Markan Passages, '*In Memoriam E. Lohmeyer* (Stuttgart, 1951) 111–15.

[2] Cf. the essays by J. Delorme and E. von Wolde in *Intertextuality in Biblical Writings. Essays in Honour of Bas van Iersel*, ed. S. Draisma (Kampen: Uitgeversmaatschappij J. H. Kok, 1989).

The search for the univocal meaning of the text that consciously or otherwise was part of the presupposition of historical study of the New Testament was clearly flawed, in that we are still no closer to definitive answers to many of the issues which that approach raised. This is neither to deny the many advances that have been made nor to ignore the continued importance of such questions in the future. The fact is that a total concentration on the past has caused us to ignore the present in which we the exegetes/readers are located and a dangerous cleavage has occurred between biblical and theological studies in the name of scientific scholarship. Various liberationist movements are today challenging such claims as they search for an emancipatory message from the foundational texts of both Judaism and Christianity. Traditional New Testament scholarship can choose either to ignore such developments and run the risk of irrelevancy, or attempt to integrate the fruits of earlier studies with new methods that will allow our texts to address our world also.[3]

Stress on the interpretative role of reading is not, therefore, a recipe for anarchy but a recognition of the possibilities of our texts. By narrowing the focus to two canonical early Christian writings we have already introduced limits that would not be acceptable in a thorough-going intertextual approach, which in theory at least should be open to all literature, past and present.[4] As late twentieth-century readers we approach two early Christian texts, interested in exploring their shared interest in the geography of Jesus' ministry, specifically the Galilee-Jerusalem dimensions of their portrayal, with a view to uncovering the significance of their shared discourse for Christian existence in the world, particularly, our world.

'Galilee of the Nations'

All the canonical gospels share a common intertext, the actual career of Jesus as this was remembered and narrated in various circles. This common narrative appears to have been acutely aware of the geographical dimensions of that career, particularly in terms of its north-south axis (see Acts 10,37–41). Viewed from the perspective of the Israelite and Jewish traditions the story of the northern prophet challenging the cultic centre was indeed an arresting feature. Elijah, Amos and Jeremiah provided partial precedents and precursors, but the Jesus story was the most daring instance of the clash between the centre and the periphery within that cul-

---

[3] Cf. W. Jeanrond, *Theological Hermeneutics: Development and Significance* (London: Macmillan, 1991), especially 78–119 on texts and readers.

[4] J. Culler, 'Presuppositions and Intertextuality,' in *The Pursuit of Signs: Semiotics, Literature, Deconstruction* (Ithaca: Cornell University Press, 1981) 100–118.

ture. It offered considerable possibilities for further elaboration and retellings as early Christian theological imagination sought new levels of meaning in this account in terms of the paradox that was at the centre of its own proclamation.

The early Christians shared a larger field of discourse with all branches of Judaism whereby earlier texts were actualised in new situations by various exegetical strategies – Midrash, Pesher, Targum and the like. In that sense it could be said without any exaggeration that all early Christian literature is profoundly intertextual.[5] Among the many earlier texts which played a significant role for the Jesus movement, the book of Isaiah seems to have had a particularly prominent role. In addition to the servant songs, the Zion and Davidic oracles and ethical statements from Trito-Isaiah, the oracle of salvation for the north (Is 9,1–6) was to prove most illuminating in regard to the geographical contours of the Jesus story both apologetically and as an aid for understanding its own tasks and mission. An oracle that was directed specifically at the north which in former times had been brought into contempt, but which could now hope for light in the person of the ideal king about to be born, was surely a text which was likely to have stirred early Christian imagination as it sought to express its own experiences in the present. Our intention here is not to document such a claim in any detailed philological or exegetical way, but to pursue the insight by seeing how it might fruitfully direct our reading of the various gospels as we seek to explore their treatment of the common intertext around the geographical contours of Jesus' ministry.

The Isaian pre-text did not demand a uniform treatment, and while our focus here is on Mark and John, a brief exploration into Matthew's and Luke's treatment will help in orienting us to the creative possibilities for narratival development that are involved. This is merely a brief testing of our initial insight, starting with Matthew who alone cites our proposed pre-text as part of his pattern of fulfilled prophecies in the career of Jesus.

Following the suggestion of Frank Kermode that the sense of an ending can be an important pointer to the writer's point of view, it is significant that Matthew directs the disciples' and our (as readers) attention to a mountain in Galilee, particularly in view of the fact that a similar location had been the scene for Jesus' great address on discipleship (Mt 5,1). The story had its beginnings in Galilee authenticated by citation of the Isaian pre-text (Is 8,23–9,1/Mt 4,15–16), even though it was the presence of the wicked Archelaus in Judea that occasioned the divinely orchestrated movement of the child Jesus there in the first instance (Mt 2,22). While the

---

[5] Cf. S. Freyne, 'Reading the Gospels in the Light of the Window of the Evangelists at Chartres Cathedral,' in *Radical Pluralism and Truth. David Tracy and the Hermeneutics of Religion*, ed. W. Jeanrond and J. Rike (New York: Crossroad, 1991) 107–20.

first journey was a secret flight, the concluding one was that of a victorious conqueror. Death in Jerusalem had indeed occurred, not however as a child at the hands of a capricious ruler, but as the result of an adult challenge to the Jerusalem religious establishment through a daring reinterpretation of the tradition of which they regarded themselves as guardians. For Matthew's perspective now, 'Galilee of the nations', was not a negative description as in the pre-text, but a challenge to the new movement, since it was from the Galilean mountain of teaching and commissioning that the word was to go forth to all nations.

Luke's ending appears to bypass Galilee with the command to stay in Jerusalem and the relegation of Galilee to a past memory (Lk 24,6). However, this was not a nostalgic recalling of the past but a vital hermeneutical key to the present so that the story could continue on into *Acts of the Apostles* and to the end of the earth (Acts 1,8). Here too, Galilee opens up the universal horizons of the story even if its place in the subsequent plot is subsumed within Luke's larger geographical schema of Judea, Samaria, and the end of the earth (Acts 9,31).[6]

Thus both evangelists are deeply conscious of the continuity that Galilee offers between the past of Jesus and the present universal perspectives of their communities. The Isaian pre-text has played an important role in articulating the conviction that the event of Jesus the Galilean has indeed universal messianic significance, even if both evangelists relate the doubt and uncertainty of the disciples. This highlights for their readers the changed perspective that is called for in the post-resurrection remembering of Galilee and all its associations as narrated in their respective accounts. Its particular contour and demand now enter into Christian faith proclamation and is assured an ongoing significance for the content of Christian belief and practice 'to the end of the age' and 'to the end of the earth' alike. For both these writers the promise of the pre-text, 'thou hast multiplied the nation, thou hast increased its joy' (Is 9,3), has been abundantly fulfilled through the community whose origins could be traced back to the memory of Jesus' Galilean career.

Great Light for a People in Darkness

The sense of universal mission is certainly not entirely absent from Mark and John, yet the fact that all scholars are agreed about the later appendices, both dealing explicitly with this theme suggest that originally it was

---

[6] For a fuller development of this reading of Matthew's and Luke's treatment of Galilee cf. my *Galilee, Jesus and the Gospels. Literary Approaches and Historical Investigations* (Dublin: Gill & Macmillan, 1988) 69–115.

not the primary focus of their compositions.[7] Their endings are directed primarily towards the proper recognition by disciples of Jesus' true identity and the implications of such a recognition. This had been the main focus of both their treatments of the career of Jesus as evidenced by the Markan messianic secret and the Johannine 'book of signs.'

Mark is certainly aware of the importance of location by suggesting in his conclusion a return to Galilee in conformity with the earlier injunction within the narrative (Mk 16,7; 14,27). Only there, it seems, can the male disciples 'see' Jesus, something that calls for further exploration presently. The dramatic tension of this ending is heightened by the women's fear and silence. Only the 'mute testimony' of the gospel's existence reassures us that the return and recognition occurred.[8] John's conclusion, on the other hand, appears to lack any connection between recognition and place, at least in terms of the Galilee-Jerusalem axis. As in Mark, a woman is given a message for the disciples about the master's movements, but with typical Johannine sense of deeper meaning the departure/return is not to another place, but 'to my Father and your Father, to my God and to your God' (20,17). The subsequent scene with the disciples in the upper room merely confirms this sense of detachment from any earthly props in John's understanding of faith. Thomas' confession, 'My Lord and my God', identifies Jesus in terms of the goal of his departure as previously indicated to Mary ('to my God and to your God'), yet his need for tangible proof is contrasted with those who in the future 'shall not see but shall believe.' Human associations of persons or place are inappropriate in this understanding (cf. 4,42).[9]

This initial comparison between our two evangelists is less than encouraging as far as their use of the shared geographical intertext is concerned. Yet the subtle way in which the pre-text has functioned in Matthew's and Luke's presentation prompts further exploration. In the prophetic oracle the coming salvation is spoken of as a great light for those who walk in darkness, a contrast that is certainly important for John in his presentation of Jesus as 'the light of the world' (1,4f.; 8,12; 9,5; 12,46). It is not unknown to Mark either (4,21) where the image of a lamp is used to express the revelatory mission that the disciples will fulfil in the future, despite the mysterious nature of their present experience. The image of

---

[7] The MSS evidence makes this clear in the case of Mark, and Jn 20,30f. is a clear literary indication of the original ending of the Fourth Gospel, as is recognised by almost all modern commentators, thus making Jn 21 either an addendum of the evangelist's or a later redactor's appendix. Cf. F. Neirynck, 'Jn 21,' *NTS* 36 (1990) 321–36.

[8] The expression is John Ashton's, *Understanding the Fourth Gospel* (Oxford: Clarendon Press, 1991) 408.

[9] Ashton, *Understanding,* 439–42.

light is undoubtedly pervasive in the Scriptures, but its association with Galilee in this particular Isaian passage is suggestive for its possibilities of opening up our two gospel texts to each other with regard to the connections between Galilee and revelatory manifestations of Jesus' true identity.

The Fourth Gospel is concerned from the outset with two levels of meaning, that sometimes, though not exclusively, is expressed in spatial terms of above and below.[10] Nevertheless, it should never be forgotten than John wrote a gospel, not a revelatory discourse, and this means that the common intertext of Jesus' earthly career was important for his purposes, so much so in fact that some recent discussions have suggested that his topographical and chronological ordering of the narrative is historically more reliable than that of the Synoptics.[11] Be that as it may, we are here interested in exploring his use of the Galilee-Jerusalem dimension of Jesus' career within his faith narrative. How, if at all, does the contrast play any role in his higher synthesis, which on the basis of his concluding chapter seems to move on a level that strives to bypass the earthly dimension entirely? Certainly, this danger of misreading the story seems to have been prevalent among the first readers of the gospel in light of the emphatic corrective of the first epistle of John.[12]

The suggestion at the end of Mark's gospel that the male disciples could hope to 'see' the Risen Christ in Galilee draws the reader's attention to the group's previous contacts with him there within the narrative. The contrast with the women who 'had followed him in Galilee,' as well as the reference to those other women who had come up with him to Jerusalem (Mk 15,41) is both deliberate and pointed.[13] Their inability or refusal to 'see' properly was one of the evangelist's ways of expressing their failures as disciples. 'Having eyes do you not see?' is one of a series of chiding questions posed to them by Jesus towards the end of the Galilean ministry (Mk 8,14–21), with special reference to the two bread miracles, but by implication to all the deeds of Jesus that they had witnessed. Their condition was deemed to be comparatively no better than 'those outside', for whom everything happened in riddles (Mk 4,10 f.). Immediately after the stern

---

[10] The temporal dimension is also employed, particularly in terms of 'remembering' in the post-resurrection context of episodes that are narrated within the time-span of the earthly ministry. See the beginning and end of the 'Book of Signs' (Jn 2,23; 12,16).

[11] E.g., J. A. T. Robinson, *The Priority of John* (London: SCM, 1985); J. Murphy-O'Connor, 'John the Baptist and Jesus,' *NTS* 36 (1990) 359–74.

[12] R. E. Brown, *The Community of the Beloved Disciple: The Life, Loves and Hates of an Individual Church in the New Testament* (London: Chapman, 1979) 109–23.

[13] R. Tannehill, 'The Disciples in Mark: the Function of a Narrative Role,' *JR* 57 (1977) 134–57; on the question of women and men as disciples in Mark's gospel cf. E. Struthers Malbon, 'Fallible Followers: Women and Men in the Gospel of Mark,' *Semeia* 27 (1984) 29–48.

cross-examination with regard to their failure to understand, and as if to make the point in the most imaginative manner possible, Jesus opens the eyes of a blind man in two stages, so that eventually he could 'see everything clearly' (Mk 8,22–26). This episode only helps to highlight Peter's short-sightedness in confessing Jesus as the Christ while rejecting the possibility of a suffering role for him, as he was about to set out on the road that lead to Jerusalem and death. Peter's and the other disciples' attitudes are sharply contrasted with another blind man, Bar-Timaeus, as that journey reaches its climax. This latter on receiving his sight followed Jesus eagerly on the way, whereas the Galilean retinue were frightened and bewildered (Mk 10,32 contrasted with 10,46–52).

By means of contrast, question and association the ideal author in Mark has left the reader painfully aware of the failures in seeing of the Galilean disciples. The light may indeed have shone in the darkness of the northern regions, but not even specially chosen ones from there have been able to comprehend it fully, despite their well-intentioned, but all too human response to the call. The concluding message, therefore, that Jesus will go before them to Galilee where they will see him as he had promised, has a mildly ironic ring in view of the previous failures, but it strikes a note of hope also for Markan readers then and now. Viewed from a post-resurrection perspective the Galilean ministry was shrouded in a strange, mysterious light that could not have been penetrated despite the best intentions (Mk 1,16–20; 3,13–19). Yet for Mark it was an essential dimension of the Christian faith-understanding about life within the world in terms of radical discipleship. The message entrusted to the women at the empty tomb was a conclusion demanded by the story itself therefore, and its intention. Otherwise Galilee would remain the symbol of unfulfilled promise, the hopes it had engendered, however imperfect, never realised. The absence of a final closing scene of reunion after the manner of Matthew and Luke is not in my opinion to be interpreted as a sign of the Markan text 'differing from itself,' as some post-modern critics suggest.[14] Rather it is an acknowledgement of the difficulties for faith and action that closeness to Jesus poses when the social dimension of his career is remembered as integral to Christian faith in the world.

'The Galileans received him' is John's positive evaluation of attitudes towards Jesus within the narrative framework of his gospel (4,45). Thus they are immediately contrasted with the Ἰουδαῖοι as the main opponents of Jesus. It is probable that these latter are not to be understood solely on

---

[14] See S. D. Moore, *Literary Criticism and the Gospels. The Theoretical Challenge* (New Haven and London: Yale University Press, 1989) 166. Contrast, E. Struthers Malbon, 'Galilee and Jerusalem: History and Literature in Marcan Interpretation,' *CBQ* 44 (1982) 242–55.

the basis of geographical origins in Judea, even though it is mainly during controversies in Jerusalem on the occasion of Jesus' visits for the great 'feasts of the Jews' that they emerge (Jn 2,18; 5,10.16; 6,41; 7,15; 8,31.48.52; 9,18.22; 10,19.24.31; 11,8.46; 12,11).[15] In most of these in- stances they are hostile characters, either in close associations with the Pharisees and other religious leaders plotting against Jesus, or positively identified with them, though in a few instances we hear of a division amongst the Jews concerning Jesus or mention that some of them believed in him. Despite these instances we are left with the overwhelming impres- sion that for the author, the Ἰουδαῖοι are negative characters with whom the ideal reader will not identify.[16] The fact that they appear in Galilee dur- ing the bread discourse (Jn 6,52) suggests that they are not to be identified simply with one geographical location, but that from the author's point of view they symbolise a closed and dismissive attitude with regard to Jesus, often cloaked in attachment to Moses instead.

The reception by the Galileans is therefore in stark contrast, particularly when one tracks down their other characteristics as portrayed by the narra- tive. The first permanent followers were initially disciples of John, and the narrator deliberately changes the scene to Galilee (1,43), where Philip of Bethsaida and Nathanael of Cana – both Galilean places in the view of the author (12,21; 21,2) – join the retinue. The former subsequently appears as the one through whom some Greeks sought an approach to Jesus (echoes here of a Johannine version of 'Galilee of the gentiles'?) and the latter is promised that he shall see 'greater things' as a reward for his initial con- fession of Jesus as 'Son of God and King of Israel', a promise that is fur- ther specified as a heavenly vision concerning the Son of Man (1,49–51). The climactic position of this typical Galilean figure in the list of those who have made an initial recognition is surely significant in terms of Gali- lean reception of Jesus later. The fact that Jesus immediately reveals his glory at Cana, Nathanael's home town, so that 'his disciples believed in him' (2,11), is equally indicative in terms of the author's positive evalua- tion of Galilean attitudes generally.[17]

---

[15] J. Ashton, 'The Identity and Function of the ΙΟΥΔΑΙΟΙ in the Fourth Gospel,' *NovT* 27 (1985) 40–75. Jn 6,52 is the only instance of Ἰουδαῖοι in Galilee in the gos- pel.

[16] R. A. Culpepper, *Anatomy of the Fourth Gospel. A Study in Literary Design* (Philadelphia: Fortress Press, 1983) 125–32.

[17] R. Fortna, *The Fourth Gospel and its Predecessor. From Narrative Source to Pre- sent Gospel* (Philadelphia: Fortress Press, 1988) 294–314, attributes the topographical interests to the final redactor and not to the putative signs source which he claims for an earlier stage of the gospel's formation. However, he attaches no particular significance to Galilee or Galileans other than as 'a foil to the Judeans' (308–10). By contrast cf. J. Bassler, 'The Galileans: A Neglected Factor in Johannine Research,' *CBQ* 43 (1981)

Once they have had the initial Cana experience there is no hint of any backsliding or desire to avoid the implications of discipleship. 'Lord to whom shall we go? You have the words of eternal life and we have believed and have come to know that you are the Holy One of God' (Jn 6,68 f.), is the response of Peter on behalf of all disciples when given the option to leave at the end of the bread of life discourse. Even though Peter is never explicitly called a Galilean in the Fourth Gospel, this confession is wholly in keeping with Galilean attitudes and is suitably located in Galilee. There are many echoes here of Mark's bread section (Mk 6,31–8,29), but most noteworthy is the contrast between the Markan disciples' utter consternation and distress at the approach of Jesus walking on the water and the Johannine disciples' joy at receiving him into the boat, admittedly after some initial fear (Mk 6,45–52 compared with Jn 6,16–21). It is the brothers of Jesus, with their admonition that 'he go to Jerusalem and show himself to the world' during the feast of Tabernacles, who in this gospel typify the inadequate response of the Markan disciples (Jn 7,1–9; Mk 9,5 f.)

It might appear from this presentation that in the Johannine perspective genuine discipleship is less demanding than for Mark. Yet we have seen that in his concluding statement on the nature of faith the author of the Fourth Gospel calls for transcending the evidence of sight, and this suggests the need for openness and trust as an essential ingredient for true disciples. Even then, however, there has to be progression from initial experience to full and trusting acceptance of Jesus and his claims. Nathanael thus becomes the paradigm of faith, the Galilean who leaves himself open to 'greater things.' One can easily imagine, given the subtlety of Johannine symbolism, that his very name is itself a hint of the 'gift' quality of such faith.

How does the author integrate the geographical indications of the intertext with this understanding of faith? While we can undoubtedly hear echoes of the Markan pattern of revelation/acceptance in Galilee and blindness/rejection in Jerusalem throughout the Johannine account, the emphasis is decidedly altered. The major part of the narrative space is devoted to the Jerusalem encounters and the visits to Galilee function more as retreats (Jn 1,43; 4,1–2.43 f. 54; 7,1.9). During these visits to be sure the two Cana miracles are performed, as well as the bread miracle and the subsequent discourse. Only the latter gives rise to any opposition, whereas the Jerusalem signs seem to generate major controversy (chs. 5, 9, 11). The effect of this change of focus is to present Jerusalem and the Ἰουδαῖοι associated with it in a very negative light and to shine the spotlight on the obstacles

---

243–57, who sees several different phases of the Johannine community mirrored in their presentation within the gospel.

to faith in the Johannine perspective. A culpable blindness is the root cause, which inhibits recognising a prophet in his own country (4,44), or as the ironic conclusion to the Book of the Signs puts it: 'They loved the praise (δόξαν) of men more than the glory (δόξαν) of God' (12,43). The very brevity of the Galilean reports by contrast highlight the uncomplicated nature of their acceptance and serves only to underline the qualities that are demanded for true faith to be possible.

This contrast between the two fundamental attitudes comes to its most pointed expression in the discussion that followed Jesus' great self-declaration 'on the last and great day of the feast' of Tabernacles (Jn 7,37 f.). The proclamation gives rise to a dialogue in which the identity of Jesus as Messiah and Prophet comes under discussion.[18] That the outcome is likely to be negative is signalled by the narrator who explains for the ideal reader that Jesus' proclamation concerned the gift of the Spirit which had not yet been given; yet later we hear of the importance of the Spirit to lead the community into a proper remembrance of Jesus' words (Jn 14,26). The Pharisees and chief priests (a little later the rulers) reject any identification of Jesus with either of these expected figures on the basis that neither the Messiah nor a Prophet could come from Galilee according to the Scriptures, of which they consider themselves to be the expert interpreters. As such they are dismissive of this 'crowd who do not know the law', and are, therefore, accursed. The slur on the crowd merely reiterates a similar implied aspersion cast on Jesus himself earlier in the same visit to Jerusalem: 'How is it that this man has learning when he has never studied?' (Jn 7,15 f.). There is deep irony here since the scholastic superiority of the Pharisees dismisses any claims that Jesus might be the prophet, while their own servants, sent to arrest him, return declaring that 'No man ever spoke like this man' (Jn 7,46). The ideal reader is only too well aware from the outset that preoccupation with the human origins of the Messiah could never disclose the true identity of the Johannine Jesus which was in God (see e.g., Jn 6,42). Yet the servants are closer to the truth in recognising the unique quality of Jesus' words, for as Peter had declared in terms of the full-blown Johannine confession: 'You have the words of eternal life' (Jn 6,68).

There is no idealisation of Galilee, or for that matter, Galileans in the Fourth Gospel. A Galilean is one who is open to the journey of faith, not one that has arrived already. Nathanael finds a counterpart in the 'Ιουδαῖοι who though never actually identified with Galilee, reject Jesus in the synagogue at Capernaum (Jn 6,59). Nicodemus, a teacher in Israel, had called for an honest appraisal of Jesus in accordance with the law,

---

[18] See especially W. Meeks, 'Galilee and Judea in the Fourth Gospel,' *JBL* 85 (1966) 159–69.

only to be rejected as being in error and being a Galilean also (Jn 7,52). With typical Johannine contrast of opposites there is no possibility of any meeting of minds. Disciple of Jesus and disciple of Moses are utterly incompatible, and yet the Johannine Christ could claim: 'Moses wrote of me' (Jn 5,46) and the narrator can comment at the close of the Book of the Signs: 'Isaiah saw his glory and spoke of him' (Jn 12,41). The passage from Isaiah that is cited is not the oracle of salvation for the north, which we have been suggesting as a pre-text for both Mark and John. It would have provided the perfect riposte to those who argued from their superior knowledge of Scripture that neither a prophet nor the Messiah could come from Galilee.

Conclusion

The tensions, real or fictive between Galilee as periphery and Jerusalem as cultic centre have left their mark on early Christian discourse about Jesus as this comes to expression in our gospels. By engaging two instances of such discourse, Mark and John, we have seen how each text has drawn on the geographical and religious polarity between the two regions in order to say something significant for Christian self-understanding in the world. Behind all these instances was the common intertext of Jesus' career in both its Galilean and Judean/Jerusalemite dimensions. Furthermore, the Isaian oracle of salvation for the north provided a common pre-text, with the aid of which the deep designs of God could be uncovered in the career of Jesus, the Galilean.

The evangelists have developed this common story line, each in his own distinctive manner. Matthew alone cites the passage, as a legitimating proof-text for his presentation of the career of Jesus as messianic, despite its deep Galilean attachments. Luke too was able to exploit the Galilean memory in a universalist direction, in line with the oracle's horizons. By contrast, Mark and John are more immediately concerned with the disclosive character of Jesus' earthly career and the challenges that this posed for Christian discipleship and authentic faith. The Isaian oracle provided a suitable pretext for this aspect of Jesus' ministry also, with its imagery of light shining in the darkness.

For both writers the tensions involved in the Galilee-Jerusalem contrasts provided the possibilities of elaborating on their understanding of discipleship in a contrasting but complementary manner. The invitation to return to Galilee in Mark underlines the radical detachment and social nature of following Jesus, in line with the Galilean narrative as a whole. The incomprehension of the disciples in the initial Galilean phase, with the promise of seeing Jesus on their return there after the Jerusalem experience of rejection and death, emphasised for all would-be disciples/readers that the possibility of finding 'the way' of Jesus as liberative within the world of human selfishness is least likely to occur at the centres of power, but rather at the margins. For John on the other hand, Galilean openness, unencumbered by any sense of superior, controlling knowledge, provided the only proper starting place for seeing in and through the career of Jesus both in Galilee and Jerusalem to an horizon that was in and with God.

Our reading of these two texts with a focus on their shared geographical outline and guided by the underlying prophetic pre-text has enabled us to uncover two contrasting but intimately related aspects of Christian life in the world, the active and the passive, the social and the contemplative. Each aspect urgently requires the other if we are not to engage in an activism without ultimate purpose or a mysticism that lacks social concern. Intertextual readings can help us, the experts, to rediscover the plain meaning of our texts for ourselves and for others. Our discipline requires such a new direction for the future even as we salute and appropriate the achievements of past methods of scholarly study of the Bible, a tradition to which Professor Neirynck has made his own distinctive and lasting contribution.

14. Christianity in Sepphoris and in Galilee

The renewal movement initiated by Jesus of Nazareth was rapidly transformed following his death by the transition from its rural base in Galilee to urban centres throughout the whole Mediterranean region. To the extent that in the first century Galilee was beginning to experience the effects of urbanisation emanating from Sepphoris and its rival city, Tiberias, as well as from the older cities on its perimeter, one might have expected that Christianity would have found a ready acceptance there also. Yet unambiguous evidence is lacking for the immediate post-Resurrection period, despite the gospels portrayal of the enthusiastic reception of Jesus by the Galilean crowds. In *Acts of the Apostles* Luke depicts the progress of the Christian mission northwards from Jerusalem to Antioch, concentrating largely on the cities of the coastal plain, mentioning Galilee only in passing (Acts 9,31). This could suggests that he had no real evidence on which to rely with regard to the new movement in Galilee in contrast to his treatment of the missionary activity of Philip and the apostles in Samaria (Acts 8,4–25).

A growing body of scholarly opinion ascribes the earliest gospel, *Q*, the putative collection of sayings of Jesus which may have undergone more than one edition, to a Galilean context, however.[1] Even if this were to be definitively established, however, the rejection experienced by the prophets of the *Q* Gospel at various Galilean centres, reflected in the document itself (*Q*Mt 10,19–20; 11,21–24; *Q*Lk 10,3.13–15; 12,11–12), suggests that they were not likely to have subsequently formed the nucleus of a permanently settled community of Christians, at least in Galilee.

Mark's Gospel has also been ascribed to a Galilean setting[2] particularly in view of the instruction by Jesus to the disciples to return to Galilee after the crucifixion (Mk 14,28; 16,7). Yet in the absence of absolute criteria for

---

[1] J. Kloppenborg, 'Literary Convention, Self Evidence and the Social History of the Q People,' *Semeia* 55 (1991) 81–88; B. Mack, *The Lost Gospel. The Book of Q and Christian Origins* (New York and San Francisco: HarperCollins, 1993) 51–68; J. Reed, 'The Social map of Q,' in *Conflict and Invention. Literary, Rhetorical and Social Studies on the Sayings Gospel Q*, ed. J. Kloppenborg (Valley Forge: Trinity Press International, 1995) 17–36.

[2] E. Lohmeyer, *Galiläa und Jerusalem*, FRLANT 34 (Göttingen: Vandenhoeck & Ruprecht, 1936) 37; W. Marxsen, *Der Evangelist Markus. Studien zur Redaktionsgeschichte des Evangeliums*, FRLANT 67 (Göttingen: Vandenhoeck & Ruprecht, 1959) 66–77.

relating texts to social realities, such claims must remain inconclusive, and southern Syria, rather than Galilee has become the preferred option for those who find the traditional Roman setting implausible.[3] Nothing in either Matthew's or Luke's Gospels suggests that either was directed to Galilean Christian communities despite the role that Galilee plays in the narrative framework of each.[4] The Fourth Gospel has a Jerusalem rather than a Galilean focus for the ministry of Jesus. The importance of Cana in Galilee as the centre of Jesus' activity in this gospel (rather than Capernaum as in the Synoptic gospels) might suggest a community of Jesus-followers in that village also at an early stage (Jn 2,1–11; 4,46). Nathanael who is said to come from Cana (Jn 21,2), but who is otherwise unknown, is listed among those who responded positively to Jesus' first appearance in Galilee, and a special revelation of 'greater things' is promised to him (Jn 1,45–51).[5]

Apart from the gospels, the only other early Christian document that has been tentatively associated with Galilean Christianity is the *Epistle of James*, on the basis of its rural imagery and its many echoes of the sayings of Jesus as these occur within the synoptic tradition.[6] The issue is complicated by our lack of knowledge of the author of this work. James, 'the brother of the Lord', might reasonably be assumed to have been a Galilean (Jn 7,1–7). He could, therefore, have retained some of his provincial outlook and interest, while being active in Jerusalem mostly, insofar as we are aware, notwithstanding the more general reference to the missionary activity of 'the brothers of the Lord', alluded to by Paul (1 Cor 9,5 f.). However, most recent scholarship sees the author of the epistle as a Hellenised Jew from the Diaspora proper, thereby diminishing considerably the possibility of direct Galilean associations of the work.[7]

---

[3] Thus for example G. Theissen, *The Gospels in Context. Social and Political History in the Synoptic Tradition* (Edinburgh: T. & T. Clark, 1992) 236–49; H. Clark Kee, *Community of the New Age. Studies in Mark's Gospel* (Philadelphia: Westminster Press, 1977) 77–105. For a criticism of the efforts to locate the gospels on the basis of internal evidence cf. E. Struthers Malbon, 'Galilee and Jerusalem: History and Literature in Markan Interpretation,' *CBQ* 44 (1982) 242–55.

[4] S. Freyne, *Galilee from Alexander the Great to Hadrian. A Study of Second Temple Judaism* (reprint, Edinburgh: T. & T. Clark, 1998) 360–72.

[5] R. Fortna, 'Theological Use of Locale in the Fourth Gospel,' in *Gospel Studies in Honour of S. E. Johnson,* ed. M. Shepphard and E. C. Hobbs, ATR Supplementary Series 3 (1974) 58–95, especially 76, note 61. Cf. also W. Meeks, 'Galilee and Judea in the Fourth Gospel,' *JBL* 85 (1996) 159–69, and J. Bassler, 'The Galileans: A Neglected Feature in Johannine Research,' *CBQ* 43 (1981) 243–57.

[6] L. E. Elliot-Binns, *Galilean Christianity* (London: SCM Press, 1956) 45–53.

[7] D. Edgar, *Has God not Chosen the Poor? The Social Setting of the Letter of James.* forthcoming, JSNT Supplement Series (Sheffield: Sheffield Academic Press).

If the gospels are at best inconclusive with regard to Galilean Christianity, the evidence from rabbinic sources raises different interpretative problems. Despite the fact that there has been a lively debate about the *minim* in Sepphoris[8], there must have been some followers of Jesus among them in light of the traditions concerning Jacob of Kefar Sekanyah (Shikhin), who is described as being a *thalmid* of Yeshua ben Panthera (or Yeshua *ha-nozri*, 'the Nazorean' in the parallel account: *t. Hul.* 2,24; *b. 'Abod. Zar.* 16b-17a). This is clearly a reference to Jesus of Nazareth since we know from Christian sources also of a contemporary report which claimed that Jesus was the child of an illicit union between his mother and a Roman soldier, named Panthera.[9] Jacob may indeed not have been a native of Sepphoris as S. Miller points out. However, the story of his meeting with Rabbi Eliezer in 'the upper street' of Sepphoris, where the famous Rabbi was arraigned before the governor for agreeing with a *minut* (unorthodox ruling) attributed to Yeshua by Jacob, points to hostility between the rabbinic sages and those of heterodox views, including presumably Jewish Christians. This Jacob should probably be identified with another of the same name, Jacob of Kefar Sama,[10] known as a healer in Yeshua's name who was prepared to heal Rabbi Eleazar ben Dama (*t. Hul.* 2,22f.; *y. Shabb.* 1,14b; *b. 'Abod. Zar.* 27b). In this instance his healing powers were rejected by Rabbi Ishmael.

Rabbinic stories are notoriously difficult to date even when referring to named sages, but they do indicate issues that were at stake at the time of the final editing of the various writings (third to fifth century CE). There were, it seems, Jewish followers of Jesus operating within the orbit of the rabbinic schools of lower Galilee who were less than popular with the rabbinic authorities there. The reason may have been partly due to fear of the Roman governor and the tight controls under which Jewish autonomy

---

[8] Thus, whereas A. Büchler, 'The *minim* of Sepphoris and Tiberias in the Second and Third Centuries,' in id., *Studies in Jewish History* (London: Oxford University Press, 1956) 245–74, has argued that the term refers to heathens opposed to Judaism and identifies many references in the sources with the inhabitants of the cities in question, S. Miller, 'The *minim* of Sepphoris Reconsidered,' *HTR* 86 (1993) 377–402, seeks to confine the number of *minim* at Sepphoris to a few non-conformist (from the point of view of the Rabbis) individuals who do not represent a Jewish Christian community in the city.

[9] Origen, *Contra Celsum*, 1,32, trans. H. Chadwick (Cambridge: Cambridge University Press, 1953) 31f.

[10] The identification of both Kefar Sama and Kefar Sekhanyah is uncertain. If the two names refer to the same place, as seems likely on the basis of the stories about Jacob, then Shikhin in lower Galilee is the most likely identification. Recently this site has been identified with Asochis of Josephus' writings and located about two kilometres north of Sepphoris: J. Strange, D. Groh, T. Longstaff, 'Excavations at Sepphoris: The Location and Identification of Shikhin,' Part I, *IEJ* 44 (1994) 216–27, and Part II, *IEJ* 45 (1995) 171–87.

could presume to operate, but also because of theological differences on various issues, including that of the messianic status of Jesus. Despite the fact that direct reference to Christians (even under such designations as 'heretics' or *nozrim*) are infrequent in the Rabbinic sources, there is literary evidence to suggest a larger and more influential presence of Jewish Christians in Galilee and Sepphoris than might initially appear. Such discussions as those concerning 'the curse on the heretics' (whether this is dealing with Jewish Christians only or has a wider reference) expelling them from participation in the synagogue worship,[11] as well as various doctrinal debates among the Rabbis, allow us to catch some glimpses of the issues at stake for Jews and Christians even after the so-called 'parting of the ways' of the two faiths in the second century CE.[12]

Among early Christian writers on heresy, Epiphanius (315–403 CE), the Palestinian-born bishop of Salamis, appears to have relevant, first-hand information about a group of Jewish Christians called Nazarenes, even if his rigid orthodoxy colours his account.[13] Along with other writers (e.g., Jerome), he locates them in Beroea, Pella and Cocabe in Transjordan (modern Golan and Hauran). It is tempting to establish links between this group and the Galilean *minim/nozrim* from Sepphoris and Kefar Sekhanyah. According to Epiphanius their orthodox belief in Jesus born of the Virgin combined with a strict observance of the Jewish law including circumcision, gave rise to hatred from the Jewish authorities (*Pan.* 29.6,7), similar to that reflected in the rabbinic sources for Sepphoris. Nor is the idea of a migration from Galilee to Transjordan improbable on other grounds. Recent analysis of pottery finds at various sites in the Golan indicates the presence of considerable amounts of Galilean ware there.[14] These finds presuppose some trading links between the two regions, thereby facilitating contacts between adherents of similar groups. As Jerome, while acknowledging their orthodox views on the nature and person of Christ, remarks: 'though they wish to be both Jews and Christians, they are neither Jews nor Christians' (*Ep.* 112,13). Indeed the discovery of lintels with

---

[11] R. Kimmelman, '*Birkath ha-Minim* and the Lack of Evidence for a Christian Jewish Prayer in Late Antiquity,' in *Jewish and Christian Self-Definition*, ed. E. P. Sanders, A. I. Baumgarten and A. Mendelson, 3 vols. (London: SCM Press, 1981), vol. 2, 226–44; W. Horbury, 'The Benediction of the *Minim* and Early Jewish-Christian Controversy,' *JTS* 33 (1982) 19–61.

[12] M. Simon, *Verus Israel: A Study of Relations between Christians and Jews in the Roman Empire* (Oxford: Oxford University Press, 1986) 183–96.

[13] Translations of Epiphanius' work are from P. R. Amidon, *The Panarion of St Epiphanius, Bishop of Salamis. Selected Passages* (New York: Oxford University Press, 1990).

[14] D. Adan-Bayewitz, *Common Pottery in Roman Galilee. A Study of Local Trade* (Ramat-Gan: Bar-Ilan University Press, 1993) 166–71 and 211–19.

what appear to be Christian (crucifix) and Jewish (menorah) symbols in the region of Transjordan could add further weight to such an hypothesis.[15]

The literary evidence leaves many unanswered questions about Christians in Galilee: the fate of the *Q* missionaries in the turbulent years leading up to the first revolt, if in fact they continued to operate in Galilee until 66 CE; the origins and subsequent history of the *nozrim* in Sepphoris; their possible relations with the followers of James, the brother of the Lord, who according to Eusebius (*Hist. Eccl.* III, v. 4), fled Jerusalem in 62 CE after James' violent death, and settled in Pella (one of the sites in Transjordan associated with the Nazarenes, according to Epiphanius); the influence, if any, of gentile Christianity prior to the conversion of the Roman Emperor Constantine in 312 CE. Archaeological investigation of Christian remains can throw light on some of these questions, particularly in view of more recent advances in that discipline in relating its data from stratified digs at particular sites to the wider, regional surveys, thereby enabling more general conclusions to be drawn on the social and cultural environment[16]

It is only with the Byzantine era (from the middle of the fourth century CE) that clear evidence of a distinctive Christian architecture and iconography begins to emerge. The Jewish population of Galilee had increased considerably in the wake of the Bar Cochba war against Rome (132–35 CE), and this trend continued in subsequent centuries on the basis of the number of settlements where synagogue remains have been recovered. These settlements appear to follow a clear pattern of concentration in eastern upper Galilee and western Golan.[17] Once a Christian presence begins to be discernible in the material culture, very few, if any traces of this are to be found in the Jewish areas, whereas in western Galilee (both upper and lower), bordering the territories of the cities of Tyre and Akko/Ptolemais, a considerable number of remains of Christian churches and burial places

---

[15] C. Dauphin, 'Jewish and Christian Communities in the Roman and Byzantine Gaulanitis: A Study of Evidence from Archaeological Surveys,' *PEQ* 114 (1982) 129–42; id., 'Farj en Gaulanitide: Refuge judéo-Chrétien?' *Proche Orient Chrétien* 34 (1984) 233–45. Cf., however, Z. Ma'oz, 'Comments on Jewish and Christian Communities in Byzantine Palestine,' *PEQ* 117 (1985) 59–67, who is highly critical of Dauphin's claims of mixed communities of Jews and Christians in the Byzantine period.

[16] E. Meyers, 'Early Judaism and Christianity in the Light of Archaeology,' *BA* 51 (1988) 69–79; id. 'The Challenge of Hellenism for Early Judaism and Christianity,' *BA* 55 (1992) 84–91.

[17] E. Meyers, J. Strange and D. Groh, 'The Meiron Excavation Project: Archaeological Survey in Galilee and Golan, 1976,' *BASOR* 230 (1978) 20; D. Urman, *The Golan. A Profile of a Region during the Roman and Byzantine Periods* (Oxford: BAR International Series 269, 1985) 75–140; Y. Tsafrir, L. di Segni, and J. Green, *Tabula Imperii Romani. Iudaea-Palestina. Maps and Gazetteer* (Jerusalem: Israel Academy of the Sciences and the Humanities, 1994), especially maps of churches and synagogues.

have come to light.[18] A similar pattern occurs to the north and east of the exclusively Jewish territories where remains of Christian churches occur in the Hermon region and in eastern Golan.[19] On the basis of this evidence it would seem that Christianity entered Galilee by way of the territories of the surrounding cities, making little if any inroads in the traditional Jewish regions.[20] The beginnings of such a development may have occurred in the second and third centuries already, even if there is no datable architectural evidence to prove this. Only very gradually does evidence of a Jewish presence in the Christian areas of western Galilee emerge in the 6th and 7th centuries.

Most scholarly attention has inevitably been devoted to those areas of Galilee where evidence of both Jewish and Christian presence has been uncovered. Epiphanius relates that a Jewish convert to Christianity, Joseph of Scythopolis, was deputed by the Emperor Constantine to build churches of Christ 'in the cities and villages of the Jews . . . where no one had been able, because there were no pagans, Samaritans or Christians in them. Especially in Tiberias, Diocaesarea (Sepphoris), Nazareth and Capernaum they take care to have no foreigners living among them' (*Pan.* 30.11,9f.). While scarcely accurate for Sepphoris and Tiberias at least, with their mixed populations from the first century already, this account nevertheless supports the suggestion of separate Jewish and non-Jewish areas in the Galilee, a pattern that becomes visible in the material remains from the Byzantine period, as already noted. It also confirms that the building of churches in the wake of the Constantinian take-over occurred in Galilee also.

This process of establishing a visible Christian presence raises the issue of the relationship between the fourth-century developments and the earlier

---

[18] M. Aviam, 'Galilee: the Hellenistic to Byzantine Periods,' in *NEAEHL* 4 vols., ed. E. Stern (Jerusalem: The Israel Exploration Society, 1994), vol. 2, 455–58; C. Dauphin, *La Palestine Byzantine du IVe au VII Siécle. Peuplement et Population*, 3 vols. (Oxford: BAR International Series 726, 1998), vol. 2, figures 43, 57, 74.

[19] Z. Ma'oz, 'Comments on Jewish and Christian Communities,' 65f.

[20] Cf. the important discussion of C. Markschies, 'Stadt und Land. Beobachtungen zu Ausbreitung und Inkulturation des Christentums in Palästina,' in *Römische Reichsreligion und Provinzialreligion*, ed. H. Cancik and J. Rüpke (Tübingen: J. C. B. Mohr, 1997) 265–98, who argues that local factors continued to inform the inculturation of Christianity in Palestine, even after the Constantinian development of the 'Reichsreligion' in the fourth century, which was heavily influenced by the urbanisation process in the region. As far as Galilee is concerned he notes its slow integration, with Chabulon on the border with Ptolemais being the only possible Galilean location mentioned in the list of bishops attending the Council of Nicea (274f.). However, Markschies recognises that this does not preclude the survival of pre-Constantinian Christian communities, especially in the villages and the need for further study of local and regional variations. Cf. B. Bagatti, *Antichi Villaggi Christiani di Galilea* (Jerusalem: Franciscan Publications, 1971).

traces of a Jewish Christianity in the rabbinic and other literary sources. According to Epiphanius, Joseph attempted to transform a temple of Hadrian in Tiberias into a Christian church but encountered difficulties with the project. The architectural remains of fifth-century churches at both Nazareth and Capernaum have been interpreted as evidence of a similar pattern of transformation of existing structures, previously belonging to Jewish Christians in both towns. At Nazareth, the remains of a small, pre-Constantinian church 'on the plan of a synagogue' with a baptismal font as well as mosaics and graffiti attributed to Jewish Christians, were found under the mosaics of the later Byzantine church.[21] Prior to that again, the process of isolating and transforming three caves that had been in ordinary domestic use from the early iron age into sacred grottos with Christian inscriptions and drawings can be discerned from the pottery and plaster remains.[22] The Byzantine church, the remains of which were uncovered in the excavations in preparation for the building of the present basilica, is also attested by the anonymous Christian pilgrim from Piacenza who stated c. 570 CE that the house of Mary is a basilica. A similar three-stage process has been suggested for Capernaum, namely, a house church (again with Jewish Christian graffiti) from the first century CE; an extended *insula sacra*, or sacred precinct, surrounded by a wall in the fourth century (also mentioned by the Piacenza pilgrim as the house of Peter), and an octagonal-shaped basilica built over it in the fifth century.[23]

It has not thus far at least been possible to trace fully a similar trajectory for Christians at Sepphoris. A dedicatory inscription, probably from the Roman period, which had frequently been taken as a *chi/rho* sign emanating from the Jewish Christians in the city, has now been interpreted as an abbreviation rather than as a Christian symbol.[24] Likewise, an inscription discovered in 1959, which Michael Avi-Yonah first thought had referred to the restoration in the time of Marcellinus (518 CE) of a church, is now considered to be associated with a municipal building.[25] However, the remains of a Byzantine church have been discovered, which the archaeologists have attributed to bishop Eutropius (late fifth or early sixth century

---

[21] B. Bagatti and V. Tzaferis, 'Nazareth' in *NEAEHL* vol. 3, 1103–5; V. Corbo, 'La Chiesa-Synagoga dell' Annunziata a Nazaret,' *Liber Annuus* 37 (1967) 333–48.

[22] B. Bagatti, *Excavations at Nazareth,* vol. I, *From the Beginning Until the Twelfth Century* (Jerusalem: Franciscan Press, 1969) 174–218.

[23] V. Corbo, *Cafarnao I. Gli Edifici della Città* (Jerusalem: Franciscan Press, 1975) 26–58, and id., 'The Church of the House of St. Peter,' in *Ancient Churches Revealed,* ed. Y. Tsafrir (Jerusalem: The Israel Exploration Society, 1993) 71–76.

[24] L. Roth-Gerson, *The Greek Inscriptions from the Synagogues in Eretz Israel* (Jerusalem: The Israel Exploration Society, 1987, [Hebrew]) 106.

[25] M. Avi-Yonah, 'A Sixth-Century Inscription from Sepphoris,' *IEJ* 11 (1961) 184–87. Cf. now E. Netzer and Z. Weiss, 'Sepphoris,' in *NEAEHL* 4, 1327.

CE), because of its proximity to the main streets which had been renovated in the time of this man. In a nearby Greek inscription which honours his achievement on behalf of the city he is described as 'our most saintly father, Eutropius, the Episcopus.'[26] The fact that this Christian bishop is associated with the renovation of the city as well as the building of a Christian basilica is consonant with the increasing civic importance of the Greek-speaking Christian church generally in the Byzantine period. In view of the literary evidence about the Jewish Christians at Sepphoris, it would come as no surprise if further archaeological evidence should come to light, either at this location or elsewhere in Sepphoris, confirming the pattern of transition from a Jewish to a Gentile Christian church, even though Sepphoris lacked any clear association with the earthly life of Jesus, unlike both Nazareth and Capernaum. The tradition linking the city with Anne and Joachim, the parents of the Virgin Mary, is preserved in the Crusader church of Saint Anne, but the legend itself is first recorded c. 570 CE by the pilgrim of Piacenza, and is often repeated by pilgrims subsequently.[27]

The process of transition from Jewish Christian to gentile Christian church in Palestine can be seen as a gradual and peaceful transformation on the analogy with what, according to Eusebius (*Hist. Eccl.* IV, v. 1–2), occurred at Jerusalem.[28] Alternatively, taking a cue from the Christian writers who treat the Jewish Christians, even the Nazarenes with their orthodox views about Christ, as heretics, the development may be understood as a new beginning after Constantine, signalling large-scale demographic changes also.[29] Unlike Jerusalem, where a list of pre-Constantinian Jewish Christian bishops is known to Eusebius, no Galilean bishop is mentioned in the list of those attending the Church Council of Nicea (323 CE), the first references being to the bishop of Tiberias at the Council of Ephesus (449 CE) and the bishop of Diocaesarea (Sepphoris) at the Council of

---

[26] E. Netzer and Z. Weiss, 'New Evidence for Late-Roman and Byzantine Sepphoris,' in *The Roman and Byzantine Near East: Some Recent Archaeological Evidence,* ed. J. Humphreys (Ann Arbor: JRA Supplementary Series 14, 1995) 164–76, especially 170–73; id., 'Hellenistic and Roman Sepphoris: The Historical Evidence,' in *Sepphoris in Galilee. Crosscurrents of Culture,* ed. R. Martin Nagy et al. (Raleigh, NC: North Carolina Museum of Art, 1996) 29–38.

[27] J. Folda, 'The Crusader Period and the Church of St. Anne at Sepphoris,' in *Sepphoris in Galilee,* 101–10; S. Miller, 'Sepphoris, the well-remembered City,' *BA* 55 (1992) 74–83.

[28] Meyers, 'Early Judaism and Christianity in the Light of Archaeology,' 71; C. Dauphin, 'De l'Église de la Circoncision à l'Église de la Gentilitè,' *Liber Annuus* 43 (1993) 223–42, especially 240–42.

[29] R. L. Wilkin, *The Land Called Holy: Palestine in Christian History and Thought* (New Haven: Yale University Press, 1992) 85; J. Taylor, *Christians and the Holy Places. The Myth of Jewish-Christian Origins* (Oxford: Oxford University Press, 1993) 18–42.

Jerusalem (519 CE). Furthermore, in view of the widening gulf between mainline Christians and Jews in Palestine, especially after the abortive Jewish revolt against Rome under Gallus (351–52 CE), it is difficult to imagine how Jewish Christians could possibly have been accommodated among an increasingly gentile population in lower Galilee.[30] The likelihood must rather be that they, like their orthodox Jewish counterparts, migrated from lower Galilee to a more congenial environment, possibly to eastern Golan.[31]

Neither the Christian nor the Jewish presence in Palestine ended with the Muslim conquest of 634–40 CE as both churches and synagogues continued to be built throughout the seventh and into the eighth century CE.[32] Many Christian churches had already been destroyed during the Persian invasion earlier in the century.[33] The evidence from coins and pottery suggests a gradual turning toward the east in terms of economic links and the consequent cutting of ties with the west for Palestinian Jews and Christians alike. Pilgrimages to the holy places, including those in Galilee continued until Jerusalem was captured by the Seljuk Turks in 1071 CE, giving rise to the Christian crusades. But that is a very different story. ·

---

[30] B. Geller Nathanson, 'Jews, Christians and the Gallus Revolt in Fourth Century Palestine,' *BA* 49 (1986) 26–36.

[31] C. Dauphin, 'Jewish and Christian Communities in the Roman and Byzantine Gaulanitis,' especially 137; Dauphin, 'Encore des judéo-chrétiens au Golan,' in *Early Christianity in Context: Monuments and Documents*, ed. F. Manns and E. Alliata (Jerusalem: Franciscan Press, 1993) 69–84.

[32] D. Groh, 'The Religion of the Empire: Christianity from Constantine to the Arab Conquest,' in *Christianity and Rabbinic Judaism. A Parallel History of their Origins and Early Development,* ed. H. Shanks (Washington: Biblical Archaeology Society, 1992) 302 f.

[33] C. Dauphin and G. Edelstein, 'The Byzantine Church at Nahariya,' and M. Aviam, 'Horvat Hesheq: A Church in the Upper Galilee,' in *Ancient Churches Revealed,* 53 and 65 respectively.

Bibliography

Adan-Bayewitz, D. *Common Pottery in Roman Galilee. A Study of Local Trade.* Ramat-Gan: Bar-Ilan University Press, 1993.
———. 'Kefar Hananya.' *IEJ* 37 (1987) 178–79, and 39 (1989) 98–99.
Adan-Bayewitz, D. and I. Perlman. 'The Local Trade of Sepphoris in the Roman Period.' *IEJ* 40 (1990) 153–72.
Adan-Bayewitz, D. and M. Aviam. 'Iotapata, Josephus and the Siege of 67: Preliminary Report on the 1992–94 seasons.' *JRA* 10 (1997) 131–65.
Aharoni, Y. 'Galilee, Upper.' In *Encylopedia of Archaeological Excavations in the Holy Land*, ed. M. Avi-Yonah, 4 vols., vol. II, 406–8. London: Oxford University Press, 1976.
Alcock, S., ed. *The Early Roman Empire and the East.* Oxford: Oxbrow Monographs 95, 1997.
Alon, G. *Jews, Judaism and the Classical World.* Jerusalem: The Magnes Press, 1977.
Alt, A. *Kleine Schriften zur Geschichte des Volkes Israels.* 3 vols. Munich: C. H. Beck 1953–64.
Amidon, P. R. *The Panarion of St Epiphanius, Bishop of Salamis. Selected Passages.* New York: Oxford University Press, 1990.
Anderson, G. *Sage, Saint and Sophist. Holy Men and their Associates in the Early Roman Empire.* London and New York: Routledge, 1994.
Applebaum, S. 'The Settlement Pattern of Western Samaria from Hellenistic and Byzantine Periods.' In *Landscape and Pattern. An Archaeological Survey of Samaria 800 B.C.E.–636 C.E.*, ed. S. Dar, 257–69. Oxford: BAR International Series 308 i, 1986.
Ashton, J. 'The Identity and Function of the 'ΙΟΥΔΑΙΟΙ in the Fourth Gospel.' *NovT* 27 (1985) 40–75.
———. *Understanding the Fourth Gospel.* Oxford: Oxford University Press, 1991.
Aviam, M. 'Galilee: the Hellenistic and Byzantine Periods.' In *NEAEHL* 4 vols., ed. E. Stern, vol. 2, 455–58. Jerusalem: The Israel Exploration Society, 1994.
———. 'Horvat Hesheq: A Church in the Upper Galilee.' In *Ancient Churches Revealed*, ed. Y. Tsafrir, 65. Jerusalem: The Israel Exploration Society, 1993.
Avi-Yonah, M. *Art in Ancient Palestine. Selected Studies.* Jerusalem: The Magnes Press, 1981.
———. *The Holy Land from the Persian to the Arab Conquest. A Historical Geography.* Grand Rapids: Baker Books, 1966.
———. 'Mt Carmel and the God of Baalbek.' *IEJ* 2 (1951) 118–24.
———. 'A Sixth-Century Inscription from Sepphoris.' *IEJ* 11 (1961) 184–87.
———. 'Syrian Gods at Ptolemais-Acco.' *IEJ* 9 (1959) 1–12.
Bagatti, B. *Antichi Villaggi Christiani di Galilea.* Collectio Minor 13. Jerusalem: Franciscan Publications, 1971.
———. *Excavations at Nazareth*, vol. I, *From the Beginning Until the Twelfth Century.* Jerusalem: Franciscan Press, 1969.
Bagatti, B. and Tzaferis, V. 'Nazareth.' In *NEAEHL* vol. 3, 1103–5.

Bagnall, R. *Egypt in Late Antiquity.* Princeton: Princeton University Press, 1993.

Bammel, E. 'The Revolution theory from Reimarus to Brandon.' In *Jesus and the Politics of His Day*, ed. E. Bammel and C. F. D. Moule, 11–68. Cambridge: Cambridge University Press, 1984.

Barag, D. 'Tyrian Currency in Galilee.' *INJ* 6/7 (1982/3) 7–13.

Barker, G., and J. Lloyd, eds. *Roman Landscapes: Archaeological Surveys in the Mediterranean Region.* Archaeological Monographs of the British School at Rome 2. London: British School at Rome, 1991.

Barker, M. *The Older Testament: The Survival of Themes from the Ancient Royal Cult in Sectarian Judaism and Early Christianity.* London: SPCK, 1987.

Bartlett, J. R., ed. *Archaeology and Biblical Interpretation.* Routledge: London, 1997.

Barzano, A. 'Giusto di Tiberiade.' In *ANRW*, II, *Principat*, 20.1, ed. H. Temporini and W. Haase, 337–58. Berlin and New York: de Gruyter, 1986.

Bassler, J. 'The Galileans: A Neglected Feature in Johannine Research.' *CBQ* 43 (1981) 243–57.

Batey, R. 'Is not this the Carpenter?' *NTS* 30 (1984) 249–58.

———. 'Jesus and the Theatre.' *NTS* 30 (1984) 563–74.

———. *Jesus and the Forgotten City. New Light on Sepphoris and the Urban World of Jesus.* Grand Rapids: Baker Books, 1991.

Bauer, W. 'Jesus der Galiläer.' In *Festgabe für Adolf Jülicher*, 16–34. Tübingen, 1927. Reprinted in *Aufsätze und Kleine Schriften*, ed. G. Strecker, 91–108. Tübingen: J.C.B. Mohr, 1967.

Baumbach, G. 'Zeloten und Sikarier.' *TLZ* 40 (1965) 727–40.

Ben David A., *Jerusalem und Tyros. Ein Beitrag zur palästinensischen Münz- und Wirtschaftsgeschichte.* Basel: Kyklos-Verlag, 1969.

Berlin, A. 'From Monarchy to Markets.' *BASOR* 306 (1997) 75–86.

———. 'The Plain Wares.' In *Tel Anafa II,i. The Hellenistic and Roman Pottery*, ed. S. Herbert, 1–36. Ann Arbor: *JRA* and Kelsey Museum, 1997.

Berman, D. '*Hasidim* in Rabbinic Tradition.' In *SBLASP 1979*, ed. P. Achtemeier, 15–33. Missoula: Scholars Press, 1979.

Bertram, W. 'Der Hellenismus in der Urheimat des Evangeliums.' *ARW* 32 (1935) 265–81.

Betz, H. D. 'Jesus and the Cynics. Survey and Analysis of a Hypothesis.' *JR* 74 (1994) 453–75.

Betz, O., K. Haacher and M. Hengel, eds. *Josephus-Studien. Festschrift Otto Michel.* Göttingen: Vandenhoeck & Ruprecht, 1974.

Beuken, W. 'Did Israel need the Messiah?' In *Messianism through History. Concilium*, ed. W. Beuken, S. Freyne and A. Weiler, 3–13. London: SCM Press, 1993.

Beuken, W., S. Freyne and A. Weiler, eds. *The Bible and its Readers, Concilium.* London: SCM, 1991.

Bickerman, E. *From Ezra to the Last of the Maccabees.* New York: Shocken Books, 1962.

Bilde, P. *Flavius Josephus between Jerusalem and Rome. His Life, his Works, and their Importance.* JSP Supplement Series 2. Sheffield: Sheffield Academic Press, 1988.

Biran, A. 'The Dancer from Dan, the Empty Tomb and the Altar Room.' *IEJ* 36 (1986) 168–87.

———. 'To the God who is in Dan.' In *Temples and High Places in Biblical Times*, ed. A. Biran, 142–51. Jerusalem: HUC-JIR, 1981.

Biran, A. and Naveh, J. 'An Aramaic Stele Fragment from Tel Dan.' *IEJ* 43 (1993) 81–98.

———. 'The Tel Dan Inscription: A New Fragment.' *IEJ* 45 (1995) 1–18.

Birnbaum, S. 'Bar Kokhba and Akiba.' *PEQ* 86 (1954) 23–33.

————. 'The Zealots: The Case for Revaluation.' *JRS* 61 (1971) 155–70.

Black, M. 'Judas of Galilee and Josephus' Fourth Philosophy.' In *Josephus-Studien. Festschrift Otto Michel*, ed. O. Betz, K. Haacher and M. Hengel, 45–54. Göttingen: Vandenhoeck & Ruprecht, 1974.

Boid, R. M. (N. Saraf). 'Use, Authority, and Exegesis of Mikra in Samaritan Tradition.' In *Mikra. Text, Translation, Reading and Interpretation of the Hebrew Bible in Ancient Judaism and Early Christianity*, ed. Martin Jan Mulder, 595–633. CRINT. Assen: van Gorcum; Philadelphia: Fortress Press, 1988.

Bokser, B. 'Wonder-Working and the Rabbinic Tradition: the Case of Hanina ben Dosa.' *JSJ* 16 (1985) 42–92.

Bottini, C., L. di Segni and E. Alliata, eds. *Christian Archaeology in the Holy Land. New Discoveries. Essays in Honour of Virgilio C. Corbo*, Studium Biblicum Franciscanum, Collectio Maior 36. Jerusalem: Franciscan Printing Press, 1990.

Brandon, S. G. F. *Jesus and the Zealots*. Manchester: The University Press, 1967.

Bremmer, J. 'Pauper or Patroness. The Widow in the Early Christian Church.' In *Between Poverty and Pyre. Moments in the History of Widowhood*, ed. J. Bremmer and L. van den Bosch, 31–57. London and New York: Routledge, 1995.

————. 'Why did Early Christianity attract Upper-Class Women?' In *Fructus Centesimus. Mélanges offerts a Gerard J. M. Barrtelink*, ed. A. A. R. Bastiaensen, A. Hilhorst and C. H. Kneepkens, 37–47. Steenbrugis: In Abbatia S. Petri, 1989.

Brooke, G. '4Q Testament of Levi (?) and the Messianic Servant High Priest.' In *From Jesus to John. Essays on Jesus and New Testament Christology in Honour of Marinus de Jonge.'* ed. M. De Boer, 83–100. JSNT Supplement Series 84. Sheffield: Sheffield Academic Press, 1993.

Brown, R. E. *The Community of the Beloved Disciple: The Life, Loves and Hates of an Individual Church in the New Testament*. London: Chapman, 1979. 109–23.

Bruneau, P. 'Les Israelites de Délos et la Juivrie Délienne.' *BCH* 106 (1982) 465–504.

Büchler, A. 'The *minim* of Sepphoris and Tiberias in the Second and Third Centuries.' In *Studies in Jewish History*, ed. A. Büchler, 245–74. London: Oxford University Press, 1956.

Büchler, A. *Der Galiläische 'am ha-'aretz des Zweiten Jahrhunderts*. Reprint, Hildesheim: G. Olms, 1968.

————. *Types of Jewish Palestinian Piety from 70 B.C.E. – 70 C.E. The Ancient Pious Man*. London: Jewish College Publications, 1922.

Buehler, W. *The Pre-Herodian Civil War and Social Debate*. Basel: Rheinhardtverlag 1974.

Bull, R. J. 'An Archaeological Footnote to "Our Fathers worshiped on this Mountain".' *NTS* 23 (1977) 460–62.

Bultmann, R. *The History of the Synoptic Tradition*. Oxford: Blackwell, 1968.

Burnett, F. W. and G. A. Philips. 'Palm Re(a)ding and the Big Bang: Origins and Development of the Jesus Traditions.' *RelSRev* 18 (1992) 296–99.

Burridge, K. L. *New Heaven, New Earth*. Oxford: Blackwell, 1969.

Byatt, A. 'Josephus and Population Numbers in First-Century Palestine.' *PEQ* 105 (1973) 51–60

Cameron, R., ed. *The Apocryphal Jesus and Christian Origins, Semeia* 49 (1990).

Cancik, H., and J. Rüpke, eds. *Römische Reichsreligion und Provinzialreligion*. Tübingen: J. C. B. Mohr, 1997.

Carney, T. F. *The Shape of the Past, Models and Antiquity*. Lawrence KS: Coronado Press, 1975.

Case, Shirley Jackson. 'Jesus and Sepphoris.' *JBL 45* (1926) 14–22.

Catchpole, D. *The Search for Q*. Edinburgh: T. & T. Clark, 1993.

Charlesworth, J. H., ed. *Jesus' Jewishness. Exploring the Place of Jesus in Early Judaism.* New York: Crossroad, 1991.

———, ed. *The Messiah. Developments in Earliest Judaism and Christianity.* Minneapolis: Fortress Press, 1992.

———, ed. *What has Archaeology to do with Faith?* Philadelphia: Fortress Press, 1992.

Chilton, B. *A Galilean Rabbi and his Bible. Jesus' Use of the Interpreted Scripture of his Time.* Wilmington: Glazier, 1984.

———. *The Isaiah Targum.* The Aramaic Bible, vol. 11. Edinburgh: T. & T. Clark, 1987.

———. 'Kingdom Come, Kingdom Sung: Voices in the Gospels.' *Forum* 3/2 (1987) 51–75.

Clermont-Ganneau, C. *Recueil d'archaeologie orientale,* 5 vols. Paris, 1903.

Coggins, R. J. *Samaritans and Jews. The Origins of Samaritanism Reconsidered.* Oxford: Blackwell, 1985.

———. 'The Samaritans in Josephus.' In *Josephus, Judaism and Christianity,* ed. L. H. Feldman and G. Hata, 257–73. Leiden: Brill, 1987.

Cohen, S. D. 'Crossing the Boundary and Becoming a Jew.' *HTR* 82 (1989) 13–33.

———. 'Ἰουδαῖοις τὸ γένος and Related Expressions in Josephus.' In *Josephus and the History of the Greco-Roman Period. Essays in Memory of Morton Smith,* ed. F. Pavente and J. Sievers, 22–38. Leiden: Brill, 1994.

———. 'Ioudaios: "Judean" and "Jew" in Susanna, First Maccabees and Second Maccabees.' In *Geschichte – Tradition – Reflexion. Festschrift für Martin Hengel zum 70. Geburtstag,* ed. H. Cancik, H. Lichtenberger and P. Schäfer, 3 vols., vol 1, 211–20. Tübingen: J.C.B. Mohr, 1996.

———. *Josephus in Galilee and Rome. His Vita and Development as an Historian.* Leiden: Brill, 1979.

———. ' Religion, Ethnicity and Hellenism in the Emergence of Jewish Identity in Maccabean Palestine.' In *Religion and Religious Practice in the Seleucid Kingdom,* ed. P. Bilde et al., 204–23. Aarhus: University Press, 1990.

Colin, J. 'La Galilée de l'Évangile et les villes paiennes de la Palestine.'*Ant. Class.* 34 (1965) 183–92.

Collins, J. J. *The Apocalyptic Imagination. An Introduction to the Jewish Matrix of Christianity.* New York: Crossroad, 1984.

———. *Apocalypticism in the Dead Sea Scrolls.* London and New York: Routledge, 1997.

———. *The Scepter and the Star. The Messiahs of the Dead Sea Scrolls and Other Ancient Literature.* New York: Doubleday, 1995.

Conder, C. R., and A. H. Kitchener. *The Survey of Western Palestine I. Sheets I–VI, Galilee.* London: Palestine Exploration Fund, 1881.

Conzelmann, H. *The Theology of St. Luke.* London: Faber and Faber, 1960.

Coote, R., ed. *Elijah and Elisha in Socioliterary Perspective.* Atlanta: Scholars Press, 1992.

Corbo, V. *Cafarnao I. Gli Edifici della Citta.* Jerusalem: Franciscan Press, 1975.

———. 'La Chiesa-Synagoga dell' Annunziata a Nazaret.' *Liber Annuus* 37 (1967) 333–48.

———. 'The Church of the House of St. Peter.' In *Ancient Churches Revealed,* ed. Y. Tsafrir, 71–76. Jerusalem: The Israel Exploration Society, 1993.

Corley, K. *Private Women. Public Meals. Social Conflict in the Synoptic Tradition.* Peabody: Hendrickson, 1993.

Cotter, W. J. 'The Parable of the Children in the Market-Place, Q(Lk) 7:31–35: An Examination of the Parable's Image and Significance.' *NovT* 29 (1987) 289–304.

Cross, F. Moore. 'Aspects of Samaritan and Jewish History in the late Persian and Hellenistic Times.' *HTR* 59 (1966) 201–11.

Crossan, J. D. *Four Other Gospels: Shadows on the Contours of the Canon.* Minneapolis: Winston Press, 1985.

———. *The Historical Jesus. The Life of a Mediterranean Jewish Peasant.* Edinburgh: T. & T. Clark, 1991.

———. 'Materials and Methods in Historical Jesus Research.' *Forum* 4/4 (1988) 3–24.

Crown, A. 'Another Look at Samaritan Origins.' In *Essays in Honour of G. D. Sixdenier. New Samaritan Studies of the Societé D'Études Samaritaines,* ed. A. Crown and L. Davey, 133–56. University of Sydney Studies in Judaica 5. Sydney: Mandelbaum Publishing, 1995.

Crown, A., ed. *The Samaritans.* Tübingen: J. C. B. Mohr, 1989.

Culpepper, R. A. *Anatomy of the Fourth Gospel. A Study in Literary Design.* Philadelphia: Fortress Press, 1983.

D'Andrade, R. and C. Strauss, *Human Motives and Cultural Models.* Cambridge: Cambridge University Press, 1992.

D'Angelo, M. Rose 'Women in Luke-Acts: A Redactional View.' *JBL* 109 (1990) 529–36.

Dalman, G. *Orte und Wege Jesu.* Gütersloh: Gerd Mohn, 1924.

Dar, S. *Landscape and Pattern. An Archaeological Survey of Samaria 800 B.C.E.–636 C.E.* Oxford: BAR International Series 308 i, 1986.

Dar, S. *Settlements and Cult Sites on Mount Hermon, Israel: Iturean Culture in the Hellenistic and Roman Periods.* Oxford: BAR International Series 589, 1993.

Dauphin, C. 'Encore des judéo-chrétiens au Golan.' In *Early Christianity in Context: Monuments and Documents,* ed. F. Manns and E. Alliata, 69–84. Jerusalem: Franciscan Press, 1993.

———. 'De l'Église de la Circoncision à l'Église de la Gentilitè.' *Liber Annuus* 43 (1993) 223–42.

———. 'Farj en Gaulanitide: Refuge judéo-Chrétien?' *Proche Orient Chrétien* 34 (1984) 233–45.

———. 'Jewish and Christian Communities in the Roman and Byzantine Gaulanitis: A Study of Evidence from Archaeological Surveys.' *PEQ* 114 (1982) 129–42.

———. 'Les *komai* de Palestine.' *Proche Orient Chrétien* 37 (1987) 251–67.

———. *La Palestine Byzantine du IVe au VII Siécle: Peuplement et Population.* 3 vols. Oxford: BAR International Series 726, 1998.

Dauphin, C., and G. Edelstein. 'The Byzantine Church at Nahariya.' In *Ancient Churches Revealed,* ed. Y. Tsafrir, 53. Jerusalem: The Israel Exploration Society, 1993.

Dauphin, C., and S. Gibson. 'Ancient Settlements and their Landscapes: The Results of Ten Years of Survey on the Golan Heights (1978–88).' *Bulletin of the Anglo-Israel Archaeological Society* 12 (1992/3) 7–31.

Dauphin, C., and J. Schonfield, 'Settlements of the Roman and Byzantine Periods on the Golan Heights.' *IEJ* 33 (1983) 189–206.

de Jonge, H. J. 'The Historical Jesus' View of Himself and his Mission.' In *From Jesus to John. Essays on Jesus and New Testament Christology in Honour of Marinus de Jonge.'* ed. M. De Boer. JSNT Supplement Series 84. Sheffield: Sheffield Academic Press, 1993.

de Jonge, M. *Jesus the Servant Messiah.* New Haven: Yale University Press, 1991.

de Lange, N. *Origen and the Jews. Studies in Jewish-Christian Relations in third-century Palestine.* Cambridge: Cambridge University Press, 1976.

Deines, R. *Jüdische Steingefässe und pharisäische Frömmigkeit.* WUNT 52. Tübingen: J.C.B. Mohr, 1993.

Derrett, J. M. 'Law in the New Testament: *Si scandalizaverit te manus tua abscide ilium.*' *RIDA* 20 (1973) 11–41.

Dessel, J. P. 'Tel Ein Zippori and the Lower Galilee in the Late Bronze and Iron Ages: A Village Perspective.' In *Galilee through the Centuries: Confluence of Cultures*, ed. E. Meyers. Winona Lake: Eisenbrauns, 1999.

Dever, W. 'Will the Real Israel Please Stand Up? Archaeology and the Religions of Israel.' *BASOR* 298 (1996) 37–58.

Diakonoff, I. M. 'The Naval Power and Trade of Tyre.' *IEJ* 42 (1992) 168–93.

Donahue, J. R. 'Windows and Mirrors'. The Setting of Mark's Gospel' *CBQ* 57 (1995) 1–26.

Draisma, S., ed. *Intertextuality in Biblical Writings. Essays in Honour of Bas van Iersel.* Kampen: Uitgeversmaatschappij J. H. Kok, 1989.

Douglas, M. *Natural Symbols. Explorations in Cosmology.* New York: Pantheon, 1982.

Downing, F. G. *Cynics and Christian Origins.* Edinburgh: T. & T. Clark, 1992.

———. 'Cynics and Christians.' *NTS* 30 (1984) 584–93.

———. 'The Social Contexts of Jesus the Teacher: Construction or Reconstruction.' *NTS* 33 (1987) 439–51.

Drexler, H. 'Untersuchung zu Josephus und zur Geschichte des jüdischen Aufstandes, 66–70.' *Klio* 19 (1925) 277–312.

Duncan-Jones, R. *Structure and Scale in the Roman Economy.* Cambridge: Cambridge University Press, 1990.

Edgar, D. *Has God not Chosen the Poor? The Social Setting of the Letter of James.* Forthcoming, JSNT Supplement Series, Sheffield: Sheffield Academic Press.

Edwards, D. 'First-Century Urban/Rural Relations in Lower Galilee, Exploring the Archaeological and Literary Evidence.' In *SBLASP 1988*, ed. D. Lull, 169–82. Atlanta: Scholars Press, 1988.

———. 'The Socio-Economic and Cultural Ethos of the Lower Galilee in the First Century: Implications for the Nascent Jesus Movement.' In *The Galilee in Late Antiquity*, ed. L. Levine, 53–73. New York and Jerusalem: The Jewish Theological Seminary of America, 1992.

Edwards, D. and C. T. McCollough, eds. *Archaeology and the Galilee. Texts and Contexts in the Graeco-Roman and Byzantine Periods.* South Florida Studies in the History of Judaism 143. Atlanta: Scholars Press, 1997.

Elborgen, I. *Die Jüdische Gottesdienst in seiner geschichtlichen Entwicklung.* Reprint, Hildesheim: G. Olms, 1967.

Elliott, J. 'Social-Scientific Criticism of the New Testament: More on Models and Methods.' *Semeia* 32 (1986) 1–33.

———. *What is Social-Scientific Criticism?* Minneapolis: Fortress Press, 1993.

Elliott-Binns, L. E. *Galilean Christianity.* London: SCM Press, 1956.

Esler, P., ed. *Modeling Early Christianity: Social Scientific Studies of the New Testament in its Context.* London and New York: Routledge, 1995.

Feldman, L. 'How Much Greek in Jewish Palestine?' *HUCA* 57 (1986) 82–111.

———. *Studies in Hellenistic Judaism.* Leiden: Brill, 1996.

Fiensy, D. *The Social History of Palestine in the Herodian Period.* Lewiston NY: The Edwin Mellen Press, 1991.

Fine, S., ed. *Sacred Realm. The Emergence of the Synagogue in the Ancient World.* New York: Yeshiva University Museum; Oxford: Oxford University Press 1996.

Finkelstein, I. *The Archaeology of the Israelite Settlement.* Jerusalem: The Israel Exploration Society, 1988.

———. 'Ethnicity and Origin of Iron I Settlers in the Highlands of Canaan: Can the Real Israel Stand Up?' *BA* 59 (1996) 198–212.

Finley, M. 'The Ancient City from Fustel de Coulanges to Max Weber.' *CSSH* 19 (1981) 305–27.

———. *The Ancient Economy.* 2nd ed. London: Chatto and Windus, 1977.

Fischer, M., A. Ovadiah, and I. Roll. 'The Epigraphic Finds from the Roman Temple at Kedesh in the Upper Galilee.' *TA* 13 (1986) 60–66.

———. 'The Roman Temple at Kedesh, Upper Galilee: a Preliminary Study.' *TA* 11 (1984) 142–72.

Fitzmyer, J. *A Wandering Aramaean. Collected Aramaic Essays.* Missoula: Scholars Press, 1979.

Foerster, G., and Y. Tsafrir. 'Nysa-Scythopolis – A New Inscription and the Titles of the City on the Coins.' *INJ* 9 (1986/7) 53–60.

Folda, J. 'The Crusader Period and the Church of St. Anne at Sepphoris.' In *Sepphoris in Galilee. Crosscurrents of Culture*, ed. R. Martin Nagy et al., 101–10. Raleigh, NC: North Carolina Museum of Art, 1996.

Fortna, R. *The Fourth Gospel and its Predecessor. From Narrative Source to Present Gospel.* Philadelphia: Fortress Press, 1988.

———. *The Gospel of Signs. A Reconstruction of the Narrative Source Underlying the Fourth Gospel. SNTSMS* 11. Cambridge: Cambridge University Press, 1970.

———. 'Theological Use of Locale in the Fourth Gospel.' In *Gospel Studies in Honour of S. E. Johnson*, ed. M. Shepphard and E. C. Hobbs. ATR Supplementary Series 3 (1974) 58–95.

Frankel, R. 'Galilee: Prehellenistic.' In *The Anchor Bible Dictionary*, ed. D. N. Freedman, 6 vols., vol. 2, 879–94. New York: Doubleday, 1992.

———. 'Har Mispe Yamim – 1988/9.' *Excavations and Surveys in Israel 9*, 100–102. Jerusalem: The Israel Exploration Society, 1989.

———. *The History of the Processing of Wine and Oil in Galilee in the Period of the Bible, the Mishna and the Talmud* Ph.D. diss., Tel Aviv University, 1984 [Hebrew].

———. 'Some Oil Presses from Western Galilee.' *BASOR* 286 (1992) 39–71.

Frankel, R., and R. Ventura. 'The Mispe Yamim Bronzes.' *BASOR* 311 (1998) 39–55.

Franzman, M. *Jesus in the Nag Hammadi Writings.* Edinburgh: T. & T. Clark, 1996.

Freyne, S. 'Bandits in Galilee. A Contribution to the Study of Social Conditions in First-Century Palestine.' In *The Social World of Formative Christianity and Judaism. Essays in Tribute of Howard Clark Kee*, ed. J. Neusner et al., 50–69. Philadelphia: Fortress Press, 1988.

———. *Galilee from Alexander the Great to Hadrian. A Study of Second Temple Judaism.* Wilmington: Glazier; University of Notre Dame Press, 1980. Reprint, Edinburgh: T. & T. Clark, 1998.

———. *Galilee, Jesus and the Gospels. Literary Approaches and Historical Investigations.* Dublin: Gill & Macmillan; Philadelphia: Fortress Press, 1988.

———. 'Galileans, Phoenicians and Itureans: A Study of Regional Contrasts in the Hellenistic Age.' In *Hellenism in the Land of Israel*, ed. J. J. Collins and G. E. Sterling. Notre Dame: University of Notre Dame Press, 2000.

———. 'The Geography, Politics and Economics of Galilee and the Quest for the Historical Jesus.' In *Studying the Historical Jesus: Evaluations of the Current State of Research*, ed. B. Chilton and C. Evans, 75–124. Leiden: Brill, 1994.

———. 'Reading the Gospels in the Light of the Window of the Evangelists at Chartres Cathedral.' In *Radical Pluralism and Truth. David Tracy and the Hermeneutics of Religion*, ed. W. Jeanrond and J. Rike. New York: Crossroad, 1991.

———. *The Twelve: Disciples and Apostles. An Introduction to the Theology of the First Three Gospels.* London: Sheed and Ward, 1968.

Friedmann, M. A. 'Babatha's *Ketubba* : Some Preliminary Observations.' *IEJ* 46 (1996) 55–76.

Funk, R., and R. Hoover. *The Search for the Authentic Words of Jesus. The Five Gospels.* New York: Macmillan, 1993.

Gager, J. *Kingdom and Community. The Social World of Early Christianity.* Englewood Cliffs, NJ: Prentice Hall, 1975.

Gal, Z. *Lower Galilee During the Iron Age.* ASORDS 8. Winona Lake: Eisenbrauns, 1992.

Garnsey, P. *Famine and Food Supply in the Greco-Roman World.* Cambridge: Cambridge University Press, 1988.

Garnsey, P., K. Hopkins, and C. R. Whittaker, *Trade in the Ancient Economy.* Cambridge: Cambridge University Press, 1983.

Gavish, D. 'French Cartography of the Holy Land in the Nineteenth Century.' *PEQ* 126 (1994) 24–31.

Geertz, C. 'Religion as a Cultural System.' In *Anthropological Approaches to the Study of Religion*, ed. M. Banton, 1–46. ASA Monograph Series 3. London, 1966.

Geller Nathanson, B. 'Jews, Christians and the Gallus Revolt in Fourth Century Palestine.' *BA* 49 (1986) 26–36.

Gelzer, M. 'Die *Vita* des Josephus.' *Hermes* 80 (1952) 67–90.

Goldstein, J. A. 'How the Authors of 1 and 2 Maccabees Treated the Messianic Promises.' In *Judaisms and their Messiahs at the turn of the Christian Era*, ed. J. Neusner, W. S. Green and E. Frerichs, 69–96. New York: Cambridge University Press, 1987.

Goodman, M. 'The First Jewish Revolt: Social Conflict and the Problem of Debt.' *JJS* 33 (1982) 417–27.

———. *Mission and Conversion. Proselytizing in the Religious History of the Roman Empire.* Oxford: Clarendon, 1994.

———. *The Ruling Class of Judaea. The Origins of the Jewish Revolt against Rome, A.D. 66–70.* Cambridge: Cambridge University Press, 1987.

———. *State and Society in Roman Galilee, A. D. 132–212.* Oxford Centre for Post-Graduate Hebrew Studies. Totowa, N.J.: Rowman and Allenheld, 1983.

Grant, F. C. *The Economic Background of the Gospels.* Oxford: Clarendon Press, 1926.

Green, W. Scott. 'Palestinian Holy Men: Charismatic Leadership and Rabbinic Tradition.' In *ANRW* II, *Principat*, 19, 2, ed. H. Temporini and W. Haase, 619–47. Berlin and New York: Walter de Gruyter, 1979.

———. 'What's in a Name? – The Problematic of Rabbinic "Biography".' In *Approaches to Ancient Judaism: Theory and Practice*, ed. W. Scott Green, 77–96. Brown Judaic Series 1. Missoula: Scholars Press, 1978.

———, ed., *Persons and Institutions in Early Rabbinic Judaism.* Brown Judaic Studies 3. Missoula: Scholars Press, 1977.

Groh, D. 'The Clash between Literary and Archaeological Models of Provincial Palestine.' In *Archaeology and the Galilee. Texts and Contexts in the Graeco-Roman and Byzantine Periods*, ed. D. Edwards and C. T. McCollough, 29–38. South Florida Studies in the History of Judaism 143. Atlanta: Scholars Press, 1997.

———. 'The Religion of the Empire: Christianity from Constantine to the Arab Conquest.' In *Christianity and Rabbinic Judaism. A Parallel History of their Origins and Early Development*, ed. H. Shanks. Washington: Biblical Archaeology Society, 1992.

Grundmann, W. *Jesus der Galiläer und das Judentum.* Leipzig: Georg Wigand, 1941.

Guérin, V. *Description géographique, historique et archéologique de la Palestine.* 5 vols. Paris, 1868–80.

Gutman, J., ed. *Ancient Synagogues. The State of Research.* Brown Judaic Studies 22. Chico: Scholars Press, 1981.

Hamburger, H. 'A Hoard of Syrian Tetradrachms from Tiberias' *Atiqot* 2. Jerusalem: Israel Antiquities Authority, 1959. 133–45.

Hamel, G. *Poverty and Charity in Roman Palestine. The First Three Centuries C.E.* Berkeley: University of California Press, 1990.

Hanson, K. C. 'The Galilean Fishing Economy and the Jesus Tradition.' *BTB* 27 (1997) 99–111.

Hanson, K. C. and D. Oakman. *Palestine in the Time of Jesus. Social Structures and Social Conflicts.* Minneapolis: Fortress Press, 1998.

Hanson, R. *Tyrian Influence in Upper Galilee.* Cambridge MA: ASOR Publications, 1980.

Harper, G. McLean. 'Village Administration in the Roman Province of Syria.' *Yale Classical Studies* 1 (1928) 107–68.

Hartel, M. 'Kh. Zemel, 1985/6.' *IEJ* 37 (1987) 270–72.

———. *Northern Golan Heights. The Archaeological Survey as Source for Local History.* Qatzrin: Israel Department of Antiquities and Museums, 1989. [Hebrew].

Hedrick, C. W., ed. *The Historical Jesus and the Rejected Gospels. Semeia* 44 (1988).

Hengel, M. 'Die Bar-Kokhbamünzen als politisch-religiöse Zeugnisse.' In *Judaica et Hellenistica. Kleine Schriften,* vol. 1, 344–50. Tübingen: J. C. B. Mohr, 1998.

———. *The "Hellenization" of Judaea in the First Century after Christ.* London: SCM, 1989. 45–52.

———. 'The Interpretation of the Wine Miracle at Cana: John 2:1–11.' In *The Glory of Christ in the New Testament. Studies in Christology in Memory of G. B. Caird,* ed. L. D. Hurst and N. T. Wright, 83–112. Oxford: Clarendon Press, 1987.

———. *Jews, Greeks and Barbarians.* London: SCM Press, 1980.

———. *Judentum und Hellenismus. Studien zu ihrer Begegnung unter besonderer Berücksichtigung Palästinas zur Mitte des 2. Jh.s v.Chr.* 2nd ed. WUNT 10. Tübingen: J.C.B.Mohr, 1973.

———. 'Messianische Hoffnung und politischer "Radickalismus" in der jüdisch-hellenistischen Diaspora. Zur Frage der Voraussetzungen des jüdischen Aufstandes unter Trajan, 115–117 n. Chr.' In *Judaica et Hellenistica. Kleine Schriften,* vol. 1, 314–43. Tübingen: J. C. B. Mohr, 1998.

———. *The Son of God.* London: SCM Press, 1976.

———. *War Jesus Revolutionär?* Stuttgart: Calwer Verlag, 1970.

———. *The Zealots. Investigation into the Jewish Freedom Movement in the Period from Herod I until 70 A.D.* Edinburgh: T. & T. Clark, 1989.

———. 'Zeloten und Sikarier. Zur Frage nach der Einheit und Vielfalt der jüdischen Befreiungsbewegung 6–74 nach Christus.' In *Josephus-Studien. Festschrift Otto Michel,* ed. O. Betz, K. Haacher and M. Hengel, 174–96. Göttingen: Vandenhoeck & Ruprecht, 1974.

Hengel, M., and A. M. Schwemer, eds. *Königsherrschaft Gottes und himmlischer Kult im Judentum, Urchristentum und in der hellenistischer Welt.* Tübingen: J. C. B. Mohr, 1991.

Hengel, M., J. Charlesworth and D. Mendels. 'The Polemical Character of "On Kingship" in the Temple Scroll: An Attempt at Dating 11Q Temple.' *JJS* 37 (1986) 28–38.

Herbert, S., ed. *Tel Anafa II,i. The Hellenistic and Roman Pottery.* Ann Arbor: *JRA* and Kelsey Museum, 1997.

Herr, C. G. 'The Iron II Period: Emerging Nations.' *BA* 60 (1997) 114–83.

Herrenbrück, F. *Jesus und die Zöllner.* WUNT 41. Tübingen: J. C. B. Mohr, 1990.

———. 'Wer waren die Zöllner?' *ZNW* 72 (1981) 178–84.

Hirschfeld, Y., and R. Birger-Calderon. 'Early Roman and Byzantine Estates near Caesarea.' *IEJ* 41 (1991) 81–111.

Hoehner, H. *Herod Antipas, A Contemporary of Jesus Christ.* SNTSMS 17. Cambridge: Cambridge University Press, 1972.

Holladay, Carl H. *Theios Aner in Hellenistic Judaism. SBLDS* 40. Missoula: Scholars Press, 1977.

Holladay, J. S., Jr. 'Religion in Israel and Judah Under the Monarchy: An Explicitly Archaeological Approach.' In *Ancient Israelite Religion. Essays in Honor of Frank Moore Cross*, ed. P. D. Miller, P. D. Hanson and S. D. McBride, 249–302. Philadelphia: Fortress Press, 1987.

Hopkins, K. 'Economic Growth and Towns in Classical Antiquity.' In *Towns in Societies: Essays in Economic History and Historical Sociology*, ed. P. Abrams and E. Wrigley, 35–77. Cambridge: Cambridge University Press, 1980.

———. 'Taxes and Trade in the Roman Empire. (200BC–400AD).' *JRS* 70 (1980) 101–25.

Horbury, W. 'The Benediction of the *Minim* and Early Jewish-Christian Controversy.' *JTS* 33 (1982) 19–61.

———. *Jews and Christians in Contact and Controversy*. Edinburgh: T. & T. Clark, 1998.

———. 'The Twelve and the Phularchs.' *NTS* 32 (1986) 503–27.

Horsley, R. 'Ancient Jewish Banditry and the Revolt Against Rome.' *CBQ* 43 (1981) 409–32.

———. *Archaeology, History and Society in Galilee. The Social Context of Jesus and the Rabbis*. Valley Forge: Trinity Press International, 1996.

———. 'Archaeology and the Villages of Upper Galilee. A Dialogue with Archaeologists.' *BASOR* 297 (1995) 5–15.

———. 'Ethics and Exegesis: "Love Your Enemies" and the Doctrine of Non-Violence.' *JAAR* 54 (1985) 3–31.

———. *Galilee. History, Politics, People*. Valley Forge: Trinity Press International, 1995.

———. 'The Historical Jesus and Archaeology of the Galilee: Questions from Historical Jesus Research to Archaeologists.' In *SBLASP 1994*, ed. D. Lull, 91–135. Atlanta: Scholars Press, 1994.

———. *Jesus and the Spiral of Violence: Popular Jewish Resistance in Roman Palestine*. San Francisco: Harper and Row, 1987.

———. 'Josephus and the Bandits.' *JSJ* 10 (1979) 37–63.

———. 'Popular Messianic Movements.' *CBQ* 46 (1984) 473–78.

———. *Sociology and the Jesus Movement*. New York: Crossroad, 1989.

Horsley, R., and J. Hanson. *Bandits, Prophets and Messiahs: Popular Movements at the Time of Jesus*. Minneapolis: Winston Press, 1985.

Humphreys, J., ed. *The Roman and Byzantine Near East: Some Recent Archaeological Evidence*. Ann Arbor: JRA Supplementary Series 14, 1995.

Ilan, T. 'The Attraction of Aristocratic Women to Pharisaism.' *HTR* 88 (1995) 1–34.

Ilan, Z. 'Galilee. A Survey of Synagogues.' *ESI* 5 (1986/7) 35–37.

Isaac, B. 'The Babatha Archive. A Review Article.' *IEJ* 42 (1992) 62–75.

Jackson, F., and K. Lake. *The Beginnings of Christianity*. 5 vols. London, 1920–30.

Josephus. *Josephus in 9 Volumes*. Trans. H. ST. J. Thackeray. The Loeb Classical Library. London: Heinemann; Cambridge: Harvard University Press, 1961–69.

Jossa, G. 'Chi sono I Galilei nella *Vita* di Flavio Giuseppe.' *RivB* 31 (1983) 329–39

———. 'Josephus' Action in Galilee during the Jewish War.' In *Josephus and the History of the Greco-Roman Period. Essays in Memory of Morton Smith*, ed. F. Paventi and J. Sievers, 265–78. Leiden: Brill, 1994.

Kaminka, A. *Studien zur Geschichte Galiläas*. Berlin, 1890.

Käsemann, E. *Essays on New Testament Themes*. London: SCM Press, 1964.

Kearney, M. *Reconceptualizing the Peasantry. Anthropology in Global Perspective*. London and Boulder: Westview Press, 1996.

Kee, H. Clark *Christian Origins in Sociological Perspective*. London: SCM, 1980.
————. *Community of the New Age. Studies in Mark's Gospel*. Philadelphia: Westminster Press, 1977.
Kelber, W. *The Kingdom in Mark. A New Time and A New Place*. Philadelphia: Fortress Press, 1974.
Kennard, J. S. 'The Jewish Provincial Assembly.' *ZNW* 53 (1962) 25–51.
————. 'Judas of Galilee and his Clan.' *JQR* 36 (1945) 281–86.
Kimmelman, R. *'Birkath ha-Minim* and the Lack of Evidence for a Christian Jewish Prayer in Late Antiquity.' In *Jewish and Christian Self-Definition*, ed. E. P. Sanders, A. I. Baumgarten and A. Mendelson, 3 vols., vol. 2, 226–44. London: SCM Press, 1981.
Kittel, G., ed. *Theological Dictionary of the New Testament*. English translation edited by W. Bromily., 8 vols. Grand Rapids: W. Eerdmans, 1964–74.
Klausner, J. *The Messianic Idea in Israel from its Beginning to the Completion of the Mishnah*. London: Allen and Unwin, 1956.
Klein, C. *Anti-Judaism in Christian Theology*. London: SPCK, 1978.
Klein, S. *Beiträge zur Geschichte und Geographie Galiläas*. Leipzig, 1909.
————. *Galiläa von der Makkabäerzeit bis 67*. Berlin, 1923.
————. *Galilee: Geography and History of Galilee from the Return from Babylonia to the Conclusion of the Talmud, by S. Klein. Completed from the Literary Remains of the Author*, ed. Y. Eltizur. Jerusalem: Translations and Collections in Jewish Studies 20, 1967 [Hebrew].
————. *Neue Beiträge zur Geschichte und Geographie Galiläas*. Vienna, 1923.
Kloppenborg, J. S. *The Formation of Q. Trajectories in Ancient Wisdom Collections*. Philadelphia: Fortress Press, 1987.
————. 'The Sayings Gospel Q and the Quest for the Historical Jesus.' *HTR* 89 (1996) 307–44.
————. 'The Sayings Gospel Q: Recent Opinion on the People behind the Document.' *Currents in Research. Biblical Studies* 1 (1993) 9–34.
————, ed. *Conflict and Invention. Literary, Rhetorical and Social Studies on the Sayings Gospel Q*. Valley Forge: Trinity Press International, 1995.
————, ed. *The Shape of Q. Signal Essays on the Sayings Gospel*. Minneapolis: Fortress Press, 1994.
Kloppenborg, J. S., and L. Vaage, eds. *Early Christianity, Q and Jesus. Semeia* 55. Atlanta: Scholars Press, 1991.
Klostermann, E. *Eusebius. Das Onomastikon der Biblischen Ortsnamen*. Leipzig: J.C. Hinrichs, 1904. Reprint, Hildesheim: G. Olms 1966.
Koester, H. *Ancient Christian Gospels. Their History and Development*. Philadelphia: Trinity Press International, 1990.
————. 'One Jesus and Four Primitive Gospels.' In *Trajectories through Early Christianity*, ed. J. M. Robinson and H. Koester, 158–205. Philadelphia: Fortress Press, 1971.
Kohl, H., and C. Watzinger. *Antike Synagogen in Galiläa*. Leipzig: Wissenschaftliche Veröffentlichung der Deutschen Orient-Gesellschaft, 1916.
Kosch, D. 'Q und Jesus.' *BZ* 36 (1992) 31–58.
Kraabel, A.T. 'New Evidence of the Samaritan Diaspora has been Found on Delos.' *BA* 47 (1984) 44–46.
Kraemer, R. Shepard. 'Ecstasy and Possession: The Attraction of Women to the Cult of Dionysus.' *HTR* 72 (1979) 56–80.
————. *Her Share of the Blessings. Women's Religions among Pagans, Jews, and Christians in the Greco-Roman World*. New York and Oxford: Oxford University Press, 1992.

Kraft, R. A., and G. Nickelsburg, eds. *Early Judaism and its Modern Interpreters*. Atlanta: Scholars Press, 1986.

Krauss, S. *Talmudische Archaeologie*, 3 vols. Reprint, Hildesheim: G. Olms, 1966.

Lang, F. '"Über Sidon mitten ins Gebiet der Dekapolis." Geographie und Theologie in Markus 7,31.' *ZDPV* 94 (1978) 145–60.

Lapin, H. *Early Rabbinic Civil Law and the Social History of Roman Galilee*. Brown Judaic Studies 307. Atlanta: Scholars Press, 1995.

Laqueur, R. *Der Jüdische Historiker Flavius Josephus*. Gießen, 1929.

Lenski, G. *Power and Privilege: A Theory of Social Stratification*. New York: McGraw, 1966.

Levine, L. *The Rabbinic Class of Roman Palestine in Late Antiquity*. Jerusalem: Yad Izhak ben-Zvi, 1989.

———, ed. *Ancient Synagogues Revealed*. Jerusalem: The Israel Exploration Society, 1981.

———, ed. *The Galilee in Late Antiquity*. New York and Jerusalem: The Jewish Theological Seminary of America, 1992.

———, ed. *The Jerusalem Cathedra*. 3 vols. Jerusalem: Yad Izhak Ben-Zvi Institute, 1981–83.

———, ed. *The Synagogue in Late Antiquity*. Philadelphia: ASOR Publications, 1987.

Lohmeyer, E. *Galiläa und Jerusalem*. FRLANT 34. Göttingen: Vandenhoeck & Ruprecht, 1936.

MacCrae, G. 'Messiah and Gospel.' In *Judaisms and their Messiahs at the turn of the Christian Era*, ed. J. Neusner, W. S. Green and E. Frerichs, 169–86. New York: Cambridge University Press, 1987.

Mack, B. 'All the Extra Jesuses: Christian Origins in the Light of Extra-Canonical Gospels.' *Semeia* 49 (1990) 169–76.

———. 'The Kingdom Sayings in Mark.' *Forum* 3/1 (1987) 3–47.

———. *The Lost Gospel. The Book of Q and Christian Origins*. San Francisco: HarperCollins, 1993.

———. *A Myth of Innocence: Mark and Christian Origins*. Philadelphia: Fortress Press, 1988.

Magen, Y. 'Mount Gerizim and the Samaritans.' In *Early Christianity in Context*, ed. F. Manns and E. Alliata, 91–147. Jerusalem: Franciscan Publications, 1993.

Malherbe, A. *Social Aspects of Early Christianity*. Baton Rouge: Louisiana State University Press, 1977.

Malina, B. *The Social World of Jesus and the Gospels*. London and New York: Routledge, 1996.

Malina, B. and Rohrbaugh, R. *A Social-Scientific Commentary on the Synoptic Gospels*. Minneapolis: Fortress Press, 1992.

Malinowski, F. *Galilean Judaism in the Writings of Josephus*. Ph.D. diss., Duke University, 1975.

Manns, F., and E. Alliata, eds. *Early Christianity in Context. Monuments and Documents*, Studium Biblicum Franciscanum, Collectio Maior 38. Jerusalem: Franciscan Printing Press, 1993.

Ma'oz, Z. 'Comments on Jewish and Christian Communities in Byzantine Palestine.' *PEQ* 117 (1985) 59–67.

———. 'The Golan: Hellenistic Period to the Middle Ages.' In *NEAEHL* 2, 234–46.

———. 'The Synagogue in the Second Temple Period. Architectural and Social Interpretation.' In *Eretz Israel* 23, *The A. Biran Volume*, 331–44. Jerusalem: The Israel Exploration Society, 1992. [Hebrew].

Markschies, C. 'Stadt und Land. Beobachtungen zu Ausbreitung und Inkulturation des Christentums in Palästina.' In *Römische Reichsreligion und Provinzialreligion*, ed. H. Cancik and J. Rüpke, 265–98. Tübingen: J. C. B. Mohr, 1997.

Martyn, J. L. *The Gospel of John in Christian History*. New York: Paulist Press, 1978.

Marxsen, W. *Der Evangelist Markus. Studien zur Redaktionsgeschichte des Evangeliums*. FRLANT 49. Göttingen: Vandenhoeck & Ruprecht, 1959.

Mason, S. *Flavius Josephus on the Pharisees: A Compositional-Critical Study*. Leiden: Brill, 1991.

———, ed. *Understanding Josephus: Seven Perspectives*. JSP Supplement Series 32. Sheffield: Sheffield Academic Press 1998.

Mattingly, D. 'Oil for Export? A Comparison of Libyan, Spanish and Tunisian Olive Oil Production in the Roman Empire.' *JRA* 1 (1988) 33–56.

McCarter, P. Kyle, Jr. 'Aspects of Religion in the Israelite Monarchy: Biblical and Epigraphic Data.' In *Ancient Israelite Religion. Essays in Honor of Frank Moore Cross*, ed. P. D. Miller, P. D. Hanson, and S. D. McBride, 137–56. Philadelphia: Fortress Press, 1987.

McLaren, J. *Turbulent Times? Josephus and Scholarship on Judea in the First Century*. Sheffield: JSP Supplement Series 29. Sheffield Academic Press, 1998.

McMullen, R. 'Market Days in the Roman Empire.' *Phoenix* 24 (1970) 333–41.

Meeks, W. 'Asking Back to Jesus' Identity.' In *From Jesus to John. Essays on Jesus and New Testament Christology in Honour of Marinus de Jonge*, ed. M. De Boer, 46–48. JSNT Supplement Series 84. Sheffield: Sheffield Academic Press, 1993.

———. *The First Urban Christians*. New Haven and London: Yale University Press, 1984.

———. 'Galilee and Judea in the Fourth Gospel.' *JBL* 85 (1966) 159–69.

Meier, J. P. 'The Circle of the Twelve: Did it Exist during Jesus' Public Ministry?' *JBL* 116 (1997) 601–12.

———. *A Marginal Jew. Rethinking the Historical Jesus*, vol. I. New York: Doubleday, 1991.

Mendels, D. *The Land of Israel as a Political Concept in Hasmonean Literature*. Tübingen: J. C. B. Mohr, 1987.

———. *The Rise and Fall of Jewish Nationalism*. New York: Doubleday, 1992.

Meshorer, Y. *City Coins of Eretz Israel and the Dekapolis in the Roman Period*. Jerusalem: The Israel Museum, 1985.

———. 'A Hoard of Coins from Migdal.' *Atiqot* 11. Jerusalem Antiquities Authority, 1968. 54–71.

———. *Jewish Coins of the Second Temple Period*. Numbers 63, 64 and 65. Tel Aviv: Am Hasefer Publications, 1967.

Meyer, B. *The Aims of Jesus*. London: 1979.

Meyer, R. 'Der 'Am ha-'ares. Ein Beitrag zur Religionssoziologie Palästinas in ersten und zweiten Jahrhundert.' *Judaica* 5 (1947) 169–99.

———. *Der Prophet aus Galiläa*. Reprint, Darmstadt: G. Olms, 1970.

Meyers, E. 'An Archaeological Response to a New Testament Scholar.' *BASOR* 297 (1995) 17–25.

———. 'The Challenge of Hellenism for Early Judaism and Christianity.' *BA* 55 (1992) 84–91.

———. 'The Cultural Setting of Galilee: The Case of Regionalism and Early Judaism.' In *ANRW* II, *Principat*, 19,1, ed. H. Temporini and W. Haase, 686–702. Berlin and New York: de Gruyter, 1979.

———. 'Early Judaism and Christianity in the Light of Archaeology.' *BA* 51 (1988) 69–79.

————. 'Galilean Regionalism: A Reappraisal.' In *Approaches to Ancient Judaism*, ed. W. Scott Green, vol. 5, 115–31. Missoula: Scholars Press, 1978.

————. 'Galilean Regionalism as a Factor in Historical Reconstruction.' *BASOR* 221 (1976) 93–101.

————. 'Judaic Studies and Archaeology: the Legacy of Avi-Yonah.' *Eretz Israel 19. Michael Avi-Yonah Memorial Volume*, 24*–27*. Jerusalem: The Israel Exploration Society, 1987.

————. 'Roman Sepphoris in Light of New Archaeological Evidence and Recent Research.' In *The Galilee in Late Antiquity*, ed. L. Levine, 321–38. New York: The Jewish Theological Seminary, 1992.

————, ed. *Galilee through the Centuries: Confluence of Cultures*. Winona Lake: Eisenbrauns, 1999.

Meyers, E., and C. Meyers. 'Expanding the Frontiers of Biblical Archaeology.' In *Eretz Israel 20. The Yigael Yadin Volume*, 140*–47*. Jerusalem: The Israel Exploration Society, 1989.

Meyers, E., E. Netzer and C. Meyers. 'Artistry in Stone: The Mosaics of Ancient Sepphoris.' *BA* 50 (1987) 223–31.

————. *Sepphoris*. Winnona Lake: Eisenbrauns, 1992.

————. 'Sepphoris: Ornament of all Galilee.' *BA* 49 (1986) 4–19.

Meyers, E., and J. Strange, eds. *Archaeology, the Rabbis and Early Christianity*. London: SCM Press 1981.

Meyers, E., J. Strange and D. Groh. 'The Meiron Excavation Project; Archaeological Survey in Galilee and Golan, 1976.' *BASOR* 233 (1978) 1–24.

Milik, J. T. 'Notes sur une lettre de Siméon Bar Kokheba.' *RB* 60 (1953) 276–94.

Millar, F. 'Empire, Community and Culture in the Roman Near East: Greeks, Syrians, Jews and Arabs.' *JJS* 38 (1987) 143–64.

Millar, F. 'The Phoenician Cities. A Case Study of Hellenisation.' *Proceedings of Cambridge Philological Society* 209 (1983) 55–71.

————. *The Roman Near East, 31 BC– AD 337*. Cambridge: Harvard University Press, 1993.

Miller, P. D., P. D. Hanson, and S. D. McBride, eds. *Ancient Israelite Religion. Essays in Honor of Frank Moore Cross*. Philadelphia: Fortress Press, 1987.

Miller, S. 'The *minim* of Sepphoris Reconsidered.' *HTR* 86 (1993) 377–402

————. 'Sepphoris, the well-remembered City.' *BA* 55 (1992) 74–83.

Moore, S. D. *Literary Criticism and the Gospels. The Theoretical Challenge*. New Haven and London: Yale University Press, 1989.

Mor, M. 'Samaritan History: the Persian, Hellenistic and Hasmonean Period.' In *The Samaritans*, ed. A. Crown, 1–18. Tübingen: J. C. B. Mohr, 1989.

Mowinckel, S. *He that Cometh*. Oxford: B. Blackwell, 1956.

Moxnes, H. *The Economy of the Kingdom. Social Conflict and Economic Relations in Luke's Gospel*. Philadelphia: Fortress Press, 1988.

Muczbik, S., A. Ovadiah and C. Gomez de Silva. 'The Meroth Mosaics Reconsidered.' In *JJS* 47 (1996) 286–93.

Murphy-O'Connor, J. 'John the Baptist and Jesus.' *NTS* 36 (1990) 359–74.

Nagy, R. Martin et al. *Sepphoris in Galilee. Crosscurrents of Culture*. Raleigh: North Carolina Museum of Modern Art, 1996.

Neirynck, F. 'Jn 21.' *NTS* 36 (1990) 321–36.

Netzer, E., and Z. Weiss. 'New Evidence for Late-Roman and Byzantine Sepphoris.' In *The Roman and Byzantine Near East: Some Recent Archaeological Evidence*, ed. J. Humphreys, 164–76. Ann Arbor: JRA Supplementary Series 14, 1995.

————. 'Hellenistic and Roman Sepphoris: The Historical Evidence.' In *Sepphoris in Galilee. Crosscurrents of Culture*, ed. R. Martin Nagy et al., 29–38. Raleigh, NC: North Carolina Museum of Art, 1996.

————. 'Sepphoris.' In *NEAEHL* 4, 1327.

————. *Zippori*. Jerusalem: The Israel Exploration Society, 1994.

Neubauer, A. *La Géographie du Talmud*. 2 vols. Paris, 1868.

Neusner, J. *Development of a Legend. Studies on the Traditions of Yohanan ben Zakkai*. 2nd ed. Leiden: Brill, 1970.

————. *Formative Judaism. Religious, Historical and Literary Studies*. Brown Judaic Studies 37. Chico: Scholars Press, 1982.

————. 'The History of a Biography. Johanan ben Zakkai in the Canonical Literature of Formative Judaism.' In *Formative Judaism 5. Religious, Historical and Literary Studies*, 79–86. Brown Judaic Studies 91. Chico: Scholars Press, 1985.

————. *A History of the Jews in Babylonia*. 5 vols. Leiden: Brill, 1968–70.

————. *Judaism and Christianity in the Age of Constantine*. Chicago: University of Chicago Press, 1987.

————. *Judaism. The Evidence of the Mishnah*. Chicago: University of Chicago Press, 1981.

————. *A Life of Rabban Yohanan ben Zakkai, ca. 1–80 C.E.* Leiden: Brill, 1962.

————. *Messiah in Context. Israel's History and Destiny in Formative Judaism*. Philadelphia: Fortress Press, 1984.

————. *Method and Meaning in Ancient Judaism*. Brown Judaic Series 10. Missoula: Scholars Press, 1979.

————. *The Rabbinic Traditions about the Pharisees before 70*. 3 vols. Leiden: Brill, 1971.

————. *The Social Study of Judaism. Essays and Reflections*, vol. I. Brown Judaic Studies 160. Atlanta: Scholars Press, 1988.

————. 'Studies in the *Taqqanoth* of Yavneh.' HTR 63 (1970) 183–98.

Neusner, J. et al., eds. *The Social World of Formative Christianity and Judaism. Essays in Tribute of Howard Clark Kee*. Philadelphia: Fortress Press, 1988.

Neusner, J., W. S. Green and E. Frerichs, eds. *Judaisms and their Messiahs at the turn of the Christian Era*. New York: Cambridge University Press, 1987.

Neyrey, J. 'Josephus' *Vita* and the Encomium: A Native Model of Personality.' *JSJ* 25 (1994) 177–206.

————, ed. *The Social World of Luke-Acts: Models for Interpretation*. Peabody: Hendrickson, 1991.

Nickelsburg, G. 'Enoch, Levi and Peter: Recipients of Revelation in Upper Galilee.' *JBL* 100 (1981) 575–600.

Nickelsburg, G., and J. J. Collins, eds. *Ideal Figures in Ancient Judaism*. Chico: Scholars Press, 1980.

Nun, M. *Ancient Anchorages and Harbours around the Sea of Galilee*. Kibbutz Ein Gev: Kinnereth Sailing Co., 1988.

Oakman, D. *Jesus and the Economic Questions of his Day*. Lewison NY: The Edwin Mellen Press, 1986. 57–72.

Oegma, G. *The Anointed and his People. Messianic Expectation from the Maccabees to Bar Kochba*. JSP Supplement Series 27. Sheffield: Sheffield Academic Press, 1998.

Oehler, W. 'Die Ortschaften und Grenzen Galiläas nach Josephus.' *ZDPV* 28 (1905) 1–26 and 49–74.

Oepke, A. 'Das Bevölkerungsproblem Galiläas.' *TL* 62 (1941) 201–5.

Oppenheimer, A. *The 'Am ha-'aretz. A Study in the Social History of the Jewish People in the Hellenistic-Roman Period*. Leiden, Brill, 1977.

Origen, *Contra Celsum*. Trans. H. Chadwick. Cambridge: Cambridge University Press, 1953.

Overholt, T. W. 'Elijah and Elisha in the Context of Israelite Religion.' In *Prophets and Paradigms. Essays in Honour of Gene M. Tucker*, 94–111. Sheffield: Sheffield Academic Press, 1996.

Overman, A. 'Recent Advances in the Archaeology of the Galilee in the Roman Period.' *Currents in Research. Biblical Studies* 1 (1993) 35–58.

———. 'Who were the First Urban Christians? Urbanization in Galilee in the First Century.' In *SBLASP 1988*, ed. D. Lull, 160–68. Atlanta: Scholars Press, 1988.

Patterson, S. J. 'The Gospel of Thomas and the Historical Jesus: Retrospectus and Prospectus.' In *SBLASP 1990*, ed. D. Lull, 614–36. Atlanta: Scholars Press, 1990.

Pavente, F., and J. Sievers, eds. *Josephus and the History of the Greco-Roman Period. Essays in Memory of Morton Smith*. Leiden: Brill, 1994.

Peacock, D. P. S., and D. F. Williams, *Amphorae and the Roman Economy*. London and New York: Longman, 1986.

Purvis, J. 'The Samaritans.' In *The Cambridge History of Judaism*, ed. W. D. Davies and L. Finkelstein, 3 vols., vol. 2, *The Hellenistic Age*, 591–693. London: Cambridge University Press, 1989.

Qedar, S. 'Two Lead Weights of Herod Antipas and Herod Agrippa I and the History of Tiberias.' *INJ* 9 (1986/7) 29–35.

Rabbinowitz, J. J. 'Note sur la lettre de Bar Kokheba.' *RB* 61 (1954) 191–92.

Rajak, T. *Josephus. The Historian and his Society*. London: Duckworth, 1983.

———. 'Justus of Tiberias.' *CQ* 23 (1973) 345–68.

Rappaport, U. 'The Hellenization of the Hasmoneans.' In *Jewish Assimilation, Acculturation and Accommodation: Past Traditions, Current Issues, Future Prospects*, ed. Menahem Mor, 1–13. Lanham: University Press of America, 1991.

———. 'John of Gischala: From Galilee to Jerusalem.' *JJS* 33 (1982) 479–90.

———. 'John of Gischala in Galilee.' In *The Jerusalem Cathedra*, ed. L. Levine, vol. 3., 46–57. Jerusalem: Yad Izhak Ben-Zvi Institute, 1983.

———. 'A Note on the Use of the Bible in 1 Maccabees.' In *Biblical Perspectives: Early Use and Interpretation of the Bible in Light of the Dead Sea Scrolls*, ed. M. Stone and E. Chazon, 175–79. Leiden: Brill, 1998.

Rathbone, D. *Economic Rationalism and Rural Society in Third-Century A.D. Egypt. The Heroninos Archive and the Appianus Estate*. Cambridge: Cambridge University Press, 1991.

Raynor, J., and Y. Meshorer. *The Coins of Ancient Meiron*. Winona Lake: Eisenbrauns, 1988.

Redfield, R., and M. Singer. 'The Cultural Role of Cities.' *Economic Development and Social Change* 3 (1954) 57–73.

Reed, J. *Places in Early Christianity: Galilee, Archaeology, Urbanisation, and Q*. Doctoral diss., University of California at Claremont, 1994.

———. 'Population Numbers, Urbanization, and Economics: Galilean Archaeology and the Historical Jesus.' In *SBLASP 1994*, ed. Eugene H. Lovering, Jr., 203–19. Atlanta: Scholars Press, 1994.

———. 'The Social map of Q.' In *Conflict and Invention. Literary, Rhetorical and Social Studies on the Sayings Gospel Q*, ed. J. Kloppenborg, 17–36. Valley Forge: Trinity Press International, 1995.

Renan, E. *Vie de Jésus*. Paris: 1863. [ET *The Life of Jesus*. Buffalo: Prometheus Books, 1991.]

Rhoads, D. *Israel in Revolution 6–74 C.E. A Political History Based on the Writings of Josephus*. Philadelphia: Fortress Press, 1976.

Rich, J., and A. Wallace-Hadrill, eds. *City and Country in the Ancient World.* London and New York: Routledge, 1991.

Richardson, P. *Herod, King of the Jews and Friend of the Romans.* Columbia: University of South Carolina Press, 1996.

Ricoeur, P. *Time and Narrative.* 3 vols. Chicago: University of Chicago Press, 1984–88.

Riesner, R. *Jesus als Lehrer.* WUNT 7. Tübingen: J.C.B. Mohr, 1981.

Rivkin, E. 'The Internal City: Judaism and Urbanisation.' *JSSR* 5 (1966) 225–40.

Robbins, V. 'Socio-Rhetorical Criticism: Mary, Elizabeth and the Magnificat as a Test Case.' In *The New Literary Criticism and the New Testament,* ed. E. Struthers Malbon and E. V. McKnight, 164–209. JSNT Supplements 109. Sheffield: Sheffield Academic Press, 1994.

Robinson, E. *Biblical Researches in Palestine and the Adjacent Regions. A Journal of Travels in the Years 1838 and 1852 by E. Robinson, E. Smith and Others.* London: J. Murray, 1856.

Robinson, J. A. T. *The Priority of John.* London: SCM, 1985.

Rodgers, Z. *Josephus: Patriot, Priest, Politician. His Vita and Contra Apionem as a Witness to his Concerns for Jews and Judaism,* Doctoral Dissertation, Trinity College, Dublin 1997. Forthcoming, Leiden: Brill, 2000.

Roll, I. 'The Roman Road System in Judea.' In *The Jerusalem Cathedra,* ed. L. Levine, vol. 3, 136–81. Jerusalem: Yad Izhak Ben-Zvi Institute, 1983.

Roth, C. 'The Constitution of the Jewish Republic, 66–70.' *JSS* 9 (1964) 295–319.

Roth-Gerson, L. *The Greek Inscriptions from the Synagogues in Eretz Israel.* Jerusalem: The Israel Exploration Society, 1987 [Hebrew].

Safrai, S. 'Teaching of the Pietists in Mishnaic Literature.' *JJS* 16 (1965) 15–31.

Safrai, S., and M. Stern, eds. *The Jewish People in the First Century.* CRINT I. Assen: van Gorcum, 1974.

Safrai, Z. *The Economy of Roman Palestine.* New York and London: Routledge, 1994.

Saldarini, A. *Pharisees, Scribes and Sadducees in Palestinian Society.* Edinburgh: T. & T. Clark, 1988.

Sanders, E. P. *Jesus and Judaism.* London: SCM, 1985.

———. *Jewish Law from Jesus to the Mishnah.* London: SCM Press, 1990.

———. *Judaism: Practice and Belief, 63 B.C.E. – 66 C.E.* London: SCM Press, 1992.

Saunders, T. *An Introduction to the Survey of Western Palestine.* London: Palestine Exploration Fund, 1881.

Sawicki, M. 'Archaeology as Space Technology: Digging for Gender and Class in the Holy Land.' *Method and Theory in the Study of Religion.* Berlin: de Gruyter (1995) 319–48.

———. 'Spatial Management of Gender and Labor in Greco-Roman Galilee.' In *Archaeology and the Galilee. Texts and Contexts in the Greco-Roman and Byzantine Periods,* ed. D. Edwards and C. T. McCollough, 7–28. Atlanta: Scholars Press, 1997.

Schäfer, P. *Der Bar Kokhba-Aufstand.* Tübingen: J. C. B. Mohr, 1981.

———, ed. *The Talmud Yerushalmi and Graeco-Roman Culture I.* Texte und Studien zum Antiken Judentum 71. Tübingen: J.C.B. Mohr, 1998.

Schalit, A. 'Josephus und Justus. Studien zur *Vita* des Josephus.' *Klio* 26 (1933) 67–95.

———. *König Herodes. Der Mann und sein Werk.* Berlin: de Gruyter, 1969.

———. *Namenswörterbuch zu Flavius Josephus.* Supplement I to *A Complete Concordance to Flavius Josephus,* ed. K. H. Rengstorf. Leiden: Brill, 1968.

Schlatter, A. *Geschichte Israels von Alexander dem Großem bis Hadrian.* Reprint, Darmstadt: G. Olms, 1972.

Schmeller, T. 'Jesus im Umland Galiläas: zu den Markinischen Berichten vom Aufenthalt Jesu in den Gebieten von Tyros, Caesarea Philippi und der Dekapolis.' *BZ* 38 (1994) 44–66.

Schottroff, W. 'Die Ituräer.' *ZDPV* 98 (1982) 125–47.

Schüpphaus, J. *Die Psalmen Solomos.* Leiden: Brill, 1977.

Schürer, E. *The History of the Jewish People in the Age of Jesus Christ* 3 vols. Revised by G. Vermes, F. Miller, and M. Black. Edinburgh: T. & T. Clark, 1973– 87.

Schüssler Fiorenza, E. *Jesus. Miriam's Child, Sophia's Prophet. Critical Issues in Feminist Christology.* New York: Crossroad, 1995.

Schwartz, D. 'Josephus and Nicolaus on the Pharisees.' *JSJ* 14 (1983) 157–71.

Schwartz, S. 'The "Judaism" of Samaria and Galilee in Josephus' Version of the Letter of Demetrius I to Jonathan. (*Antiquities* 13, 48–57).' *HTR* 82 (1989) 377–91.

Schwöbel, V. 'Galiläa: Die Verkehrswege und Ansiedlungen in ihrer Abhängigkeit von der natürlichen Bedingungen.' *ZDPV* 27 (1904) 1–151.

Scott, E., ed. *Theoretical Roman Archaeology: First Conference Proceedings.* Worldwide Archaeology Series. Aldershot: Avebury, 1993.

Shanin, T., ed. *Peasants and Peasant Societies.* Penguin Modern Sociology Readings, 1971.

Shanks, H., ed. *Christianity and Rabbinic Judaism. A Parallel History of their Origins and Early Development.* Washington: Biblical Archaeology Society, 1992.

Shatzman, I. *The Armies of the Hasmoneans and Herod from Hellenistic to Roman Frameworks.* Tübingen: J. C. B. Mohr, 1991.

Shaw, B. 'Tyrants, Bandits and Kings. Personal Power in Josephus.' *JJS* 44 (1993) 176–204.

Shepherd, N. *The Zealous Intruders. The Western Rediscovery of Palestine.* London: Collins, 1987.

Simon, M. *Verus Israel. A Study of the Relations between Christians and Jews in the Roman Empire.* Oxford: Oxford University Press, 1986.

Smith, J. Z. 'The Magician and the Temple' in *God's Christ and His Bible. Studies in Honour of Nils Alstrup Dahl,* ed. W. Meeks and J. Jervell, 233–47. Bergen: Universitetsvorlaget, 1977.

———. 'The Social Description of Early Christianity.' *RelStRev* 1 (1975) 19–25.

Smith, M. *Jesus the Magician.* New York: Harper and Row, 1978.

———. 'On the Wine God in Palestine.' *Salo M. Baron Jubilee Volume,* *815–*29. Jerusalem: Israel Academy of the Sciences and the Humanities, 1975.

———. *Palestinian Parties and Politics that Shaped the Old Testament.* New York: 1971. Reprint, London: SCM Press, 1987.

———. 'Zealots and Sicarii. Their origins and relation.' *HTR* 64 (1971) 1–19.

Spencer-Kennard, J. 'The Jewish Provincial Assembly.' *ZNW* 53 (1962) 25–51.

Stanton, G., ed. *The Interpretation of Matthew.* London: SPCK, 1983.

Stern, M. *Greek and Latin Authors on Jews and Judaism,* 3 vols. Jerusalem: Israel Academy of the Sciences and the Humanities, 1974–84.

Strange, J. 'First Century Galilee from Archaeology and from Texts.' In *Archaeology and the Galilee. Texts and Contexts in the Graeco-Roman and Byzantine Periods,* ed. D. Edwards and C. T. McCollough, 39–48. South Florida Studies in the History of Judaism 143. Atlanta: Scholars Press, 1997.

———. 'Six Campaigns at Sepphoris: The University of South Florida Excavations, 1983–1989.' In *The Galilee in Late Antiquity,* ed. L. Levine, 339–56. New York and Jerusalem: The Jewish Theological Seminary, 1992.

Strange, J., D. Groh, and T. Longstaff. 'Excavations at Sepphoris: The Location and Identification of Shikhin.' Part I, *IEJ* 44 (1994) 216–27, and Part II, *IEJ* 45 (1995) 171–87.

Struthers Malbon, E. 'Fallible Followers: Women and Men in the Gospel of Mark.' *Semeia* 27 (1984) 29–48.

————. 'Galilee and Jerusalem: History and Literature in Markan Interpretation.' *CBQ* 44 (1982) 242–55.

Sussman, J. 'The Inscription in the Synagogue at Rehob.' In *Ancient Synagogues Revealed*, ed. L. Levine, 146–53. Jerusalem: The Israel Exploration Society, 1981.

Syren, R. *The Blessings in the Targums. A Study on the Targumic Interpretation of t.Genesis 49 and Deuteronomy 33*. Abo: Abo Akademi, 1986.

Tadmor, H. *The Inscriptions of Tiglath-Pileser III King of Assyria*. Jerusalem: Israel Academy of the Sciences and Humanities, 1994.

Tannehill, R. 'The Disciples in Mark: the Function of a Narrative Role.' *JR* 57 (1977) 134–57.

Tcherikover, V. *Palestine under the Ptolemies. A Contribution to the Study of the Zenon Papyri*. Mizraim. Vols. 1V–V. New York: G. E. Stechert, 1937.

Theissen [Theißen], G. *The Gospels in Context. Social and Political History in the Synoptic Tradition*. Edinburgh: T. & T. Clark, 1992.

————. 'Gruppenmessianismus. Überlegungen zum Ursprung der Kirche in Jüngerkreis Jesu.' In *JBTh* 7 (1992) 101–23.

————. 'Historical Scepticism and the Criteria of Jesus Research. My Attempt to Leap over Lessing's Yawning Gulf.' *SJT* 49 (1996) 146–75.

————. 'Die Jesusbewegung als charismatische Wertevolution.' *NTS* 35 (1989) 343–60.

————. '"Meer" und "See" in den Evangelien: Ein Beitrag zur Lokalkoloritforschung.' *Studien zum Neuen Testament und seiner Umwelt* 10 (1985) 5–25.

————. *The Sociology of Palestinian Christianity*. Philadelphia: Fortress Press, 1977.

————. *Studien zur Soziologie des Urchristentums*. Tübingen: J.C.B. Mohr, 1983.

————. 'Die Tempelweissagung Jesu. Prophetie im Spannungsfeld zwischen Tempel und Land.' *TZ* 32 (1976) 144–58.

Theissen, G., and A. Merz. *The Historical Jesus*. London: SCM, 1998.

Theißen, G., and D. Winter. *Die Kriterienfrage in der Jesusforschung. Vom Differenzkriterium zum Plausibilitätskriterium*. Göttingen: Vandenhoeck & Ruprecht, 1997.

Thomsen, P. 'Palästina nach dem Onomasticon des Eusebius.' *ZDPV* 26 (1903) 97–141 and 145–88.

Tiede, D. L. *The Charismatic Figure as Miracle Worker*. SBLDS 1. Missoula: Scholars Press, 1972.

Tsafrir, Y., L. Di Segni and J. Green. *Tabula Imperii Romani. Iudaea-Palaestina. Maps and Gazetteer*. Jerusalem: Israel Academy of the Sciences and the Humanities, 1994.

Tzaferis, V. 'Cults and Deities Worshipped at Caesarea-Philippi. Banias.' In *Priests Prophets and Scribes. Essays on the Formation and Heritage of Second Temple Judaism in Honour of Joseph Blenkinsopp*, ed. E. Ulrich et al., 190–203. JSOT Supplements 149. Sheffield: Sheffield Academic Press, 1992.

————. 'The "God who is in Dan" and the Cult of Pan at Banias in the Hellenistic and Roman Periods.' In *Eretz Israel*, vol. 23, *A. Biran Volume*, 128*–35*. Jerusalem: The Israel Exploration Society, 1992.

Urbach, E. E. *The Sages. Their Concepts and Beliefs*. 2 vols. Jerusalem: Magnes Press, 1975.

Urman, D. *The Golan. A Profile of a Region during the Roman and Byzantine Periods*. Oxford: BAR International Series 269, 1985.

Urman, D., and P. Fletcher. *Ancient Synagogues. Historical Analysis and Archaeological Discovery*. 2 vols. Leiden: Brill, 1995.

Vaage, L. *Galilean Upstarts. Jesus' First Followers according to Q*. Valley Forge: Trinity Press International, 1994.

Vale, R. 'Literary Sources in Archaeological Description. The Case of Galilee, Galilees and Galileans.' *JSJ* 18 (1987) 210–28.

Van der Kam, J. 'Righteous One, Messiah, Chosen One and Son of Man.' In *The Messiah. Developments in Earliest Judaism and Christianity*, ed. J. H. Charlesworth, 167–91. Minneapolis: Fortress Press, 1992.

Vermes, G. 'Hanina ben Dosa. A Controversial Galilean Saint from the First Century of the Christian Era.' *JJS* 23 (1972) 28–50 and *JJS* 24 (1973) 51–64

———. *Jesus and the World of Judaism*. London: SCM Press, 1983.

———. *Jesus the Jew. An Historian's Reading of the Gospels*. London: Collins, 1973.

———. *The Religion of Jesus the Jew*. London: SCM Press, 1993.

Villeneuve, F. 'L'Économie Rurale et la Vie des Campagnes dans le Hauran Antique.' In *Recherches Archéologiques sur la Syrie du Sud a l'Époque Hellenistique et Romaine: Hauran I*, ed. J.-M. Dentzer, 63–129. Paris: Librairie Orientaliste Paul Gauthier, 1986.

Vitto, F. 'A Look into the Workshop of a late Roman Galilean Potter.' *Bulletin of the Anglo-Israel Archaeological Society* 3 (1983/4) 19–22.

Vogel, M. 'Vita 64–69, das Bilderverbot und die Galiläapolitik des Josephus.' *JSJ* 30 (1999) 65–79.

Wacholder, Ben Zion. *Eupolemus. A Study of Judeo-Greek Literature*. Cincinnati: Hebrew Union College, 1974. 155–69.

Wachsmann, S. *The Excavation of an Ancient Boat in the Sea of Galilee. Atiqot* 19. Jerusalem: The Israel Antiquities Authority, 1990.

Weeden, T. *Mark: Traditions in Conflict:*. Philadelphia: Fortress Press, 1971.

Werner, W. *Eschatologische Texte in Jesaja 1–39: Messias, Heiliger Rest, Völker*. Munich: Echter Verlag, 1982.

Whittaker, C. 'The Consumer City Revisited: the *Vicus* and the City.' *JRA* 3 (1991) 110–18.

Wild, R. 'The Encounter between Pharisaic and Christian Judaism: Some Early Gospel Evidence.' *NovT* 27 (1985) 105–24.

Wilkin, R. L. *The Land Called Holy: Palestine in Christian History and Thought*. New Haven: Yale University Press, 1992.

Wilkinson, J. *Egeria's Travels*. London: S.P.C.K. 1971.

———. *Jerusalem Pilgrims before the Crusades*. Warminster: Aris and Philips, 1977.

Williams, J. G. 'Neither Here nor There: Between Wisdom and Apocalyptic in Jesus' Kingdom Sayings.' *Forum* 5/2 (1989) 7–30.

Williams, M. 'The Meaning and Function of *Ioudaios* in Greco-Roman Inscriptions.' *ZPE* 116 (1997) 249–62.

Wright, G. E. 'The Samaritans at Shechem.' *HTR* 55 (1962) 357–66.

Yadin, Y., J. C. Greenfield, and A. Yardeni. 'Babatha's *Ketubba*.' *IEJ* 44 (1994) 75–101.

Younger, K. Lawson, Jr. 'The Deportation of the Israelites.' *JBL* 117 (1998) 201–27.

Zangenberg, J. *Frühes Christentum in Samarien. Topographische und traditionsgeschichtliche Studien zu den Samarientexten im Johannesevangelium*. Tübingen: Franke Verlag, 1998.

Zanker, P. *The Power of Images in the Age of Augustus*. Ann Arbor: University of Michigan Press, 1988.

Zeitlin, S. 'A survey of Jewish historiography: from the biblical books to the Sefer ha-Kabbalah, with special emphasis on Josephus.' *JQR* 59 (1968) 171–214 and 60 (1969) 37–68.

———. 'Who were the Galileans? New Light on Josephus' Activities in Galilee' *JQR* 59 (1973) 189–203.

Zenger, E. 'Jesus von Nazareth und die messianische Hoffnungen des alttestamentlichen Israel.' In *Studien zum Messiasbild im Alten Testament*, ed. U. Struppe, 23–66. Stuttgart: Verlag Katholisches Bibelwerk, 1974.

Index of Ancient Sources

Old Testament

New Testament

Pseudepigraphia

Josephus

Qumran

Rabbinic Writings

Graeco-Roman Authors

Early Christian Writers

Index of Subjects and Names